MULTIMEDIA PROGRAMMING

OBJECTS, ENVIRONMENTS AND FRAMEWORKS

ACM Press Books

This book is published as part of ACM Press Books – a collaboration between the Association for Computing Machinery and Addison-Wesley Publishing Company. ACM is the oldest and largest educational and scientific society in the information technology field. Through its high-quality publications and services, ACM is a major force in advancing the skills and knowledge of IT professionals throughout the world. For further information about ACM, contact:

ACM Member Services
1515 Broadway, 17th Floor
New York, NY 10036-5701
Phone: 1-212-626-0500
Fax: 1-212-944-1318
E-mail: ACMHELP@ACM.org

ACM European Service Center
Avenue Marcel Thiry 204
1200 Brussels, Belgium
Phone: 32-2-774-9602
Fax: 32-2-774-9690
E-mail: ACM_Europe@ACM.org

OTHER TITLES IN THE SERIES

MULTIMEDIA PROGRAMMING

OBJECTS, ENVIRONMENTS AND FRAMEWORKS

Simon J. Gibbs

University of Geneva

Dionysios C. Tsichritzis

University of Geneva, GMD, Bonn

 ADDISON-WESLEY PUBLISHING COMPANY

Wokingham, England • Reading, Massachusetts • Menlo Park, California

New York • Don Mills, Ontario • Amsterdam • Bonn • Sydney • Singapore

Tokyo • Madrid • San Juan • Milan • Paris • Mexico City • Seoul • Taipei

© 1995 by the ACM Press, A division of the Association for Computing Machinery, Inc. (ACM)

Cover designed by Viva Design Ltd, Oxford
incorporating the illustration from Plate IV (image editing using Adobe PhotoShop)
and printed by The Riverside Printing Co. (Reading) Ltd.
Typeset by Carol Atack, Cambridge.
Printed and bound in Great Britain by T.J. Press, Padstow, Cornwall.

First printed 1994.

ISBN 0-201-42282-4

British Library Cataloguing-in-Publication Data
A catalogue record for this book is available from the British Library.

Library of Congress Cataloguing-in-Publication Data applied for.

PREFACE

At first glance the title of this book may appear ambiguous. Is multimedia programming something one does with computers and programming languages, or does it have something to do with, as in television broadcasting, selecting 'programs' for presentation? This book is written primarily for people with a background in computers; it considers multimedia programming to be a form of computer programming – specifically, the development of software for applications where audio, video, graphics, and other media play important roles. Although we are interested in multimedia from a software perspective, on reflection it seems that this view of multimedia programming and that found in the broadcast and entertainment industries are not entirely different, that in each case the end result is information being selected for interaction and presentation.

What are our reasons for writing a book on multimedia programming? Initially we wanted to gather a set of concepts and definitions that software programmers must assimilate before working with multimedia. Many of the techniques and terms associated with multimedia are unfamiliar to programmers and rather than having to search through separate texts on graphics, image processing, digital audio, and video, it is useful if an overview of the relevant concepts can be found in one place.

If the goal were only to describe terminology, then a dictionary for multimedia programming would perhaps suffice. Instead we have organized material in a way that reflects a particular programming paradigm, that offered by object-oriented technology. This brings us to the central goal of the book, which is to formulate an approach to multimedia programming based on well-defined concepts and techniques, that tries to anticipate the needs of future applications. The approach described here emphasizes software abstractions that conceal the idiosyncrasies of particular platforms, particular devices and data formats; although in need of refinement, we hope it gives the reader a broad conceptual foundation for multimedia programming.

How multimedia technology will be used in the future is of course not known, but it is possible to make some reasonable guesses by looking at existing trends and developments. One trend, recognized since the late 1970s by Nicholas Negroponte, is that boundaries are fading between the broadcasting, publishing, and computer industries. This is evident in the recent stream of announcements describing mergers and joint projects between computer, telephone, cable, and entertainment companies. The convergence of computers with communications is one facet of a steady evolution in the role of digital technology. As technology has advanced, the role of the computer has been transformed from one of computation, to a provider of information, and finally to what can be called a tool for the *imagination*. Thus originally the computer was used primarily for numerical tasks; it was, literally, a giant calculator. Next came the information systems stage, when large computer-based systems were created for storing, distributing, and processing information. Now, as a tool for the imagination, the computer is becoming a personalized and interactive vehicle for exploration, visualization, and communication.

The driving force behind the changing role of the computer is the dramatic improvement in performance, and simultaneous reduction in cost, of digital technology. Multimedia applications in particular are technology driven – as hardware improves, new uses and forms of multimedia become possible. Among the developments likely to influence future multimedia applications are high-bandwidth networks with greater accessibility; standards and hardware for digital video compression; and faster, less-expensive, 3D graphics hardware. These developments point to a number of characteristics that can be expected in future multimedia applications:

Distributed: Computing systems in general are moving towards open systems where server-client architectures and peer-to-peer computing are prevalent. This direction is also being followed by those multimedia applications with a need either for real-time communication or for the sharing of expensive or infrequently used resources such as high-quality color printers, scanners and special-purpose processors.

Connected to large multimedia databases: The storage requirements of digital audio and video are so high that even with falling memory prices it is unrealistic to expect more than a small fraction of this material to be stored locally. Multimedia databases offer a solution to storing, sharing, and querying this information.

Support 'temporal' media, in particular video and animation: Digital video and real-time animation offer novel techniques for increasing interactivity. Both digital video and real-time animation are just now becoming feasible and are likely to play predominant roles in future applications.

Examples of applications having the above characteristics include systems for accessing public digital media collections, virtual reality, and 'palmtop conferencing'. These applications are at the edge of current technology, so naturally the tools and techniques to support their construction are not fully understood.

Among the technologies that appear promising for multimedia programming are *objects, environments,* and *frameworks*. Objects provide building blocks for multimedia applications. They allow us to encapsulate the representation of various digital media – images, audio, video, graphics, animation, music – and to specify available operations. These objects can then be combined and coordinated using services provided by multimedia environments. Environments aid in acquiring, processing, and presenting digital media by providing high-level interfaces for such tasks as device control, buffering, process scheduling, synchronization, and data conversion. They may also provide interfaces to multimedia databases and multimedia networks, and support the development of distributed applications. Multimedia environments are often tailored to particular hardware and operating systems and so must adapt as platforms change. This brings us to frameworks: generic software and generic interfaces from which specific environments can be realized. Frameworks allow new devices, new media, and new communications methods to be supported with little impact on the form of the interfaces visible to application programmers.

In this book we explore objects, environments, and frameworks for multimedia programming. The book is divided into three parts. **Part I** introduces multimedia technology and the main forms of digital media. We also look at several environments and platforms now in use, and propose a classification scheme for multimedia operations in general. This material concentrates on issues of data representation and on identifying the operations on digital media. It gives the reader an idea of what can be done with digital media, without going into details of how specific operations are implemented. **Part II** then looks at multimedia programming. We do this in the context of an object-oriented framework that provides classes and methods used to build multimedia applications. We illustrate how to model media devices, media data, and media operations using object-oriented techniques. We also describe two applications, a virtual museum and 'video widgets', which have been implemented using a prototype multimedia programming environment. Finally **Part III** speculates about the future directions of multimedia programming. Using the vocabulary provided by the object-oriented framework, current research problems including composition, synchronization, and database integration are described. The final chapter then looks at an example of a large-scale distributed multimedia system. The *Polikom* project, currently under way in Germany, illustrates both the scope of future multimedia applications and many of the challenges facing designers and users of multimedia programming environments.

Simon Gibbs
Dionysios Tsichritzis
September 1994

Note to the Reader

Depending on one's interests and background this book can be read in different ways. People familiar with multimedia technology may choose to skim Part I, or to proceed directly to the object-oriented framework of Part II. Those more interested in the technology than programming should look at Part I and perhaps Part III. In either case the glossary can be consulted for short descriptions of the various acronyms that appear throughout the book.

Index to Online Multimedia Sources

One of the authors maintains an index of pointers to multimedia-related information found on the Internet. The index can be accessed via a WWW (World Wide Web) browser; the URL is http://cui_www.unige.ch/OSG/MultimediaInfo

ACKNOWLEDGMENTS

The authors would like to thank their colleagues in the Object Systems Group at the University of Geneva for their assistance and encouragement over the past few years. Past and present members of this group, including Costas Arapis, Christian Breiteneder, Eduardo Casais, Laurent Dami, Vicki de Mey, Betty Junod, Dimitri Konstantas, Oscar Nierstrasz, Michael Papathomas, Xavier Pintado, Vassilis Prevelakis, Serge Renfer, Marc Stadelmann, and Jan Vitek, helped create the environment that made this book possible. Christian Breiteneder, Vicki de Mey, Laurent Dami, and Michael Papathomas were involved in designing and implementing the prototypes discussed in Chapter 6 and contributed to the reports and papers on which the chapter is based. Vicki de Mey and Christian Breiteneder deserve particular thanks for their aid in developing and clarifying our views of multimedia programming and for acting as test readers. We would also like to thank Josef Schaefer and Manfred Kaul of GMD for their valuable assistance in collecting information about the Polikom project, Rita Brennan of Apple, Bert Gall of Philips, and Matt Saettler of Microsoft for kindly reviewing parts of the book and helping improve its technical accuracy, and the anonymous reviewers for taking the time to provide many corrections and helpful suggestions.

The authors acknowledge the support of the University of Geneva and the *Fonds Nationale Suisse de la Recherche Scientifique.* In addition the work described in this book was aided by the *Ithaca* project of the Commission of the European Communities' ESPRIT program.

Simon Gibbs
Dionysios Tsichritzis
Geneva, September 1994

Permission acknowledgements

Plate I	Screen shot of the NeXTStep mail composition tool. Courtesy NeXT Computer, Inc.
Plate II	Screen shot of Avid VideoShop. Courtesy Avid Technology, Inc.
Plate III	Polikom video conferencing tools. Courtesy Josef Schaefer and Manfred Kaul of GMD.
Plate VI	Surface images. Images on top of page: see 'Heidi' credit below. Images at bottom of page: see 'Vase' credit below.
Plate VII	Volume images. Courtesy Silicon Graphics, Inc.

Figure 3.5	Adapted from Preston (1987).
Figure 3.7	Adapted from Preston (1987).
Figure 3.8	Adapted from Preston (1987).
Figure 3.10	Adapted from Luther (1991). © 1991, McGraw-Hill, Inc; reproduced with permission of McGraw-Hill.
Figure 3.12	Adapted from Green (1992). © 1992, Association of Computing Machinery; courtesy of the author.
Figure 3.19	Adapted from Apple Computer, Inc. (1992).
Figure 3.23	Adapted from Microsoft Corporation (1991b).
Table 3.13	Adapted from Microsoft Corporation (1991a).
Figure 3.24	Screen shot of MacroMind Director. Courtesy Macromedia, Inc.

'Barcelona Pavilion' (3D museum model, Figure 6.1, Figure 6.29) produced by Dan Baum, Efi Fogel, Dave Ligon, Jim Winget, Ben Garlick, and Rolf Van Widenfelt, all of Silicon Graphics, Inc.; courtesy Silicon Graphics, Inc.

'Heidi' (Plate VI top, Figure 6.1) courtesy Cyberware Labs., Inc.

'Vase' (Plate VI bottom, Figure 6.1 and Figure 6.2) courtesy M. Rioux of the National Research Council of Canada, Institute of Information Technology.

CONTENTS

Trademarks

386SX™, 486SX™, ActionMedia™ and DVI™ are trademarks of Intel
    Corporation.

Adobe PhotoShop™, and PostScript® are trademarks of Adobe Systems, Inc.

Alpha AXP™ and XMedia are trademarks of Digital Equipment Corporation.

Amiga®, CD32, and CDTV are trademarks of Commodore Computer.

Apple®, Macintosh®, QuickDraw™ and QuickTime™ are trademarks of Apple
    Computer, Inc.

Betacam™ and Playstation-X are trademarks of Sony Inc.

CD-i, and LaserVision are trademarks of Philips Ltd.

CompuServe® is a trademark of CompuServe, Inc.

FrameMaker® is a trademark of Frame Technology Corporation.

Helvetica™, and Times™ are trademarks of Linotype AG.

IBM PC™, Andrew™, VGA, OS/2 and MMPM/2 are trademarks of IBM
    Corporation.

Interleaf is a trademark of Interleaf Corp.

MacroMind Director® is a trademark of Macromedia, Inc.

NeXTdimension®, and NeXTStep® are trademarks of NeXT Corp.

PageMaker® is a trademark of Aldus Corporation.

RenderMan® is a trademark of Pixar Inc.

SGI™, OpenGL™ and Silicon Graphics® are trademarks of Silicon Graphics,
    Inc.

Sun™ is a trademark of Sun Microsystems, Inc.

T_EX™ is a trademark of American Mathematical Society.

UNIX® is a trademark of AT&T.

VideoToaster™ is a trademark of NewTek Inc.

VideoShop® is a trademark of Avid Technology, Inc.

VideoWindow is a trademark of Bellcore Corp.

Windows™, and Video for Windows are trademarkts of Microsoft Corp.

X Window System™, and X11™ are trademarks of Massachusetts Institute of
    Technology.

PART I

1

AN INTRODUCTION TO MULTIMEDIA

1.1 What is multimedia?
1.2 Multimedia hardware
1.3 Multimedia networking
1.4 Multimedia software: applications
1.5 Multimedia software: environments

Multimedia combines audio and visual material to enhance communication and enrich its presentation. The origin of multimedia lies in the arts and education where there is an ongoing tradition of experimentation in how information is conveyed (Ambron and Hooper, 1988; Barrett, 1992). Multimedia performances and exhibits, multimedia training material, and multimedia presentations all explore the use of various sensory channels and modes of expression. This existing tradition is now being enlarged by a new type of multimedia, one based on digital technology. Desktop computers can manipulate photographic images, audio recordings, and video clips in digital form. Digital media are readily combined and processed, and they are emerging as key elements of modern information technology.

In the original tradition of multimedia, the technology, while necessary, is of secondary importance; instead the focus is on creativity, conveying information, and engaging the imagination. One could say there is an emphasis on content rather than 'mechanics'. On the other hand, those who work with digital multimedia often need be aware of the underlying technology – the mechanics of digital media. We are at a point where this technology is rapidly changing, so exploiting the potential of multimedia requires knowing not only what is currently possible, but also what future developments are likely to bring.

This chapter summarizes several aspects of digital multimedia. We begin by discussing definitions of multimedia and its related terms. Rather than search for general definitions that satisfy all people on all occasions, we simply define some basic terms as they are used throughout the book. We then give short descriptions of many multimedia technologies, ranging from hardware devices and networking protocols to software applications and environments. A more comprehensive survey is presented by Koegel Buford (1994), and recent overviews are given by Fox (1991) and Fuhrt (1994).

1.1 WHAT IS MULTIMEDIA?

Interest in multimedia is currently pervasive – entertainment and educational groups are exploring new applications, and the computer, telecommunications, and consumer electronics industries are actively developing underlying technology. As a term, 'multimedia' is frequently used but rarely defined. Among hardware and software engineers, attempts to provide a meaning range from the whimsical 'multi-cable definition' (multimedia is when you have too many cables) to those emphasizing communication or interaction (Grimes and Potel, 1991). It is difficult to pin down the essence of multimedia since the term appears in numerous contexts, each with its own nuances. Computer users have multimedia presentations, multimedia workstations, and multimedia databases, but the people involved – the presentation authors, workstation designers, and database researchers – view multimedia from different perspectives. One point where they can agree, however, is on the essential role played by *multimedia data*. For instance, multimedia presentations, as their name suggests, involve the presentation of multimedia data, multimedia workstations deal with the processing of multimedia data, and multimedia databases with its storage and retrieval. Perhaps, then, the notion of multimedia data is a unifying thread to digital multimedia.

So what is multimedia data? Let's first look at the related notion of media data. McLuhan, in *Understanding Media*, considers media as 'extensions to man', as technologies and products giving our senses access to further forms of information. This very broad definition encompasses two more specific views. The first relates the term media to how information is conveyed and distributed; for instance, we have print and broadcast media. Second, we also use the term media when describing the materials and forms of artistic expression. This occurs when we speak of *digital media*, not in the sense of digital storage media, but in the sense of digital counterparts to *natural media*.

The distinction between natural and digital media may not always be clear-cut, but the idea is that natural media rely on physical elements – paper, stone, inks and paints, musical instruments, and the stage – while digital media rely on the computer. Suppose we call *artifacts* the objects produced in a particular medium; we can then define *media data* as machine-readable representations of artifacts.

For instance, prints, paintings, musical performances, musical recordings, films, and video clips are all artifacts; media data corresponding to these artifacts consist of digital images, digital video recordings, and digital audio recordings.

We have described three related terms: media, both natural and digital; artifacts, objects produced in media; and media data, digital representations of artifacts. Some examples are shown below.

Media	Artifacts	Media data
Photographic prints (a natural medium)	A photograph (a natural artifact)	A digital image
Computer display devices (a digital medium)	An image on a display device (a digital artifact)	A digital image

Although media data are bits and bytes used by the computer, this data can represent artifacts from both natural and digital media. Digital images produced by scanning either photographic prints or hand drawings are representations of natural artifacts, while digital images produced by a computer paint program are representations of digital artifacts.

Now that we have the notions of media, media data and artifact, we define *multimedia artifacts* as the composition of artifacts from various media. Different composition techniques are possible and will depend upon the media involved. Composition is sometimes divided into two broad categories: *spatial composition*, for instance, one image being juxtaposed with a second, and *temporal composition*, as when an audio track is added to a visual sequence. In analogy with the definition of media data, we define *multimedia data* as machine-readable representations of multimedia artifacts. Notice that the artifacts being represented may be natural, digital, or a mix of both natural and digital.

1.2 MULTIMEDIA HARDWARE

One of the stumbling blocks facing the developers of multimedia software is the variety of hardware and related equipment – tapes and disks of various shapes and sizes, cables, connectors, and switches. This section gives a classification of the types of hardware found in practice. The hardware needed by a particular application will depend on the nature of the application: whether it simply presents information, or allows creation and modification; the types of media used; and the styles of interaction supported. Rather than classify hardware on the basis of application characteristics one can rely on the intrinsic functionality of the hardware. One possibility is the following six categories (note, there is some overlap and some devices may fall in more than one category):

- Digital media devices – media-specific digital hardware

- Analog media devices – media-specific analog hardware

- General-purpose devices – non-media-specific hardware

- Synchronization devices – aid in media synchronization

- Interaction devices – allow user interaction

- Multimedia platforms – integrate several media devices

Digital media devices □ The process of creating a digital representation of a media artifact is called *capture*. The inverse process, re-creating either the artifact or a facsimile of the artifact, is called *presentation*. Both capture and presentation rely on hardware that translates between the internal digital world of the computer and the external analog world of perceivable sounds and images. Special purpose hardware is also used for *processing* media data, such as decoding a compressed representation, adding special effects, or converting from one representation to another. In other words, we can divide media-specific digital hardware into three sub-categories: capture devices, presentation devices, and processing devices. Examples of these groups are listed in Table 1.1.

Table 1.1   Examples of digital media devices.

Capture	Presentation	Processing
ASCII keyboard	Framebuffer, display driver	Video encoder or decoder
MIDI keyboard	Printer	Audio encoder or decoder
Image scanner	MIDI synthesizer	Digital video effects device
3D digitizer	Audio digital-to-analog converter	Digital audio effects device
Video frame grabber		3D graphics hardware
Video digitizer		
Audio digitizer		

Analog media devices □ Often digital media devices are in turn connected to *analog* devices such as microphones or displays. Although these devices deal with analog media they may be under computer control. As with digital devices it is possible to divide analog devices into three groups: *sources*, *sinks*, and *filters*. Sources produce analog signals while sinks are consumers. Filters convert from one analog medium to another or alter analog media in some fashion. Some examples are listed in Table 1.2.

Table 1.2   Examples of analog media devices.

Sources	Sinks	Filters
Microphone	Speaker	Analog video effects device
Video camera	Video display	Analog audio effects device
Video tape player	Video tape recorder	Audio mixer
Audio tape player	Audio tape recorder	Video scan converter
Videodisc player		Video overlay device
Photographic camera		

General-purpose devices □ The third hardware category includes devices that process or deal with arbitrary media, as opposed to being designed for a specific media type. Examples include storage devices, such as CD-ROM and magnetic disk, network interfaces, and general-purpose processors. Most devices in this category are digital; however, one can find examples of non-media-specific analog devices. For instance, oscilloscopes are used to measure both audio signals and video signals.

Interaction devices ☐ Interactive multimedia applications offer a rich range of interaction possibilities. Interaction devices give the user direct control over application behavior; they are handled, spoken to, or even worn by the user. Examples range from fairly traditional devices, such as the mouse and joystick, to the more recent electronic pens and 3D trackers. Some of the capture devices, keyboards in particular, also fall into this category.

Synchronization devices ☐ The simultaneous presentation and manipulation of multiple media often demands hardware assistance to maintain proper timing. Specialized synchronization devices, such as 'sync generators' and 'genlocks', are used in audio and video studios and other situations where synchronization requirements are particularly stringent.

Multimedia platforms ☐ Assembling a multimedia platform often entails installing boards, adding memory, selecting cables, and other time-consuming tasks. Off-the-shelf multimedia platforms reduce the *bricolage* facing end users by packaging the needed functionality into a single product; in addition they give developers a chance to target their applications at well-defined hardware environments. Current multimedia platforms include ordinary workstations, and PCs, with built-in support for several media. For instance, the workstation might come equipped with a color display, speakers and microphone, CD-ROM drive, and audio and video digitizers. Most of the major PC and workstation manufacturers now have products that can be classified as multimedia platforms.

1.3 MULTIMEDIA NETWORKING

Desktop conferencing systems and other distributed multimedia applications require digital networks for the transfer of audio and video data. Many current networks are not appropriate for these applications – the protocols that govern current networks and their limited bandwidths are ill-suited for digital audio/video traffic. *Multimedia networks*, on the other hand, provide a better match to the communication characteristics of distributed multimedia applications (Shepherd and Salmony, 1990; Ferrari *et al.*, 1992). These networks are specifically designed for multimedia traffic – especially digital audio and digital video. Multimedia networks differ from current local and wide area networks in several ways. They are distinguished by the following features:

Bandwidth ☐ One stream of digital video, even when compressed, can result in several Mbits per second. If digital video is sent at this rate, only a few video streams are needed to saturate a local area network such as an Ethernet. Multi-media networks are likely to have bandwidths of Gbits per second or more; this is essential in the long-haul sections of the network where many simultaneous video streams can be expected. Broadband ISDN and Asynchronous Transfer Mode (ATM) are examples of relevant technologies and the basis of international stand-ards for future multimedia networks. See, for example, de Prycker (1991) and Stallings (1992) for detailed descriptions of broadband technologies.

Multicasting □ Distributed multimedia applications often require multicasting, the transmission of data from one source to *many* destinations. The protocols for multimedia networks allow the set of destinations to change over time. This would be needed, for instance, in an electronic classroom where students can enter and leave as they choose.

Real-time constraints □ The transmission of multimedia data is subject to tim-ing constraints. Possible constraints include limits on transmission delay and lim-its on the 'jerkiness' of delivery (that is, applications may request that data be de-livered smoothly as opposed to being buffered and delivered in large chunks). This is essential for applications that have 'live' sources or must present synchro-nized audio and video streams.

Reliability □ In multimedia networks, reliability is a question of quality. Audio and video data, in comparison to text or numeric data, are less sensitive to errors and loss during transmission. Losing a few pixels from a video frame, or getting a few bits wrong in an audio sample, may result in barely noticeable presentation errors and so is probably not catastrophic. However, multimedia networks cannot totally ignore reliability since as errors increase, noise is added which ultimately leads to unacceptable presentation quality.

Quality-of-Service (QoS) □ Different applications have different communica-tions requirements. A conferencing system, where data is presented once and 'thrown away', can tolerate a higher error rate than an application that records a multimedia data stream for future playback. Although less sensitive to errors, the conferencing system requires fast delivery, while for the recording application long transmission delays are of no concern. One way that networks can support variations in requirements is by allowing each application to specify 'Quality-of-Service', or QoS, parameters. For example, consider an audio stream where data is produced by a source at a constant rate of 64 kbps. An application might request the following QoS parameters: a bandwidth of 64 kbps, a maximum delay of 100 ms, and a maximum loss rate of 1%. The multimedia network would then al-locate sufficient resources to satisfy the application's demands, or tell the applica-tion that the network is 'busy'.

1.4 MULTIMEDIA SOFTWARE: APPLICATIONS

User interfaces to computer software are often embellished by adding sounds, animation, and other forms of multimedia. An example would be a text editor playing audio messages to indicate errors or other events. In some sense the editor can be called a multimedia application since it uses both text and audio data. However, if multimedia applications simply make use of audio or graphics it would mean that nearly any application, after perhaps a few small changes, can be called a multimedia application. It is better to reserve the term 'multimedia application' for situations where multimedia is central to the application, rather than something gratuitous or added as an afterthought. Seen in this light, one can identify several categories for multimedia applications:

Interactive videodisc applications □ A videodisc (see page 40) holds about 50000 video frames, which is 30 minutes of video at normal playback speed. By attaching a videodisc player to a computer, software can randomly access specific frames and play selected sequences at various speeds. Computer-controllable videodisc players have been available since the mid-1970s and applications built around these devices are among the earliest examples of interactive multimedia applications. Many videodisc applications are intended for instructional use and are designed for specific learning scenarios. For example, the *Visual Almanac* (Apple Inc., 1989), an elaborate collection of video material and accompanying software, allows students to engage in such activities as exploring the solar system, listening to musical instruments, or looking at animal habitats.

Electronic games □ By far the most widely used form of interactive multimedia are the electronic games from Sega, Nintendo, and other manufacturers. These products come in several configurations including small hand-held units with LCD displays and 'consoles' which connect to external video displays. Joysticks, trigger grips, and a few buttons serve as input devices. Games are stored on cartridges which can be inserted in players. Each game is a highly interactive multimedia application that presents layered 2D animation with synchronized sound effects and music. The hardware found in game playing systems is becoming more powerful and new models often contain CD drives (for storage), video decompression hardware (for video playback), and 3D graphics hardware.

Hypermedia browsers □ Hypermedia is a way of organizing multimedia information by linking media elements. The elements being linked are called *nodes* and the entire assemblage is a hypermedia *web*. Links represent semantic relationships – when a link exists between two nodes they should be related in some fashion. For instance, a digital image can be linked to a textual description of the image which is in turn linked to related audio or video material. A hypermedia browser lets users view nodes and traverse links from one node to another.

Multimedia presentation systems □ A multimedia presentation system is an 'engine' that displays, synchronizes, provides interaction with, and generally manipulates multimedia material. This is a somewhat nebulous category that over-laps with previous categories, in particular hypermedia browsers and electronic games. Examples include 'presentation software', used to compile and display electronic 'slides', and browsers for multimedia documents (for example, a multi-media encyclopedia browser).

Multimedia authoring systems ☐ Preparation of multimedia material, in par-ticular when used for presentations, training, or entertainment, is called *authoring*. An authoring system is a collection of software tools that help in the many steps of multimedia production. These steps include:

- Media capture: Media data can be obtained by 'capturing' existing artifacts. Multimedia authoring systems streamline data capture by providing interfaces to a range of image scanners, video digitizers, and other capture devices.

- Media conversion: It is a fact of life that images, audio clips, animation sequences, and video clips exist in a variety of formats. A well-equipped multimedia authoring system will have a set of utilities for converting between many of the commonly used formats.

- Media editing: After data has been captured and converted to the native format of the authoring system it may need further massaging before it is suitable for presentation. For instance, noise can be removed from audio clips, images touched up, and graphics rearranged. Multimedia authoring systems provide media-specific editors for these operations.

- Media composition: At the core of a multimedia authoring system is a tool for combining media and specifying their spatial and temporal relationships. The tool may offer several views of the artifact under construction. Useful views include a document-like layout for spatial composition and a timeline for temporal composition.

- Adding interactivity: Multimedia authoring systems provide ways for embedding interactivity in multimedia material. Possibilities include attaching 'interactors', such as buttons, menus, and dialog boxes, to media elements. The interactor is stored with the media data and is activated on presentation. Powerful authoring systems also have scripting languages which are used to attach arbitrary procedures to media elements.

- Media mastering: The final step in multimedia production is preparing the material for distribution. This can include, for example, determining a CD-ROM layout that gives good performance, or preparing different playback formats for different platforms. An authoring system can help keep track of the elements that appear in a multimedia production and assemble them in a distribution format.

Multimedia mail systems ☐ A multimedia mail system handles electronic mes-sages containing audio, graphics, and other media. Three components are needed – one for creating messages, a message transfer service, and a component for presenting messages. Standards are critical so that a message created using one system can be presented on another. Several products supporting multimedia mail are now in use; an example is shown in Plate I.

Desktop video systems □ Desktop video systems use workstations or PCs for video capture, editing and 'post-production' (for instance, the addition of titles and effects). The first desktop video systems dealt with analog video – the computer is used to control analog video equipment and video is stored in analog form, usually on video tape. More recent desktop video systems digitize the video and store it in compressed form on magnetic disk. An example of a digital video editing system is shown in Plate II.

Desktop conferencing systems □ A desktop computer equipped with microphone, speakers, and a video camera, and placed on a multimedia network, can establish audio and video connections between other, similarly equipped, machines. This is the basis of desktop conferencing, where the computer plays the role of a multimedia communications device. A 'conference' may be a short two-party conversation or a lengthy meeting between several participants, some of whom come and go as the conference proceeds. The power of desktop conferencing is increased by adding *multi-user tools*, such as group editors. These tools allow conference participants to share documents and other forms of data. Participants can simultaneously edit the shared objects and view each other's changes. An example system, including several multi-user tools, is shown in Plate III.

Multimedia services □ Finally, many multimedia applications fit under the broad heading of 'multimedia services'. Examples include interactive shopping, banking, educational and medical services where multimedia is used to enrich the interface; and *video-on-demand*, where users play back remotely stored digital video in their homes.

1.5 MULTIMEDIA SOFTWARE: ENVIRONMENTS

The previous section listed several categories of multimedia applications. At the moment commercial products are available in each category so although we are in the early stages of building multimedia networks, and although there are still many questions concerning standards and platforms, multimedia applications are already here.

As multimedia applications grow in number and sophistication, lower-level support software becomes more important. For instance, by providing well-defined interfaces to audio and video devices, operating systems can simplify application development and improve portability. An operating system with audio and video support is one example of a *multimedia environment* – a set of services, abstractions, interfaces, and libraries intended for multimedia programming. Other examples include multimedia database systems and multimedia toolkits. Perhaps not surprisingly, multimedia environments are less mature than multimedia applications. Products have appeared as questions of standards and infrastructure are still being resolved. The situation is now improving – multimedia environments are receiving greater attention than before and are the focus of much research and industrial activity.

Multimedia operating systems □ The high data rates of digital audio and digital video place heavy demands on computing resources – processor cycles are needed for decoding and encoding, bus bandwidth is needed for pulling data off storage devices. Furthermore, these tasks are subject to timing constraints deriving from video frame rates and audio sampling rates. Multimedia operating systems, like real-time operating systems, help manage time-sensitive tasks. Tokuda (1994) gives an overview of operating system support for multimedia applications. The question of what functionality is needed by multimedia operating systems is an active research area; however, current proposals often include:

- Real-time process scheduling: Multimedia applications are generally time-sensitive. Various forms of synchronization arise, such as 'lip sync' between audio and video, or the triggering of activities as animation scripts are played. Some processes have real-time deadlines. For instance, a music synthesizer has to produce notes on time; similarly a renderer may have to produce frames at a specific rate. Real-time schedulers allow processes to declare their timing requirements. The scheduler then attempts to ensure that all processes with timing requirements are given sufficient processor cycles. For example, consider a process that requires activation at regular intervals – perhaps it is involved with video frame processing or data acquisition. A real-time scheduler would ensure this process was not kept waiting by lower priority non-real-time processes.

- Continuous media abstractions: Digital audio and video are sometimes referred to as *continuous media* since both input (recording) and output (playback) are ongoing activities. Traditional file systems are not designed for continuous access. As a result, applications during playback may have to contend with buffer underflow (since the file system is not providing data fast enough). Similarly, during recording, buffers will overflow if the file system cannot keep up with the input data rate. Each case leads to unacceptable quality, such as clicks or stutters in an audio track. Multimedia operating systems offer special services for continuous media. They allow applications to create and control streams of continuously flowing data. For example, 'ropes' (Terry and Swinehart, 1988; Venkat Rangan *et al.*, 1991), are continuous media abstractions that combine notions of file access, data flow, and synchronization. Applications manipulate ropes via a high-level interface (such as 'play rope') and do not deal with buffering or data access. Furthermore, the operating system will ensure that the file system provides or consumes data at the appropriate rate.

Multimedia database systems □ Traditional database management systems (DBMSs) deal primarily with numeric and character data. Multimedia database systems, in comparison, manage text, image, graphics, audio, and video data. Full-fledged multimedia database systems are only in the early stages of development, at least as commercial products, although specialized DBMSs for text or image storage are available. The additional features and functionality likely to be found in multimedia database systems include:

- Large data values: Digital images and video have immense sizes so special storage techniques are needed to optimize access. As an example, there have been proposals for adding so-called 'blobs' (binary large objects) to database systems. Blobs are accessed piece-by-piece, rather than all at once. Applications can then store and retrieve arbitrarily large values directly in the database rather than having to fall back to the file system.

- Additional attribute types: In addition to storing large values, multimedia databases need to know something about the *type* of data being stored. Generally database systems interpret, in a limited sense, the data they contain. For instance, each attribute in a relational database has an attribute type. This information is used by the database manager to detect meaningless requests, such as adding a salary to an age, and to perform type-specific operations, such as determining if one date is before or after another. Common attribute types include those used for dates, monetary values and character strings. Multimedia databases have additional attribute types for audio-valued and video-valued attributes and other forms of media data. The database manager can then perform media-specific operations and does not simply treat media data as uninterpreted 'blobs'.

- Extended query languages: Current database manipulation and query languages, such as SQL (Date and Darwen, 1993), are not appropriate for accessing some forms of multimedia data. Consider retrieval: with SQL the SELECT statement is used to find data satisfying a query predicate and transfer it from the database to the application. This style of exchange between applications and the database does not fit the continuous flows that occur during the recording and playback of media data. Instead, query languages for multimedia databases need operations that create stream-like connections between the database and applications. In this way streams of media data, perhaps audio samples or video frames, can be exchanged.

- Long real-time operations: Concurrency control in traditional database systems involves the scheduling of short operations that read and write items in the database. For example, transferring an amount from one bank account to another is realized by a few database operations that select and update the appropriate records. Each of these operations have short durations (likely in the sub-second range). This gives the concurrency manager considerable leeway in scheduling, since changes in the execution order of operations are not likely to seriously delay applications. Hence operations are scheduled so as to maximize database performance while maintaining data integrity. This approach to concurrency control is not suitable for multimedia databases where recording and playback operations can take minutes or hours to complete. Furthermore, both recording and playback are real-time operations; they cannot be arbitrarily interrupted by other database requests. Thus multimedia databases must support long operations with real-time constraints and ensure that sufficient resources are allocated for their duration.

Multimedia toolkits   □   Software toolkits reduce the time needed for application development. Toolkits have been particularly successful for user-interface programming, often a lengthy activity resulting in disproportionately large parts of application code. Multimedia and user-interface programming have many similarities. They both coordinate the presentation of information, they both deal with multiple input and output devices, and both are sensitive to timing issues. Because of these similarities, and because multimedia applications are potentially time-consuming and difficult to implement, toolkits can also greatly simplify multimedia programming. Components of multimedia toolkits range from low-level device drivers, to higher-level subroutine and class libraries, and to special-purpose interpreted languages that border on the scripting languages found in multimedia authoring systems. One of the earliest examples is the *Andrew Toolkit* (Borenstein, 1990) developed by Carnegie Mellon University and IBM. The Andrew Toolkit provides objects and classes for presenting, structuring, and interacting with text, graphics, and other media; it is also extensible so programmers can add new forms of media and interaction mechanisms. A second early example is the *Muse* toolkit (Hodges *et al.*, 1989; Hodges and Sasnett, 1992) developed as part of Project Athena, a large project in the educational use of computers that was sponsored by MIT, Digital Equipment Corporation, and IBM. Muse combines elements of user-interface and document management with multimedia authoring. More recently, NeXT's software environment – *NeXTStep* – has illustrated how object-oriented programming can encapsulate and integrate a variety of media devices and services (NeXT Inc., 1992). NeXTStep contains classes for 2D and 3D graphics, audio and music; there is also some support for video capture, compression and output.

Toolkits simplify development by encapsulating low-level services (for instance, those of the operating system, the window system, and network) by a set of easier to use and interrelated abstractions. The choice of abstractions, and the concepts on which they are based, is a crucial issue. In the second part of this book we motivate an approach to multimedia programming where the primary abstractions are interconnectable media components. To prepare for this we first look in more detail at the primary media types and existing multimedia environments.

I MULTIMEDIA MAIL: NeXT's mail composition tool is used to create multimedia messages. The message being created appears in the main lower window; immediately above is a row of icons for performing mail operations and importing sounds and images. For example, pressing the 'Lip Service' icon brings up a small audio recording panel.

II   DESKTOP VIDEO: Avid's VideoShop. The upper windows contain audio tracks, video tracks, and folders. Video tracks are indicated by 'micons' – icons that, when selected, cycle through a series of icon-sized frames. Movies are composed by sequencing tracks in the lower window.

2

MEDIA TYPES

2.1 Nontemporal media types
2.2 Temporal media types
2.3 Other media types
2.4 Comparisons

The applications discussed in the previous chapter operate on many forms of data. These forms, such as text and video, are called *media types* because of their prominent roles in traditional media. For instance, the *video type* is central to broadcast media, while print media are based on a *text type*. This chapter surveys the main media types, summarizes related concepts and terminology, and gives references for further reading. The selected references are not intended to be exhaustive, but to provide starting points for exploring specific topics.

Media types and data types □ The term 'media type' often appears in informal descriptions of multimedia applications and systems as a way of indicating the different forms of data that are present. This chapter is based on a more precise notion of media type, one derived from the notion of data type found in programming languages. When programmers define a new data type, they give a specification of a data structure plus the operations that can be applied to the structure. Examples of data types familiar to programmers include lists, stacks, and arrays. Media types, like data types, specify both a representation, or data structure, and a set of operations. The difference is that media types include operations of a special nature, operations used to present and capture data in some medium. For instance, a two-dimensional numeric array can be used to represent image data, but if the only operations are things like array multiplication and inversion it does not seem natural to call this a media type. However, the same specification becomes a media type when it is extended with operations for presenting arrays as images on the printed page or some other medium. Similarly a text data type deals with representations and operations on sequences of characters, while a text media type would also specify operations for formatting or printing the text.

The following survey of media types anticipates the object-oriented approach that will be used later in the book. We want to classify media types based on similarities in their representations and operations so as to help understand how to model media types using object-oriented techniques. Questions concerning implementation of operations, algorithm design, and user-interface design are beyond the scope of the book – instead the focus of the survey is on grouping operations on media types into broad categories and discussing their general nature.

The following sections summarize the more common media types; also covered are several new media types which, although less commonly used, offer great potential for interactivity. As an aid in making comparisons and organizing the material, many of the media types will be introduced using a *media type template*:

Media type \<name\>
 Representation
  \<aspects of representation\>
 Operations
  \<categories of operations\>

The template identifies various aspects and forms of representation associated with the media type and divides operations on the media type into a number of broad categories.

2.1 NONTEMPORAL MEDIA TYPES

At a high level, one can divide media types into two groups: temporal and non-temporal (related terminology includes dynamic/static, time-based/non-time-based, and continuous/discrete). The temporal media types include audio, video, music, and animation; their nontemporal counterparts are text, images, and graphics. We begin by discussing the more traditional nontemporal media types.

2.1.1   TEXT

Media type Text
      Representation
            ASCII
            ISO character sets
            Marked-up text
            Structured text
            Hypertext
      Operations
            Character operations
            String operations
            Editing
            Formatting
            Pattern-matching and searching
            Sorting
            Compression
            Encryption
            Language-specific operations

Text may not be as visually exciting as some of the other media types, but it often conveys essential and precise information. With the development of digital video, interactive 3D animation, and multimedia in general, we should not overlook the importance of textual data.

Text representation

Data representations for text range from simple character encodings to elaborate page description languages used to specify not only the characters comprising a text but also its appearance on the printed page.

ASCII □ Consider first the simpler representations. The most commonly used character encoding is ASCII (American Standard Code for Information Interchange), a 7-bit encoding developed by the American national standards body. ASCII codes are usually stored in 8-bit bytes, but a byte can represent 256 values, twice as many as the 128 needed for ASCII. The result is that text editing systems tend to appropriate the unused values for their own purposes, perhaps to represent 'non-ASCII' characters (such as '£') or to embed formatting information. This of course leads to incompatibilities between text editing systems and difficulties in interchanging information, problems that ASCII was meant to overcome.

ISO character sets □ Perhaps the main shortcoming of ASCII is its lack of support for non-English text (even with 'English' text there can be problems, as seen with the sterling symbol above). Recently, extensions to ASCII have been standardized by ISO, the International Organization for Standardization. For example, 'ISO Latin' (ISO, 1987b) is a superset of ASCII which provides an encoding for the accented characters found in many European languages. ISO, in cooperation with national standard bodies, has also standardized encodings for non-Latin character sets. The ISO encodings are becoming widely used, appearing, for example, in the X window system, PostScript, and 'international versions' of software packages. There is also a considerable literature on representing and processing non-Latin text including Chinese, Japanese, and Korean (IEEE, 1985a); Arabic (Becker, 1987); and Chinese and Arabic (ACM, 1990a).

Marked-up text □ Printed text has both form and content. While content may be represented by a sequence of characters, the form of a document, its visual presentation structure, remains an elusive quantity. Clearly content itself does not specify presentation structure and additional information is needed. One approach is to 'mark up' text by embedding special character sequences which identify structural boundaries or specify formatting operations. For example, in *troff* (Ossana, 1976), a text formatting system found on UNIX systems,

```
.ce
This is a line of text.
```

indicates that 'This is a line of text.' should be centered on the page.

A potential problem with marked-up text is mixing logical structure, such as where paragraphs start and stop, with layout structure, such as the positioning of margins. If these two structures are separated it is easier to perform global formatting operations, for instance, changing the point size of all section titles. Ease of reformatting makes the document less dependent on the display device and so more portable. SGML (Standardized General Markup Language), an ISO standard (ISO, 1986; Bryan, 1988; Goldfarb, 1990), separates layout from logical structure by the use of *document types*. In SGML, a document type identifies possible document components and their layout properties, while a *document instance* is text marked up with tags identifying components. By manipulating the document type definition it is then possible to change the overall layout of the document.

Marked-up text can be carried to great extremes. Troff, in addition to supporting a large number of formatting operations, provides control structures, variables, and the ability to define macros. This 'markup language' has been used to define extensions for mathematical equations, tables, references, and line drawings, which simplify the use of troff. Similarly, the use of T_EX (Knuth, 1984), another powerful markup language, is simplified by the L^AT_EX (Lamport, 1986) macro package. Finally, those markup languages that support document types can be extended by defining types for particular domains. For instance, SGML document types have been defined for musical works (see the discussion of SMDL on page 66) and for documents containing time-based information (see the discussion of HyTime in section 3.7).

Structured text ☐ When tags are used, structural information is dispersed throughout the text. Document editors must scan and parse the text in order to extract this information and build representations that can be processed more efficiently. Processing-oriented representations, called *structured text*, use data structures to represent logical and layout organization. As an example, the logical organization of a document might be a series of sections, each with a title and subsections, which in turn are composed of paragraphs. This organization can be represented by a tree-like data structure; another tree-like structure might be used for the breakdown of the layout into pages, blocks and columns. Most document processing and page layout programs have their own proprietary representations for structured text. Some relevant standards, however, do exist. For instance, ODA, the *Office Document Architecture* (Horak, 1985; ISO 1989b), is an international standard that specifies how the logical and layout components may be composed and interrelated. ODA also specifies an interchange format in which the layout and/or logical structures are embedded in a byte stream with the document content.

Hypertext ☐ Although traditional text has a hierarchical structure from the perspective of layout and logical organization, it is also, in many ways, very linear – it has a beginning and an end, and is often intended to be read in a particular order. Hypertext (Conklin, 1987), or nonlinear text, has instead a graph-like structure. With hypertext one speaks of *nodes*, small 'chunks' of text, being connected by *links*. The reader meanders through hypertext by following links of interest. A hypertext browser is a computer-based presentation system that quickly displays nodes and traverses links, thus increasing the sense of interactivity associated with hypertext.

Hypertext nodes range from paragraph-sized or page-sized blocks of text to complete documents. Layout of hypertext generally shares the same concerns as layout of traditional text, although node size and the fact that hypertext is usually displayed on computer monitors rather than printed on paper may influence layout requirements. The difficulty, and essential problem, in hypertext representation is the handling of links. Different forms of links are used by different hypertext systems. Some links are bidirectional, others can be traversed in only one direction. Some links are anchored to nodes, others to sub-parts (such as words or phrases within a node). Links may have attributes (for instance, the link's author) or operations to be performed when the link is followed. At the time of writing, several standards-related activities for hypertext representation are underway (Moline *et al.*, 1990; ISO 1992a; ISO 1992b; Berners-Lee and Connolly, 1993).

Text operations

Here we summarize the main categories of text processing operations; for a more detailed overview of text processing the reader is referred to the survey by Smith (1990).

Character operations ☐ The simplest operations on text deal with individual characters and are the building blocks for more complicated text processing. Many programming languages support a 'character' data type. Variables of this type can be assigned values and accessed by name. It is also possible to compare the lexical ordering of two characters (character encodings, such as ASCII, define a *collating sequence* – an ordering on the character set, allowing one to say, for example, 'a' < 'b').

String operations ☐ Characters are often grouped into *strings* – data structures containing sequences of characters. Common string operations include string comparison ('abc' < 'abd'), string concatenation ('abc' + 'def' → 'abcdef'), and extracting and manipulating substrings.

Editing ☐ Editing operations are used to modify the form and content of documents. The simplest editing operations are the familiar insert/delete and cut/copy/paste. The effect of these basic operations depends on the text representation used by the editor. If the editor views text as simply a long sequence of characters, a string, then these operations correspond to string operations; for instance, paste inserts a substring. If the editor has some notion of document structure then it must do more work: when a block of text is first cut and then pasted the editor repairs the structural information associated with the text. In either case a representation of the *selection* of text to be operated upon is needed. In addition to insert/delete and cut/copy/paste, many text editors provide more complex editing operations for manipulating document structure. Examples include adding paragraphs or creating numbered lists. Meyrowitz and van Dam (1982) survey early editing systems and discuss editor design.

Formatting ☐ Formatting is the process of applying layout specifications to text. Text formatting is either interactive or noninteractive. In the first case, the formatter operates in parallel with an editor. Such a combination is called a WYSIWYG ('what you see is what you get') editor and typically displays formatted text on a computer display as the user edits the text. With noninteractive formatting the user first edits the text and then invokes a formatter which either displays the formatted text on a computer display or sends it to a printer. Furata *et al.* (1982) survey document formatters and compare various approaches.

The output of the formatter may be a bitmap-like image of the formatted text or detailed text positioning information specified in a *page description language*. Page description languages provide device-independent and compact representations of formatted text. At present the most common page description language is PostScript (Adobe Systems Inc., 1990), which is used extensively by laser printers and other high-resolution output devices.

The essence of high-quality text formatting is the rendering of text in different *fonts*. Strictly speaking, a font is a particular *typeface* (such as Times Roman or Helvetica) in a particular *point* size (a point is a unit of measurement used in typography; 1 point is 1/72 of an inch). Early formatting systems used bitmapped fonts. While these fonts can be rendered quickly they have many defects: lack of device independence, large storage requirements or low resolution, and poor quality when scaled or rotated. More flexible fonts are obtained by designing a geometric description of each character within a typeface. This approach has been explored by Knuth (1986) and is used by PostScript. A large number of traditional typefaces are now available in the PostScript *Type 1* format (Grosvenor *et al.*, 1992) which, in addition to geometric character descriptions, employs *kerning* – the variation of spacing between characters (Von Ehr, 1988) – and alignment 'hints' to produce high quality output.

Pattern-matching and searching ☐ Most editors provide a 'search and replace' command based on the ability to recognize a *pattern* (a string, possibly containing special 'wildcards' which match more than one character) within the text. A wide range of patterns can be formally represented by *regular expressions*; table-driven scanners are commonly used to recognize such patterns (Aho and Ullman, 1972). When the pattern is a fixed string more efficient algorithms are possible since scanning time can be improved by skipping over parts of the text (Boyer and Moore, 1977).

Scanning becomes impractical for large bodies of text. Furthermore, finding exact pattern matches becomes less important – instead it is often useful to search for text passages pertaining to particular subjects. A number of database and information retrieval techniques are used for searching large texts. These methods include 'full text inversion', requiring an index of word locations, the use of hashing to create compressed 'signatures' which can then be scanned, and techniques based on the clustering of 'similar' texts. Faloutsos (1985) describes text retrieval methods in more detail.

Sorting ☐ Sorting algorithms have been exhaustively studied by computer scientists and their time and space requirements are well known. Knuth (1973) provides an extensive survey of sorting algorithms.

Compression ☐ ASCII uses 7 bits per character, yet information theoretic arguments estimate 1–2 bits per character being sufficient for natural language text. In a sense there are 5 bits of redundant information per character. Text compression schemes remove this redundancy and reduce the storage requirements of text. Two common methods are Huffman coding and Lempel-Ziv coding. Huffman coding varies the number of bits used to represent characters – it attempts to shorten the code as frequency increases. The Lempel-Ziv algorithm identifies repeating strings and replaces them by pointers to a table. Both methods compress English text to between one-half and two-thirds its original size. Descriptions of the Huffman and Lempel-Ziv algorithms, and comparisons with a number of additional text compression algorithms, are provided by Bell *et al.* (1989).

Encryption ☐ Text encryption is increasing in use with the spread of electronic mail and other network services. One commonly used method is *DES* (Data Encryption Standard) (National Bureau of Standards, 1977). More versatile and more secure encryption can be achieved using *public key* algorithms (Rivest *et al.*, 1978). A number of such algorithms have been developed and are in use. Recently the use of encryption, in particular within the telephone system, has become a topic of much controversy (ACM, 1993b).

Language-specific operations □ The operations described above are language-independent – they can be applied to text containing English, French, or any other language for which a character encoding exists. There are other operations which make use of knowledge about specific languages. These operations include spelling checking, parsing, and the statistical analysis of writing style. Smith (1990) gives an introduction to this aspect of text processing.

2.1.2   IMAGE

Media type Image
>   **Representation**
>>   Color model
>>   Alpha channels
>>   Number of channels
>>   Channel depth
>>   Interlacing
>>   Indexing
>>   Pixel aspect ratio
>>   Compression
>   **Operations**
>>   Editing
>>   Point operations
>>   Filtering
>>   Compositing
>>   Geometric transformations
>>   Conversion

In this section we discuss *digital images* – two-dimensional arrays of pixels of varying color or intensity. Although we assume an array-like structure, it is possible that other data structures are used for image storage. Arrays should be considered as a conceptual, or abstract, representation – we are always free to talk about particular pixels at particular coordinates, whether or not they are actually stored in an array. Also, it is useful to differentiate between image types and the data types from which images are *produced* through some computational process. For example, two pairs of numbers can be interpreted as line end-points, the line can be drawn and an image obtained. Are line coordinates then an image type? Here we choose to classify data types used to produce images as *graphics types*. Admittedly there are borderline cases. Yet the division between image data and graphic data often appears in practice, and, although the boundary may blur, we will continue to make the distinction.

Digital images are clearly an important media type; they are essential to many professions and are commonly used in, for instance, film and video production, meteorology, medicine, and publishing. However, these areas have different requirements and tend to have their own preferred image representations and operations.

Image representation

Although there are many different formats for image data, these formats can be compared along certain dimensions. These dimensions include:

Color model □ Digital color images require some form of encoding color. A procedure for specifying colors is called a *color model* (or *color space*). There are two main types of color models: those related to color production on some output device, and those based on theories of human color perception. Foley *et. al* (1990) provide an introduction to color models, and further information is given by Thorell and Smith (1990); here we just mention the more common models:

> *CIE color space*:   An international standard for color specification created by the *Commission Internationale de l'Éclairage* and used as a reference to calibrate other color models. The original CIE color space, known as CIE XYZ, was developed in 1931 and is based on the *tristimulus* theory of color specification which implies that the perceived color of any light source can be specified by three parameters. A number of extensions to the CIE XYZ space have been developed; many are compared by Thorell and Smith (1990).

> *RGB*:   Colors are represented by a numeric triple specifying red (R), green (G), and blue (B) intensities. This model is convenient for video display drivers since the numeric values can be easily mapped to voltages for the red, green, and blue guns in color CRTs.

> *HSB*:   Colors are represented by a triple representing *hue* (the dominant color of a sample; hue is represented by an angular value varying from red to green to blue at 120° intervals), *saturation* (the intensity of the color) and *brightness* (the amount of gray in the color, brighter colors have less gray).

> *CMYK*:   Computer displays emit light; they produce colors by adding red, green, and blue intensities. Paper, on the other hand, reflects light. To print a particular color on a white page one must apply inks that subtract (absorb) all colors other than the one desired. For this reason printers use inks corresponding to the *subtractive primaries* – cyan, magenta, and yellow – the complements of the red, green, and blue. Mixing equal quantities of pure cyan, magenta, and yellow inks produces black. However, in practice inks are not pure and a special black ink (the 'K' in CMYK) is used to give better blacks and grays.

> *YUV*:   A color model used within the television industry. There are a variety of YUV-like color models with names such as YIQ, YCbCr and YPbPr (Thorell and Smith, 1990). Here we use YUV loosely as referring to these models in general. Y represents *luminance*, and can be thought of as the black-and-white portion of a video signal. UV are *color difference signals* (they involve the difference between Y, and B and R respectively). UV

forms the color portion of a video signal and is called *chrominance*, or simply *chroma*. YUV is suited for video broadcast since it makes efficient use of bandwidth: the human eye has greater sensitivity to changes in luminance than to color changes, so it is possible to better utilize available bandwidth by allocating less to chroma and more to luminance.

Alpha channels □ In addition to color information, images may have one or more alpha channels defining regions of full or partial transparency. Alpha channels can be used to store selections and to create masks and blends when compositing images (Porter and Duff, 1984).

Number of channels □ This quantity is the number of pieces of information associated with each pixel. This is typically the dimensionality of the color model used by the image (for instance, four channels for CMYK, three for RGB) plus the number of alpha channels present.

Channel depth □ A channel's depth is the number of bits-per-pixel used to encode the channel values. Typical depths are 1, 2, 4, and 8 bits. Less common are 5, 6, 12, and 16 bit depths. In a multiple-channel image it is quite possible that different channels will have different depths. For instance, if 16 bits are available per pixel and the RGB model is used, then one might allocate 5 bits to each of two colors and 6 bits to the remaining color.

Interlacing □ The storage layout of a multiple-channel image may separate channel values (as when R values for all pixels are stored, followed by all G values, followed by all B values) or use interlacing (RGB for the first pixel, followed by RGB for the second, and so on).

Indexing □ A number of image formats allow pixel colors to be represented by an index in a *color map* or *color lookup table* (CLUT). The color map may be predefined (for instance, a default map used by a window server) or may be specified as part of the image data.

Pixel aspect ratio □ This term refers to the ratio of pixel width to height. Images with square pixels are simpler to process; however, some displays and scanners work with rectangular pixels. If the pixel aspect ratios of an image and a display monitor differ, the image will appear stretched or squeezed when displayed.

Compression □ Digital images consume large amounts of storage. For instance, a page-sized 24-bit color image (8 bits for each of RGB) produced by a medium-resolution scanner (producing 300 pixels per inch) takes up about 20 Mbytes. In order to reduce image size, many image formats compress the pixel data. Commonly used techniques include run-length coding, LZW coding (Lempel-Ziv and Welsh, a variation of Lempel-Ziv coding), predictive coding, and transform coding. See Netravali and Limb (1980) for a description of many image coding techniques.

Image compression methods are classified as *lossless* (compression followed by decompression preserves the image) and *lossy* (some information is lost). Methods based on transform coding are lossy; however, these methods have high compression ratios. Transform coding represents an image by the coefficients of some mathematical transform of the image. The *discrete cosine transform*, or DCT, is frequently used and is the basis of an international standard known as *JPEG*, named after ISO's and CCITT's 'Joint Photographic Experts Group' (Wallace, 1991). With JPEG it is possible to control the amount of compression, and the resulting image quality. Typically, JPEG can compress images to one-fifth of their original size without noticeable loss of quality.

Generally, the amount of compression achieved by a particular method will depend on image content. For example, synthetic images, such as those produced by drawing and paint programs, often contain large regions of constant color, and run-length coding will work well. For natural, continuous-tone images, such as those originating from scanners or video digitizers, transform coding is more appropriate.

Given the number of choices that can be made in determining image representation, it is not surprising that a number of image formats have evolved. Two examples are GIF and TIFF. GIF (Graphics Interchange Format) was developed by CompuServe for the exchange of images over dial-up lines. It uses LZW coding to compress images and so reduce transfer times. TIFF (Tagged Image File Format) is a flexible format that supports a wide range of pixel depths and compression methods. For more information on image file formats, a comprehensive survey is given by Kay and Levine (1992).

Image operations

Image processing operations may operate directly on pixel data or on higher-level features such as edges, surfaces, and volumes. Operations in the second group fall under the domains of image analysis and image understanding; they are beyond the scope of this book. Instead we focus on operations which are commonly used in collecting and preparing image material for presentation and display. We divide these operations into six categories: editing, point operations, filtering, composition, geometric transformations, and conversions. Support for a variety of image operations is now becoming available in page-layout and paint programs. To illustrate these operations we give examples of their use in Photoshop, a powerful image editor (Adobe Systems Inc., 1991).

Editing □ The most basic image editing operation is changing individual pixels. This ability is needed for delicate image touch-up, and is the basis of 'paintbrush operations' such as airbrushing and texturing. Image editors also support cutting, copying, and pasting selected *groups* of pixels. A selection might be a simple rectangular sub-image or, more usefully, an arbitrarily-shaped region. For example, Plate IV(c) shows a mask which selects the foreground of the image in Plate IV(b). Such detailed and complex selections are either drawn by the user or calculated by software (for instance, by examining color differences between neighboring pixels).

Point operations □ A point operation consists of applying a function to every pixel in an image (or selection). The function is of a special form – in calculating a new pixel value, the only image data used is the pixel's current value. (For instance, looking at neighboring pixels is excluded.) Examples of these operations include:

Thresholding: A pixel is set to 1 or 0 depending upon whether it is above or below the threshold value. This creates monochrome (binary) images which are often used as masks when compositing.

Color correction: An image may be modified to increase or reduce contrast, brightness, to alter *gamma* (changing gamma affects the brightness of midtones and has less effect on highlights and shadows), and to strengthen or weaken particular colors.

Filtering □ Filter operations, like point operations, involve applying a function to every pixel in an image or selection. The function determines a pixel's new value based on its current value and that of neighboring pixels. Depending on the definition of the function, filtering is used to blur or sharpen an image, introduce distortions, and produce a variety of special effects (several examples are shown in Plate IV).

Compositing □ Image compositing is the combining of two or more images to produce a new image. Alpha channels are frequently used to control blending and masking. An example is shown in Plate IV(h) where the chameleon from Plate IV(b) has been placed on a computer-generated background. In general, compositing is specified by mathematical relationships between the various images, for instance one image might be produced from the sum of two existing images. An immense variety of effects are possible. Examples are given by Holzmann (1988) who describes a language for composing images.

Geometric transformations □ Basic geometric transformations include displacing, rotating, mirroring, and scaling an image. Other geometric transformations include skewing (slanting) an image and warping (Wolberg, 1990). An example of the latter is mapping a rectangular selection to an arbitrary four-sided polygon.

Conversions □ With the variety of image formats there is a frequent need to convert from one format to another. Fortunately there are a number of public domain software packages which handle many format conversion tasks; in addition, image processing software will usually import and export images in a number of formats. Besides format conversion, there are other operations that can be considered forms of conversion. These include image compression or decompression, changing color models, and changing image depth or resolution. The latter operations are particularly important when producing hard copy. To print an image containing a range of colors, the image is usually converted to the CMYK color model. This conversion, known as *color separation*, allows plates for the four printing colors to be produced. The quality of color printing depends on, among other factors, the resolution of both the image and the printer. In some cases print quality can be improved by *resampling* the image and obtaining a better match between printer and image resolutions. Resampling, whether up (adding pixels) or down (dropping pixels), can be viewed as a conversion from one resolution to another.

2.1.3   GRAPHICS

Media type Graphic
   Representation
     Geometric models
     Solid models
     Physically based models
     Empirical models
     Drawing models
     External formats for models
   Operations
     Primitive editing
     Structural editing
     Shading
     Mapping
     Lighting
     Viewing
     Rendering

In classifying media types it is important to be as general as possible and to bring out the essential characteristics of the different types. What then is the basis of a 'graphics type'? Graphics data and image data are often confused with each other. What is needed is a concept shared by the many graphics representations yet differentiating graphics types from image types. Fortunately there is such a concept: a central notion of graphics is *rendering,* which is an operation that takes graphics data and produces image data. Using this notion one can then define a graphics type as a data type *plus* a rendering operation. Instances of the graphics type are called *models.*

Graphics representation

The above definition for graphics types raises two issues: what are models and how are they rendered? We now enumerate various forms of models used in graphics and discuss operations on these models and their relationship to rendering. This material just skims the surface of graphics; for further information the reader is referred to standard graphics texts (Newmann and Sproull, 1979; Harrington, 1987; Foley *et al.*, 1990).

   One note about the terminology used in the discussion of graphics modelling: here the term 'object' refers to elements of a scene being modelled, for instance a table leg or a flower pot. In general, a graphics model will contain groups of such graphics objects. This informal use is common when discussing graphics models. However, there are also more precise uses of the term 'graphics object'. In particular, in *object-oriented graphics* programming (Wisskirchen, 1990), graphics objects are instances of classes specified by an object-oriented programming language.

Geometric models □ Geometric models consist of collections of 2D and/or 3D geometric *primitives*. Two-dimensional primitives include lines, familiar shapes such as rectangles and ellipses, plus more general polygons and curves. Three-dimensional primitives include the above plus surfaces of various forms. Curves and curved surfaces are often described by parameterized polynomials. Primitives are first defined in local or *object coordinates*, for example a circle might be centered at the origin. Groups of primitives are then arranged in a common *world coordinate* system by applying *modelling transformations*. These transformations include rotation, translation, and scaling. It may be possible to organize primitives into *structural hierarchies*. For instance, a bookcase might be represented by structures for the shelves and the sides. Each structure can be broken down into lower-level structures and primitives.

Geometric modelling is perhaps the simplest and most well-understood form of modelling. It is the basis of several standard device-independent graphics libraries. Examples are GKS, the *Graphic Kernel System* (ISO, 1985); PHIGS, the *Programmer's Hierarchical Interactive Graphic System* (ISO, 1989a); and *OpenGL* (OpenGL Architecture Review Board, 1993). GKS is an early 3D graphics standard. Primitives include lines, points, text, and images. These are grouped into *segments*, which can be operated on as a whole (such as to be made visible or invisible, translated, or scaled). PHIGS introduces a wider range of primitives and hierarchical collections called *structures*. PHIGS+, an extension to PHIGS, adds further primitives and more elaborate forms of lighting and shading (Howard *et al.*, 1991). Also related to PHIGS is PEX, or the *PHIGS Extensions to X*, which adds 3D graphics to the X window system (Clifford *et al.*, 1988). Finally, OpenGL is a portable version of a widely used graphics library from Silicon Graphics.

Solid models □ Special techniques have been developed for modelling complex solids. These techniques include:

> *Constructive solid geometry (CSG):* Solids are combined using union, intersection, and difference operations. For example, a thinly walled cylinder can be formed by taking one solid cylinder and subtracting another of slightly smaller diameter.

> *Surfaces of revolution:* A solid is formed by rotating a 2D curve about an axis in 3D space. This is referred to as *lathing*. For instance, wine glasses and candlesticks can be formed in this way.

> *Extrusion:* A 2D outline is extended in 3D space along an arbitrary path. For example, circles can be extruded to form straight (or curved) pipes.

Model construction, using the above techniques, is less time-consuming than when dealing with geometric primitives. However, there is a trade-off – although solid modelling is very powerful, rendering these models is likely to be expensive.

Physically based models □ Realistic images can be produced from physical models describing the forces, stresses, and strains on objects. For example, when one deformable object hits another, contact forces develop and alter their shapes. By specifying physical properties of objects – their mass and velocity, degrees of freedom, rigidity, and so on – it is possible to determine their shape through numerical methods.

Empirical models □ Complex natural phenomena, for example clouds, waves, fire, and plants, are difficult to describe realistically through the use of geometric or solid modelling. In addition, physically based models are often impractical in these cases – it may be infeasible to derive physical equations governing the phenomena, or the equations may be computationally intractable. The alternative is to develop models based on observation, rather than physical laws. Such models do not necessarily embody the underlying natural processes that cause these phenomena, but, nevertheless, produce realistic images. Some well-known examples of this form of modelling include: fractals, used to model mountains and other land features (Fournier *et al.*, 1982); probabilistic graph-grammars, used to model branching plant structures (Smith, 1984); and particle systems (statistically described collections of particles), used for fires and explosions (Reeves, 1983).

Drawing models □ Another form of modelling is to describe an object in terms of drawing (or painting) actions. The description, which may contain conditions, loops and other programming constructs, can be viewed as a sequence of commands to an imaginary drawing device. Examples of this approach include PostScript and the 'turtle graphics' of LOGO (Abelson and diSessa, 1981).

External formats for models □ In practice, the models we have been referring to exist as data structures used by graphics packages and rendering algorithms. It is useful if models can be exported and imported between applications. In other words, we want to save these models in an external format which can be read by other applications. Examples of such formats include CGM, the Computer Graphics Metafile (ISO, 1987a; Arnold and Bono, 1988), and file formats used by computer-aided design software. One can also include PostScript and RIB, RenderMan Interface Binary (Upstill, 1990), as external formats. However, these last two examples are best thought of as 'render-only' formats since it is difficult to modify a model once it has been expressed in either PostScript or RIB. Many graphics file formats are discussed by Kay and Levine (1992).

Graphics operations

It is difficult to identify operations that apply to graphics models in general. There are basically two reasons for this. First, as shown above, there are many forms of modelling in use and there are operations which are possible in some representations but not others. Secondly, various forms of modelling are often combined and used to represent different parts of a single scene. Yet despite the variety of representation, we can identify operations common to many of the above representations. These operations include:

Primitive editing □ The most basic operations deal with specifying and modifying the parameters associated with model primitives. In the case of geometric primitives, this involves specifying the type of each primitive (whether a straight line, a curve, a polygon, or some other primitive) and specifying geometric information such as vertex coordinates and surface normals.

Structural editing □ In general a model is a collection of primitives of various forms. Structural editing refers to creating and modifying these collections, and establishing spatial relationships between members. Specific examples include arranging objects in structural hierarchies and specifying modelling coordinate transformations.

Shading □ A distinction is sometimes made between *shape* and *shading* (Upstill, 1990). Shapes can be specified by any of the modelling techniques mentioned above – geometric modelling, solid modelling, and so on. However, to produce an image of the model, additional information is required. This additional 'shading' information specifies how light interacts with the various objects within the model. It includes the color of an object (or more precisely, the frequencies of light which the object reflects) and how light is reflected (that is, does the object have a mirror-like surface or does it reflect light diffusely?). If an object transmits light then an index of refraction may also be specified.

Several general-purpose methods have been devised for calculating the colors of objects given information about surfaces and light sources. With many of these shading methods, surfaces are first described using meshes of small polygonal surface 'patches'. The simplest method, *flat shading*, results in each patch having a constant color. More sophisticated methods involve interpolating color or surface normals across a patch; these are known as *Gouraud shading* and *Phong shading* respectively. Finally *ray tracing* and *radiosity* are based on physical models of light behavior and give highly realistic results.

The generation of photorealistic images requires extremely flexible shading. The powerful renderer known as RenderMan (Upstill, 1990) achieves this flexibility through the support of programmable *shaders*. A shader is a procedure written in a special shading language and can be attached to object surfaces. Shaders have access to information about the surface and incoming light; this can be used to produce a variety of effects, such as simulating wooden or marble surfaces. Furthermore, by simply replacing shaders one can completely alter the appearance of an object.

Mapping □ Computer graphics makes use of a variety of techniques for enhancing the visual appearance of objects. Many of these can be grouped under 'mapping', and include:

> *Texture mapping:*   An image (the texture map) is applied to a surface. This requires a mapping from 3D surface coordinates to 2D image coordinates. Given a point on the surface, the image is sampled and the resulting value used to color the surface at that point. Refinements of texture mapping include *solid textures* (textures are obtained from a 3D space rather than a 2D

space) and *procedural textures* (textures are calculated rather than sampled). Both solid and procedural textures can be obtained from shaders as described above.

Bump mapping: Like texture mapping, except the image map is used to modify the surface's normal vector rather than color. Bump mapping is used to mimic minor surface perturbations such as scratches and scrapes.

Displacement mapping: Introduces local modifications to a surface's position, for instance to produce ridges or grooves.

Environment mapping: This technique, also known as *reflection mapping*, is used to simulate limited forms of reflection. (Reflection is handled more generally by renderers incorporating ray-tracing algorithms.)

Shadow mapping: Similar to environment mapping in that it produces a particular lighting effect, in this case shadows, without resorting to the more expensive ray-tracing and/or radiosity methods.

Some examples of mapping are shown in the accompanying figures. A simple model containing a cube, a background plane, and two light sources is shown in Figure 2.1. In Figure 2.2 a flower-shaped texture map has been applied to one of the surfaces of the cube, and in Figure 2.3, a procedural texture (providing a granite-like surface for the cube), an additional texture map (the brick background), a displacement map (causing the flower to stand out), and shadow maps have been added.

Lighting □ In addition to the graphics objects contained within a model, lights are used to illuminate the scene. Common light sources include *ambient light* (background lighting, comes from all directions with equal intensity), *point lights* (come from specific points in space, intensity follows the inverse-square law), *directional lights* (a source located at infinity in some direction, its intensity is constant), and *spot lights* (can be thought of as illuminating a cone-shaped volume). In each case various parameters associated with the source (such as its color) can be specified.

Viewing □ Producing an image of a 3D model requires a transformation which projects 3D world coordinates to the 2D coordinates of the image. This transformation must be applied to those parts of the model within the *viewing volume*, the region of model space that appears in the image. View specification consists of selecting the projection transformation and the view volume. (A simpler form of view specification is needed when rendering 2D models.) Parallel and perspective projections are most commonly used. Sophisticated renderers also allow 'camera attributes' such as focal point and depth of field to be specified (Upstill, 1990).

Rendering □ The rendering operation converts a model (including shading, lighting and viewing information) into an image. Rendering software often allows the selection and fine-tuning of various control parameters. Examples include the output resolution (the width and height of the output image in pixels, and the pixel

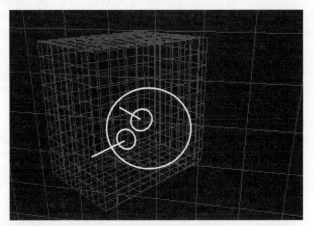

Figure 2.1   A 3D model; circles indicate light sources.

Figure 2.2   Rendered model, with shading and texture mapping.

Figure 2.3   Rendered model, with displacement and shadow mapping.

depth) and approximate rendering time (for instance, is a quick and low-quality preview image sufficient, or is an accurate, but slow to produce, high-resolution image required?).

2.2 TEMPORAL MEDIA TYPES

The second major grouping of media types – audio, video, music and animation – share the property of being extended in time. It makes sense, for instance, to refer to the fourth minute of a video clip or the tenth beat in a score. Instances of the temporal media types are dynamic and continually changing, whereas text, images and graphics, are in a sense timeless.

The first temporal media types we consider are analog and digital video. Video, whether in analog or digital form, is an electronic representation of a sequence of images. These images are called *frames*. When video is broadcast or recorded, provisions are made for including one or more audio tracks. Consequently, we often think of video as containing an audio component. This can lead to some confusion in discussing video as it may not be clear whether audio information is present or not. Here we treat video as being purely visual. Combinations of video and audio are a form of multimedia and more the topic of the next chapter.

2.2.1   ANALOG VIDEO

Media type Analog video
    Representation
        Frame rate
        Number of scan lines
        Aspect ratio
        Interlacing
        Quality
        Component versus composite
    Operations
        Storage
        Retrieval
        Synchronization
        Editing
        Mixing
        Conversion

Analog video is not stored and manipulated within the computer and so is not strictly a data type but, for a number of reasons, knowledge of analog video is relevant to multimedia programming. First, an understanding of analog video and traditional video practice is needed to appreciate the capabilities of digital video. Second, at the moment video systems contain both analog and digital components. Computer and video hardware may handle video in digital form, yet it often enters and leaves as an analog signal – there is input from analog cameras and output to analog monitors. So, for at least the present, we need to be concerned with mating analog and digital video components. Finally, a number of analog video devices, in particular videodisc players, provide flexible computer interfaces. Software cannot access analog video directly, but it can certainly control its recording and playback.

We now briefly delve into analog video representations and operations. A full understanding of this subject requires a background in electronics and signal theory – here, though, we discuss analog video informally. For technical information the interested reader can consult one of the standard references on video technology (such as Blair Benson and Whitaker, 1990; Zettl, 1984). Krupnick (1990) provides an introductory description of video equipment and practice.

Analog video representation

Analog video is an electrical signal; visual information is encoded by changes in signal amplitude. Not all electrical signals can be considered video signals. For each of the various video formats there are rules governing signal structure. These rules determine the breakdown of the signal into frames, frames into horizontal *scan lines*, the way in which color is represented, and the placement of synchronization information. Synchronization is one of the recurrent themes of multimedia and we will discuss many forms of synchronization in the following chapters. When dealing with analog video, synchronization refers to adjusting the timing of one video signal against another or against some reference signal.

When a video frame is displayed, it is swept out on the screen as a series of horizontal scan lines. Boundaries between scan lines, and between frames, are identified by rectangular 'sync pulses' occurring in 'blanking intervals'. The general form of a video signal is shown in Figure 2.4. This figure shows only overall structure; more accurate signal descriptions with precise timing information can be found in video reference books (such as Blair Benson and Whitaker, 1990).

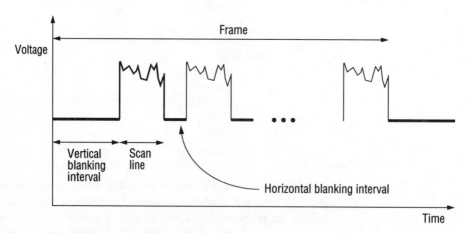

Figure 2.4   A video signal (approximate frame structure).

At present, different video signal formats are used by the broadcast industry and the computer industry. However, it is possible to compare the formats along a number of key dimensions. These dimensions include:

Frame rate □ The frame rate is simply the number of frames per second produced by a video signal. Common rates are 25–75 Hz (that is 25–75 frames per second, or *fps*). The disadvantage of low frame rate signals is that they flicker when displayed. Also, at lower frame rates moving objects may appear blurred within individual frames and motion is jerky.

Number of scan lines □ Video formats divide frames into scan lines. Each frame has the same number of scan lines. The *scan rate* is the number of lines scanned per second, that is, the product of the frame rate and number of scan lines per frame.

Aspect ratio □ The aspect ratio is the ratio of the width of a video image to its height. Current broadcast video formats have a 4:3 aspect ratio.

Interlacing □ As mentioned above, low frame rates produce noticeable (and irritating) flicker. The flickering can be reduced by interlacing: frames are divided into two *fields*, the first containing the odd-numbered scan lines, the second the even. During display, the entire first field is drawn and then the entire second field. The result is that the display appears to refresh at twice the original frame rate. This form of interlacing is called 2:1, since there are two fields per frame. Other field-to-frame ratios are possible but not commonly found.

Quality □ The video marketplace is divided into three sectors: consumer, professional (or industrial), and broadcast. Video equipment manufacturers produce different lines of equipment for the three sectors. The main difference between product lines, besides cost, is the 'quality' of the video produced. Quality is measured in objective terms including signal-to-noise ratio and image resolution. A consumer and a broadcast video camera may both produce the same format, but the quality of the second will be better.

Composite video versus component video □ Broadcast television standards have been designed so that color broadcasts can be displayed by black-and-white receivers. This was achieved by separating color information (chrominance) from intensity information (luminance). With composite video, the luminance and chrominance signals are combined into a single electrical signal. With component video there are multiple signals. Generally component video gives better quality; its disadvantages are more elaborate cabling and the need to maintain synchronization between the different components.

There are several forms of component video. *YUV* video has three components, a luminance signal (Y) and two chrominance signals (U and V). (See the discussion of the YUV color model on page 23.) *S-video* (for separated video) and *Y/C* video (for luminance/chrominance) have two components, a luminance signal and a single chrominance signal. Through signal splitters and other signal converters it is possible to connect composite and component video equipment. Unfortunately conversions add noise and reduce quality.

The major analog video signal formats are listed below:

(1)   *NTSC (National Television Systems Committee)*:   A television standard developed in the USA, NTSC is used throughout North America, Central America and Japan, and some parts of the South Pacific and South America.

(2)   *PAL (Phase Alternation Line)*:   A European television standard used in much of western Europe, India, China, Australia, and parts of Asia and South America.

(3)   *SECAM (Séquentiel Couleur avec Mémoire)*:   The French television standard, used also in Eastern Europe, Russia, and parts of Africa and the Middle East.

(4)   *RGB*:   A component video signal format with separate red, green, and blue signals. RGB video is commonly used for computer displays. There is no single RGB standard; instead different computer and monitor manufacturers have evolved their own formats. One example is VGA, developed by IBM and now an industry standard for PCs and other computers.

(5)   *HDTV (High Definition Television)*:   A number of analog HDTV signal formats have been developed and are in various stages of use. The earliest HDTV system, Japan's Hi-Vision, is used for daily broadcasts in Japan. Hi-Vision is also known as MUSE[1], SMPTE 240M[2] and '1125/60' since it gives 60 fields per second and 1125 scan lines. In Europe there are broadcasts in a similar analog HDTV format known as HD-MAC or '1250/50'. In addition to there being differing analog HDTV signal formats, the newer proposals are for digital HDTV systems. However, the characteristics which distinguish HDTV in general from other broadcast formats include a wider aspect ratio (16:9 as compared to 4:3) and more scan lines (of the order of 1000 as compared to 500 to 600).

The three broadcast video standards, NTSC, PAL and SECAM, have both composite and component representations. The component version of NTSC is often called YUV 525/60[3], indicating 525 scan lines at 60 fields per second (see Table 2.1). The component versions of PAL and SECAM are identical and are called YUV 625/50. In addition there are slight variations of these formats used from one country to another. Another twist are proposals for *Extended Definition Television*, which give an intermediate step from current broadcast formats to HDTV.

---

[1]   MUSE, or *Multiple Sub-Nyquist Sampling Encoding*, actually refers to the method used to reduce the bandwidth of Hi-Vision broadcasts.

[2]   SMPTE 240M is the name of a standard based on Hi-Vision.

[3]   More precisely, this should be 525/59.94. The frame rate for NTSC was originally 30 frames per second, or 60 fields per second. When color was added, there was interference between the new color 'subcarrier' and the audio carrier used for broadcast transmission. The interference was removed, and compatibility with existing black-and-white receivers maintained, by reducing the frame rate by 0.1% to 29.97 frames per second or 59.94 fields per second.

Table 2.1 Comparison of analog video signal formats.

Signal format	Components	Frame rate (Hz)	Scan lines	Aspect ratio	Interlacing
NTSC	1	29.97	525	4:3	2:1
YUV 525/60	3	29.97	525	4:3	2:1
PAL	1	25	625	4:3	2:1
SECAM	1	25	625	4:3	2:1
YUV 625/50	3	25	625	4:3	2:1
RGB	3	~25–75	~200–1000	Varies	Usually 1:1
1125/60 (aka SMPTE 240M, Hi-Vision, MUSE)	3	30	1125	16:9	2:1
1250/50 (aka HD-MAC)	3	25	1250	16:9	2:1

A comparison of the above signal formats is shown in Table 2.1. In the case of RGB, where there is no single standard, the table gives only typical values.

Analog video operations

The preparation of a video recording is often divided into three stages: pre-production, production and post-production. Various tasks take place in each stage; however, the basic activities are: *pre-production*, the script is written and shots are planned; *production*, the video is shot; and *post-production*, the video is edited. If we think in terms of how video material is processed and modified, it is the third, or post-production, stage which is of greatest interest. In order to understand what operations take place at this point, consider the equipment found in a typical post-production studio (see Figure 2.5). This equipment includes:

Video sources: Equipment that produces a video signal. Examples are cameras, tape players, and videodisc players.

Video sinks: Video sinks consume video signals. Monitors and tape recorders fall into this category. (Note that some devices, in particular video tape machines, can act as both sinks and sources.)

Routing switch: A routing switch simply connects sources to sinks. It may also provide signal 'duplication' so that, for instance, a single source can be connected to multiple sinks without a loss in signal strength.

Edit controller: An edit controller is a device that controls the positioning, playback and recording of a number of video devices (usually video tape recorders). Edit controllers are either special-purpose devices produced by video equipment manufacturers or small computers, such as a PC or Macintosh, with appropriate software and interface hardware.

Video mixer: A video mixer (also known as a *video switcher* or *vision mixer*) combines a number of input video signals and produces one or more out-

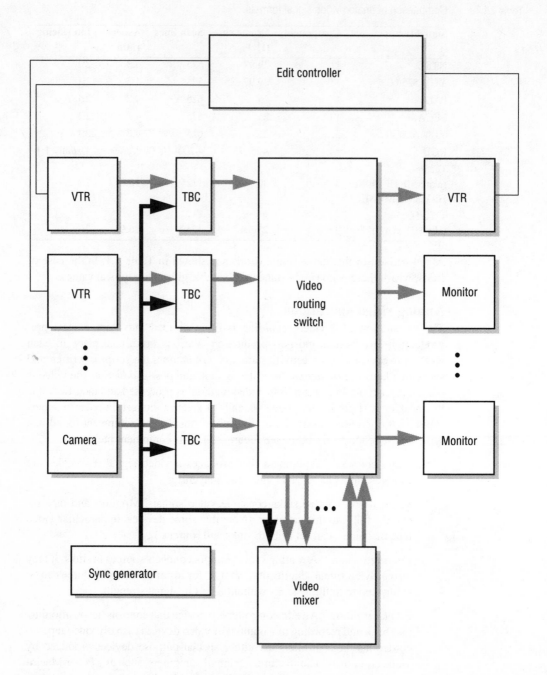

Figure 2.5   Video post-production equipment.

put signals. Mixers are often used to make transitions from one signal to another, perhaps a fade or a wipe.

Video synchronization equipment: In order for video to be edited and mixed cleanly (without the image breaking up during transitions) the various signals must be *synchronized*. In particular, each signal must start a new frame at the same time. Equipment used to ensure synchronization includes the *sync generator* and *timebase correctors* (see page 43).

Fully exploiting the resources of a video studio to produce precisely edited video sequences containing complex transitions and special effects requires mastery of the studio equipment. As each studio component is likely to have a number of functions and controls, it can be difficult to grasp the overall capabilities of a studio. However, if we consider the basic purpose of each component we can break down the available operations as follows:

Analog video storage □ Post-production deals mainly with recorded video, so some means of video storage is needed. In the early days of television, before video tape was available, video was recorded by *kinescoping*. This involved aiming a motion-picture camera at a video monitor and recording onto film. The video would be replayed by running the film through a coupled projector and video camera (known as a *telecine*). Now, though, the primary storage media for analog video are video tape and videodisc:

Video tape: Magnetic video tape is available in a number of formats (see Table 2.2) of varying tape width, recording capability, and capacity. The larger tape widths have better video quality and can record more tracks (for example, additional audio and timing tracks), but they are bulkier and more expensive.

Table 2.2   Analog video tape formats.

Tape format	Width	Signal	Quality
Type B	1"	Composite	Very high
Type C	1"	Composite	Very high
Betacam	1/2"	Component	Very high
MII	1/2"	Component	Very high
U-matic	3/4"	Composite	Good to very good
Hi8	8mm	Component	Good
S-VHS	1/2'	Component	Good
Video8	8mm	Composite	Fair
VHS	1/2"	Composite	Fair

Tape drives for the various video tape formats have mechanical differences, but, in principle, during recording a rotating head writes the video fields diagonally across the tape. This is shown in Figure 2.6 and is called *helical-scan*. A second spinning head is used for playback (since the head rotates, a tape player can produce a signal even when the tape is 'paused'). Video

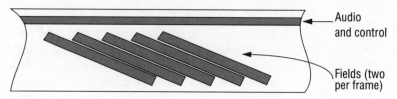

Audio
and control

Fields (two
per frame)

Figure 2.6   Video tape layout.

tape, like magnetic tape in general, does not provide quick access – it can take minutes to seek to a particular location. However, there is another problem with tape that mere patience cannot overcome: when an analog signal is recorded and then re-recorded, each succeeding *generation* has more noise and less quality. With broadcast equipment, loss of picture quality may be noticed in as few as three to five generations; with consumer equipment the degradation is more rapid. Besides the loss of quality when copying, even repeatedly playing a tape will, in the long run, lead to a poor signal as the tape is stretched and magnetic material on its surface wears off.

Videodisc: Optical videodiscs overcome many of the problems of tape. Like tapes, videodiscs come in many formats, however *LV* or *Laser Vision* is the most common. LV is read-only; there are write-once and write-many videodisc systems, but these are more expensive and are not fully compatible with the LV format (that is, it is not possible to play a videodisc written by one of these systems on an LV player). LV technology is a forerunner of the popular audio CD. An LV disc is produced by using a laser to form small pits on a master disc's surface. A 'stamper' is then created from the master and used to mold discs for distribution. Like CDs, an LV disc is read by a low-powered laser beam which detects the recorded pits. Unlike CDs, this binary pickup signal is converted immediately to analog within the player, so it is not possible to obtain digital data from an LV player.

LV discs are produced in two formats: CAV, or constant angular velocity, and CLV, or constant linear velocity (see Table 2.3 for a comparison). In each case, the pits on the disc are arranged into a long spiral track starting near the center of the disc and ending near the outer rim. On CAV discs, the portion of the track corresponding to a single frame extends for exactly one revolution about the disc. This means that all frames start at the same angular position of the disc. As a result, CAV discs offer flexible playback: the player can, without changing the rotational velocity, freeze a frame and play in forward or reverse at various rates, simply by repositioning the pickup head during vertical blanking intervals.

CLV discs do not have the playback flexibility of CAV. When playing a CLV disc, the drive changes its rotational velocity, in order to maintain a constant linear velocity, as the pickup head moves away from or towards the center of the disc. The need to mechanically accelerate or deaccelerate the disc significantly increases access time. Furthermore, frames do not occur

Table 2.3 Laser Vision (LV) videodiscs.

	CAV	CLV
Capacity[a]	30 min (NTSC)	
(duration/side)	36 min (PAL)	60 min
(frames/side)	54 000 frames	(not frame addressable)
Access time[b]		
(worst case)	3 s	10 s
Drive revolution	1800 rpm (NTSC)	600–1800 rpm (NTSC)
	1500 rpm (PAL)	570–1500 rpm (PAL)
Quality	High	High

a. Capacity data is for 12" discs.
b. Access times will vary from player to player.

at regular angular positions so variable-rate playback is not possible. Even simple freeze-frame is difficult without some form of frame memory within the player. The one advantage of CLV discs over CAV is that they have twice the capacity, allowing up to two hours of video if both sides of the disc are used. As a result CLV is found in situations where interactivity is not so important but capacity of greater than one hour is needed. For instance, LV film recordings are typically in CLV format.

Analog video retrieval ☐ In order to locate segments of video, whether on tape or videodisc, some method of video addressing is needed. The simplest solution is to use frame numbers. For instance, on CAV LV videodiscs, frames are numbered from 1 to 54 000. An LV player can be told to seek to frame n, or play back frames n through m. With video tape, frame-accurate retrieval is more difficult. First, not all video tape players support frame addressing. In the absence of this capability, tape can be positioned manually by operating the tape transport controls while watching the output signal or a 'revolution counter'. This, of course, is awkward and imprecise. A second difficulty with frame-accurate positioning of video tape is the need for *pre-roll*: for instance, if a tape is to start recording at frame n, it must first seek for some frame before n (typically a few seconds earlier) and then start the tape transport mechanism. This ensures that the tape is moving at the correct velocity by the time the recording head is located over frame n. However, only when the tape reaches this frame is the recording head activated and the actual recording started.

Video tapes that support frame addressing make use of a *time code*: an 8-digit value of the form:

hh:mm:ss:ff

where the four components refer to hour, minute, second and frame number respectively. To use time code addressing, a time code must first be written on the tape. This can occur during the actual recording of video footage or during an earlier tape preparation stage. There are two commonly used techniques for adding time code to video tape:

(1) Longitudinal Time Code (LTC): The time code is written on a 'longitudinal' track running along the length of the tape.

(2) Vertical Interval Time Code (VITC): The time code is inserted on the 'transverse' video track during the vertical blanking interval.

VITC has the advantage that, since it is part of the video signal, it is detected by the spinning video head and so can be read even when the tape is paused. LTC, on the other hand, is simpler to extract from a rapidly moving tape.

In addition to machine-readable time code such as LTC or VITC, it is possible to 'burn in' time code as part of the video image. The 'hh:mm:ss:ff' digits will then appear whenever the video is viewed and without the need for time code reading equipment. Since burned-in time code is not machine-readable (without some form of optical character recognition) and destroys parts of the original video, its uses are limited.

Time code formats have been standardized by broadcasting organizations in the USA and Europe. For PAL and SECAM video there is *EBU time code*, a 25 frame per second format defined by the European Broadcast Union. For NTSC, the Society of Motion Picture and Television Engineers (SMPTE) has developed a format known as *SMPTE Time Code*. When dealing with NTSC and SMPTE time code, a complication arises because of NTSC's non-integer valued frame rate. Recall that NTSC is actually 29.97 frames per second. This has led to two variants of SMPTE time code:

(1) Non-drop frame SMPTE time code: Frame numbers run from 0 to 29, that is, as if there were 30 frames per second. The result is that the hour/minute/second portion of the time code is incremented slightly slower than real time (the discrepancy is about 3.5 seconds per hour).

(2) Drop frame SMPTE time code: Drop frame time code increments the hour/minute/second portion of the time code at the same rate as real time. This is done by skipping certain frame numbers. The rule is that frame numbers 0 and 1 are 'dropped' from every minute not divisible by 10.

Analog video synchronization □ Video special effects equipment and professional video editing equipment require that input signals be synchronized. In describing video signal synchronization, the term *timebase* refers to signal timing, that is, when frames and scan lines start and stop. Synchronization errors are also called timebase errors and can be divided into two categories: *timebase jitter* and *timebase phase shift*. Timebase jitter is slight variation in the timing of the signal, for instance small changes in the frame period. Tape players in particular are prone to timebase jitter caused by tape friction and stretching, and by variation in motor speed. Two signals may have a stable timebase, but not be synchronized, for instance one may always be half a frame behind the other. Such a 'timebase phase shift' will be found in signals coming from independent sources; also a signal running over a long cable will emerge with its timebase shifted (as compared to where it entered the cable).

Synchronization is a matter of degree; it is not possible to perfectly synchronize two signals but the amount by which they are out of sync can be decreased.

In a video studio this is achieved through the use of a variety of equipment, including the following:

(1) Sync generator: A sync generator provides a very stable timing signal (essentially a black video signal) used as a reference by other equipment. This signal is often called the 'house sync'.

(2) Genlock: A video source which is 'genlockable' will synchronize its output to a reference signal provided as an input.

(3) Timebase corrector (TBC): A timebase corrector removes timebase jitter from an input signal. It produces an output signal with the same color and luminosity as the input but with a stable timebase. Some TBCs can also remove timebase phase shift by genlocking the output to a reference signal.

Analog video editing ☐ Editing of analog video is primarily a question of copying video segments from one tape to another, a process known as *dubbing*. Two commonly used procedures are:

cuts-only editing: This form of editing is the video tape version of copy and paste. It requires two tape drives (a player and a recorder) and an edit controller. A video segment on the play tape is specified (for instance, by starting time code and duration) and an insert point (a time code) on the record tape. The edit controller positions and pre-rolls the two tapes and then turns on recording for the specified duration. It is called 'cuts-only' because successive segments on the edited (record) tape start immediately after each other (cut from one to another) rather than overlap (as in a dissolve, for example).

A-B roll editing: The more versatile 'A-B roll' editing requires two players ('A and B'), a recorder, a video mixer, and again an edit controller. The output from the players is sent through the mixer. The mixer produces a single output, which may be either one of the player signals or a 'mixed' signal such as a dissolve or wipe. It is the mixer's output signal which is recorded. Specifying an editing operation now requires selecting the start points of both players and the recorder, the duration of the segment to be recorded, and the actions to be taken by the mixer. The edit controller must position and pre-roll all tapes and, at the appropriate moment, request the mixer to execute an effect (unless the mixer is being operated manually).

A notation known as an *edit decision list* (EDL) is often used to specify video editing operations. Using software, an EDL can be constructed 'offline' and then loaded onto an edit controller for execution. The software also allows the EDL to be modified and saved for future use.

Analog video mixing ☐ The video mixer is the source of many of the special effects and transitions seen on television broadcasts. The basic purpose of a mixer is to combine one or more input signals to produce an output signal. A mixer may operate on analog inputs directly, or first digitize the inputs, then manipulate these signals in digital form, and finally convert back to analog for output – this is called a *digital video effect*, or *DVE*.

The operations of a video mixer can be divided into two main groups: *transitions* and *effects*. Suppose a mixer has two video inputs, A and B. At the start of a transition, output comes directly from one of the inputs, say A. During the transition A and B are combined in some manner, and finally at the end of the transition only B is present. Transitions are often performed by pulling a 'T bar' on the mixer's console; the position of the T bar controls the amount of mixing, and the speed by which it is pulled determines the transition's duration. With an effect, the mixer continuously applies some transformation – effects are generally longer lasting than transitions and may involve only a single input signal. Some of the more common transitions and effects include (examples are shown in Plate V):

Cut: A transition where the mixer simply switches from input A to input B during the vertical blanking interval (so as to avoid obtaining a frame with parts of both inputs).

Fade: A transition from a single input to a constant background, usually black. The contribution of the input is gradually reduced and replaced by the background.

Dissolve (cross-fade): A transition during which the output is a weighted sum of the two inputs. The contribution of A is lowered while that of B is increased.

Wipe: A transition where A is pulled or 'wiped' away to reveal B. Simple wipes resemble scrolling operations, a more complex example is the 'page turn' where one input is lifted away, much like a page of a book, to reveal the second.

Tumble: A transition where B tumbles in to cover A. For instance, a reduced version of B might appear in the top right corner of A and then rotate and enlarge as it fills the screen.

Wrapping: An effect where one input is 'wrapped' around a simple 3D object such as a sphere or cube. The result is somewhat like texture mapping, except the texture is now a 25 fps or 30 fps video signal.

Keying: An effect used to overlay two inputs. A *key signal* controls when a mixer's inputs are present in the output. For instance, a key signal resembling a square wave would result in the mixer repeatedly switching from one input to the other. A key may be provided as an additional input to the mixer or it may be derived from one of the input video signals. With *chroma keying*, a color is chosen (typically blue) and wherever this color is present in one signal the mixer switches to the second signal. The result is that blue regions in the first signal are replaced by the second. *Luminance keying* is similar, except the key is determined by thresholding the luminance of one of the input signals.

Both effects and transitions can be parameterized. Parameters include the input selections (a mixer generally has a large number of inputs) and the duration of the effect or transition. In some cases, parameter values may be specified at a few intermediate points within a transition and then interpolated while the transition is executed. For example, to construct a complicated tumble, the mixer operator might select a few points along the desired trajectory and specify the position and orientation of tumbled frames at these points. Some mixers allow the operator to edit and save such specifications.

Analog video conversion □ The final operation on analog video that we will consider is conversion from one video signal format to another. The hardware which performs this feat is known as a *scan converter* and has an input for one video format and an output for the second. For example, the high-resolution RGB video signals displayed on computer monitors can be connected to a scan converter and then recorded on video tape or viewed on a NTSC monitor. Scan converters are also used to change from one broadcast format to another, such as from NTSC to PAL, a process also known as *standards conversion*. Conversion of analog video signals is not fully invertible. While it is possible to convert from one signal format to a second and then back to the first, the resulting signal will be of lower quality than the original.

2.2.2   DIGITAL VIDEO

Media type Digital video
    Representation
        Analog formats sampled
        Sampling rate
        Sample size and quantization
        Data rate
        Frame rate
        Compression
        Support for interactivity
        Scalability
    Operations
        Storage
        Retrieval
        Synchronization
        Editing
        Effects
        Conversion

Digital video is well established in the broadcast industry, and now, with the emergence of powerful compression standards, it is appearing on workstations and in consumer products. However, the digital video used in television studios is quite different from what one might find on a personal computer. It is natural to ask, then, just what is the essential characteristic shared by the various forms of digital video. Recall from the previous section that analog video is a sequence of frames, encoded by a continuous electrical signal and occurring at some constant rate, the frame rate. With digital video we again have a sequence of frames; the frames are now digital images, perhaps compressed in some manner. But the key concept we wish to associate with a media type for digital video is the notion of *timing:* digital video is not just any sequence of images, but a sequence with accompanying information indicating the durations frames are to be displayed. Often, as with analog video, frame durations are constant, in which case there is also a constant frame rate. However, this is not always so and many digital video sequences have varying frame rates.

In this section we give an overview of existing data representations for video and discuss how operations on digital video differ from their analog counterparts covered in the previous section. Further information on digital video can be found in Watkinson (1990), which covers much of the underlying technology; also ACM (1991) describes a number of recent developments in digital video compression.

Digital video representation

As with other media types we have discussed, the digital video types can be characterized along a number of dimensions, each helping to determine possible data representations. Since digital video is a sequence of frames, where each frame can be considered a digital image, the various dimensions that were discussed for image representation are applicable now to the representation of frames. However, the temporal nature of digital video, the fact that frames are meant to occur at a particular rate, lead to additional dimensions:

Analog formats sampled ☐ Digital video frames are generally obtained in two ways: *synthesis*, usually by computer program, and *sampling* (of an analog video signal). In the second case, the characteristics of the underlying analog signal will influence the form of the digital representation. As we have seen in the previous section, analog video signals have different frame and scan rates, various methods for color encoding, and come in both composite and component formats. These factors are relevant in determining such quantities as sampling rate and sample size.

Sampling rate ☐ The choice of sampling rate is crucial in specifying a digital format for sampled analog video, since its value determines storage requirements and data transfer rates. Sampling theory gives a lower limit for the frequency at which to sample in order to faithfully reproduce a signal. This limit, the *Nyquist rate*, is twice the highest frequency within the signal; sampling below the Nyquist rate introduces artifacts that result in distortion of the original signal. In selecting a sampling frequency one should also consider the subsequent processing of video frames, for instance applying compression algorithms or producing digital video effects. Generally video processing is simplified if each frame and each scan line give rise to the same number of samples. This requires the sampling frequency to be an integer multiple of the scan rate.

Sample size and quantization ☐ Sample size is the number of bits used to represent sample values, while quantization refers to the mapping from the continuous range of the analog signal to discrete sample values. Factors that influence the choice of sample size include the signal-to-noise ratio of the sampled signal, the sensitivity of the medium used to display frames, and, ultimately, the sensitivity of the human eye. Regarding quantization, digital video commonly uses *linear quantization*, where quantization levels are evenly distributed over the analog range. This form of quantization (as opposed to, for instance, *logarithmic quantization*) is convenient for the arithmetic processing of sample values. (Quantization is also discussed in the context of audio sampling on page 56.)

Broadly speaking we can divide digital video representations into two categories: *high data rate* formats and *low data rate* formats. The high data rate formats are primarily used in professional video production and post-production. There is little or no compression, and picture quality and ease of processing are of primary importance. The low data rate formats are intended for both interactive computer-based applications and transmission over general-purpose data networks. In order to achieve a low data rate (with acceptable picture quality) compression is necessary.

Consider first the high-quality professional formats and other high data rate formats. Examples of this category (see Table 2.4) include:

Digital component video (CCIR 601): The *International Consultative Committee on Broadcasting* (abbreviated as *CCIR*) has developed a family of digital video formats known as CCIR Recommendation 601. The 601 format is obtained by sampling a component video signal; a base sampling rate of 3.375 MHz has been chosen for use with both component NTSC (YUV 525/60) and component PAL (YUV 625/50). In other words, the data rates for sampled NTSC and PAL are the same. The sample size (for each of the components) is generally 8 bits, but in some cases 10 bits may be used.

As mentioned, CCIR 601 is a family of formats. A particular member is often written '*m:n:l*', indicating that the first component (Y) is to be sampled at m times the base rate, while U and V are sampled at n and l times this rate. The rate multipliers, m, n and l, can take on the values 1, 2, 3, and 4. As specific examples, the 4:4:4 format gives the highest data rate and the most accurate color information and is suitable for working with synthetic images where abrupt color changes are possible; 4:2:2 is commonly used for video post-production and is supported by digital VTRs; 4:1:1 is adequate for final conversion to analog video.

Digital composite video: Video studios often prefer composite video to component; cabling is simpler, and composite equipment is readily available. As a result many video studios find a composite digital format easier to incorporate than component digital. To meet this demand, a composite digital format has been developed by equipment manufacturers. The sampling rate is set at four times the color subcarrier frequency, f_{sc}. (For NTSC, $f_{sc} \approx$ 3.58 MHz, for PAL $f_{sc} \approx$ 4.43 MHz.) Sample size is generally 8 bits, although, as with digital component video, 10 bits are also used.

CIF and QCIF: The *Common Intermediate Format* (CIF) and *Quarter-CIF* (QCIF) are two digital video formats approved by the CCITT for use in video conferencing. CIF is obtained by sampling a YUV signal and, like CCIR 601 4:1:1, the chrominance (UV) components are sampled at 1/4 the rate of the luminance (Y) component. One can think of CIF, and QCIF in particular, as bordering between the high data rate and low data rate formats – the data rate (and quality) of CIF is considerably lower than CCIR 601, while QCIF is still lower again (see Table 2.4).

Digital HDTV: There is no *High Definition Television* (HDTV) standard for digital video. HDTV refers to a set of technologies, in various stages of realization, all of which aim to improve upon the existing video broadcast standards such as NTSC and PAL. Additionally, some HDTV systems are analog while others are digitally based. However, despite these qualifications, there is a strong connection between HDTV in general and digital video. Recent HDTV systems make use of a digital representation at some point of the video production, broadcast, reception, and display process; perhaps for capture, perhaps for storage, or perhaps for transmission. Early background information on HDTV activities is provided by Frenkel (1989); Poynton (1994) gives a recent update.

In general HDTV proposals use a 16:9 aspect ratio (compared to 4:3 for NTSC and PAL), frame rates similar to those of NTSC and PAL, but horizontal and vertical resolutions that are approximately doubled. The result is a 'raw' (uncompressed) data rate for digital HDTV that is an order of magnitude greater than the rate for conventional digital video.

Digital component, digital composite, CIF/QCIF and HDTV are compared in Table 2.4. As mentioned above, there is no digital HDTV video standard; however, a plausible frame resolution and data rate are provided for the sake of comparison. The second category of digital video formats, those intended for interactive applications and/or transmission over data networks have much lower data rates than the formats in Table 2.4. Dimensions for comparing these formats include:

Data rate □ The high data rate formats can be converted to lower rate formats by a combination of: data compression, reducing the horizontal and vertical resolution, and reducing the frame rate. For example, starting with a broadcast quality digital video format of approximately 10 Mbytes/s, one could divide the horizontal and vertical resolutions by two (giving VHS quality resolution), and also divide the frame rate by 2. If one could compress the result by a factor of 10 the data rate would be roughly 1/100th the original, about 1 Mbit/s. This is comparable to the data transfer rates of local area networks and optical storage devices (such as CD-ROM[1]) and so suitable for a variety of computer-based applications.

---

[1] The CD-ROM data rate is a target for digital video formats since even compressed video requires large amounts of storage. If this rate can be obtained then an hour's worth of video data can be stored on a CD-ROM and played back using a conventional CD-ROM drive.

Table 2.4   Digital video formats.

Digital video format	Analog formats sampled	Sampling rate (MHz)	Sample size	Approximate video data rate (Mbyte/sec)[a]	Frame resolution[b]
Digital component (CCIR 601)	525/60 YUV 625/50 YUV	13.5[c]	8/10	30.9, 20.6, 15.4[d]	720 × 500 720 × 600
Digital composite	Composite NTSC Composite PAL	14.3 17.7	8	11.2 13.7	768 × 510 948 × 608
CIF				4.5	360 × 288[e]
QCIF	Various	Various	8	1.1	180 × 144[e]
Digital HDTV[f]	NA	NA	NA	~125[g]	~1600 × ~900

a. The video data rate is not simply the product of the sampling frequency and sample size since not all parts of a video signal contain visible picture information.
b. These numbers refer to samples per line and numbers of lines sampled.
c. This refers to the sampling frequency of the Y component, the color difference signals are sampled at fractions of this rate (specifically 1/2 this rate or 6.75 MHz is used for CCIR 601 4:2:2, 1/4 this rate for 4:1:1).
d. These values refer to the data rates for CCIR 601 4:4:4, 4:2:2 and 4:1:1 respectively using 8-bit samples.
e. This is the resolution of the Y (luminance) data. Chrominance data has one quarter this resolution.
f. There is no standard digital HDTV format, the data rate and frame resolution given here are estimates.
g. Based on 24 bits per pixel, 1600×900 pixels per frame, and 30 frames per second.

Frame rate □ The basic question here is whether the format is intended for playback at analog video frame rates (25 or 30 frames per second). This is often called *full-motion* video. When the frame rate is reduced to 10 or 15 frames per second, motion is less accurately depicted and the playback image flickers; however, the data rate is also much reduced.

Compression □ Compression is the key to low data rate digital video and there has been much work recently in devising suitable compression techniques and algorithms (Steinmetz, 1994). Methods for video compression can be compared along three dimensions:

(1)   *Lossy* versus *lossless* compression: Generally video compression can afford to be lossy (see the discussion of image compression on page 24) since it is often not critical that the reconstituted video data exactly match the data prior to compression. This allows the use of powerful compression techniques where compression factors of 1/10th or more are possible without noticeable loss in picture quality.

(2)   *Real-time* compression: If digital video is stored in a compressed form, then real-time decompression is needed for playback. However, if an application uses only prerecorded (as opposed to live) video, then real-time compression is not necessary. Thus a digital video format might choose to forfeit the ability to record in real time in favor of better image quality, or a lower data rate. Compression schemes which have near equal compression and decompression times are said to be *symmetric*.

(3) *Interframe* versus *intraframe* (or *relative* versus *absolute*) compression: Successive video frames tend to be similar. Interframe (also called frame-to-frame) compression schemes exploit temporal redundancy and predict, or interpolate, intermediate frames from independently coded *key frames*. Here a key frame is one that differs significantly from preceding (or following) frames – for example, the first frame in a scene. With intraframe schemes, all frames are independently coded and no interpolation or prediction takes place.

The video quality at a given data rate depends upon the techniques used; in other words, one can compare the low data rate digital video formats by comparing their image quality (resolution *and* frame rate) at a particular data rate. The goal of a video compression algorithm is to avoid sacrificing too much video quality in attaining a particular data rate, while allowing decompression (and perhaps compression) to be done in real time by inexpensive hardware.

Support for interactivity ☐ Requirements for interactive applications include random access to video frames, the ability to play back at different rates and in reverse, and the ability to cut and paste video segments. Support for these features will depend upon the compression techniques used. For example, predictive coding, where frames are derived from previous frames, makes reverse play difficult.

Scalability ☐ Scalable video allows control over video quality. Lippman (1991) identifies two forms of scalability:

(1) *Transmit scalability*: The encoded data rate is chosen at compression time from a range of rates, thus matching the encoded rate to transmission and processing constraints and/or matching the resulting data size to storage constraints.

(2) *Receive scalability*: The decoded data rate is chosen at decompression time in order to match playback requirements. For example, consider an application which receives a 3 Mbits/s digital video value representing a 640 × 480 image at 30 frames per second. Suppose the application's user is not interested in the video at the moment and has relegated it to a small window (perhaps 160 × 120), where it is updated at 15 frames per second rather than 30. Since the resolution has been reduced to 1/16th the original and the frame rate to 1/2 it would appear that only 1/32 of the 3 Mbits/s should be needed to produce the displayed image. If the video representation were scalable then the decoder would, in effect, ignore parts of the received data. In addition the decoder can switch between multiple video sources. For instance, the user could request to display one video sequence at full resolution or two concurrent sequences at half resolution.

Transmit scalability is present in current approaches to low data rate digital video since there is flexibility in choosing frame resolution, frame rate, and compression factors. Receive scalability is a very attractive feature; it is not directly supported by current video coding standards but may appear in the future.

The following lists some current approaches to low data rate digital video:

DVI: The David Sarnoff Research Center has developed a digital video technology, now acquired by Intel, known as *Digital Video Interactive* or *DVI* (Luther, 1991). DVI is discussed in more detail in Chapter 3; here we just mention some characteristics of its digital video formats. DVI supports two digital video formats: *Production-Level Video* (PLV) and *Real-Time Video* (RTV). PLV uses a proprietary compression algorithm allowing VHS-quality video to be produced from a data rate of about 1[1] Mbit/s. The algorithm performs *interframe* compression which exploits similarities between successive frames. This requires considerable computation, and even with costly hardware is difficult to achieve in real time. A few years ago compression times of 2–30 seconds per frame were reported for various parallel computer configurations (Tinker, 1989); with current specialized video processing hardware, real-time PLV compression is just becoming possible. In comparison to compression, PLV decompression is much simpler and can be performed by relatively inexpensive PC boards in real time. Thus PLV is intended for application playback but not recording. Applications that must record digital video use the second DVI format. RTV results in data rates similar to those of PLV; however, the video quality will be poorer and the frame rate may be reduced.

MPEG: The *Moving Pictures Expert Group* (MPEG), an ISO working group, has developed a video compression standard based on interframe coding and DCT techniques (Le Gall, 1991). The standard also addresses audio encoding and combined audio/video streams. The initial standard for video, known as MPEG-1, leads to data rates of about 1 Mbit/s for VHS-quality video. This is in the same range as DVI's PLV mentioned above. A more recent proposal, MPEG-2, is intended for broadcast quality video and HDTV at data rates between 2 and 15 Mbits/sec. In addition, an MPEG proposal for very low date rates (64 Kbits/s and under) is being planned. One problem with interframe coding is that editing and random access are difficult to implement since one frame depends on another. MPEG (and PLV) allow certain frames to be independently coded; these frames then serve as random access entry points. MPEG encoding requires considerably more computation than decoding – like PLV it is easier to achieve real-time playback than recording. Recently, however, products for both MPEG-1 and MPEG-2 encoding in real time have been announced.

JPEG: The JPEG image compression standard (discussed on page 25) can be used with digital video by treating each frame as an image to be compressed independently, a technique referred to as *motion JPEG*. Hardware implementations of JPEG are capable of compressing and decompressing medium resolution images (640 × 480 pixels) at video frame rates and are the basis of several computer-based digital video editing systems. For a given frame rate and resolution, JPEG-compressed video will have a higher

---

1. Data rates for compressed video depend on a number of factors, including quality, frame rate, and source material. The 1 Mbit/s figure quoted, and other values given for compressed video data rates, are only approximations.

data rate than interframe compression techniques such as MPEG and DVI's PLV, but since frames are compressed independently, it is an easier matter to rearrange the order of the frames and to play back in reverse or at variable rates.

px64: CCITT Recommendation H.261 describes a video coding standard intended for video applications using ISDN, or Integrated Services Digital Network (Liou, 1991). The standard is known as px64 since it produces data rates that are multiples of the ISDN's 64 Kbits/s B channel rate; the multiplier, *p*, can range from one to 30. The H.261 coding standard influenced the more recent MPEG proposals and, like MPEG, px64 involves both interframe coding and transform techniques. The px64 standard is intended for video conferencing and 'videophone' applications, and so requires that both encoding and decoding be in real time. At small values of *p*, the extremely low data rates of px64 result in very low-quality video and low frame rates, a form which may be acceptable for video telephony but is not intended for many other applications. At higher *p* values, px64's video quality improves, but since px64 is constrained to perform real-time compression, at a given data rate MPEG compressed video and DVI's PLV will be of better quality.

Digital video operations

A digital representation for video has many advantages: it opens the way for software manipulation of video material, storage of video in file systems and databases, its transmission over data networks, and its rapid and error-free duplication. The following looks at some of the technology used to handle digital video and the operations that are provided.

Digital video storage □ Digital video can be stored, like other data, using any of the digital storage technologies available. However, to record or play back the video in real time, the storage system must be capable of sustaining data transfer at the video data rate. Currently, the four main forms of storage for digital video are:

Magnetic tape: The high data rate digital video representations lead to massive storage requirements. For example, one hour of CCIR 601 4:2:2 consumes 72 Gbytes, while an hour of digital HDTV approaches the terabyte range. At present, only magnetic tape can provide these capacities at practical costs. There are a number of tape formats used by digital VTRs (DVTRs); see Table 2.5. This equipment is intended for professional video production and post-production and storage of frequently used material (such as a broadcaster's library of commercials).

Special purpose magnetic storage systems: Short durations (for instance, 30 seconds to 1 minute) of high data rate digital video can be stored on special-purpose, magnetic disk based, storage systems. These systems provide digital video inputs and outputs, so can be connected directly to external digital video equipment. A possible configuration is shown in Figure 2.7. In this example a network connection to a host computer allows digital frames to

Table 2.5   Digital video tape formats.

Tape format	Tape size	Video format	Manufacturers
D1	3/4"	CCIR 601 (8-bit)	Sony, BTS
D2	3/4"	Digital composite	Ampex, Sony
D3	1/2"	Digital composite	Panasonic
DCT	3/4"	CCIR 601 (8 bit, 2:1 compressed)	Ampex
D5	1/2"	CCIR 601 (10-bit) and digital composite	Panasonic
Digital Betacam	1/2"	CCIR 601 (10 bit, 2:1 compressed)	Sony, BTS

be transferred between the host and storage system. (Such transfers need not occur in real time and would primarily be used for single-frame recording of computer-generated or computer-modified frames.)

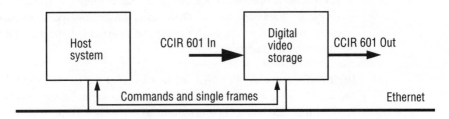

Figure 2.7   Digital video storage system.

Video memory boards: Several manufacturers produce boards equipped with very large amounts of semiconductor memory (several hundred Mbytes or more) and capable of storing short durations of uncompressed digital video. Like the special-purpose magnetic storage systems, digital video inputs and outputs are also provided for recording and playback.

General-purpose magnetic and optical storage systems: Many of the low data rate digital video representations were specifically designed so that conventional general-purpose storage devices (magnetic disks, writable, write-once and read-only optical media) could be used for real-time video playback and possibly recording. However, even at low data rates, video can quickly fill magnetic disks. For instance, at 1 Mbit/sec, a 100 Mbyte disk is filled in about 13 minutes, a 1 Gbyte disk in a little over two hours.

Digital video retrieval □ As with analog video, retrieval of digital video requires some method of frame addressing. Again time codes and frame numbers can be used. There are complications, though. First, the low data rate formats generally result in variable-sized frames; an index giving frame offsets is then needed for random access. Second, interframe compression techniques rely on similarities between frames. Only key frames are independently coded, others are derived from these frames. Random access is a two-step process: finding the nearest preceding key frame, and using this frame to decode the desired frame. This implies that the access method must be able to determine the nearest key frame for any frame; however since an index is already needed to cope with variable frame sizes, this information can be added easily.

Digital video synchronization ☐ The playback of digital video can exhibit the same synchronization problems – timebase jitter and timebase phase shift – that one finds with analog video. The synchronization techniques developed for analog video, such as genlocking and timebase correction, are also applicable to digital video. To give one example, a digital video timebase corrector aligns an incoming digital stream with a timing reference – as samples arrive they are momentarily buffered and then released in sync with the timing signal. Perhaps the main difference between analog and digital video synchronization is that digital systems are inherently more flexible than analog systems. As a result, a new range of synchronization-related operations are possible. For example, a software-based digital video player that is dropping out of sync might be directed to produce frames at a lower resolution. By reducing the computational load on the player it can then output frames at the appropriate rate.

Digital video editing ☐ There are two forms of digital video editing: *tape-based* and *nonlinear*. Tape-based editing involves the same fundamental procedures as used with analog video tape. The crucial difference is that generation loss is no longer an issue. With a DVTR, each copy has the same quality as the original (although there is debate about the effects of the slight compression found in the newer digital video tape formats). With error-free copies, complex compositions become possible where video material is layered together using keying or some other mixing operation.

With nonlinear editing, the video material is placed in random-access storage. This streamlines the editing process since there is no need to wait for tapes to cue and rewind. Graphical interfaces, where icons and timelines represent particular sequences, allow video segments to be selected and copied from one sequence to another. Copying and rearranging digital video need not result in massive data transfers on the storage device; instead the frame index can be modified so pointers, rather than the data itself, are moved.

Digital video effects ☐ With video in a digital form, a variety of special effects and transformations are possible. Video effects, like video processing in general, can be divided into two categories: real-time and non-real-time. The real-time effects include those discussed in the section on analog video mixing (in fact, many analog video effects are produced by way of intermediate digitization). So real-time tumbles, wipes, and fades are possible given the appropriate equipment.

Where digital video differs from analog is in the possibility for non-real-time processing. Any general-purpose computer, from small laptops to supercomputers, can be used for the generation and modification of digital video frames *if* frames need not be produced in real time. The complexity of the processing is no longer constrained by the frame rate, but rather by the computing resources available (and the patience of the user). For example, a desktop video editing system, rather than relying on expensive effects equipment to produce a tumble or some other transition, could calculate the transition in non-real time. The resulting frame sequence would be handled by the editor in the same way as sequences coming from cameras or other sources, that is, there is no distinction between natural video sequences and those that have been synthesized.

Digital video conversion □ With the variety of digital video representations, it is often necessary to convert from one format to another. Also, within some formats, varying degrees of compression are possible, and so one can speak of conversions within a single format that result in compression or decompression. As with effects processing mentioned above, conversion techniques fall into two categories: real-time and non-real-time. Real-time conversion typically requires special hardware, while non-real-time conversion can be performed with general-purpose computing equipment.

2.2.3 DIGITAL AUDIO

Media type Digital audio
    Representation
        Sampling frequency
        Sample size and quantization
        Number of channels (tracks)
        Interleaving
        Negative samples
        Encoding
    Operations
        Storage
        Retrieval
        Editing
        Effects and filtering
        Conversion

Digital audio appears in two main areas: telecommunications, where digital transmission of telephone calls is commonplace, and the entertainment industry, where a variety of digital audio recording media are used, the most well known being the audio CD. This section looks at commonly used representations for digital audio and discusses operations on digital audio that are of particular relevance to multimedia application programming. Further information can be found in texts on digital audio such as that of Pohlmann (1989).

Digital audio representation

Digital audio is produced by sampling a continuous signal generated by a sound source. An *analog-to-digital converter* (or A/D converter, or simply ADC), takes as input an electrical signal corresponding to the sound (coming from a microphone or some other source) and produces a digital data stream. The analog signal is reproduced from this data by a *digital-to-analog converter* (or D/A converter, or DAC) which consumes the data stream and outputs an analog electrical signal to be connected to an amplifier and speakers. The question we are concerned with is the format of the data used by ADCs, DACs, and other digital audio equipment. We first discuss some of the dimensions to digital audio representation.

Sampling frequency (rate) □ Sampling theory has shown that a signal can be reproduced without error from a set of samples provided the sampling frequency is at least twice the highest frequency present in the original signal. This fundamental result gives the lower limit when selecting a sampling frequency to be used in practice. For instance, the telephone networks allot a 3.4kHz bandwidth to voice-grade lines; thus an 8kHz sampling frequency, allowing some tolerance in component design, is used for digital telecommunications. The human ear is sensitive to frequencies of up to about 20kHz, so to digitize arbitrary perceivable sounds, a sampling frequency of over 40kHz is required.

Sample size and quantization □ During sampling, the continuously varying amplitude of the analog signal must be approximated by digital values. This introduces a *quantization error*, the difference between the actual amplitude and the digital approximation. Quantization error, on reconversion to analog form, is manifest as distortion – a loss in audio quality. The error can be reduced by increasing the sample size, that is, by allowing more bits per sample and thus improving the accuracy of the digital approximation.

The term *quantization* refers to breaking the continuous range of the analog signal into a number of intervals, each associated with a unique digital representation. While the number of intervals will depend on the sample size, there is freedom in choosing the intervals themselves and how they are coded. The simplest scheme, known as *linear quantization*, uses equally spaced intervals (this is also called uniform quantization). For instance, suppose the maximum variation of the analog signal is 5.0 (the units need not concern us) and suppose the sample size is 3 bits, then each quantization interval would span $5.0/2^3$ or 0.625 units of signal amplitude. In comparison, *nonlinear quantization* uses non-equally spaced intervals. With logarithmic quantization, a commonly used nonlinear encoding, low amplitude intervals are more closely spaced than those at higher amplitude, the result being greater sensitivity at lower amplitudes – an advantage, since this is also where the ear is most sensitive to noise. Generally nonlinear quantization, in particular logarithmic quantization, can provide better audio quality than a linear scheme using the same sample size. However, when digital audio is filtered or transformed, linear quantization is needed since the techniques of digital signal processing are then easier to apply.

Number of channels (tracks) □ Stereo audio signals contain two channels – the left and the right. Some consumer audio products use four channels, while professional audio editing equipment deals with 16, 32, or more channels. A digital audio format can specify the encoding of a fixed (or variable) number of channels, or, alternately, consider only a single channel and leave open the representation of multi-channel values.

Interleaving □ A multi-channel audio value can be encoded by interleaving channel samples, or by providing separate 'streams' for each channel. The advantages of interleaving include easier synchronization of channels; in other words, since channel values are contiguous they tend to be processed together and output together (one would not want a CD player that played the left track slightly in advance of the right). Additionally, storing and transmitting a multi-channel value in its entirety can be more efficient when the value is interleaved than when the channels are treated separately. A disadvantage of interleaving is that an interleaved format can waste space or bandwidth if not all channels are needed. Also single-channel operations can be more expensive because of accesses to the other channels; for example, when filling a buffer with samples from disk, samples from all channels will be read only to be discarded if not from the channel of interest. Interleaving also 'freezes' the synchronization relationships between channels, if one channel is to be temporally shifted with respect to another, the samples must be re-interleaved. A final disadvantage is that interleaving may not allow variation in the number of channels.

Negative samples □ The voltages found in analog audio signals alternate between positive and negative values and so negative-valued samples occur. One possibility is to code samples using unsigned integers (where 0 would correspond to the lowest negative voltage); however, if processing is anticipated then signed integers are more convenient in which case a two's complement, one's complement, or sign-magnitude representation may be used.

Encoding □ A number of methods have been developed for encoding audio data so as to reduce storage and transmission costs. Compressed audio also provides better quality when compared to uncompressed audio at the same data rate. Descriptions of audio coding can be found in Pohlmann (1989); here we mention two methods commonly used in multimedia applications.

> PCM: *Pulse code modulation* refers to how a digital signal can be formed from a series of pulses (see Figure 2.8). PCM signals make better use of bandwidth and are less 'jumpy' than other simple methods of transmitting digital data (such as 'pulse amplitude modulation' – a series of pulses of varying amplitude). In the context of audio coding, a PCM value is simply a sequence of uncompressed samples. As a result PCM acts as a reference format against which more complex coding methods can be compared.

> ADPCM: *Adaptive delta pulse code modulation* reduces the PCM data rate by encoding differences between sample values. There are variations of this technique but in one approach each sample is replaced by a single bit indicating the sign of the difference between it and the previous sample. During decoding, reconstituted samples are formed by scaling the difference and adding it to the previous decoded sample. This previous value indexes a table of scaling factors and so determines the amount to scale the difference. The scale factors depend on the original samples and are calculated during encoding. ADPCM is related to a number of other methods including differential pulse code modulation and delta modulation. ADPCM is widely used,

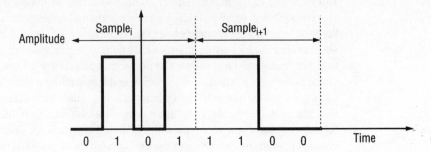

Figure 2.8   Pulse code modulation of sample data (sample size = 4 bits).

for instance both CD-i and DVI (two multimedia systems discussed in the next chapter) process ADPCM encoded audio; in addition ADPCM standards exist (such as CCITT G.721). Typical compression ratios are from 4:1 to 2:1.

Specific examples of audio formats are listed in Table 2.6. The table entries can be divided into two groups. The first group (CD audio and DAT) are high data rate formats intended for musical recordings, the second group (G.721, A-law and μ-law) are low data rate formats used for telephony.

Table 2.6   Some digital audio formats.

	CD audio	DAT	G.721	A-law[a] μ-law
Sampling rate (kHz)	44.1	48[b]	8	8
Sample size (bits)	16	16	16/4[c]	8
Quantization	Linear	Linear	Linear	Log
Number of channels	2	2	1	1
Data rate per channel (10^3 bit/sec)	705	768	32	64
Encoding	PCM	PCM	ADPCM	PCM
Quality	Very high	Very high	Moderate	Telephone

a. A-law is used within European telephone systems, while μ-law is North American.
b. DAT has a number of audio formats – three sampling frequencies are possible (32 kHz, 44.1 kHz and 48 kHz) and the 32 kHz rate may use either 16-bit linear quantization or 12-bit nonlinear; in the second case two or four tracks may be recorded. The numbers listed are for the highest quality DAT format.
c. This first number refers to the decoded sample size, the second to the encoded size.

Digital audio operations

Digital audio storage □ It is possible to record digital audio, even at the data rates of the high-quality formats, on general-purpose magnetic storage systems. For instance, a magnetic disk with a sustainable data transfer rate of 5 Mbytes per second could, in theory, record or play back about 50 channels of CD-quality digital audio. This number of channels is not possible without highly optimized data layout and buffering, but one or two channels are well within the reach of current magnetic storage devices and the buses for small computer systems.

An hour of stereo digital audio, at the CD audio data rate, requires over half a gigabyte of storage space. As a result, applications involving large amounts of digital audio make use of 'tertiary' storage media. For instance, a multimedia authoring environment could store most of its audio resources offline, but in a form that can be easily mounted. DAT cassettes or CD discs are suitable for this purpose. When a user requires a particular audio sequence, the corresponding disc or tape would be mounted and perhaps the value copied into secondary storage. Mounting may be done manually or automated by use of 'jukeboxes'.

Digital audio retrieval   □ Random access of digital audio is the ability to quickly retrieve and play back portions of a digital audio sequence. The basic technical problems are finding the data and reading it so as to ensure a continuous flow of samples to the digital-to-analog converter. Portions of audio sequences, often called *segments*, can be identified by their starting time and duration. To locate a segment involves mapping the starting time to a 'segment address' – an offset within the audio value. (The segment address must then be mapped to a physical address on the disk; however, this is usually performed by a file system.) With constant rate formats it is a simple matter to convert time code to a segment address. In situations where there is no direct mapping, random access requires an index identifying the addresses of segments given their time code. The second problem, ensuring a continuous flow of data, is not difficult with a dedicated storage device. However, since the data transfer rates of magnetic disks are significantly higher than those required for digital audio, it is feasible to read (and write) many audio values simultaneously. In this case the scheduling of disk operations, block and buffer sizes, and data layout on the disk must be carefully selected and controlled (Gemmell and Christodoulakis, 1992).

Digital audio editing   □ As with digital video, there are two main forms of digital audio editing – tape-based and disk-based. The random access provided by disk-based systems immediately simplifies and streamlines the editing process. Time consuming tape mounting and rewinding are no longer necessary and high-speed copying is possible. Whether tape-based or disk-based, the basic editing operations involve cutting, copying, and inserting audio segments. Simply inserting one sequence of samples in the midst of another can produce an audible click – the editor must take care to preserve the continuity of the waveform. One technique is to calculate a *cross-fade* by scaling and adding the amplitudes of the original segment and the inserted segment about the insertion point (see Figure 2.9).

Digital audio also supports a technique known as nondestructive editing. With this form of editing, segments of the original captured data are accessed via a *play list* – a data structure identifying segment offsets, their durations, and the order in which they are to be joined. As with the similar 'edit decision lists' used in video editing, play lists keep track of actions taken during an editing session. For instance, cuts, copies, and inserts can be performed by manipulating and rearranging play list entries. An advantage of nondestructive editing is that it preserves the original captured data; it also avoids large and time-consuming copying

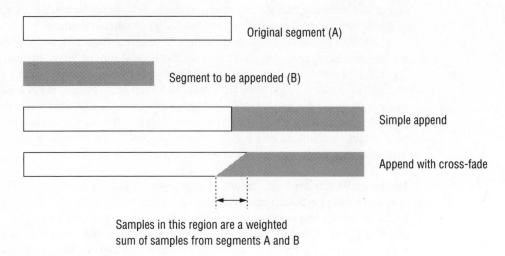

Original segment (A)

Segment to be appended (B)

Simple append

Append with cross-fade

Samples in this region are a weighted
sum of samples from segments A and B

Figure 2.9   Audio cross-fade.

operations. A play list can be 'previewed' by playing back the segments to which it points; a play list can also be 'collapsed' and a new audio segment created reflecting the editing actions present within the play list.

When editing audio, at some point it is necessary to select where segments start and stop. This can be extremely difficult, requiring much trial and error, since the audio value 'moves' as one listens to it. Traditionally, professional editors often select an edit point by adeptly pulling the tape back and forth within the player. Digital systems can provide many alternatives. One possibility is to display the waveform graphically, thus giving visual clues as to when audio events start and stop. Another possibility is to allow regions to be marked while listening to the track; the user can then go back and select more precisely within the marked region. A graphical display of markers, placed either on the waveform or against a timeline, also aids in quickly finding and selecting regions.

In addition to cutting, copying and inserting segments, a host of other editing operations can be performed on audio in digital form. Modifying volume levels by scaling sample values is one crucial example. Other useful operations include, when editing a multi-track recording, the ability to add and delete tracks, mix tracks together, or change the relative timing by shifting one track with respect to the other. These operations can be implemented on personal computers and workstations, however high-quality professional audio editing is often performed on dedicated 'audio workstations'. These workstations have special-purpose signal processing hardware, bus and storage architectures designed for audio recording and playback, and numerous interfaces for connection to studio equipment.

Digital audio effects and filtering □ Audio workstations, and to a lesser extent audio editing programs on general-purpose computers, can perform a number of special effects through the application of digital filtering techniques. Depending upon the complexity of the effect, the number of tracks involved, and the available computational resources, processing may or may not take place in real time. Some of these effects include:

Delay: By introducing delay and feedback, effects such as echoing and re-verberation are produced.

Equalization (EQ) – Digital filtering techniques are used to emphasize, re-duce or balance various frequency bands within a segment.

Normalization : A segment is scaled so that its peak amplitude is the maxi-mum allowed value.

Noise reduction: Digital signal processing is used to reduce unwanted noise, such as a background hiss or hum.

Time compression and expansion: Segment duration is increased or de-creased without changing pitch.

Pitch shifting: A segment's pitch is changed without altering its duration.

Stereoization: A single track is split into two stereo tracks with differing au-dio content.

Acoustic environments: The 'signatures' of particular acoustic environ-ments, for instance the slight echo of a cathedral or the dampened sound of a small club room, are applied to an existing track.

Digital audio conversion □ A final set of useful operations on digital audio deals with conversion from one format to another, or alteration of encoding pa-rameters within a single format. An example of the first form of conversion would be uncompressing an ADPCM track and converting it to PCM. An example of al-tering encoding parameters would be resampling a PCM track at a lower frequen-cy and lower amplitude resolution.

2.2.4   MUSIC

Media type Music
> **Representation**
>> Operational versus symbolic
>> MIDI
>> SMDL
> **Operations**
>> Playback and synthesis
>> Timing
>> Editing and composition

With the advent of powerful, low-cost digital signal processors, many computers can now record, process, and generate music. Since music is often essential to multimedia compositions, the programmers of multimedia applications require a 'music type' allowing them to call upon a computer's musical capabilities. In this section we look at some of the issues involved in representing music and the operations commonly performed on musical data. These issues are central to the field of computer music which explores software and hardware techniques for the composition, performance, recording, and 'processing' of music. For more information on computer music the reader is referred to survey articles (ACM, 1985) or texts (Roads and Strawn, 1987; De Poli *et al.*, 1991; Howell *et al.*, 1991; Rowe, 1993).

Representation of music

Operational versus symbolic □ In general, a musical representation is a means of specifying the information needed to produce a piece of music. This simple definition, though, immediately raises difficult questions. First, what is perceived as music varies from culture to culture and person to person. Thus, unless the musical representation is to account for arbitrary sounds, there must be some notion of the representation's *expressibility,* that is, just what forms of sound it intends to encompass. Second, performances of a piece of music vary, from musician to musician and instrument to instrument. Furthermore, a musician can choose to interpret one piece in different styles. The question is, then, to what degree a musical representation specifies its performance. At one extreme are representations based on the exact timings and physical descriptions of sounds to be produced, at the other extreme representations involving highly symbolic descriptions of the form of the music and allowing great leeway in their interpretation. These can be identified as *operational* versus *symbolic* representations. We term both of these *structural* representations, since as opposed to representing music by audio samples, there is information about the internal structure of the music.

We now describe two examples of data representations for music. The first, MIDI, is a widely used protocol allowing the connection of computers and musical equipment. It is an example of an operational representation. The second,

SMDL, is a proposal for a standard structure for documents containing musical information. SMDL has both operational and symbolic aspects.

MIDI □ The *Musical Instrument Digital Interface*, or MIDI, standard was designed during the early 1980s by the manufacturers of musical equipment. MIDI defines a set of *messages* for this equipment. It has been highly successful and is found on a variety of products including electronic keyboards and synthesizers, drum machines, *sequencers* (used to record and play back MIDI messages), and devices used to synchronize music with video or film.

Any MIDI device has one or more *ports* by which it can be connected, using a standard cable, to other MIDI devices. These ports come in three types: a MIDI OUT port allows a device to send to other devices any MIDI messages it has produced, a MIDI IN port receives MIDI messages from another device, and a MIDI THRU port repeats received messages, thus allowing daisy-chaining of MIDI devices. A simple configuration is shown in Figure 2.10, where a keyboard/synthesizer is used to generate and process MIDI messages. These messages can be recorded by the sequencer (typically a special-purpose MIDI device or a computer with MIDI ports and sequencer software). On playback the sequencer outputs the recorded MIDI messages, which are then processed by the keyboard/synthesizer and passed on to other MIDI devices for further processing.

How a MIDI device processes a MIDI message, or, more specifically, how it responds to messages received on its MIDI IN port or generated internally, varies from device to device. In the example above, the sequencer responds by logging messages. Other devices, such as synthesizers, may respond by producing sound; however, the sound is *not* entirely determined by the MIDI message. Instead the message merely directs the synthesizer to select a sound from a 'palette' of sounds. One can think of a palette as defining the set of notes produced by some instrument. For instance, a drum machine will have a palette of drum-like sounds,

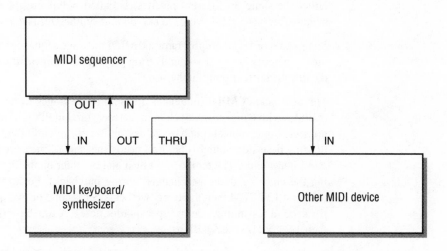

Figure 2.10   Example MIDI system configuration.

while a more general synthesizer will have palettes for many instruments, such as a violin or clarinet, and possibly allow the definition of new palettes. The result is that, since palettes vary from synthesizer to synthesizer, different MIDI devices can produce different sounds when supplied with the same data.

We now describe MIDI's message set; complete specifications and very practical descriptions of MIDI are provided by Rona (1987; 1990) and Rothstein (1992). Since MIDI is widely used, yet perhaps not well known outside the MIDI community, we will treat it in more detail than some of the other media types examined so far. Before describing specific messages we introduce a few important MIDI concepts:

Channel: A MIDI connection has sixteen message channels; most messages include a code indicating their channel number. MIDI devices can be set to respond to all channels or only messages on a specific channel.

Key number: Notes are identified by key numbers of which there are 128 (in comparison, a standard keyboard has 88 keys).

Controller: Operational characteristics of a MIDI device can be altered by changing the values of controllers. There are 128 controllers. For example, controller number 4 is the 'foot controller'; changing its value typically alters how sounds are produced. Not every device will support every controller, and in fact many controllers are left undefined by the MIDI protocol. This allows new devices with new features to make device-specific extensions to MIDI.

Patch/program: An audio palette is called a program or patch. Patches are identified by a patch number. A synthesizer may be capable of having many patches active at the same time, in which case it is called *multi-timbral*.

Polyphony: The ability of a synthesizer to play many notes at a time (using either the same or different patches) is called polyphony. A *monophonic* synthesizer has a single voice, a *polyphonic* synthesizer has many.

Song: A recorded or preprogrammed MIDI message sequence in a MIDI device's memory is called a song. During playback, a *song position pointer* indicates the current point in the song.

Timing clock: A MIDI sequencer timestamps messages using a clock that operates with a *timebase* (clock interval) measured in PPQ – *parts per quarter note*. Some typical timebase values are 24, 96, and 480 PPQ. To convert the timebase into actual time, one needs the *tempo*, measured in BPM – *beats per minute*. The tempo is set by a dial or slider on the device containing the clock (and can be changed during playback). For example, if the tempo is 120 BPM then there are two beats per second or two quarter notes per second (assuming one beat per quarter note). A timebase of 24 PPQ is then $1/24 \times (1/2)$ sec ≈ 20 ms.

MIDI synchronization: MIDI devices containing clocks can be set to *external sync* or *internal sync*. When set to internal sync, a device is known as a *master* and produces on its MIDI OUT port a special 'Timing Clock' message at 24 PPQ. *Slave* devices, those set to external sync, use the Timing Clock message in place of their clock. This allows many MIDI devices to maintain synchronization by sharing a single clock. Furthermore, adjusting the tempo of the master device controls the timing of the entire system.

MTC: MIDI Time Code (MTC) is used to synchronize MIDI with film or video. As a film or video is played, its SMPTE Time Code is extracted and read by an MTC generator which produces 'MIDI Time Code' messages at a rate of four times per frame. These messages are used to trigger sound effects or musical sequences. MTC was not part of the original MIDI specification, but was added as MIDI became more widely used.

The MIDI protocol is based on an 8-bit code for messages, each consisting of a single *command byte* (also called the *status byte*) and possibly one or more *data bytes*. Command and data bytes are distinguished by the value of the high-order bit ('1' for commands, '0' for data). Table 2.7 lists all MIDI messages. They can be divided into the following categories:

(1)   Channel voice messages (8c–Ec): Determine the actual notes played, how quickly they are hit and released and with what pressure, and the values assigned to controllers.

(2)   Channel mode messages (Bc, with controllers 121–127): Used to select the *mode* of a synthesizer. For example, should it respond to one channel or all channels; should each channel be separately voiced, or all voices used for one channel.

(3)   System messages (F0–FF): Perform general system functions and do not have channels. The Timing Clock and MIDI Time Code messages mentioned above are in this category; other system messages include a System Reset and messages for starting and stopping devices. For instance, to play back in a multi-device MIDI system the master device first sends a Start message. A clock-based device receiving this message will start to play from the position of its song pointer.

The modularity and flexibility of MIDI have led to its wide use, but this in turn has revealed its limitations. For instance, MIDI operates at a baud rate of 31 250 bits per second; at this rate about 500 notes can be sent per second. Complex pieces using many instruments may require higher rates. A second problem area is the limited number of channels, lack of device addressing, and, in general, the difficulties in configuring large MIDI networks. Another potential problem is the device dependence of MIDI data, due, in part, to the arbitrariness of patch numbers – without some convention for patch numbers, different synthesizers produce different sounds from the same data. Finally, MIDI is now being used in ways it was not originally intended, such as controlling stage lighting and special effects equipment. Recent MIDI developments address some of these issues. An extension to the MIDI specification, known as *General MIDI* (or *GM*), defines a patch numbering scheme, and deals with other problems related to device independence. A MIDI file format (*SMF* or *Standard MIDI Files*) and recommendations for extending MIDI beyond the musical domain have also been developed.

Table 2.7   MIDI message formats.

Command name	Command code (Hex[a])	Number of data dytes	Data
Note Off	8c	2	Key number, velocity value
Note On	9c	2	Key number, velocity value
Key Pressure	Ac	2	Key number, pressure value
Control Change	Bc	2	Controller number, control value
Program Change	Cc	1	Program (patch) number
Channel Pressure	Dc	1	Pressure value
Pitch Bend Change	Ec	2	Pitch bend value
System Exclusive	F0	n[b]	Arbitrary
MIDI Time Code	F1	1	Frame number
Song Position Pointer	F2	2	Song position pointer value
Song Select	F3	1	Song number
undefined	F4		
undefined	F5		
Tune Request	F6	0	
End of Exclusive	F7	0	
Timing Clock	F8	0	
undefined	F9		
Start	FA	0	
Continue	FB	0	
Stop	FC	0	
undefined	FD		
Active Sensing	FE	0	
System Reset	FF	0	

a. A 'c' indicates the lower four bits are used for a channel number.
b. All following bytes, until an End of Exclusive message, are considered as data. This message is commonly used to download large amounts of data (such as patch memory) from one MIDI device to another.

SMDL ☐ The *Standard Music Description Language*, or SMDL, originates from the Music Information Processing Standards (MIPS) committee within ANSI. The goal of the MIPS committee is to create a standard for encoding music and associated information such as a piece's title or the name of its composer. SMDL addresses many uses of music-related material. It encompasses the representation of music for electronic dissemination and production by software, the representation of scores and musical examples in printed documents, and the representation of musical annotation and attributes used for musical analysis or by music databases (ANSI, 1988a).

SMDL is an application of *Standard Generalized Markup Language* (SGML), the document markup language discussed in Section 2.1.1. Specifically, SMDL introduces an SGML document type used for what are called *musical works* or simply *works*. Each work has four hierarchically structured sections: the *core* section, *gestural* section, *visual* section, and *analytical* section (ANSI,

1988b). The core consists of musical events, such as note sequences, which form the work. There is one core per work and it provides a canonical representation of the work. The gestural section contains performances of the core. Performances may differ in interpretation (as when notes are stressed differently) or perhaps by the introduction of new 'ad lib' events. The visual section is used to display the core in printed form. This section contains one or more scores; a score in turn contains events, which generally correspond to musical events within the core but may also include formatting information used to enhance the visual presentation and additional information (such as lyrics). Finally, the analytical section allows a number of theoretical analyses, referring to the core, its score, and performances, to be included within the work.

SMDL has recently been subsumed by the more general 'HyTime' standard for documents containing time-based media. HyTime is discussed in Section 3.7.

Operations on music

It is interesting to compare the representation of music in symbolic or operational form to the capture of music by audio sampling. Generally musical representations are more abstract than audio representations; they contain less performance-related information. If the goal is to reproduce a specific performance then a musical representation would not be appropriate, unless it were a hybrid allowing aspects of real performances to be included.

The above suggests that musical representations are best for the earlier stages of music production while audio representations are preferable for the final 'product'. However, there are many advantages of musical, as opposed to audio, representation. First, the musical representation is likely to be more compact, thus reducing costs of storage and transmission. In addition a musical representation is 'portable'; it can be synthesized with a fidelity and complexity suited to the available hardware and output devices. A further advantage is that while digital audio has inherent noise, musical representations are noise-free. Perhaps, though, the most significant advantage is that a musical representation makes possible many operations that would be infeasible, or require extensive processing, if they were to be performed on audio data. These operations include:

Music playback and synthesis □ Whether music is encoded in audio form or by a structural representation, there is always the possibility of playback, or 'performing' the music. Where the two forms differ is in the flexibility of control during playback. During audio playback, the listener has limited influence over musical aspects of the performance. The listener may change the volume, or engage some processing module, but these are operations of an audio, rather than musical, nature. In comparison, if the music is produced by synthesis from a structural representation, many forms of control and interaction become possible. For instance, the listener can independently change pitch and tempo – with digital audio this is difficult since simply altering the playback speed will in turn alter the pitch. Control over individual instruments is also possible. The listener may be able to increase or decrease instrument volumes or modify the sounds they produce. In other words, musical representations offer a greater potential for interactivity than is found with audio representations.

Music timing □ In a structural representation the timing of musical events is more explicit than in an audio representation (where, for instance, finding the start of a particular note sequence may require searching and listening). The availability of timing information, and the ability to modify tempo, makes it possible to alter the timing of groups of musical events and to adjust the synchronization of musical events with other events (such as video frames).

Music editing and composition □ Current music software (see Yavelow (1992) for a discussion of many examples) supports a large repertoire of editing and composition operations. Basic editing operations deal with modifying primitive events and notes. More complex operations refer to musical aggregates – chords, bars, and higher-level groupings. Examples would be repeating a phrase or replacing a melody. Music composition software simplifies the tasks of generating, combining, or rearranging tracks and automates the printing of a score in conventional music notation.

2.2.5   ANIMATION

Media type Animation
  Representation
      Cel models
      Scene-based models
      Event-based models
      Key frames
      Articulated objects and hierarchical models
      Scripting and procedural models
      Physically based and empirical models
  Operations
      Graphics operations
      Motion and parameter control
      Rendering
      Playback

Animation, in a general sense, is the depiction of objects as they vary over time. Traditional animation relies on individually drawing or photographing large numbers of images which when viewed in succession create an illusion of life-like motion. Computer animation also results in sequences of images, in this case produced by software rather than by being hand-drawn or photographed.

Since animation, like video, relies on sequences of images, introducing an 'animation type' needs a way of distinguishing between it and the video type. One possibility is based on image content: we could reserve the video type for sequences of images deriving from natural sources (such as via video cameras), and use the animation type for synthetic image sequences. Unfortunately there are many problems with this approach. While information about content is certainly useful (for example, in aiding retrieval, or in selecting a compression algorithm) using it as the basis of differentiating between animation and video leads to two types

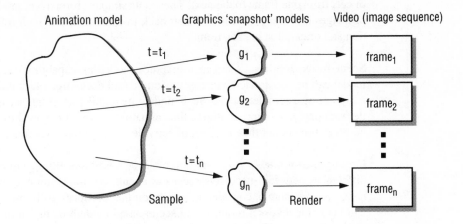

Animation model   Graphics 'snapshot' models   Video (image sequence)

Figure 2.11   Animation sampling and rendering.

which are very similar – both supporting essentially the same set of operations – so it seems little is gained. Also it is not clear which type to assign to image sequences containing some natural and some synthetic images, or containing images composed from both natural and synthetic sources.

Instead one can base the distinction on modelling. This approach is similar to the situation with images and graphics, where graphics types provide models which are rendered to produce images. In analogy, we will say that animation types also provide models, but when these models are rendered the result is video, that is, a sequence of images. Thus animation models are *evolving*, or time-dependent; while graphics models are independent of time. By *sampling* an animation model at a particular time, a graphics 'snapshot' model is obtained which is then rendered to produce an image. Figure 2.11 depicts this process.

Computer animation is evolving quickly and new techniques and methods appear regularly. The area is driven by the continual increase in rendering and processing power and the continual need for novelty in entertainment and advertising. The following is a short classification of animation representations and operations. Readers interested in a more thorough discussion of animation, or descriptions of advanced techniques, should consult available textbooks (Weinstock, 1986; Magnenat-Thalmann and Thalmann, 1990; Vince, 1992) or conference proceedings.

Animation representation

Cel models □ Early animators drew on transparent celluloid sheets, or 'cels'. Different sheets contained different parts of a scene, and the complete scene was assembled by overlaying the sheets. Movement of an object within the scene could be achieved by shifting the corresponding sheet.

Cel modelling can be carried over to computer animation. Cels are implemented as digital images containing a transparency channel. A scene is rendered by drawing the cels back to front, and movement is added by changing the position of cels from one frame to the next. Thus in its simplest form a 'cel model' is a set of images plus a specification of their back-to-front order and their relative position and orientation in each frame.

Scene-based models □ Given a graphics modelling capability, an animation model can be constructed by simply taking a sequence of graphics models, each representing a complete scene. Such models are highly redundant (scenes vary little from one to another) and force the animator to work at the level of individual points in time rather than in terms of activities taking place over time.

Event-based models □ A variation of scene-based modelling is to express the differences between successive scenes as events that transform one scene to the next. As an example, consider an animation that produces 20 frames showing a ball bouncing across a room. Using scene-based modelling, the animator would have to construct 20 graphics models, each describing the room and the ball at its current position. With event-based modelling, the animator constructs an initial model of the room and ball, and then specifies events that displace the ball from scene to scene. While this technique again forces the animator to work at the level of individual time points, it is useful for interactive animation where the events are no longer entered manually, but recorded from input devices 'attached' to pieces of the model (as when a mouse is used to specify the trajectory of the ball by dragging it across the room).

Key frames □ A pervasive technique borrowed from traditional animation is the use of key frames. Here, in essence, the animator models the beginning and end frames of a sequence and lets the computer calculate the others. Key framing is used in conjunction with other techniques. For example, two cel models or two geometric models might be identified as key frames. The 'in-between' frames are then determined by interpolating parameters of these models (parameters would include cel positions in the first case, and the positions of geometric objects and lights in the second case).

Articulated objects and hierarchical models □ Key framing removes much of the drudgery of the animator's task yet complex sequences require more powerful modelling techniques. One problem is that specifying key frames is extremely time-consuming if objects must be placed individually. A second problem is that the paths produced by interpolating between the key frames may not be what is desired. Hierarchical models address both problems to a certain degree by allowing the construction of articulated objects – jointed assemblies where the configuration and movements of sub-parts are constrained. For example, consider a clock object consisting of a face and two hands. The model may specify that the hands lie parallel to the face and can only rotate about a single axis perpendicular to the face. This allows the animator to deal with the clock as a single unit where proper relative positioning is maintained. Furthermore, the constraints are upheld during interpolation – if the clock happens to be in different positions in two key frames, the entire assembly will be correctly displaced in the intermediate frames.

Scripting and procedural models □ Current state-of-the art animation modelling systems have interactive tools allowing the animator to specify key frames, preview sequences in real time, and control the interpolation of model parameters. Scripting languages are an additional feature of many such systems; they provide the animator with the ability to express sequences in a concise form and are particularly useful for repetitive and structured motion. Scripting languages include many of the features of general-purpose programming languages, for instance parameterized operations and control flow. Where scripting languages and programming languages differ is that the former also include high-level operations, such as 'stretch' or 'detect collision', intended specifically for animation. The most powerful scripting languages go beyond simple actions to tasks and goals. The animator then gives directions such as 'close the door' or 'kick the football into the net' and leaves the complex task of calculating object trajectories to the modelling software.

Physically based models and empirical models □ A final modelling technique is to take into account physical forces and interactions. This approach is used to produce sequences depicting evolving physical systems (such as flowing water, or changes in global weather patterns). The animator uses a mathematical model of the system derived from physical principles or from empirical data. In either case the model is 'solved', numerically or through simulation, at a sequence of time points, each solution resulting in one frame of the animation sequence.

Animation operations

Graphics operations □ Since animation models are graphics models extended in time, the graphics operations (primitive and structural editing, lighting, viewing, shading, and so on) are also applicable to animation models.

Motion and parameter control □ The essential difference between graphics and animation operations is the addition of the temporal dimension. Objects are no longer fixed in place but can be assigned complex trajectories. Similarly, instead of static lights, it is also possible to specify the behavior of lights over time (as when a light changes position or color). Commercial 3D animation systems often include separate 'modelling' and 'animation' tools. The modelling tools are used to construct 3D objects (graphics models), while the animation tools add temporal information to these objects (and so produce animation models).

Animation rendering □ There are two basic forms of animation rendering: real-time and non-real-time. In the first case the model is rendered as frames are displayed. Ten or more frames per second are needed to avoid jerkiness, so real-time rendering is only feasible with simple models or with special hardware. The alternative is to pre-render frames, spending minutes, hours, or more on each frame, and storing the result as a video sequence. Pre-rendered animation offers higher visual quality than real-time animation. Temporal quality is also usually higher since a constant frame rate is easily obtained (by sampling the model at regular intervals), while with real-time animation the frame rate may depend on model complexity and so vary considerably.

Animation playback ☐ If animation is pre-rendered, playback offers the same operational possibilities as with digital video, that is, control over playback rate and direction. The playback of animation rendered in real time, in comparison, is more flexible. In this case it is possible to modify the model interactively as play-back proceeds. For example, model objects can be added and removed, lights turned on and off, and the viewpoint changed. In other words, real-time animation is potentially highly interactive and modifiable.

2.3 OTHER MEDIA TYPES

Text, graphics, images, video, audio, music, and animation – these are familiar media types, but are there others? The notion of 'media type' is very broad; it is used to classify the various representations of information to which we are ex-posed. If some representation has distinctive characteristics – perhaps it allows control over some aspect of presentation that is not possible with other media types, or permits some new form of user interaction – then it may be useful to make this distinction explicit by forming a separate media type.

Much of the information one currently encounters can be grouped under the types we have mentioned so far. There are other forms of information, less com-monly used but with interesting capabilities. Examples include:

2.3.1   EXTENDED IMAGES

'Extended images' are a hybrid of the graphics and image types. Like images, they have a simple structure and may be acquired by some form of sampling apparatus. But, like graphics, there is freedom in selecting viewing position and direction. This freedom permits a range of interaction possibilities, adding the flexibility of graphics to image-like data. We give two examples of extended images:

Surface images ☐ A 'surface image' consists of a 2D digital image with an ad-ditional channel giving depth information. The depth channel can be visualized as a 3D grid over which the 2D image is laid (the effect is similar to texture map-ping). A surface image is shown in Plate VI; both the grid and the composed image are illustrated. Scanning devices have been developed for producing surface im-ages and are now available commercially. The interactive display and manipula-tion of surface images requires significant processing power. However, these ca-pabilities are now within the range of personal computers so it is likely that surface images will be of importance to interactive 3D applications.

Volume images ☐ A volume image is a 3D grid with an 'intensity' associated to each point. These images are often derived from physical data, for example medical scans, and the intensities then refer to some measurable value such as material density. A grid point, called a *voxel* or 'volume element', may have an opacity value in addition to its intensity. Volume images are rendered into 2D images in a variety of ways. The volume can be viewed from arbitrary directions and positions, and, by making parts of the volume transparent, it is possible to progressively reveal inner structure (see Plate VII). This addition of one more dimension to image data dramatically increases size and processing cost; however, volume images, like surface images, have much potential for interaction. For instance, an interactive anatomical atlas has been based on a voxel model of the human head (Höhne *et al.*, 1992).

2.3.2   DIGITAL INK

Representations of the hand-drawn characters and sketches common to pen-based interfaces are referred to as 'digital ink'. More than a simple bitmap, digital ink contains information that aids in pattern and character recognition, for instance stroke direction and pen pressure. A platform-independent format, called *Jot*, is currently being specified by several manufacturers of pen-based products.

2.3.3   SPEECH AUDIO

In the discussion on representations for digital audio, no assumption was made concerning the content of the audio – an audio value could contain a film sound track, a radio newscast, bird calls, or any other imaginable sound. Certain applications, for example voice mail, do not need this generality – they can take advantage of data representations intended specifically for speech.

Speech encoding □ For speech-only audio signals, low data rates can be obtained by exploiting knowledge of the process of speech production. The audio coding methods mentioned in Section 2.2.3 are classified as time-domain techniques; they code a time-varying waveform in terms of digitized sample values. Alternately, a digital representation for audio can be based on a description of the frequencies present within the signal or some other aspect of signal structure. The amount of compression obtained will depend on the nature of the signal. A pure tone, for instance, is best described in terms of frequencies, but this may not be the case for noisy signals. Speech coding techniques rely on the inherent structure within speech signals. One example, *linear predictive coding* (LPC), like some of the PCM variants, predicts samples from previous samples. LPC uses a model of speech production to predict samples; this results in very low data rates. For instance, an LPC standard known as LPC-10 has a data rate of approximately 2400 bits/sec, or about 1/15th the lowest data rate audio encoding listed in Table 2.6. The quality of LPC-10 speech is low and would not be suitable for many applications. However, speech coding methods are certainly relevant in situations where storage is limited and large speech segments are required.

Speech synthesis □ An alternative to producing speech from encoded recordings is to synthesize speech directly from text. A number of low-cost commercial text-to-speech synthesizers exist; also current workstations have sufficient power to run text-to-speech software. The input data rate of text-to-speech synthesis is very low, a few hundred bits per second – an hour's worth of speech can be produced from perhaps 150 kbytes. However the resulting speech quality is fairly low and lacking in intonation and stress. Quality is improved by using text marked up with stress and timing information, but producing the markup is difficult and being restricted to marked-up text would reduce the versatility of text-to-speech synthesis.

2.3.4   TEMPORAL SEQUENCES

The temporal media types – digital audio and digital video, music and animation – are examples of *temporal sequences*, that is, sequences of data elements, each element having a starting time and duration. A general characteristic of multimedia systems is the ability to process temporal sequences – to set up activities that produce and consume temporal sequences subject to their timing constraints. A common example is a video decompression activity which must consume an incoming digital video value and produce a sequence of uncompressed frames. If it is the processing of temporal sequences that is intrinsic to multimedia systems, then forms of temporal sequences other than those listed above may appear in multimedia systems. Such data, while not clearly identifiable as 'media' data, can be usefully mixed with media data. Some possible examples include recordings of user input (for instance, logs of mouse movement), timestamped message and event logs (for instance, messages sent to a server process), logs of instrument data, and data annotating other temporal sequences (for instance, a sequence identifying the set of people appearing in each frame of a corresponding video sequence).

2.3.5   NONTEMPORAL VIDEO AND ANIMATION

Frame sequences associated with conventional video and animation are ordered by a single value – time. The *frame access function*, which selects a frame given a time value, is a linear mapping from time to frames. With nontemporal video and animation, the frame access function need no longer be linear and may depend on variables other than time. In cases where the access function depends on several variables, different frame sequences are obtained by, for instance, holding one access variable constant and varying the others. This can be visualized by thinking of access variables as coordinates of a 'frame space', a frame sequence is then a path through frame space.

An example of nontemporal video is shown in Figure 2.12. Here video frames depict a single scene viewed from different directions. The result is a two-dimensional frame space and an access function of the form $frame = f(\theta, \phi)$. The right-hand side of the figure shows the frame space and one possible frame sequence. Such frame spaces are called *navigable movies* (Yawitz *et al.*, 1992) since they offer the user the ability to move around a scene. The extra degrees of freedom within navigable movies offer many novel possibilities for interaction and playback.

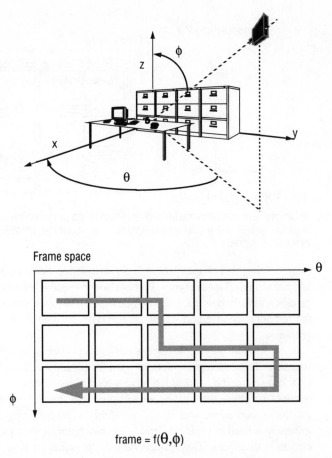

Frame space

frame = f(θ,ϕ)

Figure 2.12   An example of nontemporal video. Video frames of a scene viewed from various angles are captured and then accessed using angular values. Frame space is two dimensional.

An example of nontemporal animation is shown in Figure 2.13. In this case, a three-dimensional frame space is obtained from a physical model. For instance, suppose the model describes stresses on an aircraft wing. The frame space is constructed by selectively varying three model parameters, perhaps the angle of the wing, wind speed, and air pressure, and rendering a frame for each combination of parameter settings.

2.4 COMPARISONS

It is interesting to look back at the media types described in this chapter and ask whether any patterns or similarities can be seen. Considering the media types themselves, there seem to be two ways to group similar types. First, as was used

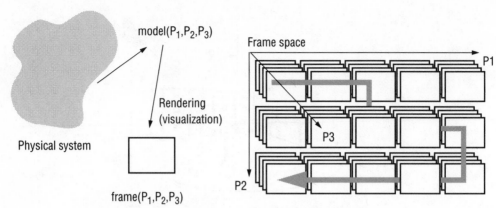

Figure 2.13   An example of nontemporal animation. Frames are rendered from a model of a physical system; the model contains three independent parameters. Frame space is three dimensional.

in organizing this chapter, there is the distinction between temporal media types and nontemporal media types. Perhaps not so evident is that members of these two groups naturally pair up with each other. For instance, one can consider video as the temporal counterpart of the image type, or animation as the counterpart of graphics.

A second way of grouping the media types is by complexity of internal structure. The data representations used for certain media types, in particular 'flat' text, images, audio, and video have very little structure – they are basically sequences of characters, pixels or samples. On the other hand, 'structured' text, graphics, animation, and music are richly organized aggregates – hierarchical grouping is used to build up complex values from simpler parts. Note that text occurs in both groups. This reflects how the presence or absence of structure is not inherent in a media type, but rather is determined by the choice of representation. In other words, one can envisage enriching the representation of the unstructured media types with internal relationships and sub-structures. An example of a form of structured video is discussed by Bruckman (1991).

The structured and unstructured media types are related by *synthesis* and *recognition*. These relationships are depicted in Figure 2.14. Synthesis proceeds from structured media types to their unstructured counterparts, and results in a loss of information (but, somewhat paradoxically, often leads to more data). Recognition takes place in the opposite direction and attempts to re-establish structure. To give an example, a graphics representation can be used to synthesize an image – this is the rendering process. The inverse operation, pattern recognition, is the identification of graphics structures, such as edges and regions, within an image. Another observation is that structured types are both highly portable – their presentation is device independent, and scalable – presentation quality improves with increased resources. Both properties derive from decoupling presentation from representation. By altering the synthesis operation, presentation quality can be matched to the characteristics of different output devices. PostScript is a good example since the quality of the presentation (the synthesized bitmap) improves as

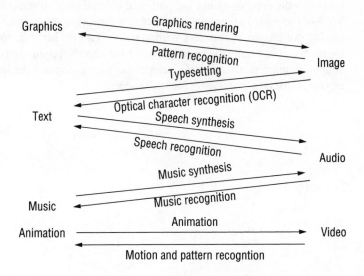

Figure 2.14   Synthesis and recognition relationships between structured media types (left) and unstructured media types (right).

printer resolution improves. Other examples are MIDI, where different synthesizers will have different audio quality, and graphics, where quality depends on the rendering algorithm.

Now consider operations on media types. Here again it is also possible to identify general patterns. Looking over the operations discussed in the previous sections, some major groupings emerge. These are:

Creation: Operations that deal with the acquisition, storage, retrieval, and presentation of media values.

Modification: Operations that alter or replace selected parts of a value. The primary example is editing.

Transformation: Operations that produce a new value by applying some function to existing values; furthermore, the values are of the same media type. Examples include image filtering and resampling, compressing an audio value, changing from one animation format to another, and video special effects.

Conversion: Operations that convert a value from one media type to another. Examples include the forms of recognition and synthesis shown in Figure 2.14.

Timing: Operations that influence the synchronization and presentation rate of a media value. Timebase correction falls into this category, as do operations that scale or invert temporal sequences.

This brings to an end our discussion of media types. No doubt there are many topics which the reader would have preferred to have seen presented in more detail. We have provided numerous references so that those seeking more information can use this chapter at least as a starting point. Our goal here has not been to cover the media types exhaustively. Instead we have introduced some basic terminology and, more importantly, a certain perspective that anticipates the later chapters on an object-oriented framework for multimedia.

3

MULTIMEDIA ENVIRONMENTS

3.1 The CD family

3.2 CD-i

3.3 DVI

3.4 QuickTime

3.5 MPC/MME

3.6 Director

3.7 Standards for multimedia

The previous chapter described the basic building blocks of multimedia – text, graphics, images, audio, video, music, and animation. In this chapter we look at how these elements are combined and manipulated as a whole. As in the previous chapter, we view things from a programmer's perspective; the issues that concern us are data representations and operations.

The examples given in this chapter focus on *multimedia types*. Like data types in general, a multimedia type is a specification – it specifies mechanisms for combining data from various media and operations which apply to these combinations. The most basic operation is presentation, but many other operations, including support for interaction, are associated with multimedia types. Because operations on multimedia data have real-time constraints, multimedia types are often designed for specific operating environments. A *multimedia environment* is the mix of hardware and software used to support a multimedia type – one could say that the environment implements the type since it specifies and realizes the programming interface for the type. A *multimedia application*, in turn, draws on the services of a multimedia environment and provides added functionality to the user, or to other applications. So in principle there is a distinction between multimedia types, their implementation, and their clients – the applications. In practice, though, the lines are unclear; for instance, authoring software can be considered as both part of the implementation of a multimedia type and a client of the type.

In the following sections we describe several widely used multimedia environments and discuss the data representations, operations, and particular hardware platform for each. A quick overview of the examples we have chosen is given in Table 3.1. Other examples of multimedia environments include *NeXTStep* (NeXT Inc., 1992), an object-oriented environment originally developed for NeXT workstations and now available on Intel and other platforms; *MMPM/2*, multimedia extensions for IBM's OS/2; *XMedia* (Digital Equipment Corp., 1991); and multimedia toolkits such as *Muse* (Hodges *et al.*, 1989) and *Andrew* (Borenstein, 1990).

Table 3.1   Multimedia environments and multimedia types.

Multimedia environment	Multimedia type	Media types[a]
CD-i	'Real-time' format	Audio, video, image
DVI	AVSS format	Audio, video, image
QuickTime	QuickTime movie format	Audio, video, image, music (MIDI), text, graphics, SMPTE time code
MPC/MME	RIFF format	Audio, video, image, music (MIDI), text, graphics
Director	Director movie format	Audio, video, image, music (MIDI), text, graphics, animation

a. This column lists media types directly supported by the multimedia type. Other media types may be indirectly supported since most of the multimedia types allow arbitrary data to be present; however, interpretation of this data is then a responsibility of the application rather than the environment.

We begin, however, by giving some background information on CD technology since it plays a prominent role in many multimedia environments.

3.1 THE CD FAMILY

The compact disc is seen by many as a fitting storage medium for multimedia data and a number of standards based on the CD are in use. The low costs of duplicating CDs (as compared to magnetic media), their portability and resilience, and recent demonstrations of digital video playback indicate that the CD is likely to become a routine instrument for multimedia storage and exchange. In this section we give some background information on the CD in order to better understand its

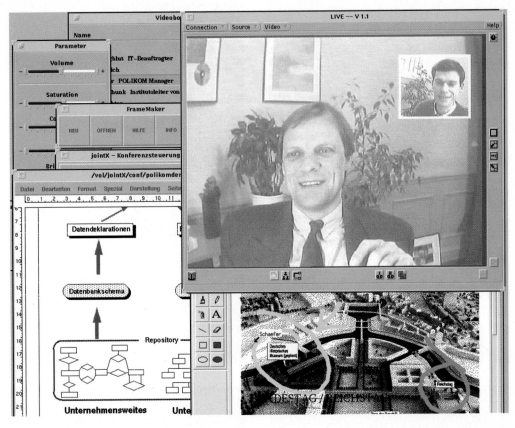

III   DESKTOP CONFERENCING: GMD's Polikom project. The display includes video windows showing conference participants and several shared tools.

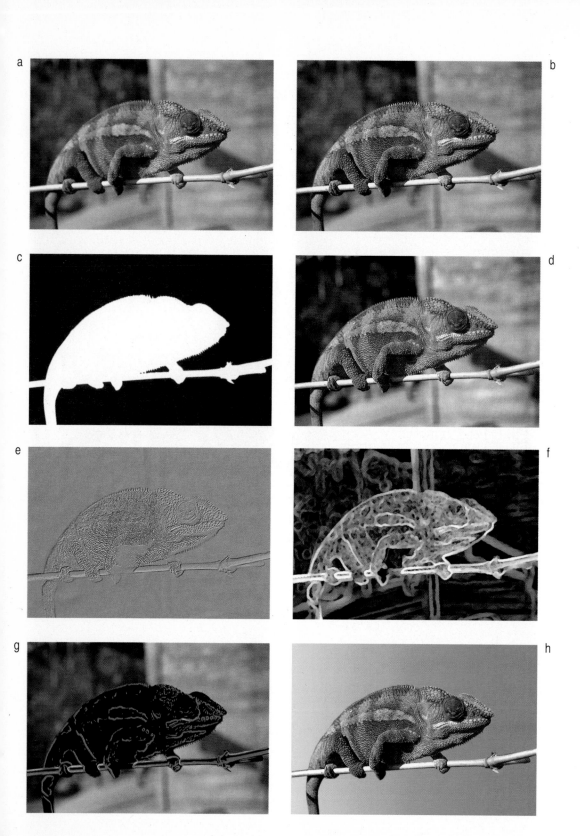

IV IMAGE EDITING: *(opposite)* (a) the original image; (b) after sharpening; (c) a selection mask; (d) the background reduced to grayscale; (e) an 'emboss' filter followed by change of tone; (f) several filters applied to highlight edges; (g) similar to preceding, but filters applied to a selection; (h) a composite. These images were produced using Adobe Photoshop.

V VIDEO EFFECTS AND TRANSITIONS: *(above)* (a) input signal A; (b) input signal B; (c) a dissolve; (d) a wipe; (e) a wrap; (f) luminance keying. These images were produced with the aid of NewTek's Video Toaster.

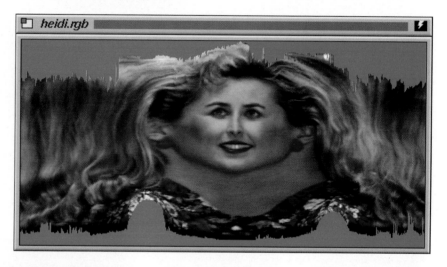

VI SURFACE IMAGES. Two examples of surface images; the first, an image of a woman's head, was created using a 3D scanner from Cyberware Labs. The second, a vase, was created by researchers at the National Research Council of Canada.

capabilities and limitations. A more comprehensive description of CD technology and formats is provided by Pohlmann (1992).

Compact disc formats are specified in a series of documents named from the colors of their covers. Some of these documents are proprietary, while others, such as the CD-DA and CD-ROM specifications, have become international standards. Listed in chronological order, we have:

Red Book (1982) covers physical specifications of the CD and CD-DA

Yellow Book (1985) CD-ROM

Green Book (1988) CD-i

Orange Book (1991) CD-R

White Book (1993) Video CD

CD technology was developed during the late 1970s, primarily by Philips and Sony, and the first audio CD players were commercially introduced in 1982. Since that time the CD has become highly successful as a digital audio storage medium, and, because of its large capacity and low costs, numerous extensions have been proposed for taking the CD beyond the audio domain.

The CD is a close relative of the LV videodisc (see page 40) and is based upon similar optical storage technology. There are two important differences, however. First, although LV stores information as discrete pits on the disc surface, it only provides information in analog form. The CD, on the other hand, is a true digital storage medium. Properly configured, the CD allows storage of arbitrary digital data and can be used in much the same way as a magnetic storage device. Second, recall that LV discs come in both CAV (constant angular velocity) and CLV (constant linear velocity) formats. The CD, however, uses only the CLV format. This allows more data to be stored on discs, but, unfortunately, leads to longer access times since the rotational velocity must be changed as the reading mechanism moves across the disc.

The physical specifications of the CD are laid out in the Red Book, a document compiled by Philips and Sony and the basis of the compatibility between different CDs and different CD players. The standard CD is 12 cm in diameter and consists of three layers: a transparent substrate, a thin metallic layer, and an outer layer of protective acrylic.

The metallic layer contains a long sequence of small pits (about 0.5 micrometers in diameter) strung together to form a spiral winding from near the center of the disc to its outer edge. Pit boundaries are detected by a laser beam within the player and result in a digital sequence, where 1s represent a boundary and 0s represent no boundary. This raw data sequence, called *channel data*, comes off the disc at a rate of about 4.3 million bits per second.

Channel data is not used directly; it contains encoded application data and must first be decoded. The reason for encoding, which takes place during the CD production process, is to ensure greater robustness and longevity of the medium. CD data encoding uses two techniques: Cross-Interleave Reed-Solomon Code (CIRC), an error detection / correction scheme, and eight-to-fourteen modulation (EFM), a procedure for removing successive 1s (and so ensuring that pit

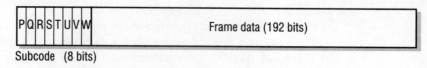

Subcode   (8 bits)

Figure 3.1   A CD frame.

boundaries are not too close). A detailed description of CD encoding is provided by Philips (1982) and Pohlmann (1989; 1992).

During decoding, channel bits are grouped into *frames*, the smallest unit of data independently decoded by a CD player. A frame consists of 588 channel bits, however after decoding this is reduced to 200 bits organized as shown in Figure 3.1.

At the start of a frame are 8 bits of 'subcode'. CD subcode is accumulated over groups of 98 successive frames; this forms eight 98-bit values (called P, Q, R, S, T, U, V, and W) which contain organization and control information. For example, all CDs consist of a lead-in area, a program area containing from 1 to 99 'tracks', and a final lead-out area. The P and Q subcodes delimit these areas and identify track boundaries.

The subcode within a CD frame is followed by 192 bits of data. What this data represents will depend on the use to which the CD is being put. It may contain audio samples, or it may contain data used for images, text, or anything else.

We now look at some specific CD formats. First, though, we summarize some of the characteristics of CDs in general in Table 3.2.

Table 3.2   CD characteristics.

Disc diameter	12 cm
Maximum playing time	74 minutes
Channel data rate	4.32×10^6 bits/s
Maximum channel data capacity[a]	19×10^9 bits
Frame rate	7350 frames/s
Bit error rate	approximately 10^{-10}
Encoded frame size (channel bits per frame)	588 bits
Decoded frame size	200 bits
Frame data size[b]	192 bits (24 bytes)
Frame data rate	1.41×10^6 bits/s
Maximum frame data capacity[a]	6.2×10^9 bits
Maximum number of frames[a]	32.6×10^6
Linear velocity	1.2–1.4 m/s
Rotational velocity	3.5–8 rev/s

a. These quantities refer to a CD with maximum playing time.
b. Decoded frame size minus subcode bits.

3.1.1   CD-DA

Compact Disc - Digital Audio refers to a 'standard' CD, one containing a digital audio recording. Recall that the sampling rate used for CD audio is 44 100 Hz and that each sample is 16 bits. Since two channels are present, CD audio has a data rate of $(44\,100 \times 16 \times 2) = 1\,411\,200$ bits per second. This is exactly the CD frame data rate. In other words, all data bits of a frame are used for audio samples. Since a frame contains 192 data bits, this allows each CD-DA frame to hold twelve audio samples, six for each channel.

The program area on a CD-DA disc holds one or more musical tracks, perhaps separated by pauses. The Q subcode bits provide a track table of contents and timing information. The table of contents identifies the number of tracks on the disc, their location and duration. Timing information indicates such things as the elapsed and remaining playing time for the disc or track, and the track number.

3.1.2   CD+G, CD+MIDI

CD-DA uses the P and Q subcode bits; but R–W, or 6 of the 8 subcode bits, are left unused. This amounts to over 20 MB of available space on one CD. *Compact Disc plus Graphics* and *Compact Disc plus MIDI* are two early CD formats that store text (such as song titles) and either simple graphics or MIDI data in the unused subcode. Playback of the audio portion of these discs is possible on any CD-DA player since the additional data will simply be ignored. However, modified players are needed to extract the graphics or MIDI information. The use of CD+G and CD+MIDI is not very common and both have been surpassed by more recent developments.

3.1.3   CD-ROM

The *Compact Disc - Read Only Memory* is a storage medium for arbitrary digital data. The main difference between the CD-ROM and the CD-DA formats is an additional layer of error detection and correction. While an undetected error in audio data poses no serious risk, this is not the case for arbitrary data (one certainly would not want bit errors appearing in program executables placed on a CD).

The CD-ROM format is defined by the Yellow Book, a successor to the earlier Red Book of CD-DA. A CD-ROM disc is divided into consecutive sectors, each formed from a group of 98 frames. A sector contains a single data block. Since the frame data size is 24 bytes, 98 frames gives 2352 bytes per CD-ROM block. The block is the unit of random access: knowing a block address, a CD-ROM reader can locate the appropriate sector and read the block from the disc. Block addresses are similar to video time code: they indicate the playing time from the start of the disc to the block.

CD-ROM blocks come in two formats, called Mode 1 and Mode 2 (see Figure 3.2). Each block begins with a synchronization field followed by a three-byte address field and a field identifying the mode of the block. The use of the remaining bytes depends on a block's mode. Mode 2 blocks leave all this data for application use. Mode 1 blocks reserve 288 bytes for error detection and correction, leaving 2048 bytes for application use. Mode 1 is intended for text and numeric

Mode 1

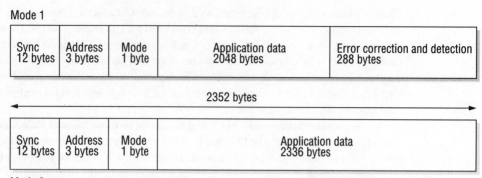

Figure 3.2   CD-ROM block formats.

data. Mode 2 is more appropriate for audio and image data, but since Mode 1 blocks can be used for this purpose, many early CD-ROM drives only supported Mode 1. However, Mode 2 is the basis of more recent CD formats (CD-i, CD-ROM XA, Photo CD, Video CD) and so is supported by newer CD-ROM drives.

CD-ROM characteristics, such as numbers of blocks per disc, block sizes, and data rates are summarized in Table 3.3. An important development, affecting the data rates listed in this table, are *multi-speed* CD-ROM drives. These drives are capable of spinning the disc at two or more times the speed of earlier drives; data transfer rates are correspondingly higher, and access times slightly lower.

Table 3.3   CD-ROM characteristics.

Block rate	75 blocks/s
Frames per block	98
Block data size	2352 bytes
Application data per block	2048 bytes (Mode 1) 2336 bytes (Mode 2)
Application data rate[a]	150 kB/s (Mode 1) 171 kB/s (Mode 2)
Maximum number of blocks[b]	283,500 (63 min) 330,000 (74 min)
Maximum application data capacity	550 MB (Mode 1, 63 min) 630 MB (Mode 2, 63 min) 645 MB (Mode 1, 74 min) 735 MB (Mode 2, 74 min)
Bit error rate (Mode 1)	10^{-15}
Average access time	approx. 500 ms[c]

a. Some newer CD-ROM players revolve at two or more times the speed of earlier players and can sustain data transfer at multiples of the rates listed here.

b. Two standard durations are used: 63 minutes and 74 minutes.

c. Includes seek time, sensing, and rotational delay; values will vary from player to player.

The CD-ROM format specifies the physical format of data on a CD, but it does not specify logical format, that is, how data is organized into files. This problem is addressed by ISO standard 9660 (ISO, 1988). The standard evolved from an earlier CD-ROM file organization proposed by the *High Sierra Group,* a group of representatives from CD-ROM producers and other interested parties. ISO 9660 defines how a CD-ROM can be organized into a hierarchical file system which can then be mounted by a computer operating system. Because CD-ROMs have much slower access times than magnetic hard disks, it is not practical to search for files by first reading directory entries from the disc. In order to allow the operating system to quickly find files on a CD-ROM, ISO 9660 specifies an index structure called a path table. The path table performs a file path name to file address mapping and is meant to be loaded into main memory in order to improve file access times.

3.1.4   CD-i

The CD-ROM format and ISO 9660 determine how a hierarchical file system can be laid out on a CD. However, the content of the files is unspecified – there is no indication, for example, whether a particular file contains image or audio data. *Compact Disc-Interactive* provides a complete specification for the storage of multimedia data on a CD-ROM. In addition, CD-i specifies the player hardware and software needed to extract, present, and interact with the data. In other words, CD-i is a complete delivery platform for multimedia applications. The data representation employed by CD-i is an example of what we call a multimedia type and is discussed further in Section 3.2.

3.1.5   CD-ROM XA

CD-ROM Extended Architecture, developed by Philips, Sony and Microsoft, can be considered an 'open' form of CD-i. Whereas CD-i players are essentially self-contained systems, CD-ROM XA players can be used as computer peripherals and so are platform-independent. CD-ROM XA introduces Form 1 and Form 2 blocks, a refinement of CD-ROM Mode 2, used by many of the other CD formats. Like CD-i, CD-ROM XA specifies how compressed audio data (ADPCM), text, and imagery can be interleaved on a CD-ROM. Since the XA format is similar to CD-i, which will be examined in detail, we will not discuss CD-ROM XA further.

3.1.6   CD-V

Compact Disc-Video is a hybrid analog video / digital audio format. Three disc sizes are used: 12 inch, allowing 60 minutes of video per side, 8 inch, allowing 20 minutes, and the standard 12 cm (4 3/4 inch) CD, called a CD-V single, allowing about 6 minutes of video. (The 12 inch and 8 inch discs are usually referred to as *Laser Discs* or LD.) In each case the video is accompanied by a digital audio (and possibly analog audio) sound track. The CD-V single disc is divided into two regions, one containing the 6 minutes of audio/video material, the other an additional 20 minutes of digital audio. The second region can be played on a standard CD-DA player. The CD-V video format is based on that used by LV, and CD-V players can play back LV discs. Like LV, CD-V must be recorded in either NTSC or PAL video format and may use either CAV or CLV scanning. Taking into account video format, scanning format, and disc size there are twelve possible CD-V configurations. Fortunately, 'omni-players' exist which will play many of these configurations, in addition to audio CD and LV discs.

3.1.7   PHOTO CD

Photo CD technology, developed by Eastman Kodak and Philips, offers an alternative to prints or slides by recording digitized photographs on a CD. There are four formats for Photo CD discs:

- Photo CD Master: Intended for 35 mm consumer photography, stores up to 100 images per disc.

- Pro Photo CD Master: Intended for professional photographers using 35 mm or larger film sizes (70 mm, 120 mm, 4" × 5"), stores from 6 to 100 images per disc.

- Photo CD Portfolio: Combines audio, text, and graphics with low-resolution images, up to 800 images per disc.

- Photo CD Catalog: Intended for storage of large numbers of low-resolution images (up to 6,000 per disc).

Photo CD Master discs are prepared by scanning 35 mm film at about 2000 samples per inch – samples contain 12 bits for each of red, green, and blue. This produces a very high resolution ($3072 \times 2048 \times 36$ bit) RGB raster image; however, this is not the form stored on disc. First, the raw RGB values are converted to the PhotoYCC color model (this model is similar to YUV in that colors are represented by one luma and two chroma components). Each PhotoYCC component is allotted 8 bits, so 24 bits per pixel are required. During conversion to PhotoYCC, the film type, determined by a bar code reader, can be used to help better approximate original colors. Finally, each image is stored on the disc in five resolutions (see Table 3.4), ranging from a low-quality preview resolution up to the full film-quality resolution. Because of their large size, the two higher-resolution versions of the image are stored in compressed form. The intermediate 'Base' version, with a resolution of 768×512 pixels, is intended for viewing on television monitors (however, since the 4:3 aspect ratio of television monitors differs from that of 35 mm film, part of the image is clipped when viewed). Typically the images are written on a write-once CD by the photo-developer; Photo CD thus relies on recordable CD technology. During a recording session, the entire disc may be filled or images may be appended to a disc already partially full. Discs recorded in more than one session are called *multisession* discs.

Photo CD images can be viewed on a television set by using either CD-i players or special Photo CD players, both of which connect directly to television sets. The advantage of Photo CD players is that they provide additional viewing capabilities, such as hardware pan and zoom. Since Photo CD conforms to the CD-ROM XA format it is possible to place audio, text and graphics on a Photo CD disc. It is also possible to read the images from a Photo CD disc using either a

Table 3.4   Photo CD image types.[a]

Name	'Quality'	Resolution	Aspect ratio	Bits per pixel	Image size
Base/16	Preview	192×128	3:2	24	72 kB
Base/4	Low video	384×256	3:2	24	288 kB
Base	High video	768×512	3:2	24	1.1 MB
4Base	HDTV	1536×1024	3:2	24/4[b]	0.5–1 MB[c]
16Base	Film	3072×2048	3:2	24/4[b]	2–4 MB[c]

a. Entries refer to the consumer Photo CD Master format used with 35 mm film; the professional format is available for 70 mm, 120 mm and other high-resolution film.
b. Bits per pixel for an uncompressed image and approximate value for a compressed image.
c. Approximate size of compressed image.

CD-ROM or CD-ROM XA drive; the images can then be displayed on a computer screen or manipulated by software. However, older CD-ROM players can only read the first session on multisession discs. This has been corrected with newer players.

3.1.8   CD-R, CD-WO

Compact Disc-Recordable and *Compact Disc-Write Once* are examples of CD WORM (write-once, read many) technologies. CD-WO and CD-R can be used for archiving and for producing CDs in small quantities, but for mass production the traditional duplicating process is more efficient and less costly. Although the physical construction of writable discs differs from read-only discs, playback on standard players is possible. For example, existing CD-R systems can record discs in a variety of formats including CD-DA, CD-ROM, CD-ROM XA, CD-i and Photo CD. Any player compatible with the format selected during recording can be used for playback. (As mentioned in the discussion of Photo CD, some drives, particularly older models, are only capable of reading the first session of a multisession disc.)

3.1.9   VIDEO CD

Video CDs contain up to 74 minutes of MPEG-1 video and accompanying audio. This new format is specified by a document called the White Book and is based on the Karaoke CD standard developed by Philips and JVC. Playback is possible on dedicated Video CD players, CD-i players (using an MPEG decoder extension for CD-i players), CD-ROM XA players (using an MPEG decoder on the host), and adapted CD-DA players equipped with digital outputs (using an MPEG decoder that connects directly to the digital outputs). The format of the analog video signal produced by a Video CD player is determined by the player, not the disc, so any Video CD can be viewed on NTSC, PAL, and SECAM displays.

3.1.10   FUTURE OPTICAL STORAGE TECHNOLOGIES

Optical storage is following several trends. First, there is the inclusion of more and more media types. There has been a progression from audio, to images, to video (see Table 3.5). Second, there is the development of writable and erasable CDs. Here existing magneto-optical technology may become more widely used. Third, like magnetic storage, optical technology is progressing towards smaller dimensions and higher densities. For example, Sony has recently announced its recordable MD or *Mini Disc* system. MD disc diameter is half that of the CD, but the audio playback duration is still 74 minutes (MD compresses audio data; the actual data capacity is about 140 MB at the same density as CD). In addition, as storage density increases, CLV may be abandoned for the lower capacity but more flexible CAV format. CAV drives offer not only improved access times and transfer rates, but also multiple playback speeds and durations.

Table 3.5   Summary of capabilities of CD formats.[a]

Capability	CD-DA Red Book	CD-ROM Yellow Book	CD-i Green Book	CD-ROM XA	CD-R Orange Book	Photo CD	Video CD White Book
Audio (PCM)	✓	✓	✓	✓	(✓)		
Application data		✓	✓	✓	(✓)		
Audio (ADPCM)			✓	✓	(✓)		
Image (RGB)			✓	✓	(✓)		
Image (PhotoYCC)					(✓)	✓	
Video (MPEG-1)			(✓)		(✓)		✓
ISO 9660		(✓)		(✓)	(✓)	✓	
Multisession		(✓)		(✓)	✓	✓	
Players supporting this format	CD-DA CD-ROM CD-i CD-ROM XA Photo CD Video CD	CD-ROM CD-ROM XA	CD-i	CD-ROM XA CD-ROM[b] CD-i[c]	Depends on format recorded	CD-ROM XA CD-i Photo CD	CD-DA[d] CD-ROM XA[e] CD-i[f] Video CD

a. The checked entries in parentheses indicate a possible capability. For example, CD-ROM discs can be in ISO 9660 file format, but other file formats are also possible. CD-R has many entries in parentheses since a CD-R drive can write arbitrary data but it may not be capable of playing or interpreting the data.
b. The CD-ROM XA extensions are now part of the CD-ROM specification (the Yellow Book) so new CD-ROM players should support the additional CD-ROM XA capabilities.
c. To play a CD-ROM XA disc (or any of the formats based on CD-ROM XA, in particular Photo CD and Video CD) on a CD-i player requires a CD-i application file be stored on the disc. This is called a CD-ROM XA bridge disc.
d. Requires an adapted CD-DA player equipped with digital output and a separate MPEG decoder.
e. Requires an MPEG decoder on the host machine.
f. Requires an MPEG decoder extension on the CD-i player.

3.2 CD-i[1]

3.2.1   CD-i OVERVIEW

Compact Disc-Interactive is specified by the Green Book, a document which, like the earlier Red Book and Yellow Book, was prepared by Philips and Sony. A detailed description of CD-i is also provided by Preston (1987). CD-i is a complete system, designed so that the data and software used by an interactive multimedia application can be combined on a CD and then played by any CD-i player. The Green Book specification encompasses the physical and logical organization of multimedia information on a CD, hardware interfaces for CD-i players, and software interfaces for CD-i programs. CD-i requires a video monitor and audio equipment for presentation; however, CD-i players connect to existing consumer electronic products (NTSC or PAL television receivers, stereo equipment) and so are targeted to the home and educational markets.

3.2.2   CD-i MEDIA TYPES

The Green Book specifies a CD-i 'base case decoder' which has hardware support for a variety of audio and image media types. The CD-i media types are summarized below.

Audio □ Four digital audio formats are supported by the CD-i decoder. They are ordered in terms of audio quality and have been designed so that changing from one quality level to the next alters the data rate by a factor of two. The four CD-i audio types are:

- CD-DA: Certain portions of a CD-i disc can be dedicated to high-quality digital audio stored in the same format as used on a CD-DA disc.

- Level A: Corresponds to very good 'hi-fi'-quality audio.

- Level B: Similar to the quality of FM radio.

- Level C: About the same quality as AM radio; can be used for music, but is more appropriate for voice material.

The four audio types are compared in Table 3.6. Generally, when selecting a particular audio format, the CD-i author must balance quality against data rate.

Image □ A CD-i image is characterized by its type, size, and resolution. Several types are available; these are listed below. The image size is simply the width and height of the image measured in pixels, while the resolution is one of 'normal', 'double', or 'high'. The size of the largest possible image, that occupying a full screen, depends on whether the player generates an NTSC or PAL video signal, and which of the three resolutions is used. Full-screen image sizes are listed in Table 3.7. CD-i authors preparing discs for international use are advised to keep

---

[1.] Formerly CD-I, but renamed by Philips to avoid confusion with CD-"one".

Table 3.6   CD-i audio types.

	CD-DA	Level A	Level B	Level C
Sampling rate (kHz)	44.1	37.8	37.8	18.9
Bits per sample[a]	16	16/8	16/4	16/4
Encoding	PCM	ADPCM	ADPCM	ADPCM
Number of channels[b]	2	4	8	16
Encoded data rate per channel (KB/s)[c]	86	42.5	21.3	10.6
Capacity[d]	74 min	4hr 20 min	8 hr 40 min	17 hr 20 min

a. For the ADPCM formats, the first number refers to the decoded sample size, the second to the encoded size.
b. This row gives the maximum number of mono channels that can be placed on a disc; half this number of stereo channels are available.
c. For the ADPCM formats, the encoded data stream contains parameters needed by the decoder in addition to sample data.
d. Approximate maximum play time for a single channel from a 650 MB disc (except for the CD-DA column where the play time of the single stereo channel is given).

important information within a 'safety region'. This region is visible on both NTSC and PAL monitors (slight distortion will occur owing to the different pixel aspect ratio of images as they appear on NTSC and PAL monitors).

Table 3.7   CD-i full screen image sizes (width × height in pixels).

	Normal	Double	High
NTSC	360 × 240	720 × 240	720 × 480
PAL	384 × 280	768 × 280	768 × 560

The image types supported by CD-i include:

- RGB 5:5:5: Uses the RGB color model with 5 bits per color. RGB 5:5:5 is intended for complex images containing a large range of colors. Because encoding and decoding can be done quickly, this format is useful when images are modified by the user.

- DYUV: Based on the YUV color model. A differential coding scheme is used, so pixels are represented by differences from their neighbors. In addition, UV ('chroma') values are supplied for alternating pixels, while every pixel has a Y (luminance) value. In this respect DYUV resembles some of the digital video formats (such as CCIR 4:2:2, see page 47). DYUV is intended for continuous-tone images; it is appropriate for scanned photographs or digitized video frames.

- CLUT: Pixels are represented by an index in a color lookup table (CLUT). Three table sizes are possible: 256, 128 or 16 entries. The corresponding formats are called CLUT-8, CLUT-7 and CLUT-4. These formats are appropriate for computer-generated images with limited numbers of colors.

- RL: Based on run-length coding. A color lookup table is again used, either of 128 or 8 entries. The corresponding formats are called RL-7 and RL-3.

Table 3.8   CD-i image types.

	Bits per pixel	**Bytes per pixel**	**Bytes per image**[a]	**Images per disc**[b]
RGB 5:5:5	15	2[c]	172,800	3944
DYUV	8	1	86,400	7888
CLUT-8	8	1	86,400	7888
CLUT-7	7	1[d]	86,400	7888
CLUT-4	4	1/2	43,200	15776
RL-7[e]	7	1	varies	varies
RL-3[e]	3	1/2	varies	varies

a. A full screen, normal resolution, NTSC image (360 x 240 pixels).
b. Using 650 MB per disc.
c. The 16th bit is used for transparency.
d. One bit is unused.
e. Following entries give bits and bytes for a single pixel run.

The RL formats are intended for graphical material containing large areas of fixed color.

The above image types are compared in Table 3.8.

Video □ A recent extension to CD-i, MPEG-1 encoded video, allows full-screen, full-motion video playback (van de Meer, 1992). Existing players are up-graded by attaching an 'FMV cartridge' containing the MPEG decoder and additional memory. Without the extension, full-screen full-motion video is not possible. However, it is possible to produce a video-like effect by working with sequences of images and keeping the image size small, or restricting motion to parts of the image, or using low frame rates. (Somewhat confusingly, image sequences used in this manner are often referred to as video in early CD-i documentation.)

Text and graphics □ CD-i developers can place graphics and text data on a disc; however, the interpretation of this data is the responsibility of the application. To aid applications in handling text and graphics, the CD-i software development environment contains a set of commands allowing the display of text in various fonts and the drawing of simple 2D geometric objects.

3.2.3   CD-i MEDIA ORGANIZATION

The organization of a CD-i disc can be viewed at three levels: sectors, files and tracks. At the lowest level, CD-i, like CD-ROM, partitions the disc into consecutive sectors. Each CD-i sector contains a single CD-ROM Mode 2 block with the Mode 2 data area divided into an 8-byte sub-header and a region for CD-i data. A portion of the CD-i data region can be used for additional error detection and correction, similar to that of CD-ROM Mode 1, or the entire data region may be available for CD-i program use. These variations, shown in Figure 3.3, are called Form 1 and Form 2 respectively (and also appear in CD-ROM XA).

CD-i sectors are further categorized on the basis of the type of data they contain. There are three possibilities:

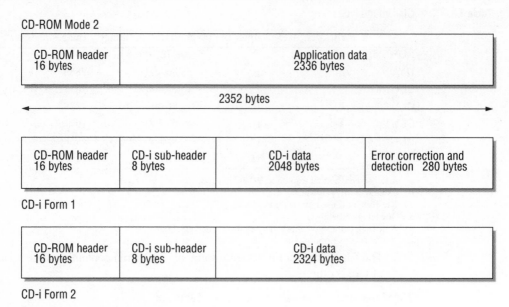

Figure 3.3   CD-i block formats.

Audio sectors: These hold a Form 2 block containing Level A, B, or C audio.

Video sectors: These hold a Form 2 block containing image data (or MPEG data).

Data sectors: These hold a Form 1 block containing arbitrary program-related data. For example, text and graphics data would be stored in sectors of this form.

Audio and video sectors are called *real-time sectors*, since these parts of the disc are meant to be 'played', as opposed to being read, by a CD-i application. When a sequence of sectors is played the sectors are retrieved from the disc continually at a specific data rate; one can think of a stream of data flowing from the disc. The application must ensure that the stream is processed at the same rate it is produced. For audio sectors this basically involves directing the stream to appropriate decoding and digital-to-analog conversion hardware. For video sectors it involves loading image data into a memory buffer (or MPEG data into the MPEG decoder).

In addition to a data region, each CD-i block contains a sub-header. The sub-header gives information about the contents of the block; it indicates whether the block is Form 1 or Form 2, whether the block contains audio, image, video, or program-related data, what encoding method is used, and whether the block is a 'trigger' (used for synchronization, see below).

At the highest level of organization, that of tracks, a CD-i disc is comprised of one or more CD-i tracks (regions of the disc containing Form 1 and Form 2 data sectors). These are then followed by CD-DA tracks, if any are present on the disc. The contents of a CD-i track can be thought of as a complete application, that is, the application's code and any data needed by the application. (It is certainly possible to lay out a CD-i disc so that a single application spans more than one track, but there is little need to do so since CD tracks, unlike those on magnetic disks, are of variable length.) There is some compatibility between CD-i and CD-DA. In particular, the CD-DA tracks on a CD-i disc can be played by a conventional CD-DA player. Similarly, a CD-i player can play CD-DA discs.

At the two extremes – sectors and tracks – the CD-i organization is fairly simple. The complexity and versatility of CD-i become apparent at the intermediate level, that of files. CD-i files, like those on a CD-ROM disc, are groups of sectors. CD-i also follows the approach of the ISO 9660 standard and specifies both a hierarchical file system and a path table located at a well-defined position on the disc. Where CD-i goes beyond CD-ROM and ISO 9660 is in the internal structure of files. We have already seen that blocks are tagged (by the CD-i sub-header) according to their content. In addition, CD-i files have two sub-structures: *records* and *channels*.

A record is a logical component of a file, and may contain interleaved audio, video, and data sectors. If audio or video sectors are present, the record is called a *real-time record*. The first sector of a real-time record, known as the *real-time control area*, contains a group of instructions which are activated as the record is played. These instructions determine how the record is processed and help synchronize audio and video during playback.

Within a real-time record, a channel is a sequence of sectors storing the same type of data and meant to be played one after the other. (Thus channels are always sequences of real-time sectors.) Each channel has a data rate which can be expressed as a fraction of the disc data bandwidth; sectors within the channel are spaced at regular intervals governed by this fraction.

As an example of a real-time record, consider an application which displays a series of images with audio accompaniment. The audio consists of an 'ambience' track, encoded as a Level B stereo value (thus requiring 1/4 the CD-i bandwidth), plus English and French narration, each using Level C mono (and so each requiring 1/16th the CD-i data bandwidth). The image material is allocated a further 1/2 of the CD-i data bandwidth. A possible organization of this data into a single CD-i real-time record is shown in Figure 3.4. Here four channels are used, the first three for the background audio and narration, the fourth for the image sequence. During playback, one of the narration channels can be masked out. As can be seen, not all of the CD-i bandwidth is used. The remaining portions can be allocated to other records, other files, or additional channels in the example record.

3.2.4   CD-i ARCHITECTURE

The main components of a CD-i player are shown in Figure 3.5. The architecture can be visualized in terms of streams of data (heavy arrows in the figure), originating from the disc, perhaps being stored in memory, and then terminating at the two primary output devices – a video monitor and speakers. A variety of input devices allow interactive control over the data streams. A description of player components follows.

CD player: This component contains the disc drive and the optical scanning mechanism. It supports basic functions such as starting, stopping, and

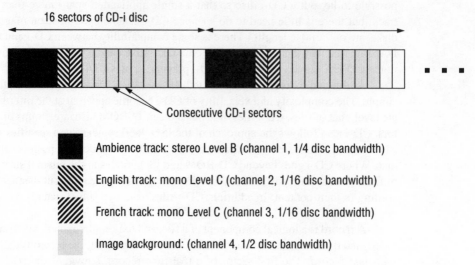

16 sectors of CD-i disc

Consecutive CD-i sectors

Ambience track: stereo Level B (channel 1, 1/4 disc bandwidth)

English track: mono Level C (channel 2, 1/16 disc bandwidth)

French track: mono Level C (channel 3, 1/16 disc bandwidth)

Image background: (channel 4, 1/2 disc bandwidth)

Figure 3.4   A CD-i real-time record. The record consists of four interleaved channels. The pattern shown repeats over intervals of 16 sectors.

pausing the drive and controlling physical positioning of the scanning mechanism.

CD-DA decoder: This component decodes the raw data stream coming from the player and produces either a CD-DA stream (PCM samples) or a CD-i stream (CD-i blocks).

Audio processing unit: The audio processing unit receives PCM samples and converts these to a pair of analog signals. In addition this component can produce limited audio effects such as mixing and gain control.

The above components are similar to those found on any CD-DA player. The remainder are specific to CD-i.

CD-i controller: The CD-i controller de-interleaves incoming data blocks by examining the CD-i sub-header; this results in streams of ADPCM samples, image data, and arbitrary application data which are then passed to other components. The controller also implements channel masking: applications can select particular channels within a real-time record, and only blocks belonging to these channels will be passed by the CD-i controller.

ADPCM decoder: The ADPCM decoder produces PCM samples from Level A, B and C audio. The PCM samples are passed to the audio processing unit for digital-to-analog conversion.

Main processor: At the heart of a CD-i player is a microprocessor used to control disc activity and interpret user input. The processor runs CD-RTOS, the *Compact Disc-Real-Time Operating System*, a multitasking operating system with extensions for playing CD-i real-time records. (CD-RTOS is

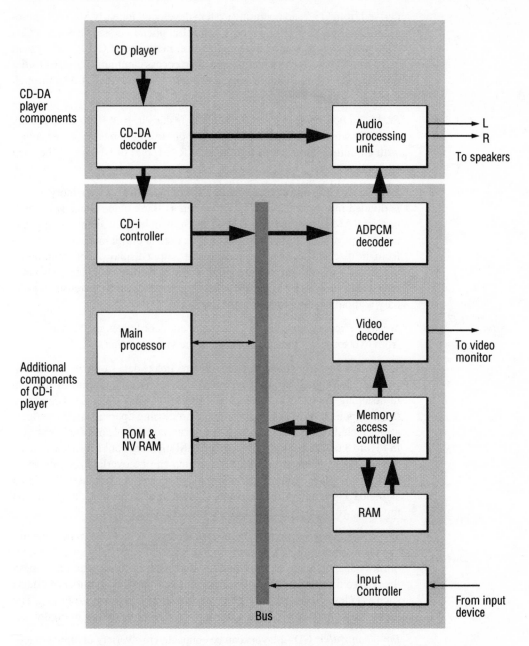

Figure 3.5   CD-i player: components and data/control paths. High data rate streams are indicated by heavy arrows.

derived from OS-9, an operating system developed for early Motorola processors and now used for process control applications and in some PCs.) CD-i applications, loaded in from the disc, make use of CD-RTOS system calls for process synchronization and interprocess communication, CD-i file operations, reading input devices, and controlling the flow of data through the CD-i system.

ROM and *non-volatile RAM:* CD-RTOS resides in ROM and so is readily available when a CD-i player is powered on. In addition each player comes with a minimum of 8 kB of non-volatile RAM, part of which may be used by applications.

RAM: Each CD-i player comes with 1 MB of random access memory, which is divided into two 512 kB regions known as Bank 0 and Bank 1. A small part of RAM is used by CD-RTOS; the remainder is available to applications. Typically the bulk of this memory is used to buffer image data coming from the disc and destined to appear on the output display. Another common use is for applications to store small audio and image segments ('soundmaps' and 'drawmaps') in RAM. These segments can then be reused repeatedly without needing to access the disc.

Memory access controller: This component coordinates memory accesses from two sources – the system bus and the video decoder.

Video decoder: The video decoder converts image data stored in RAM to an analog video signal suitable for display on a television monitor. In addition to decoding the CD-i image formats, RGB 5:5:5, DYUV, CLUT, and RL, this component provides various image processing operations. These operations include the ability to compose images, an example of which is shown in Figure 3.6. The contents of the two RAM memory banks form two image planes, called Plane A and Plane B, which can be overlaid on a constant background plane (some CD-i players also accept an external video signal as the background). A fourth plane, containing the cursor, then appears on top of the combined background and image planes.

The video decoder supports a number of techniques that govern how the image planes are combined. These techniques include the use of color keys, arbitrarily shaped matte regions, and the transparency information present in the RGB 5:5:5 format. The video decoder also supports a number of effects such as fades and dissolves, wipes, cuts, scrolling, and limited zooming. The hardware components used to achieve these effects are shown in Figure 3.7.

Input controller: CD-i players can be connected to a variety of input devices used for pointing and selection. Possibilities include a mouse or joystick, infrared keypad, lightpen, or track ball. Some CD-i players also provide a keyboard interface.

As mentioned above, the CD-i architecture can be visualized in terms of streams. These streams contain either CD-DA or CD-i data and are processed in real time (at the same rate as they are produced) by the components in the player. For

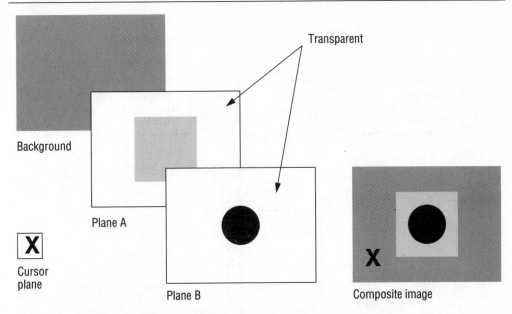

Transparent

Background

Plane A

Cursor
plane

Plane B

Composite image

Figure 3.6   Example of CD-i image composition.

CD-DA streams there is only one path available: from the disc to the CD-DA de-coder, and then leaving the system via the audio processing unit. CD-i streams, which contain audio, image, or application data, offer more possibilities. For in-stance, an ADPCM stream may be produced by the CD-i controller, which de-in-terleaves CD-i data coming from the disc; it may then go either to the ADPCM decoder or to a location in memory. ADPCM streams also originate from memory, the soundmaps referred to earlier, in which case the path would be from memory to the ADPCM decoder. Given the stream-like nature of CD-i, the responsibility of the application is largely that of directing the flows of data. Typically these ap-plications are event-driven, where events are generated by the streams themselves (as when a real-time record ends) or by user input.

3.2.5   CD-i OPERATIONS

Programmers control the capabilities of the CD-i hardware, and manipulate the many media types, by drawing from a large repertoire of operations intended for CD-i application developers. These operations are provided by libraries, which in turn make use of the CD-RTOS kernel. In addition there is an interpreter for the real-time control areas found in some CD-i records. The overall structure of the CD-i software environment is shown in Figure 3.8.

Rather than look at CD-i operations on single media, the details of which can be found in specification documents, we will consider more general *multi-media operations* – operations that apply to several media types, or that rely on a multimedia environment. First we present a classification of multimedia opera-tions similar to that of Chapter 2 where operations on media types were divided into a number of groups such as editing, compression, and conversion. The

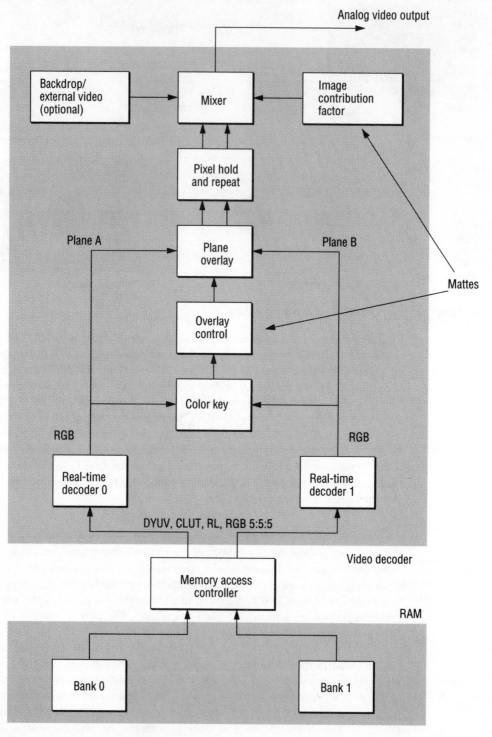

Figure 3.7   CD-i image processing hardware.

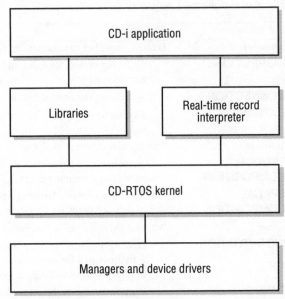

Figure 3.8   CD-i software environment.

classification of multimedia operations is based on three main categories: *config-uration, composition,* and *activation.*

Descriptions and examples of the three categories are listed in Table 3.9. A few words of explanation are in order. First, the purpose of the classification is to help identify operations that emerge as media are combined and that are difficult to reduce to operations on single media. These 'non-reducible' operations offer a higher-level and more abstract view of multimedia environments than descriptions in terms of operations on specific media. Second, the scheme does not encompass all multimedia operations; for instance, there is no mention of user interaction or multimedia authoring. Instead the scheme identifies basic, or elementary, operations. For example, user interaction, whether specified via scripting languages, event models, or some other means, relies on synchronization and other activation operations. Finally, the categories are very general so there is considerable latitude in how they are realized in any particular environment. Since operations are described in general terms the classification scheme also serves as a tool for comparing different environments.

Looking over the classification scheme several views of a multimedia environment are evident. First, there is a component-oriented view that considers the environment as a collection of interconnectable devices and other elements. The *configuration* category comes from this rather static view, it is concerned with basic housekeeping of components. Second, a data-oriented view emphasizes how multimedia data is organized and structured. The *composition* category derives from this view – composition operations are used to combine data from different media. Yet another view is activity-oriented; it focuses on the dynamics of the environment by identifying the activities that take place. The *activation* category, based on this view, is concerned with the management of groups of activities.

Table 3.9   Classification of multimedia operations.

Type of operation	Examples
Configuration	Overall control of the multimedia environment
INSPECTION	Querying system for types and capabilities of components
CONNECTION	Specifying the flow of data among components
EXTENSION	Adding new components, adding new media types, support for scalable media
Composition	Specify how different media are to be combined
TEMPORAL COMPOSITION	Associating an audio track with a video track, specifying dynamic effects and transitions
SPATIAL COMPOSITION	Specifying the overlay of two images or the placement of text and graphics, specifying static effects
Activation	Activate the multimedia environment
INSTANTIATION	creating and terminating groups of cooperating activities (used for presentation, capture, the execution of effects and transitions), allocating resources
TIMING	Ensuring that time-based media flow at the proper rates, responding to events generated by activities, scheduling and synchronizing activities
TUNING	Controlling dynamic characteristics of activities (such as output volume, screen position, visual quality, audio fidelity)

CD-i configuration operations □ The INSPECTION operation is supported in CD-i by a data structure called a *configuration status descriptor* which is available to applications and describes the devices in the system. Since CD-i is meant to be a standard platform with little variation in the capabilities of different players, the ability to inspect the system and determine what components are present is not of great importance; however, it is still needed if applications are to take advantage of MPEG decoders and other optional equipment. A limited form of EXTENSION exists since arbitrary data can be placed in CD-i data sectors, but interpretation of data sectors is the responsibility of the application. Where CD-i is flexible is in the CONNECTION of components. Here there are two relevant mechanisms:

> *Channel masks:* The application can construct a channel mask. The mask is loaded into the CD-i controller which then only passes data from the un-masked channels to the rest of the system.

> *Source/destination selection:* The application can explicitly select the sources and destination of data flows. For example, the application can play ADPCM data from the disc or from a soundmap in memory. Similarly the application can route ADPCM data to the audio processing unit or to a memory buffer.

CD-i composition operations □ CD-i is a programmable system and so it is possible for applications to construct their own mechanisms for combining and presenting data from different media. For instance, an application could read text and graphics from a CD-i data sector and then display this data as a document. Here the composition of the text and graphics is the responsibility of the application, not the environment. CD-i does, however, provide some underlying support for media composition. There are two primary mechanisms:

> *Data interleaving:* CD-i supports TEMPORAL COMPOSITION through the interleaving of image and audio data on the disc. The placement of data within a real-time record is designed so that the channels can be played simultaneously.

> *Display control program:* In CD-i, SPATIAL COMPOSITION is performed by a 'display control program' which the application loads into the video decoder. However, the specification of spatial composition is not part of the CD-i image format; display control programs are placed in ordinary data sectors and so require application intervention.

CD-i activation operations □ Activation operations are divided into three main groups – those dealing with the INSTANTIATION of activities, those dealing with activity TUNING, and those dealing with activity TIMING. The 'play' command is a good example of an activity instantiation operation in CD-i; it creates a data stream that issues from a real-time record and follows a path through the system as specified by configuration operations. Other activity instantiation operations include invoking special effects such as fades, scrolls, cuts, wipes, dissolves, and zooms. Examples of activity TUNING in CD-i include setting audio attenuation, controlling audio mixing, selecting the screen resolution, and manipulating the color lookup table.

CD-i has extensive support for activity TIMING. The simplest mechanism, greatly reducing application involvement in synchronizing CD-i presentation activities, is data interleaving. For example, two audio channels played simultaneously from the disc will not drift or 'jitter' if interleaved in a real-time record. In this example data would flow directly from the disc, through the ADPCM decoder, and out to the audio processing unit. In other cases, where sources other than the disc are used, or data is buffered in memory, some application control is needed to ensure, for example, that a particular sound is heard just as an image is presented on the display. In such cases, CD-i applications can make use of the synchronization mechanisms provided by CD-RTOS – these include a signal facility, shared memory, and interprocess communication. Since CD-i applications involve a number of asynchronous components, the disc, the input devices, the decoders, and the application itself, the signal facility is heavily used and a number of special signals are generated as aids in synchronization:

> *Triggers:* By setting a bit in the CD-i sub-header, sectors within a real-time record can be marked as triggers. During playback, a signal is generated when such sectors are encountered. For example, an application needing to know when a particular audio event occurs could use a trigger attached to the audio sector containing the event in question.

> *Display signals:* The display control programs loaded in the CD-i video decoder contain two instruction lists: the *field control table* (FCT) and *line*

control table (LCT). The first is executed when a new field is about to be displayed (that is, 60 times per second for NTSC systems), the second when a new line is about to be displayed. Execution of both the FCT and LCT generate signals. These signals allow the application to synchronize events to display activities. For instance, by catching the FCT signal an application could perform a cut to a new image while simultaneously starting the playback of a soundmap from memory.

Real-time records: As a real-time record is played, the instructions located within its control area can issue signals back to the application. In addition, the CD-i controller signals the application when playback of a real-time record is completed (termination of soundmap playback also generates a signal). Finally, signals are generated as buffers being filled by real-time data are completed. These signals keep the application informed of progress of real-time record playback and are used to synchronize playback with other activities.

This concludes our discussion of CD-i. The above material has covered both CD-i disc format and CD-i player architecture. While the architecture and technical specifications may be showing signs of age, it should be realized that CD-i constitutes one of the first systems that could credibly be called a multimedia platform and that the number of CD-i titles continues to grow.

3.3 DVI

3.3.1 DVI OVERVIEW

DVI, or *digital video interactive*, appeared briefly in the last chapter during the discussion on low data rate digital video representations. This section provides a more complete description of DVI – the media types it supports, the basic hardware and software components used by DVI, and the functional capabilities of DVI.

The literature on DVI makes the distinction between DVI technology and DVI systems. DVI technology consists of several basic components: storage formats for digital audio and video, compression and decompression algorithms for these formats, and hardware and software allowing applications to capture and play back data in these formats. The integration of these components into a particular host hardware and software platform is called a DVI system. To the application developer, it is important that DVI applications run on any DVI system; the underlying hardware is of less consequence. From the developer's perspective then, DVI can be viewed as an *application programming interface* (API). How this interface is implemented will depend on hardware design and may vary from platform to platform.

The early development of DVI took place at RCA's David Sarnoff Research Center during the mid 1980s. However, the main source of DVI products is Intel, who acquired the rights to DVI technology and now markets DVI chip and board sets (notably the *ActionMedia* boards for the PC). In the following, references to DVI and DVI systems are to the hardware and supporting software as provided by Intel. Further information on DVI, and digital video in general, is provided by Luther (1991). Additionally, a series of articles by the developers of DVI provides a good introduction to this technology and indicates the direction in which it is evolving (Ripley, 1989; Harney et al, 1991; Green, 1992).

3.3.2   DVI MEDIA TYPES

DVI systems perform operations on video, audio, image, graphics, and text data. Like CD-i, DVI specifies a number of formats, or what we call media types. However, these media types should be considered only as the 'predefined' types of DVI. It is possible for the application developer to incorporate other formats by reprogramming the DVI hardware (although this may reduce portability).

Video □ The DVI hardware was originally developed with two digital video formats in mind: *Real-Time Video* (RTV) and *Production-Level Video* (PLV). To the application developer, the main difference between RTV and PLV is that the first supports both record and playback, while with the higher-quality PLV format, only playback is possible. Thus RTV is used when an application must generate or modify video – for instance, an authoring tool; RTV is also used to test an application and its data prior to converting to PLV. When the video material needed by an application is known, PLV should be chosen since, bit-for-bit, it provides better quality than RTV.

PLV uses a proprietary compression algorithm (Tinker, 1989), and conversion of video material to PLV is not done by application developers but rather by special service facilities established by Intel. The developer submits analog video which is digitized to produce a series of YUV images. Y is sampled at a resolution of 256×240 samples per video frame, and U and V are each sampled at 1/16 this rate, which is 64×60 samples per frame. The sample size is 8 bits, resulting in 69 120 bytes per frame, or an average of 9 bits per pixel. The digitized frames are stored on disk where they can be read by the compression hardware. The PLV compression algorithm is a lossy, interframe coding scheme. The amount of storage consumed by the compressed video is determined by a handful of interrelated factors which can be specified by the application developer. These factors include:

- Quality: The spatial resolution and color depth of the decoded video. For example, if low-resolution video is required (perhaps it will only appear in a small window) then sampling could take place at a lower resolution than the standard 256×240.

- Frame rate: The number of decoded frames per second. For some applications, full motion video (25 or 30 frames per second) is not needed and so can be traded for better quality or reduced storage.

- Data rate: The average data rate for the encoded video. Control over this parameter allows matching the video data rate to the transfer capacity of the storage device used by the application.

● Decode time: The average amount of time to decode a frame. If an application plans to use the DVI hardware simultaneously for video decoding and some other purpose (such as image or graphics operations), a decode time less than the frame period is needed.

● Key frame selection: The location and frequency of key frames (recall that in video compression, key frames are those compressed without reference to other frames). Key frames are needed for random access; the application developer can request they be generated at a specific frequency or inserted at particular points. However, key frames require about three times as much data as interpolated frames.

In comparison to PLV, RTV uses a simpler compression algorithm – allowing the DVI hardware to compress video frames in real time. The application developer still has control over such factors as the data rate and frame rate; however, frames are independently coded (intraframe compression) so key frame selection is not an issue. For given quality, RTV will occupy several times the storage of PLV. When RTV is used for prototyping, it may be desired to allocate the same amount of storage to the RTV data as will be used for the final PLV data. (The prototype and final application then operate with data at the same rate.) Matching RTV and PLV storage requirements can be achieved by reducing the RTV quality and lowering its frame rate – for example, dropping from 30 to 10 frames per second.

Audio □ DVI systems support a number of audio types and so offer different quality versus data rate alternates. As an example, Ripley (1989) mentions three DVI audio formats: FM, 'mid-range' and 'near AM'. A CD-ROM disc can contain up to five hours of FM stereo audio, 20 hours of mid-range mono audio, and 40 hours of near AM mono audio. DVI, like CD-i, makes use of a form of ADPCM to compress recorded audio data; the data is then decompressed by DVI hardware during playback.

Image □ DVI systems can process and display images stored in a number of formats. These include RGB, YUV, and monochrome images, color mapped images, and images containing an alpha channel. Processing operations are generally implemented on the DVI hardware and include still-image compression and decompression (various algorithms, both lossless and lossy, are supported), blending (of two images), adjustment of contrast, brightness, and saturation, scaling, and warping (reshaping a polygonal region of an image).

Text and graphics □ The DVI software provides functions for rendering text and graphics data. These functions produce bitmaps, image-like data structures which can be combined with images and other bitmaps. The rendering functions rely on DVI hardware for efficiency; examples are structured graphics operations (for instance, rendering 2D primitives such as lines and polygons), and simple text formatting (for instance, rendering text using a bitmap font).

3.3.3   DVI MEDIA ORGANIZATION

DVI specifies a multimedia format, known as the *AVSS file format*, allowing a number of *data streams* to be interleaved into a single file. (AVSS, the *Audio/Video Support System*, will be described when we look at DVI operations.) An AVSS data stream is analogous to a CD-i record and, as with CD-i, we can distinguish between real-time data and non-real-time data. In AVSS there are three kinds of streams containing real-time data:

- Digital audio stream: A sequence of digital audio samples in one of the DVI audio formats.

- Digital video stream: A sequence of RTV or PLV frames.

- 'Underlay' stream: A sequence of data elements that are delivered to the application as the AVSS file is played. A common example is time code; other examples are the coordinates of a moving object in a video stream and the location of regions sensitive to user selection.

AVSS streams can also contain still images or arbitrary application data. Such streams do not have real-time constraints so the data need not be processed at a specific rate.

3.3.4   DVI ARCHITECTURE

Current DVI products are based on two chips from Intel, a *pixel processor* and a *display processor*. Two generations of these chips have been produced: the 'A-series' consisting of the 82750PA pixel processor and the 82750DA display processor, and the more recent 'B-series' containing the 82750PB and the 82750DB. These chips are known as the PA and DA and the PB and DB respectively. Collectively the pixel processor and display processor form the i750 video processor, and the i750 is in turn the main component of the ActionMedia boardset. The most recent version, ActionMedia II, uses the B-series chips while the earlier ActionMedia I is based on the A-series chips. The high-level architecture of a DVI/ActionMedia system is shown in Figure 3.9; there are three main groups of components: the host system, the ActionMedia delivery board, used for RTV and PLV playback, and the optional ActionMedia capture board, used for RTV recording.

> *Host system:*   ActionMedia boards are intended to run on a host system; current possibilities for the host include an IBM PS/2 or a PC-AT compatible computer. The configuration of the host system can vary; however, it must contain a main processor, memory, and input devices (in particular, a keyboard and mouse). Some form of secondary storage, such as a floppy disk, hard disk or network server, is also needed (for start-up of the host system and loading the DVI runtime environment). Finally, the host system is likely to have a video adaptor (such as VGA); it may then have its own display monitor or it may share a monitor with the delivery board.

> *Host/DVI Interface:* The ActionMedia boards use an internal bus, the DVI bus, for communication among components. The Host/DVI interface is a

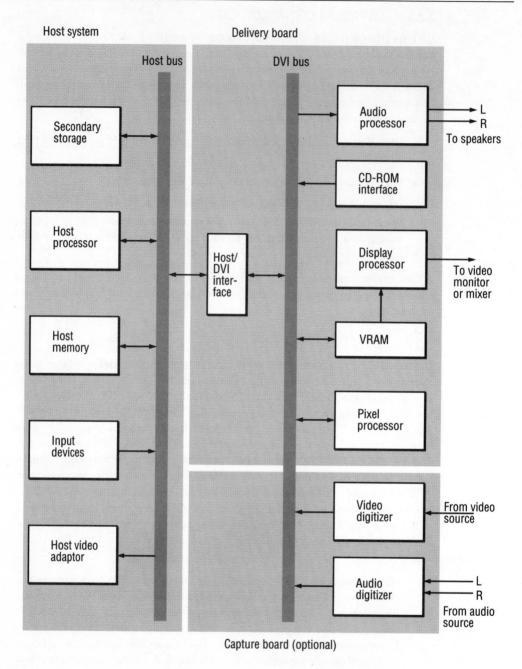

Figure 3.9 DVI (ActionMedia) high-level architecture and data/control paths.

bridge from the host's bus to the DVI bus. During playback, data read from the storage device (magnetic disk or CD-ROM) is passed via this interface to the delivery board, and similarly, during recording, data is passed back to the host system from the capture board. In addition to simple exchange of data, the Host/DVI interface permits the host system to control the DVI components. For example, code for the pixel, display, or audio processors is downloaded over this interface.

VRAM: An ActionMedia delivery board comes with at least 1 MB of video RAM. This special purpose memory supports two simultaneous modes of access (such memory is called *dual-ported*): a random access mode, used to read and modify randomly addressed memory locations, and a serial access mode, used to rapidly read out long consecutive stretches of memory. In the ActionMedia boards, the main role of VRAM is buffering of video frames as they are being decoded and displayed. Typically a compressed frame will be placed in VRAM by the host system; the pixel processor then decodes the frame and the result is also placed in VRAM. The decoded frame is read out of VRAM, scan line by scan line, by the display processor using the high-speed serial access mode. In addition to video frame data, VRAM is used to buffer audio data (either going to the audio processor or coming from the audio digitizer) and to hold other forms of data, such as fonts, that may be needed for presentation.

Pixel processor: The pixel processor is the powerhouse of the ActionMedia boards. Its primary responsibility is real-time decoding of RTV and PLV video frames; for this task it is capable of reaching rates of 30 frames per second with full-screen frames. The pixel processor is micro-programmable; this is exploited by many DVI operations which download code and execute on the pixel processor rather than on the host CPU. Examples of operations implemented in this manner include graphics and text rendering, image processing operations, various compression schemes, and video effects and transitions.

Display processor: The display processor generates an analog signal suitable for viewing on a video monitor. It reads pixel data from VRAM, converts it to an RGB format, and then passes the converted pixels to digital-to-analog converters. Images stored in VRAM occur in a variety of formats, differing in the number of bits per pixel, color model, use of a color map, and presence of an alpha channel. In converting to an RGB format the display processor must perform such tasks as UV interpolation, YUV to RGB conversion, and color map lookup. By modifying internal registers, signal timing and other characteristics of the output signal can be controlled, so allowing connection to a variety of monitors including NTSC, PAL, and RGB monitors. The display processor has the ability to genlock to an external signal and can produce a key signal from an image's alpha channel. This allows the DVI video signal to be mixed with other video signals, such as an external video signal or the signal generated by the host system's video driver.

CD-ROM interface: DVI data is often stored on CD, so a CD-ROM interface and player are useful. Placing the interface on the delivery board has the advantage of not loading the host bus during playback.

Audio processor: The ActionMedia delivery board contains an audio processor and associated digital-to-analog conversion and filtering hardware. The audio processor obtains encoded audio data from VRAM, decodes this data, and passes it to the digital-to-analog converters. It is capable of driving two channels, and so can produce a stereo audio signal or two independent mono signals.

Audio and video digitizers: The ActionMedia capture board contains both audio and video digitizers. The video digitizer takes as input an analog RGB signal and samples this at a resolution of 768×480 samples per frame (the sample size is 8 bits per channel). The digitized frame is accumulated in VRAM and can then be stored on the host's secondary storage device in a DVI image format. Alternatively, the pixel processor can be directed to perform RTV compression on the digitized frame and the compressed frame is then stored as part of a sequence of RTV frames. The separate audio digitizer allows audio capture to proceed in parallel with video capture if need be – the digitized audio is placed in VRAM and can then be stored with the accompanying video data.

3.3.5　DVI OPERATIONS

Application developers control the functionality of a DVI system through an extensive runtime software environment. The architecture of the DVI software environment has gone through two generations: *AVSS* (Audio/Video Support System) and *AVK* (Audio/Video Kernel). We now describe both AVSS and AVK and then discuss the multimedia operations supported by DVI.

AVSS □　The software environment for an application using AVSS is shown in Figure 3.10. The environment includes interfaces to four software components: AVSS itself, and components supporting graphics and image operations, a real-time executive responsible for scheduling and synchronization (RTX), and assorted error handling and memory functions (STD). These four components in turn rely on operating-system-level 'drivers' which directly control host system hardware and hardware on the ActionMedia boards.

If we consider multimedia operations, as opposed to single media operations, the two components of central importance are AVSS and RTX. The primary function of the AVSS component is to play back AVSS files. Playback and, in general, applications implemented using AVSS consist of a number of cooperating *tasks* administered by the real-time executive – RTX. The real-time executive is an extension to the host operating system that allows multitasking. RTX is given control of the host processor every thirtieth of a second and determines whether any tasks are runnable. Tasks are scheduled by priority and those with lower priority are preempted by those with higher priority. RTX also handles input

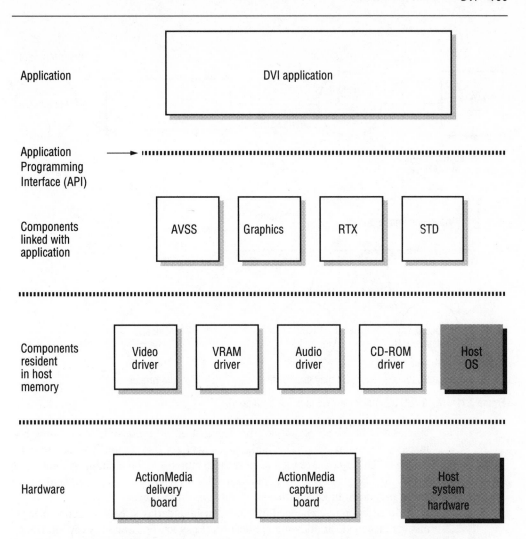

Figure 3.10   AVSS software environment. DVI components are shown unshaded, host system components are shaded.

devices such as the keyboard and mouse. Applications respond to input events by calling an RTX function; they are then scheduled when the event occurs.

The tasks involved in AVSS playback are shown in Figure 3.11. Here the highest priority task is the *reader task*, which de-interleaves the streams within an AVSS file and stores the data in buffers to be processed by other tasks. Typically the file is located on a secondary storage device such as a hard disk or CD-ROM; however, if there is sufficient space it can be loaded into main memory prior to playback. Video, audio, and image streams are sent to VRAM buffers for processing by the DVI hardware, while underlay and ordinary data streams are sent to RAM where they are picked up by application tasks. Two other tasks play a

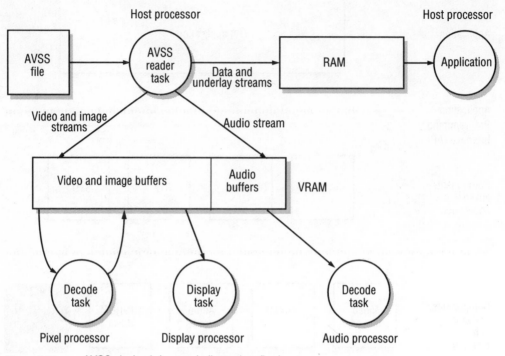

Figure 3.11   AVSS playback (arrows indicate data flow).

crucial role in AVSS playback. The *decode task* is responsible for creating bit-maps by decompressing video and image data (it is also responsible for audio decoding). The *display task* then outputs these bitmaps to the monitor. Although the decode and display tasks are administered by RTX, they are executed on the DVI hardware and so involve little use of host system resources.

In addition to embedded time code in an underlay stream, a second mechanism is provided for allowing applications to synchronize with AVSS playback: AVSS *hook routines* are application-defined functions that are called at specific points during stream processing. Some specific hook routines are:

HookOnIn: Called after the reader task has read a video frame.

HookBeforeDecode: Called as the decode task is about to start frame decompression.

HookAfterDecode: Called after the decode task has completed frame decompression.

HookOnVbi: Called as the display task generates a vertical blanking interval. (Recall from Section 2.2.1 that a vertical blanking interval, or VBI, is an analog signal sent to the monitor, allowing it to retrace before a new frame is drawn.)

As an example, an application that wishes to apply a video effect during playback could invoke the effect from a HookAfterDecode routine. To superimpose graphics (such as a special cursor) on moving video, a HookOnVbi routine could be used. However, the application developer must take care with the design of hook routines (and application tasks in general) since they may be preempted by the higher priority reader, decode, and display tasks.

AVK □ The AVSS environment has certain shortcomings – it is difficult to port to a new host platform (since RTX interacts intimately with the host operating system) and it is not designed for the handling of multiple video streams (for example, although AVSS files can contain a number of video streams, typically only one would be selected for playback at a time). To overcome these limitations and provide a more flexible environment, a second generation of DVI software, known as AVK, or Audio/Video Kernel, has been designed (Green, 1992).

AVK is based on a conceptual model called the *digital production studio.* This model views a DVI system in terms of a number of components which operate on streams of audio and video data. Components are analogous to the mixers, routers and other equipment found in a traditional production studio (for instance, see Figure 2.5). The various components of the digital production studio model and their possible connections are shown in Figure 3.12.

We now give a brief description of the components appearing in the digital production studio model. First, the *analog interface* is responsible for all analog-to-digital and digital-to-analog conversion. It connects to external analog devices, such as monitors, speakers, microphones, or cameras, and maps these connections to *physical channels*, unidirectional paths available to data streams. Another component, the *stream manager*, is similar to the AVSS reader task in that it can read and de-interleave the AVSS file format; this produces data streams which flow through *logical channels*. The stream manager can also write streams to storage and for this reason the logical channels are bidirectional (although a logical channel can only be used in one direction at a time). The mapping between physical channels and logical channels is carried out by the *audio/video mixer.* For example, two audio streams, arriving from external devices over two physical channels, could be mixed and mapped to a single logical channel leading to storage. Similarly two video streams, arriving over logical channels, could be mixed, perhaps using effects provided by the *effects processor*, and then sent for display. The final components are the *display manager*, which is used to select particular image and/or video mixes for viewing, and the *sampler,* which allows resampling of audio or video data within the system (for example, it can produce an image by 'sampling' a video stream).

AVK provides the application programmer with a software library allowing the application to control streams and connect components in different configurations. The two basic configurations would be for recording and playback; however, others are possible. The AVK software also provides a notification service so that the application can respond to events taking place among the components.

The AVK architecture is extensible in a number of ways. For example, as the hardware underlying individual components becomes more powerful, more streams can be handled by the component. It should also be possible to enhance

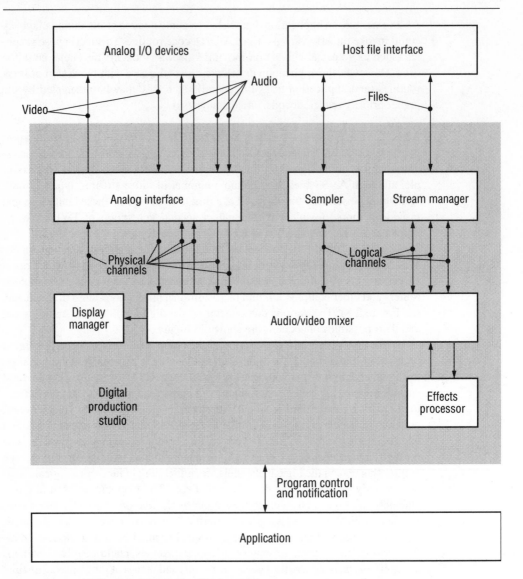

Figure 3.12   DVI's *Digital Production Studio* model.

the system by adding components that perform specialized services (for instance, a music synthesizer which generates an audio stream). These new components would then be connected by applications in the same manner as the existing components.

This completes our overview of AVSS and AVK; we now look at multimedia operations provided by DVI. As explained in the previous section, we divide multimedia operations into three categories: configuration, composition, and activation operations (see Table 3.9). Our discussion of what DVI offers in terms of the three categories is based on the more powerful AVK environment, but there will be some references to AVSS since AVK retains the capability to play and record the AVSS file format.

DVI configuration operations □ The configuration operations are INSPECTION, CONNECTION and EXTENSION. For DVI, examples of inspection include determining the size of VRAM, or whether RTV capture is supported, or whether a CD-ROM drive is present. The connection operation is explicitly supported by AVK – applications connect components within the digital production studio to perform particular functions, such as recording or playback. Extension mechanisms include adding components to the digital studio subsystem and micro-programming the pixel processor (this sounds forbidding, but microcode development tools are available from Intel).

DVI composition operations □ The two forms of multimedia composition, TEMPORAL COMPOSITION and SPATIAL COMPOSITION, are supported by DVI through the following mechanisms:

> *Data interleaving:* Temporal composition is reflected by the interleaving of audio and video data in an AVSS file. Like the notion of a real-time record in CD-i, the physical placement of a data stream within an AVSS file implicitly specifies its timing relative to other streams.

> *Pixel processor programming:* The DVI pixel processor performs spatial composition of image, video, and graphics data. For example, by suitable programming of this processor, graphics can be written over still or moving video, or a transition can be made from one image to another. Furthermore, the ability to generate a key signal allows the video output of the display processor to be mixed (composed) with other video sources. However, and again like CD-i, spatial composition is not specified by data structure (in this case the AVSS file); instead, it is the responsibility of the application to determine when and how spatial composition is to occur.

DVI activation operations □ Activation operations are divided into three main groups – those dealing with the INSTANTIATION of activities, and those dealing with their TUNING and TIMING. Instantiation can be thought of as 'turning on' the components in AVK's digital production studio; once the studio is running each component performs one or more activities. The application can tune the behavior of ongoing activities in a number of ways: at a low level there is the possibility of reprogramming the pixel processor and setting registers in the display processor, while at a higher level the application can control the mixer and other components in the digital production studio. Mechanisms related to the timing of activities include the hook routines of AVSS and the use of notification in AVK. Additionally, underlay streams can be used to synchronize applications with playback activities.

3.4 QUICKTIME

3.4.1 QUICKTIME OVERVIEW

QuickTime is an extension to the Macintosh operating system allowing the creation, playback, compression, and editing of time-based data. Of central importance within QuickTime is a flexible multimedia type, called the QuickTime *movie* format, which governs how groups of *tracks*, each usually referring to digital audio or digital video data, are assembled and presented.

QuickTime has an open architecture permitting the addition of new media types, new compression algorithms, and new hardware devices. The basic environment is entirely software-based and can play low-resolution movies on a Macintosh without the use of additional hardware. Better quality playback is achieved through adding special decompression hardware. Other extensions allow the recording of conventional video in the QuickTime movie format. Extensions to networked environments are also planned. While QuickTime originates from the Macintosh, QuickTime players are now available for the PC and for workstations. The following is a description of the 2.0 release of QuickTime. A much more detailed description can be found in the QuickTime documentation[1] (Apple, 1992), while a general overview is provided by Wayner (1991).

3.4.2 QUICKTIME MEDIA TYPES

Prior to QuickTime the Macintosh was already an established multimedia platform and commonly used in such areas as graphic design, computer animation, and computer music. QuickTime builds upon the Macintosh's existing support for sound and graphics and its existing media types. In particular, QuickTime extends the role of Apple's PICT format, previously used for mixed image, graphics and text data, by adding a temporal dimension and supporting temporal sequences of PICT images. The following summarizes the media types relevant to QuickTime.

Video and image □ As indicated above, both video and image data are based on the PICT format, a representation allowing a range of pixel depths and either indexed or non-indexed color information. PICT itself offers only minimal compression and is not suited for real-time playback at video frame rates. QuickTime introduces several additional compression algorithms which can be applied to sequences of, or individual, PICT images. These algorithms require no special hardware, those found in QuickTime include:

MPEG compression: QuickTime includes an implementation of the MPEG-1 standard. Real-time decompression in software is possible, while compression, without special hardware, usually takes much longer. This algorithm is suited for sequences of continuous-tone images. Compression is generally lossy. A quality factor, specified prior to compression (and

---

[1] At the time of writing (June 1994) QuickTime 2.0 documentation had not yet been released, and consequently some of the material in this section is based on private conversation with Apple.

possibly modified during compression), controls quality loss: at high quality factors there is no noticeable change in video quality, but the compression ratio is low; at low quality factors, quality is lost but the compression ratio is high.

Compact video compression: This algorithm (developed by SuperMac Technology Inc.) is intended for real-time decompression of digital video. For example, with a frame resolution of 320×240 pixels (a common size for QuickTime movies) and a pixel depth of 24 bits, decompression rates of 15 or more frames per second are possible without hardware acceleration. The algorithm is not symmetric so compression will take longer than decompression. Like MPEG compression, compact video compression is appropriate for continuous-tone material and is lossy (although again a 'quality factor' can be specified prior to compression).

Video compression: This is a simpler algorithm than compact video compression. Video compression, or 'Road Pizza' (the well-known development name), provides faster compression time than compact video compression at the cost of lower quality or increased compressed data size.

The video and compact video algorithms can both compress frames independently or achieve higher compression ratios by using interframe techniques. In the latter case a key frame rate is specified prior to compression and can be adjusted during compression. Applications can also select specific frames to be key frames.

Animation compression: Like MPEG, compact video, and video compression, the animation compression algorithm is used for image sequences, but works best with synthetic or computer-generated sequences rather than natural continuous-tone sequences. The algorithm relies on run-length coding, both spatially and in the temporal domain, and for this reason compression ratios depend greatly on image content. A lossy and lossless mode are available; for the lossy mode, decompression time is similar to that of the video compression algorithm – this allows animation compression to be used for real-time playback.

Photo compression: The QuickTime implementation of the JPEG image compression standard is called photo compression. It is intended for continuous-tone images and leads to compression ratios of between 10:1 and 20:1 without serious loss of image quality. Compression times are longer than those of the other methods, so photo compression is used primarily for single images rather than image sequences.

Graphics compression: This algorithm is intended for the special, but common, case of 8-bit images and image sequences. It gives higher compression ratios than animation compression, but decompression times are longer and it is not intended for real-time playback.

Raw compression: This algorithm alters pixel depth, for instance the conversion of a 32 bit per pixel image to 8 or 16 bits per pixel. It is often applied before the other algorithms, some of which require specific pixel depths.

Determining which compression scheme to use for a given image sequence involves trade-offs between decoded image quality, decode time, frame rate, compressed data size, and compressed data rate. Furthermore, some of these trade-offs depend not only on the compression scheme, but also on image content, the playback platform, and the choice of compression parameters (such as the quality factor, the key frame frequency). Thus selection of a compression scheme and accompanying parameters is a complex decision, but in practice heuristics come into play and not all alternates need be considered or evaluated.

Audio □ QuickTime supports a range of audio sample rates, the maximum being just over 65 kHz. A PCM representation is used with a sample size of 8, 16, or 32 bits. Audio values are either mono or stereo; in the second case samples from the two channels are interleaved when stored. QuickTime can make use of an audio compression algorithm developed by Apple (called *Macintosh Audio Compression and Expansion*, or MACE), which gives either 3:1 or 6:1 compression, with some loss of quality. The 65 kHz sample rate and 32-bit sample size are upper limits; the audio hardware may only support lower sample rates or smaller sample sizes. For instance, the standard audio DAC on the Macintosh operates at about 22 kHz with 8-bit samples. When the audio hardware used for playback does not support the sample size or sample rate used for recording, the audio data is converted by software during playback so as to maintain compatibility.

Text □ QuickTime movies can include tracks that contain text data and associated timing information. Subtitles are one obvious use of text tracks.

Music □ QuickTime also supports MIDI tracks. During playback, software synthesis is possible, or the MIDI data can be transferred to external MIDI devices.

Graphics □ Graphics primitives can be embedded in PICT data and so can be included within movies. This form of data is largely ignored by QuickTime but is passed on to the display software and so would appear during movie playback.

SMPTE time code □ While not strictly a media type in the sense we have been using, SMPTE time code can be placed in QuickTime movie tracks. Such tracks are useful for editing and may help synchronize QuickTime players with professional audio and video equipment.

3.4.3   QUICKTIME MEDIA ORGANIZATION

QuickTime provides an elegant data model for composing time-based media. The model governs the relative timing of audio, video, and other movie elements and their mixing when several elements are presented simultaneously; it can accommodate alternate forms of presentation, such as dual language sound tracks, and can map movie elements to different storage devices. In addition, the model can be realized by 'practical' data structures in the sense that editing and modification are possible without the need for copying large blocks of information.

Since the QuickTime data model is rather complex, we will follow a database approach, and describe media organization within QuickTime at two levels: a conceptual level which identifies the entities that appear in a QuickTime movie, and their attributes and relationships; and a physical level which determines how the conceptual entities are represented by storage structures. Also we will concentrate on the organization of audio and video data, although other media are supported. First, however, it is necessary to say a word about the role and representation of time in QuickTime.

Time in QuickTime □ The timing of a QuickTime movie, for instance when a particular track starts or stops, is specified by time values placed within the movie. Thus timing is explicit, rather than being implicit in the storage layout of data. Time values are represented by unsigned integers and refer to a *time coordinate system*. Each time coordinate system has a *time scale* indicating the number of units occurring per second and a *duration* indicating the maximum time value. For instance, a natural coordinate system for an NTSC video clip could have a scale of 30, since the number of units per second then corresponds to the number of frames per second; the duration would correspond to the number of frames in the clip.

In essence, a time value is simply an integer referring to some time coordinate system. There is, however, a complication: during playback the *rate* of presentation may change. For instance, the user may play a movie at twice its normal rate, or in slow-motion or even in reverse. The notion of playback rate is expressed by a quantity called a *timebase*. During playback there is a current timebase which serves as an additional scale factor when converting between actual time and time values within a movie.

Conceptual organization of media in QuickTime □ The QuickTime data model includes four basic entities: *data*, *media*, *track*, and *movie*. These are grouped into hierarchies so that a single movie entity is composed of a group of track entities, each of which is based on a media entity that in turn refers to a data entity. Proceeding from the bottom of the hierarchy up, we have:

> *Data entity:* A data entity represents the actual storage used for audio and/or video data and is typically part of a file on hard disk or CD-ROM. The storage associated with a data entity is referenced by one or more media entities, which may belong to the same or different movies.

> *Media entity:* A media entity is a temporal sequence, that is, a sequence where each element has a start time and a duration. These quantities are measured in *media time* – a time coordinate system defined by the media entity. Associated with each media entity is a media type, which may be either audio or video. Sequence elements do not contain the video or audio data; instead they are references (pointers) to a storage region represented by a data entity. In case of a video media entity, elements are references to

frames; for an audio media entity, the elements are references to audio samples.

As an example, suppose we have four video frames stored in a data entity and referenced by r1, r2, r3 and r4. Consider the media entity, $vMedia_{30}$, formed from the following sequence:

$vMedia_{30}$ =
$<r1, 0, 1>$,
$<r2, 1, 3>$,
$<r3, 4, 1>$,
$<r4, 5, 1>$

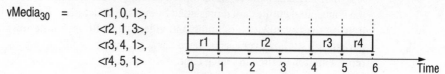

Here the subscript on the entity name is the time scale and elements are <frame reference, start time, duration> tuples. The first element, $<r1, 0, 1>$, indicates that the frame referenced by r1 starts at media time 0 and has a duration of 1 unit, which, since the time scale is 30, is 1/30th of a second. It is followed by r2, and so on. In this case adding the duration to the start time of one element gives the start time of the next element – there are no gaps or overlapping elements in the sequence. Such media are sometimes called *continuous* and have the property that any media time value falls within the span of a single media element.

Track entity: A track entity is a reordering of a media entity; it may also exclude or duplicate some of the elements of the media entity. Each track entity is contained in one movie entity and measures time in the coordinate system of the movie. For example, suppose the movie time scale is 60 and a track entity is constructed from $vMedia_{30}$. This track would resemble:

$vTrack_{60}$ =
$<r1, 0, 2>$,
$<r2, 2, 6>$,
$<r3, 8, 2>$,
$<r4, 10, 2>$

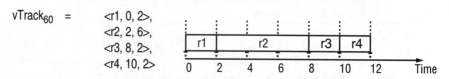

Since the time scale of $vMedia_{60}$ is twice that of $vMedia_{30}$, its start times and durations are multiplied by a factor of two. Now suppose the track is modified by removing the first frame and placing the third and fourth frames at the beginning of the track. After editing, the track becomes:

edited-$vTrack_{60}$ =
$<r3, 0, 2>$,
$<r4, 2, 2>$,
$<r2, 4, 6>$

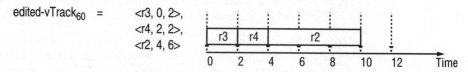

Rather than represent tracks as explicit sequences, QuickTime uses a list of edit operations that produce the track sequence when applied to a media sequence. The representation of the edited $vMedia_{60}$ then resembles:

$$\text{edited-vTrack}_{60} \ = \ \text{vMedia}_{30} + \text{CUT(r1)} + \text{MOVE(r3 thru r4 before r2)}$$

For long sequences the edit list form is a more condensed representation and allows efficient implementation of editing operations.

Movie entity: A movie entity is essentially a group of track entities. (Tracks can also be grouped into secondary structures, called *layers,* but this need not concern us for the moment.) A movie specifies a time scale, used by all its tracks, and specifies a duration. Tracks are offset within the movie; the offset is measured in movie time and results in a translation when converting between media time and movie time. For example, suppose the edited vMedia$_{60}$, as listed above, is offset by four units. The track, in explicit form, then becomes:

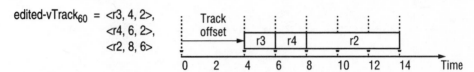

$$\text{edited-vTrack}_{60} = \langle r3, 4, 2\rangle,$$
$$\langle r4, 6, 2\rangle,$$
$$\langle r2, 8, 6\rangle$$

As can be seen, changing the offset alters the start times of all elements, but has no effect on their duration.

An example of a QuickTime movie consisting of two tracks, aTrack$_{60}$ and vMedia$_{60}$, is shown in the upper part of Figure 3.13. The lower part of the figure shows the hierarchy of entities that underlie the movie. As in the above examples, subscripts on entity names indicate time scale. The movie and track entities use a time scale of 60 while the two media entities use 8000 and 30 (corresponding to possible audio and video sample rates) respectively. Note there is only one data entity (the 'arc' on the storage device) and both media entities refer to the same region of storage (so, in this example, audio and video data are interleaved).

Physical organization of media in QuickTime □ The preceding discussion concentrated on the conceptual basis of QuickTime and intentionally excluded a number of issues that add to its complexity. We have not mentioned the mechanisms for controlling the spatial positioning and composition of tracks, the role of media element 'descriptors', or the intricacies of media entity to data entity referencing. We now discuss such issues and describe QuickTime at a more detailed level, that of the structures used by QuickTime movies when stored in files or loaded into memory.

The basic storage unit used by QuickTime, called an *atom,* consists of three parts: a size in bytes, a four-character code, and a content section. Atoms are used for external storage of software data structures; the four-character code identifies the 'type' of the data structure, and the content section contains its fields. Fields may be simple values, such as integers or strings, or they may be other atoms, so it is possible to build up atom hierarchies. Of course, the program storing an atom and the program reading it must agree on the meaning of the type codes. This can be accomplished by sharing header files that define the corresponding data structures.

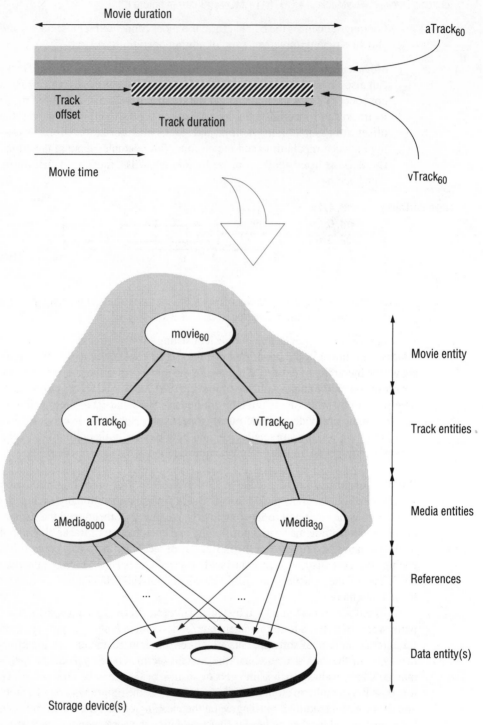

Figure 3.13   Conceptual view of a QuickTime movie.

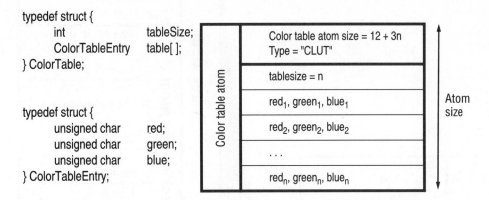

```
typedef struct {
        int                    tableSize;
        ColorTableEntry        table[ ];
} ColorTable;


typedef struct {
        unsigned char     red;
        unsigned char     green;
        unsigned char     blue;
} ColorTableEntry;
```

Figure 3.14   A (C) data structure and corresponding 'CLUT' atom.

For instance, consider an atom used to store color lookup tables. The type code might be 'CLUT' and the content section could be arranged so that there is a color table size followed by table entries consisting of red/green/blue values. Figure 3.14 shows a ColorTable data structure and the form of the corresponding CLUT atom.

The movie, track, and media entities associated with a single QuickTime movie are stored in an atom hierarchy, the root of which is a movie atom. The movie atom contains a list of track atoms, each containing a media atom (see Figure 3.15). We now consider some of the fields found in movie, track and media atoms (for a complete description the reader is referred to QuickTime documentation).

> *Movie atom:* A movie atom specifies the movie's time scale and duration, preferred playback rate, and preferred playback volume. It identifies the movie's *poster* (a single video frame representative of the movie) and *preview* (a short sequence of frames also representative of the movie). The movie atom allows storage of a *current selection* and *current time*, useful for editing and suspended playback. Finally a *movie matrix* and a *clipping atom* determine the spatial coordinate system and clipping region used by the movie (similar information is found in track atoms). During playback a series of spatial coordinate transformations, clipping, and matte operations take place, the purpose of which is to compose track frames in the playback window. For instance, Figure 3.16 shows a *standard movie controller window* (used to control movie positioning, playback volume, and so on) in which frames from two video tracks appear simultaneously.

> *Track atom:* A track atom specifies a track's offset within the movie, its volume relative to other tracks, and its spatial display information. It contains a media atom and an *edit atom*; the latter lists the segments of the media sequence appearing in the track sequence. Finally the track atom contains *layering information* used to group 'alternate' tracks. The standard

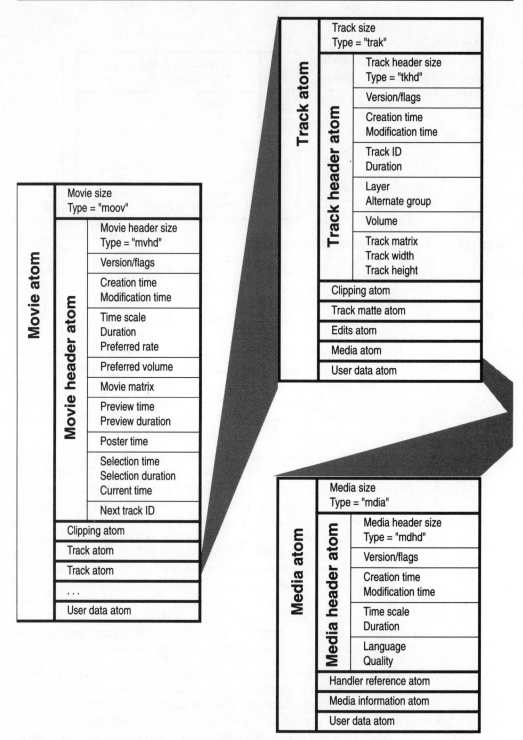

Figure 3.15   Data structure for movie, track and media atoms.

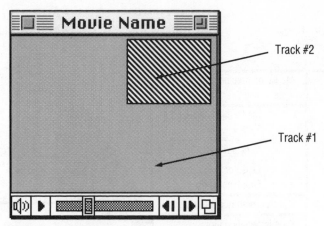

Track #2

Track #1

Figure 3.16 A QuickTime standard movie controller window showing two video tracks.

example is a movie with two or more sound tracks, each in a different language. During playback only one is selected from the group.

Media atom: A media atom specifies the time scale and duration of a media sequence. Within a media atom the *language* and *quality* fields indicate audio content and audio/video quality, the *handler atom* identifies the software component responsible for interpreting media data, and the *media information atom* (see Figure 3.17) provides additional media-specific information such as channel balance (for stereo audio media) or the graphics 'paint' operation used to overlay frames (for displaying video media). The media information atom also contains a *data information atom* identifying the storage region for media elements, a *handler atom*, identifying, in this case, the software component used for accessing media data, and a *sample table atom*.

Below the level of media and media information atoms, a variety of table structures come into play. These are found in sample table atoms; their purpose is to provide access to individual elements, called *samples*, in a media sequence. The principal form of access during playback is the retrieving of samples in temporal order; however, a simple media-time-to-sample-address mapping is not possible since samples can vary in size and duration. It is also possible for two or more media sequences to be interleaved within a single data entity, or the ordering of samples within a media sequence to differ from their storage order.

The mapping from media time to sample address relies on intermediate, performance-oriented structures called *chunks*. A chunk is a group of consecutive samples placed in contiguous storage. Chunking optimizes data access – groups of samples can be read or written with fewer storage operations than are needed to access samples separately. Chunking also improves the efficiency of the mapping from media time to sample address. Samples and chunks are characterized by the following information:

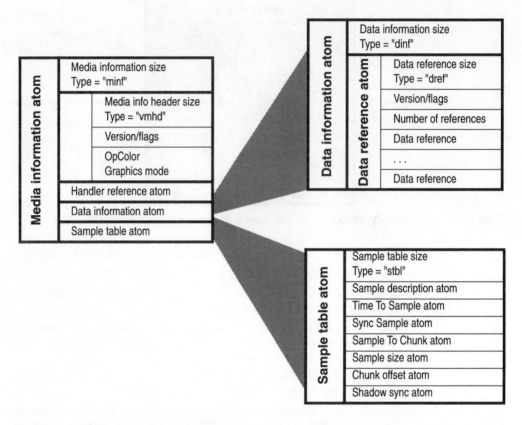

Figure 3.17   Data structure for media information, data information, data reference, and sample table atoms. Media information atoms are media-specific; the example shown here is for video media.

Sample: A media value is a sequence of samples. The actual storage is provided by the data region identified by a data reference atom. Each sample is characterized by:

- Sample number: The index of the sample within the media sequence.

- Sample offset: The location of the sample in the data region.

- Sample size: The number of bytes occupied by the sample in the data region.

- Sample duration: The number of units of media time occupied by the sample.

- Sample descriptor: Media-specific information needed to interpret the sample. For instance, descriptors for 'video samples' (that is, video frames) identify such things as the compression type, color depth, and compression quality factors. Information found in descriptors for audio samples includes the sample size and sample rate.

Chunk: Chunks are groups of consecutive samples, each chunk is characterized by:

- Chunk number: The index of the chunk within the media sequence.

- Chunk offset: The location of the chunk in the data region.

- First sample: The sample number of the first sample appearing in the chunk.

- Number of samples: The number of samples within the chunk.

- Chunk descriptor: All samples within a chunk use the same sample descriptor, hence it is possible to associate a unique sample descriptor that serves as the descriptor for the chunk.

Sample table atoms demarcate samples and chunks within the data region and provide the information needed to map media time to sample addresses. In addition, sample table atoms keep track of sample descriptors. This is accomplished using several tables:

Time-to-Sample Table: Maintains information about sample durations and provides a mapping from media time to sample number.

Sample-to-Chunk Table: Provides a mapping from sample number to chunk number and identifies chunk descriptors.

Chunk Offset Table: Gives the chunk offset for each chunk. In other words, it maps chunk numbers to chunk offsets.

Sample Size Table: Maps sample number to sample size.

In addition, the *Sample Description Table* maintains all sample descriptors; it is indexed by a field from the *Sample-to-Chunk Table*; and finally the *Sync Sample Table* lists the sample numbers for all key frames – those which can be decompressed independently of preceding (and succeeding) frames.

Using the above tables (and the information found in track atoms), the following lists the steps needed to find the sample occurring at a particular value of movie time:

(1)   Map from movie time to media time by using the track offset and its Edits atom.

(2)   Map from media time to sample number using the Time-to-Sample table.

(3)   Map from sample number to chunk number using the Sample-to-Chunk table.

(4)   Map from chunk number to chunk offset using the Chunk Offset table.

(5)   Determine the sample size and the sample's offset within the chunk by examining the Sample Size table.

(6)   Add the sample offset within the chunk to the chunk offset and access the data region at this point.

This access procedure may appear excessively indirect, but the table lookups are needed if one allows variable-sized samples, samples appearing non-consecutively in the data region, interleaving of samples from different media, and the possibility of editing tracks without modifying the underlying media or data region. Furthermore, there are common situations where some of the tables reduce to a single entry. For example, if samples have constant size then the Sample Size table, and perhaps the Sample Description table, can be replaced by a single entry; if samples have uniform duration then the Time-to-Sample table is not necessary.

Returning to movie organization, each QuickTime movie is described by a movie atom – a hierarchy of track, media, and other atoms. The atom hierarchy and the sample data can be stored in two basic ways. First, it is possible to place a movie atom in one file and then reference other files in which sample data is stored. In this way the same data can be referenced by many movies. It is also possible to 'flatten' the movie by bundling the movie atom and the external data together in a single file. This second form is self-contained and so easier to transfer from one system to another.

3.4.4   QUICKTIME ARCHITECTURE

QuickTime has been designed so that playback is possible without additional hardware on a range of Macintosh models; their basic architecture is shown on the left of Figure 3.18. The difficulty with supporting multiple playback platforms is coping with differences between platforms. In particular, it is necessary for Quick-Time to adapt to differences in such things as processing power, storage device access times and data transfer rates, and video monitor characteristics. The adaptability of QuickTime is largely provided by two mechanisms. First, if the playback platform cannot access, decompress, or display video frames at the rate they are to be played, whether owing to a slow processor or a slow storage device, then QuickTime adapts by dropping frames while maintaining the continuity of audio playback. Second, the device independence of the Macintosh graphics software allows QuickTime movies to be displayed on monitors of differing resolution and color depth.

While any 'off-the-shelf' Macintosh is sufficient for playback, for recording existing video material in the QuickTime format, certain additional hardware may be required. Examples of hardware extensions that aid in QuickTime recording include:

Audio digitizer: Some Macintosh models have only a single digital-to-analog converter (DAC) providing low- to medium-quality audio output. Audio input, audio output of higher quality, or stereo output requires additional audio hardware on these models.

Video digitizer: A video digitizer captures, in digital form, entire video sequences in real time (as opposed to video 'frame grabbers' which are more suited for capturing single frames). A video digitizer may allow the resulting digital video stream to be displayed in a window, compressed and

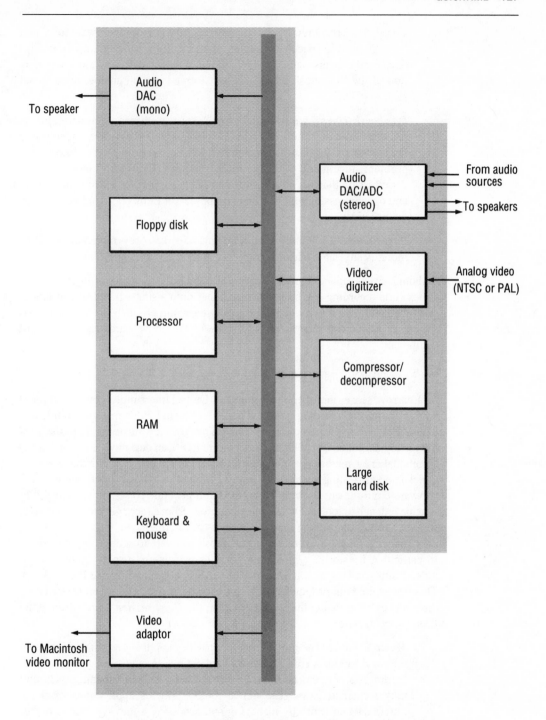

Figure 3.18   Basic Macintosh configuration (left) and possible additional hardware components for QuickTime recording (right).

stored, or stored directly. Video digitizers often support hardware 'pan' and 'zoom' (used to specify the region of an incoming video frame to be digitized) and may also support video output, in which case a window, or a portion of the Macintosh display, is transformed into an analog video signal such as NTSC.

Hardware compression: QuickTime's software-based decompression is pressed to produce mid-resolution output (240 × 320 pixels) at video frame rates even on the fastest Macintosh models. Recording poses more of a problem since many of the algorithms require significantly more time for compression than decompression. Hardware support for video compression and decompression relieves the main processor of this task and gives better quality video.

Large hard disk: Finally, a large magnetic disk, of several hundred MB or more, is advisable when recording or authoring with QuickTime.

Although listed separately above, many of the hardware components needed for QuickTime recording can be bundled together onto a single board. In particular, combined audio digitizer/video digitizer/compression products are available. Also, newer Macintosh models include some of the above hardware as standard equipment.

3.4.5   QUICKTIME OPERATIONS

In a narrow sense, the operations found in QuickTime simply govern the playback, editing and recording of digital audio and digital video material. While this itself is a significant accomplishment, such a narrow view misses perhaps the most interesting aspect of QuickTime: the software has been designed so that it can accommodate new media types and new forms of compression. Rather than viewing QuickTime as dealing specifically with audio and video, it is better viewed as a software environment for time-based media in general. To see how extensibility is achieved, and to look at QuickTime operations from a more general perspective, we now discuss the software architecture of QuickTime.

QuickTime relies on existing Macintosh software to access output devices. In particular, it uses the *QuickDraw* graphics package to display decompressed video frames and the *Sound Manager* to perform audio output (see Figure 3.19). This leaves the bulk of QuickTime's duties to be performed and orchestrated by three pieces of software: the *Movie Toolbox*, the *Compression Manager*, and the *Component Manager*.

Movie Toolbox: The movie toolbox provides applications with a high-level interface to QuickTime. It allows applications to control playback and recording, to perform editing operations, and to modify media, track, and movie characteristics. The movie toolbox shields applications from the movie data structure by managing and accessing a movie's atoms. It provides the standard movie controller window and it configures the other software components needed for QuickTime operation. For instance, if during

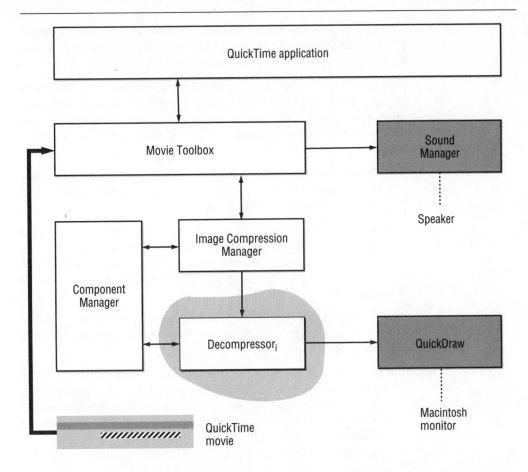

Figure 3.19 QuickTime playback software environment. The Sound Manager and QuickDraw are not part of QuickTime but are needed for playback. The decompressor is an example of a QuickTime 'component' – software which is dynamically loaded into the environment.

playback a track requires decompression, then the movie toolbox ensures that the appropriate decompressor is available.

Image Compression Manager: The image compression manager acts as an intermediary between the movie toolbox (or applications wishing direct access to compression facilities) and the various components performing specific compression or decompression services. It provides a uniform high-level interface to these services irrespective of the compression algorithm used and whether it is implemented by hardware (using a compressor board) or by software.

Component Manager: In QuickTime the term 'component' has a special meaning. A component is a piece of software with an interface of a particular form. The interface specifies the *requests* the component can handle and is identified by a four-character code called the *component type*. Clients, such as applications or the movie toolbox, can create instances of component types and then invoke the requests supported by the component. Quick-Time calls this *connecting* to the component.

Components are the key to extensibility in QuickTime. The component manager is responsible for keeping track of available components, registering new components, and allowing clients to connect to and communicate with component instances. Among the components found in QuickTime are:

- Movie controller: This component drives the standard movie controller window. Other user interfaces for QuickTime movies can be provided by replacing this component.

- Codecs: Components used to compress and decompress frames. The QuickTime 2.0 release contains codecs for each of the compression algorithms dicussed on pages 114–15. Others codecs can be added. Codecs can be entirely software-based or interfaced to compression hardware.

- Clock: A component that provides timing services, such as establishing a clock running at a certain rate. This component is used primarily by the movie toolbox.

- Grabbers and digitizers: Components used when acquiring digital video and audio data from external devices. These components, like device drivers, carry out low-level communication with devices and so are specific to particular device types or models. For instance, the manufacturer of a video digitizing board should provide a digitizer component if the board is to be QuickTime compatible.

Among a component's requests, some are needed by the component manager for housekeeping while others are intended for clients. The requests used by the component manager aid in opening and closing connections, in component registration, and in component identification. The component manager can also ask a component whether it can perform a particular request.

We now summarize QuickTime by considering it in light of the three general categories of multimedia operations introduced earlier in this chapter: configuration, composition, and activation (see Table 3.9).

QuickTime configuration operations □ Configuration operations are grouped into those for INSPECTION, for CONNECTION, and for EXTENSION. Support for configuration inspection is primarily provided by the component manager since it allows applications to determine which components have been registered and so gain information about available hardware and software. QuickTime does not explicitly support the connection of components (in the sense of establishing dataflow paths between components). Rather the routing of data is controlled by the movie toolbox in response to high-level requests from applications and the nature of the data being presented or recorded. The primary extension mechanism in QuickTime is the ability to add components.

QuickTime composition operations □ QuickTime supports TEMPORAL and SPATIAL COMPOSITION through its use of the movie format. Aggregation and placement of tracks within a movie determine their relative timing, that is, their temporal composition. Their spatial composition is specified by the 'spatial information' found in movies (in particular, the movie and track matrices and clipping atoms).

QuickTime activation operations □ The activation operations are INSTANTIATION, TUNING, and TIMING. In QuickTime, the notion corresponding to activity instantiation is called 'component connection', which in fact involves creating a component instance. Once an activity has been instantiated, its component interface provides a way of modifying its running behavior. Activity timing is under control of the movie toolbox but can be influenced by applications through the adjustment of the timebase or by modifying timing information within the movie. Events under application control can be synchronized to movie playback by using callbacks triggered by movie events (such as reaching a particular frame).

3.5 MPC/MME

MPC refers to *Multimedia PC* – an industry standard identifying the hardware and software for a multimedia platform based on the PC. MPC system software is called *MME*, or *Microsoft Multimedia Extensions*, a set of software components and services found in Windows 3.1. MME includes an API for multimedia application developers, specifications for a wide range of media types, and an extensible approach to organizing media devices which also aids application portability.

3.5.1   MPC OVERVIEW

MPC software and hardware requirements are specified by a group of vendors called the *MPC Marketing Council*. The marketing council has also developed a certification procedure allowing members to attach a special logo to their products provided compatibility conditions are met. For hardware products this means compliance with the MPC hardware requirements, for software the ability to run on an MPC platform. Thus MPC guarantees a degree of compatibility between applications and platforms. The lack of well-defined platforms has often plagued multimedia applications developers in the past but the risk of platform standards is that developers may become tied to old technology. MPC appears to be avoiding this pitfall by specifying a series of platforms, each upwardly compatible with the preceding. Currently there are two levels of MPC hardware requirements (see Table 3.10); the second specifies newer and more powerful hardware than the first.

The software development kit for Windows 3.1 includes a set of authoring tools that aid in preparing MPC titles; for example, there are tools for converting

Table 3.10 Summary of MPC hardware requirements.

	Level 1	Level 2
CPU	16 Mhz 386SX or compatible	25 Mhz 486SX or compatible
RAM	2 MB	4 MB 8 MB recommended
Magnetic storage	30 MB hard drive 1.44 MB 3.5 inch floppy	160 MB hard drive 1.44 MB 3.5 inch floppy
Optical storage	CD-ROM drive with digital audio outputs 150 KB/s sustained data transfer rate 1 s maximum average seek time	CD-ROM drive with digital audio outputs 300 KB/s sustained data transfer rate 400 ms maximum average seek time
Display	640 × 480, 8-bit color	640 × 480, 16-bit color
Audio	8-bit ADC/DAC, 11.025 kHz and 22.05 kHz sampling rate Microphone input Analog audio mixing capabilities	16-bit ADC, 11.025 kHz sampling rate (22.05 kHz and 44.1 kHz optional) 16-bit DAC, 11.025 kHz and 22.05 kHz sampling rate (44.1 kHz optional) ADPCM support recommended Microphone input Analog audio mixing capabilities
MIDI synthesizer	8-note polyphonic, multi-timbral MIDI synthesizer	8-note polyphonic, multi-timbral MIDI synthesizer
User input devices	101-key keyboard Two-button mouse	101-key keyboard Two-button mouse
I/O interfaces	MIDI IN/OUT ports Serial port Parallel port Joystick port	MIDI IN/OUT ports Serial port Parallel port Joystick port

between numerous media formats and editing image or audio data. As with the other multimedia environments considered in this chapter, we shall not cover authoring or application design. What we will discuss are the media types found in MME, and we will also consider how different media can be combined and composed. For further information on MPC and MME the reader is referred to the series of books from Microsoft (1991a–c) and Windows 3.1 documentation.

3.5.2 MME MEDIA TYPES

The designers of MME have been eclectic in their choice of media – MME contains a broad range of media types which, in many cases, are based on commonly used existing formats. The media types supported by MME include:

Audio □ MME uses the flexible 'waveform audio file format' (WAVE). There are three basic sampling frequencies (11.025, 22.05 and 44.1 kHz), two sample sizes (8 and 16 bits), and two possibilities for the number of channels (mono and stereo). The resulting data rates range from that of CD-DA (172 kB per second) to 1/16th of this, or about 11 kB per second. Both PCM and compressed representations are possible. For instance, MME supports the ADPCM algorithm of DVI (an algorithm now standardized by the Interactive Media Association, see page 146).

Music □ MME supports MIDI synthesis and recording. In addition MME incorporates the *General MIDI* extension which helps ensure device independence of MIDI data (when MIDI data is played on synthesizers adhering to General MIDI, the results should sound similar).

Image □ MME image representation is based on the *Device Independent Bitmap* (DIB) format originally defined for OS/2. DIB allows 1, 4, or 8 bits per pixel of indexed color (with indexed color, a color map, or *palette*, is used), or 24 bits per pixel true color (no palette). Applications can use image formats other than DIB; however, DIB is recommended because of its portability. The DIB format increases portability through two mechanisms. First, the format contains information about the 'importance' of color table entries (this would be provided by the image designer or image editing software; presumably important colors are those that predominate in the image). This information is useful when the display device is not capable of producing the number of colors in the image and a smaller set must be chosen. The second portability mechanism deals with target screen resolution – the DIB format identifies the desired resolution (in number of pixels per meter) at which to display the image. The application can then determine whether the image matches a particular display device (and perhaps scale the image if necessary).

Text and graphics □ MME supports a document representation known as RTF, or *Rich Text Format* (Microsoft Corp., 1987). RTF documents contain a mix of text and graphic material, and information governing their layout – paragraph styles, fonts, and so on. Document components are identified by tags coming from a simple but extensible markup language; additionally an ASCII encoding simplifies interchange of RTF documents among word processors and various document formatting systems.

Video □ Video for Windows (VfW) is a digital video framework based on MME. VfW bears many resemblances to QuickTime and so will only be described briefly. Like QuickTime, VfW supports multiple codecs and allows new codecs to be added to the framework. An example of a VfW codec is *Indeo*, a software implementation of DVI's RTV. Video for Windows provides a programming interface for video playback and recording, and specifies a file format called *AVI*, or Audio Video/Interleaved. VfW codecs are also used for the compression and decompression of DIB images and WAVE audio values.

3.5.3   MME MEDIA ORGANIZATION

MME supports the *Resource Interchange File Format* (RIFF), a flexible file format developed by IBM and Microsoft. Using RIFF, data from the MME media types can be bundled together in a single file – a system of tags allows the various parts to be recovered by applications.

RIFF files are built from *chunks*[1], each consisting of a four-character *chunk type*, followed by an integer indicating the amount of data in the chunk, and then the actual data. Chunks can contain other chunks so, in general, RIFF files are hierarchical. The root chunk has 'RIFF' as its chunk type, and the first four bytes of the data field are then reserved for a *form type*, which, like a chunk type, serves to identify the structure of the following data. RIFF is extensible since new media types can be accommodated by adding new chunk or form types. (An application encountering an unknown type would simply ignore the accompanying data.) To ensure portability of RIFF files, applications must agree on form types and chunk types. Microsoft allows developers to register types so potential clashes can be avoided. Examples of currently registered form and chunk types are given in Table 3.11.

Table 3.11   Some RIFF form and chunk types.

Form type or chunk type	Data contained in chunk
PAL	A color palette
RDIB	A DIB image
RMID	A MIDI sequence (a Standard MIDI File)
RTF	Text and graphics
WAVE	Audio samples
LIST	A list of subchunks
INFO	Information about the file (such as copyright holder, creation date, comments)

A simple example of a RIFF file is shown in Figure 3.20. Here a 200-byte MIDI sequence has been placed in a RIFF chunk. Other information, perhaps an audio segment or some images, could be added to the file by creating new chunks and then concatenating these as shown in Figure 3.21. In this case the chunks are essentially independent of each other; there is no information describing how to compose the chunks during playback. However, by defining suitable form and chunk types, composition information can be represented. For instance, it is possible to define form types for AVSS files or QuickTime movies.

---

[1] A word concerning terminology: RIFF chunks are not the same as QuickTime chunks (instead they resemble QuickTime atoms). Chunks, as used in QuickTime, have no counterpart in RIFF.

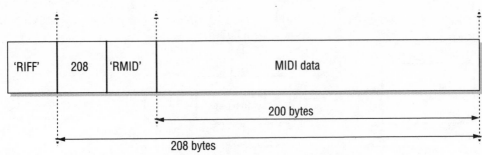

Figure 3.20 A RIFF file (the chunk type is RIFF and the form type is RMID).

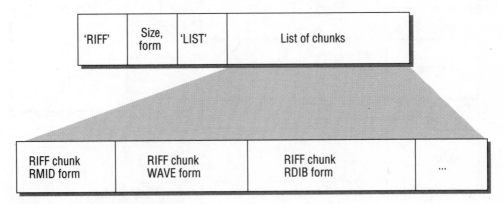

Figure 3.21 A multimedia RIFF file.

3.5.4 MPC ARCHITECTURE

In describing the architecture of MPC systems there are two points to bear in mind. First, one of the goals in designing MME was to allow for future hardware developments. This has led to an extensible environment where new kinds of hardware can be added easily. Second, the MPC specification, given at the beginning of this section, identifies only the minimal requirements for an MPC system. In addition to the hardware found in a minimal MPC system, MME supports optional devices such as videodisc players and video overlay boards (used to digitize an incoming analog video signal and display the result in a window). As a result MPC systems fall into a range of configurations, and further configurations will become possible as support for new devices is added.

One possible MPC system is shown in Figure 3.22. Here the components one would expect in a conventional PC appear towards the left-hand side while the multimedia extensions appear on the right. The extensions include the required audio and MIDI devices (in practice both of these, and the mixer, usually reside on the same board) and a CD-ROM drive. In addition some optional components are shown – a videodisc player and video overlay device, and a joystick.

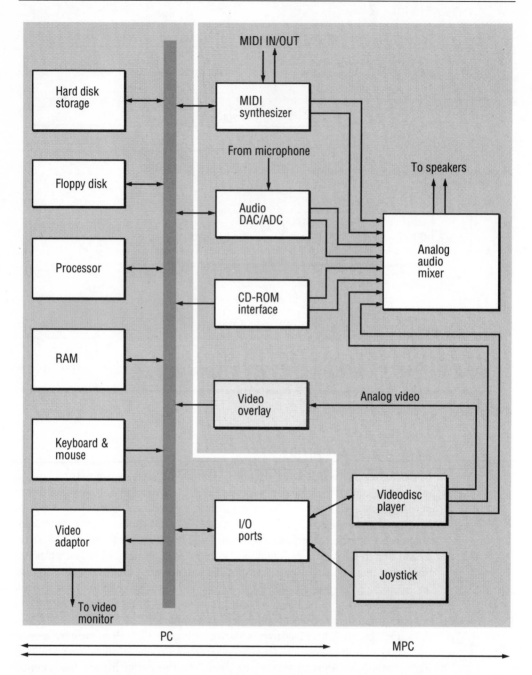

Figure 3.22   A possible MPC system and its main data/control paths (lightly shaded components are optional).

3.5.5   MME OPERATIONS

The key to MME's extensibility lies in its organization of devices and their operations. Two techniques are used: first, devices are classified into *device types* that
specify the operations supported by the device, and, second, operations are classified into various device-independent and device-specific categories. The basic
steps in adding a new device are to define its device type and then implement the
required device-independent operations and any device-specific operations.

Some MME device types are listed in Table 3.12. The shaded entries are optional device types and not available on all MPC systems. Generally a device type,
or more accurately an instance of a device type, corresponds to a piece of hardware. There are cases, however, where the device is 'emulated' by software. Devices that play back video or animation sequences fall into this category – each
player instance corresponds to a process running on the MPC processor. Software-
based devices are extremely flexible. For example, since many copies of a video
player process can be created it is possible, in principle, to play two or more video
sequences simultaneously (in practice though, playback may not proceed smoothly owing to resource contention).

Table 3.12   MME device types.

Device type	Description
cdaudio	CD audio player
dat	Digital audio tape player
digitalvideo	Displays digital video in a window
overlay	Displays analog video in a window
scanner	Image scanner
sequencer	MIDI sequencer
vcr	Video tape recorder or player
videodisc	Videodisc player
waveaudio	Digital audio player

The operations specified by MME device types are divided into three categories:

Required operation category: Every device must support these operations.
They include a capability operation, used to determine the capabilities of the
device, status and info operations which provide additional information
about the device, and open and close operations.

Basic operation category: These operations are optional, but if supported
their arguments and return values must be of a standard form. Examples include loading data onto the device and saving data from the device (called
the load and save operations), play/record/stop/pause/resume operations, a
seek operation, and a set operation for adjusting the state of the device. The
basic category also specifies a number of additional arguments for certain
required operations (in particular, the status operation).

Extended operation category: This is the device-specific category.

Operations here may apply only to the device in question, or introduce device-specific arguments to the required and basic operations.

As an example, the MME specification for the cdaudio device type is listed in Table 3.13. Here each row corresponds to an operation/argument combination and shading is used to distinguish between combinations that are basic (dark shading), required (light shading) and extended (no shading). Generally operations take a number of arguments so a device type specification must identify those that are required and those that are optional. By convention '{}' is used to enclose required arguments, '[]' to enclose optional arguments, and 'l' to indicate alternatives. Furthermore, bold face is used for literals (operation and argument names, constants) and italics for parameters which may be associated with these.

Table 3.13   The MME cdaudio device type. Shading is used to distinguish between operation/argument combinations that are basic (dark shading), required (light shading) and extended (no shading).

Operation	Arguments	Description
capability *device_name*	{ **can eject**	returns **true** or **false** (depends on **status**)
	l **can play**	returns **true** or **false** (depends on **status**)
	l **can record**	returns false
	l **can save**	returns false
	l **compound device**	returns false
	l **device type**	returns cdaudio
	l **has audio**	returns true
	l **has video**	returns false
	l **uses files** }	returns false
close *device_name*		closes the device
info *device_name*	[**product**]	returns product name and model
open *device_name*	[**alias** *device_alias*]	specifies a name to use for the device
	[**shareable**]	allows the device to be shared
	[**type** *device_type*]	used for compound devices, no effect for **cdaudio**
pause *device_name*		pauses playback (same as **stop** for **cdaudio**)
play *device_name*	[**from** *position*]	starts playback at this position
	[**to** *position*]	stops playback when *position* is reached
resume *device_name*		has no effect for **cdaudio**
seek *device_name*	[**to** *position*	moves to *position*

Table 3.13   The MME cdaudio device type. Shading is used to distinguish between operation/argument combinations that are basic (dark shading), required (light shading) and extended (no shading).

Operation	Arguments	Description
	I to start	moves to the beginning of the CD
	I to end]	moves to the end of the CD
set *device_name*	[audio all off	disables audio output
	I audio all on	enables audio output
	I audio left off	disables the left audio channel
	I audio left on	enables the left audio channel
	I audio right off	disables the right audio channel
	I audio right on	enables the right audio channel
	I video off	has no effect for **cdaudio**
	I video on]	has no effect for **cdaudio**
	[door closed	attempts to close the disc tray door
	I door open]	attempts to eject the disc
	[time format milliseconds	time is measured in milliseconds
	I time format ms	time is measured in milliseconds
	I time format msf	time is measured in minutes/seconds/frames
	I time format tmsf]	time is measured in tracks/minutes/seconds/frames
status *device_name*	{ current track	returns number of current track
	I length	returns duration of disc
	I length track *track_number*	returns duration of *track_number*
	I media present	returns **true** or **false** (depends on whether a disc has been inserted)
	I mode	returns one of **not ready, open, paused, playing, seeking,** or **stopped**
	I number of tracks	returns number of tracks on disc
	I position	returns current position
	I position track *track_number*	returns starting postion of *track_number*
	I ready	returns **true** or **false** (depends on whether a disc has been inserted and the door closed)
	I start position	returns starting position of disc
	I time format }	returns current time format
stop *device_name*		stops playback

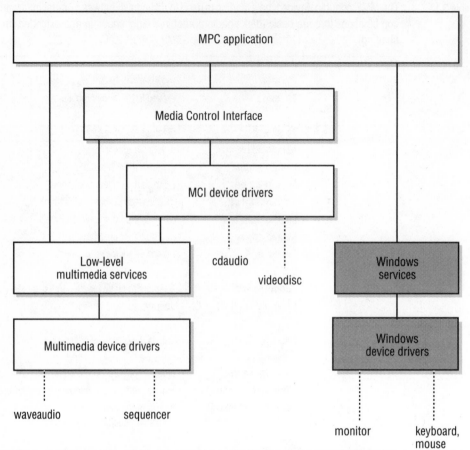

Figure 3.23   MME software environment. MME components are shown unshaded, Microsoft Windows components are shaded. Examples of devices are shown in italics.

Looking at the cdaudio specification, one can see that the only extensions provided by this type are two arguments to the set operation and the media present argument for the status operation. However, cdaudio is a relatively simple example and the other MME device types make more use of device-specific extensions.

The device type abstraction is made available to application programs by what is known as the *Media Control Interface* (or MCI), see Figure 3.23. A description of this, and other components of the MME software environment, follows:

MPC application: MPC applications, or 'titles', have available two interfaces to the multimedia environment: a high-level interface provided by MCI, and a low-level interface requiring greater involvement in I/O operations, buffer management, and timing. Applications also use callbacks to respond to events (called messages in MME) generated by the environment. Examples of events are a play operation ending and a period of time elapsing.

Media Control Interface: The MCI supports the device type abstraction. Applications can invoke operations on devices either by sending parameterized events (essentially data structures) to the MCI or by sending textual command strings. The two methods are equivalent, so choosing which to use is a question of programming convenience. Examples of command strings (comments have been added for clarity) are:

```
open videodisc alias vsrc  // open a videodisc, use vsrc as device name
set vsrc time format hms   // measure time in hours/minutes/seconds
seek vsrc to 0:10:00       // position at the 10th minute
play vsrc speed 120        // play at 120 frames/second
```

When invoking a device operation the application can choose to wait until completion or to proceed asynchronously – in which case it can also request that a notification event be generated on completion.

In addition to acting as an intermediary between applications and devices, the MCI performs a small number of system operations. The most notable among these is sysinfo, which, given a device type, allows applications to determine the number of instances of the type present, their names, and which instances are currently open.

MCI device drivers: Every multimedia device has an MCI device driver responsible for converting MCI operations to a form the device understands and sending this information to the device. Devices (and MCI device drivers) can be divided into two main groups. First, there are devices incapable of exchanging media data directly with an application (here 'directly' means without the aid of another device). VCRs and videodisc players fall into this category – since to actually obtain video data from a video tape or videodisc, another device, a digitizer, is needed. For such devices the MPC plays the role of an elaborate remote control mechanism; it only exchanges control information with the device, and only needs an MCI driver. Devices in the second category are capable of exchanging data with the application and require a multimedia device driver (see below). An MCI driver is still present but it communicates with a lower-level driver rather than with the device directly.

Low-level multimedia services: Multimedia services include extended file I/O services (such as support for RIFF files, buffered file I/O and memory files), timer services (such as requesting timer events to be generated at specific times), and low-level interfaces to those devices capable of exchanging media data with applications.

Multimedia device drivers: Certain devices, for instance the MIDI sequencer, the digital audio player, and the VfW player, allow applications to read or write media data (or, and it amounts to the same, to save and load media data). A low-level device driver is needed for such devices; it is responsible for communication with the device hardware, or the software emulating the device.

In summary, MPC applications can use the device type abstraction as provided by MCI, or use the lower-level multimedia services (it is also possible to work at both levels). The operations provided in each case are similar; the difference is the degree of control. We now discuss MME in terms of the three general categories of multimedia operations introduced earlier in this chapter: configuration, composition, and activation (see Table 3.9).

MME configuration operations □ Configuration operations are grouped into INSPECTION, CONNECTION, and EXTENSION. Very general support for inspection is provided by the MCI sysinfo and capability operations. Connection is not explicitly supported, other than the ability to control the analog audio mixer (which, in effect, connects different audio sources to the external speakers). Extension is possible through adding codecs to Video for Windows, adding chunk and form types to RIFF files, and adding device types to MCI.

MME composition operations □ Generally MME does not directly support TEMPORAL and SPATIAL COMPOSITION; this is left to specific devices and applications. An example of composition provided by applications is Video for Windows and the AVI file format (temporal composition of audio and video).

MME activation operations □ Two groups of activation operations, INSTANTIATION and TUNING, are directly supported by MME. Activity instantiation occurs when an MCI play or record operation is issued; modification is provided by the set operation. For the third group, TIMING, there is less complete support. A certain degree of synchronization is possible using the existing event notification mechanism. Fine-grain synchronization, for instance synchronizing movie playback with playback of a DAT recording, is more difficult. The generation of time code events is required (for instance, the MIDI sequencer should generate events as it encounters MIDI Time Code commands, video devices should generate events corresponding to SMPTE Time Code), and also a way of locking devices to a source of these events. Admittedly though, this could require changes to the MPC hardware specifications in addition to the software environment.

3.6 DIRECTOR

CD-i, DVI, QuickTime, and MPC/MME have no built-in media type for animation. Since we have not yet seen an example of animation we will briefly look at an authoring system, which, because of the presence of a powerful scripting language, can also be considered a multimedia programming environment. The example we will look at is *MacroMind Director* (MacroMind Inc., 1991), a popular authoring tool that runs on the Macintosh. Director is used to create interactive 'movies' for several platforms – there is both a player for the Macintosh and an MPC compatible player for Director movies.

A Director movie can contain audio, video, image, music, text, and graphics elements. Yet the focus is on animation – essentially a Director movie is a sequence of structured frames, each frame containing layered visual elements, the so-called 'castmembers'. During playback, a sequence of images is produced by rendering and composing the castmembers in each frame. This matches the definition of an 'animation media type' as a model that evolves and is rendered to produce an image sequence.

The model underlying a Director movie is called its *score,* a two-dimensional grid-like structure specifying the layout and timing of all movie elements. An example of a score grid is shown in Figure 3.24. Entries within the grid are called *cells.* Columns of cells correspond to frames of the model, and they are ordered in the score such that time progresses from left to right. Rows of cells are called *channels.* There are various kinds of channels, not all of which need be used; running down the rows in Figure 3.24, the channels appearing in a score are:

Tempo channel: Cells in the tempo channel (indicated by the clock icon) contain timing instructions. For instance, the tempo cell of frame #11 (the last column in the score) specifies a 3-second delay.

Palette channel: The palette channel manipulates the color maps used during frame rendering. In Figure 3.24, the palette cell for frame #11 indicates that the 'system' color map is to be cycled.

Transition channel: This channel specifies visual transitions, such as fades and wipes.

Sound channels: There are two channels used to identify sounds produced during playback. Sounds include digital audio segments, MIDI sequences, and speech synthesized from text.

Script channel: The script channel supports interactivity and other complex behavior. Scripts are sequences of commands written in a high-level language called *Lingo*; they are identified by unique script numbers. A script may be attached to a particular frame, in which case the number of the script appears in the frame's script channel. As a simple example, the following script detects a mouse click and then instructs the movie player to go to the frame labelled p2 (which is frame #10 in Figure 3.24):

```
on mouseUp
        go to "p2"
end mouseUp
```

Lingo contains a large number of built-in functions for handling user input and manipulating movie elements. In addition, 'external functions', written in a programming language such as C or Pascal, can be made accessible from within Lingo scripts. External functions allow Lingo scripts to communicate with and control external devices (for instance, videodisc players or audio boards) and external software systems (for instance, remote database servers).

Animation channels: The score in Figure 3.24 shows three animation channels, but many more may be used. Animation cells specify the rendering of visual castmembers. Among the information present in an animation cell are

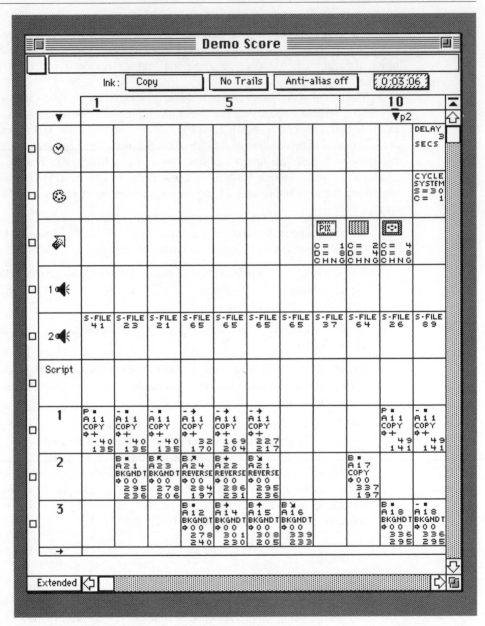

Figure 3.24   Score window produced by MacroMind Director.

the castmember number (like scripts, castmembers have unique identifiers), its type (possibilities include image, graphics, and text), the position where the castmember is to be rendered, and the *ink effect* to use while rendering.

A player for Director movies is essentially a score interpreter. During playback it successively generates frame images and displays these in a 'stage' window; it should also execute scripts and perform any actions specified in the tempo, palette, transition, and sound channels. The key step is rendering animation cells. The basic procedure is to start with the cell in the first animation channel and then overlay those from succeeding channels. One can think of the animation channels as being ordered from background to foreground. Often the castmember from one cell will overlap castmembers from earlier cells. Here the upper cell's 'ink effect' is crucial in determining the result. Possible ink effects include making the castmember opaque or partially transparent.

Although Director is a higher-level environment than the others discussed in this chapter, the classification scheme for multimedia operations (see Table 3.9) would still seem to apply. Examples of the various operation categories – configuration, composition, and activation – can all be found in Director. Composition, both spatial and temporal, is particularly well supported, but perhaps a weakness of Director and Lingo is to be found in the area of activities and synchronization.

3.7 STANDARDS FOR MULTIMEDIA

Standards are crucial to promoting multimedia – in the absence of standards, developers are not sure of stable platforms or accepted data formats and risk producing software and other products with little market value. Because of extensive commercial interest in the communications, computer, and entertainment industries, there are many groups involved in standards and many sides to basic issues. For example: should standards focus on data formats, or also include presentation platforms? Is it too early to standardize, or would even premature standards be a boon to multimedia development? and who should formulate standards, the traditional standards bodies or newly formed manufacturers' and users' groups?

Multimedia standards should incorporate existing single-media standards and conventions, but go beyond these and address how different media can be combined and interrelated. Important issues include data representation, exchange of multimedia information, and presentation platforms. We now discuss several activities that show what form multimedia standards may take. A more extensive list, containing both multimedia and media-specific standards, is presented by Adie (1993).

HyTime □ HyTime refers to an ISO standard, the *Hypermedia/Time-based Structuring Language* (Markey, 1991; Newcomb, 1991; ISO, 1992a; Koegel *et al*, 1993), which is in turn an application of SGML, the document markup language. In SGML, users define document types that reflect the structure of their documents, for example the US Department of Defense has defined an SGML document type for online manuals. HyTime specifies a group of building blocks (called 'architectural forms') that can appear in SGML document type definitions. The result, a HyTime-compliant document type, allows the structuring of multimedia and hypermedia information. For instance, coordinate systems can be established and used for the layout and timing of components, and a rich linking mechanism is available, allowing documents to contain links between elements of different media. HyTime is particularly suited for time-based documents, those where components have a temporal nature – music scores and animation sequences are examples.

MHEG □   MHEG is the abbreviation of *Multimedia and Hypermedia Information Coding Experts Group*, an ISO working group that is developing a standard for representing multimedia information. This group's proposal, known as the MHEG standard (Markey, 1991; ISO 1992b; Price, 1993), is not yet complete but the focus is clearly on structuring and linking components of different media. MHEG specifies a coding for what it calls multimedia objects. The objects are built from text, graphics, audio, image, or video components and can contain links to other multimedia objects. The MHEG coding provides mechanisms for representing dynamics and interactivity. These mechanisms include links with triggerable actions, and interaction objects such as menus and buttons. MHEG implementations are likely to be based on an 'MHEG engine' – a software component which responds to user input and coordinates the presentation of MHEG objects. For example, a collection of MHEG objects placed on a CD-ROM could be browsed though and presented by an MHEG engine reading the CD. MHEG coding is suitable for situations like this, where information has been prepared and is stored ready for presentation. MHEG is not intended for authoring or other applications that require extensive editing of multimedia information.

PREMO and HyperODA □   PREMO (Stenzel *et al.*, 1994) is a proposed ISO standard addressing presentation techniques for multimedia information. It focuses on the configuration, extension, and distribution of flexible presentation environments. HyperODA (ISO, 1993) extends the earlier ODA document standard by adding support for hypermedia and temporal relationships.

IMA □   The *Interactive Multimedia Association*, or IMA, is a trade association with over 200 members, primarily coming from the computer and entertainment industries. The goal of the IMA is to promote the use of multimedia technology. To this end it acts as a forum allowing industrial groups to meet and explore relevant issues. Noticeably it is sponsoring a 'Compatibility Project' with the explicit aim of encouraging interoperability among multimedia hardware and software vendors. One result has been the Recommended Practices for Multimedia Portability (Interactive Multimedia Assoc., 1991), which, like MCI (see Section 3.5) deals with interfaces to multimedia devices and services. Other areas being addressed by the Compatibility Project include data formats and platform architectures.

OMF □ The *Open Media Framework*, or OMF, is a group of media system vendors including animation software companies and broadcast equipment manufacturers. The OMF was founded by Avid, a company known for its nonlinear video editing systems. The goal of the OMF is to foster interchange of digital media among different products by developing formats for data exchange and storage. In doing so the OMF seeks to apply an open-systems approach to the hardware and software used for video and film production. In comparison to the IMA, the OMF is more concerned with high-end equipment and formats; however, the two organizations do cooperate and the IMA has recently approved a data exchange format submitted by the OMF.

PART II

4

OBJECT-ORIENTED MULTIMEDIA

4.1 Why objects?
4.2 Objects, classes, and related terms
4.3 Multimedia frameworks
4.4 A note on C++
4.5 An example class hierarchy

The previous chapters have described the forms of media data and the characteristics of platforms used for interactive multimedia applications. This chapter returns to the goal of the book, which is to identify software abstractions for multimedia programming. The approach we follow, called object-oriented multimedia, models media types, their properties and operations, using the techniques of object-oriented programming. This gives a set of building blocks, known as *classes*, that can be incorporated into programs directly or extended to provide further functionality.

4.1 WHY OBJECTS?

Object-oriented multimedia seems almost inevitable. Several of the environments mentioned in Chapter 3 have object-oriented features and there is a wealth of literature on object-oriented graphics – see, for example, Wisskirchen (1990). Object-oriented techniques have also been used for image, music, and animation software and, most recently, for video (NeXT Inc., 1992; Schnorf, 1993). There appears to be a natural fit between multimedia programming on one hand and object-oriented programming languages on the other. Some reasons for this affinity include:

Encapsulation □ Multimedia programmers face a challenging environment. First, concepts from many areas, including audio recording, video production, animation, and music, appear but are novel to many programmers and not normally part of their training. Second, multimedia applications often involve special hardware with idiosyncratic interfaces and operating procedures. One of the strengths of object-oriented programming is its ability to encapsulate information and help shield programmers from many of the details of particular media and pieces of hardware.

Modularity □ The equipment used in audio and video studios relies to a larger and larger extent on digital technology. The result is that entire product lines, from video and audio mixers to editing suites and special effects devices, are becoming programmable and more interconnectable. At the same time, the media processing functionality of studios is moving to the desktop and becoming available to applications running on personal computers. Object-oriented programming is well suited to capturing the complex interfaces of media processing services in a modular form which is easy for application developers to use.

Extensibility □ Unlike more established areas, the requirements and the nature of multimedia applications are evolving and far from stable. Database systems for multimedia, virtual environments, desktop conferencing systems, and other applications should be able to adapt to changes in interface technology, media formats, and hardware platforms. Object-oriented programming addresses the need for extensibility by offering mechanisms for enhancing and extending existing code.

Portability and cross-platform development □ Ideally multimedia applications should run on different platforms and tolerate hardware variations within platforms. Porting from one platform to another, or adding support for a new piece of hardware, should not require rewriting the application. Object-oriented interfaces can make platform dependencies more explicit and so simplify both cross-platform development and development targeted for heterogeneous platforms.

Software legacy □ A final reason for the affinity between object-oriented languages and multimedia programming is that multimedia applications are still in their infancy. Many software developers face a *legacy* problem – the need to maintain compatibility with earlier applications, but multimedia presents the opportunity to start with (at least nearly) a clean slate. Since the design of multimedia applications is less constrained by existing software, developers are relatively free to exploit new techniques such as object-oriented programming languages.

4.2 OBJECTS, CLASSES, AND RELATED TERMS

Many object-oriented programming languages, including Smalltalk, C++, Objective C and Eiffel, have taken their place among the languages used for commercial applications and software product development. While there are notable differences between these languages, in particular the extent to which compile-time type checking is used to detect errors, they share several underlying concepts. An extensive survey of the conceptual foundations of object-oriented programming is found in Wegner (1990). The purpose of this section is to review many of these key concepts. This section should familiarize the reader with the vocabulary of object-oriented technology, but is not intended to serve as a guide in applying or using the technology. Information of this nature can be found in the many textbooks on object-oriented programming and object-oriented design (Meyer, 1988; Wirfs-Brock *et al.*, 1990).

Objects, instance variables and methods □ It is frequently said that objects encapsulate both state and behavior. More specifically, an object is a programming language construct that identifies a collection of data items plus a collection of operations. The data items are called the object's instance variables and the operations its methods. As an example, consider an object named myCdPlayer[1] with an instance variable named currentTrack. A method for this object might be PlayTrack(trackNumber). Invoking a method can be visualized as sending a message to an object; the message contains both the method name and any arguments needed by the method. The syntax of method invocation differs from one language to another, but a common form is to append the method name after the object name as in myCdPlayer.PlayTrack(4). The result of invoking a method often leads to a change in the object's state. For example, executing myCdPlayer.PlayTrack(4) will set the currentTrack instance variable to the value 4 (assuming no error takes place). In general an object's methods specify allowable operations on the object and so serve as an interface to the object. In many object-oriented programming languages, methods are meant to be the *only* interface by which objects are manipulated (in which case it is not possible to bypass methods and modify an object's instance variables directly).

Classes, types, and signatures □ Applications often require many objects of similar form – objects that have the same instance variables and identical methods.

[1.] This chapter uses a sans-serif font (Helvetica Narrow) for all programming examples. Class and method names begin in upper case while names of objects and instance variables begin in lower case.

A class is a specification of common properties of objects: it specifies their instance variables and their methods, and possibly provides implementations for the methods. A class resembles a 'template' (Wegner, 1990) for creating objects. Objects belonging to a class are called its instances, and creating a new object of a class is called instantiation. For example, objects representing compact disc players could be instantiated from a class called CdPlayer. The definition of this class would specify PlayTrack and currentTrack and other methods or instance variables possessed by all CdPlayer objects. Class definitions may also specify type information, such as the types of instance variables and the types of arguments and return values of methods. What constitutes a type varies from language to language but is likely to include basic data types and user-defined classes. Another useful concept is that of a method signature, which is essentially the name of a method plus the type of its arguments and return value.

Class variables and class methods □ While objects belonging to the same class have similar instance variables, the values for these variables differ from object to object. Class variables, on the other hand, have the same value for all members of a class. One use of class variables is to aid in modelling constraints. For example, the engineering specifications for CD discs state that a disc can have no more than 99 tracks. Should this value be needed by the CdPlayer class, it is natural to assign it to a class variable such as maxTrack. Class methods are invoked by messages sent to classes rather than instances. A standard example is the method that creates a new object. As an example, the CdPlayer object might be created by an expression of the form CdPlayer.New. Here New is a class method, so the name appearing to the left of the '.' is a class name, not an object name.

Single and multiple inheritance □ Inheritance is a central feature of object-oriented languages, and is an important technique for reusing class definitions and their implementations. Inheritance takes place in the context of subclass/superclass relationships between classes. A subclass inherits methods and instance variables from its superclasses – both its immediate 'parent' superclasses and their superclasses in turn. Languages supporting single inheritance allow a subclass to have a single parent superclass, while with multiple inheritance many parents are possible. As an example, consider a new 'Model X' player produced by a manufacturer of CD players. A subclass of CdPlayer, named ModelXCdPlayer, can then be specified. ModelXCdPlayer will inherit PlayTrack and other methods of CdPlayer (and its superclasses); it may also introduce methods only relevant to Model X players or provide alternative implementations for inherited methods.

Abstract classes, concrete classes, virtual methods, and dynamic binding □ Abstract classes group together methods and instance variables shared by several subclasses, but their definition is incomplete in the sense that method implementation is, at least partially, deferred to the subclasses. In comparison concrete classes are fully defined. A deferred method, or one whose implementation is overridden by a subclass, is called a virtual method. Languages that allow virtual methods require dynamic binding, the ability to link at runtime to the code providing a method's implementation. As an example, suppose CdPlayer is an abstract class with two concrete subclasses, ModelXCdPlayer and ModelYCdPlayer. If different manufacturers' CD players differ in how they are controlled then the PlayTrack method can be declared as a virtual method of CdPlayer and its implementation deferred to ModelXCdPlayer and ModelYCdPlayer. At runtime, an expression such as myCdPlayer.PlayTrack(4) will require dynamic binding so that the appropriate implementation of PlayTrack is selected (depending upon whether myCdPlayer is an instance of ModelXCdPlayer or ModelYCdPlayer).

Polymorphisn: □ Dynamic binding and inheritance result in polymorphic functions, functions that can be applied to objects of different types. This is seen in the above example where the method PlayTrack can be used with both ModelXCdPlayer and ModelYCdPlayer objects. Polymorphic functions are in a sense open-ended since they may extended for use in new contexts; this helps in designing extensible software. However it is possible to overuse polymorphism, as when the same name is used in too many contexts and its meaning becomes unclear.

Delegation and prototypes □ One disadvantage of classes is that they can be too rigid in determining the behavior of objects. Changing environments, where object behavior and structure are uncertain, need flexibility. One alternative is to do away with classes and allow objects to delegate methods to other objects. This technique is used in conjunction with prototype objects that provide default behavior. As an example, suppose the two objects protoModelXCdPlayer and protoModelYCdPlayer serve as repositories for the default behavior of Model X and Model Y CD players. A method invocation such as myCdPlayer.PlayTrack(4) would then pass control to one of these prototype objects – which prototype is chosen is entirely up to myCdPlayer. Because objects can choose (and change) to whom they delegate methods, there is the potential for a high degree of flexibility and adaptation in object behavior.

Active objects □ Active objects, like ordinary or passive objects, have state (instance variables) and behavior (methods). In addition, an active object may spontaneously perform actions, even when no messages are sent to the object. Again consider the CD player object as an example. After starting a CD player and directing it to play a track, as in myCdPlayer.PlayTrack(4), the object continues to transfer audio data from the CD disc to digital-to-analog converters until the disc ends or some other event occurs such as receiving a myCdPlayer.Stop( ) message. Active objects introduce concurrency to applications. For instance, the following plays two tracks simultaneously:

```
myCdPlayer.PlayTrack(4);        // myCdPlayer starts to play
yourCdPlayer.PlayTrack(7);      // myCdPlayer continues playing, yourCdPlayer
                                //    starts to play
myCdPlayer.Stop( );             // myCdPlayer stops, yourCdPlayer continues
                                //    playing
yourCdPlayer.Stop( );           // both players are stopped
```

Here there is true concurrency (assuming that myCdPlayer and yourCdPlayer represent actual physical devices). It is also possible that active objects encapsulate software processes, in which case there is 'quasi-concurrency' (where, assuming a single processor, what appears to be concurrency is brought about through sharing the processor among the active objects). Whether active objects provide true or quasi-concurrency will depend on their implementation. Furthermore, by reimplementing a class, active objects can be 'moved' from hardware to software (or in the other direction) without impacting the interface seen by application programmers. Thus some subclasses of CdPlayer may represent particular models of real CD players, while other CdPlayer subclasses could be based on the emulation of CD players in software. An application programmer using only the methods from the CdPlayer class need not be aware of whether CdPlayer instances correspond to real CD players or software processes.

Persistent objects □ The objects created by a program written in an object-oriented language are usually stored in transient data structures. An object may represent a real-world entity, or even communicate with the external world (as when a CdPlayer object sends commands to a CD player), but once the program ends the storage is released and the object disappears. Subsequent programs can recreate the object, but it is their responsibility to ensure that the object's state is correctly restored. Persistent objects, on the other hand, outlive applications or program executions. Non-volatile storage, whether a simple file system, an object management system, or a full-fledged database system, is used to save object state. Support for persistence can be deeply ingrained within an object-oriented language, in which case storage and retrieval of objects is transparent to the programmer. Otherwise objects require explicit 'exporting' and 'importing' to and from storage.

Distributed object environments □ Environments supporting objects located on different processors (hosts) are a further extension to object-oriented technology. These environments coordinate communication between local and remote objects and provide facilities for naming and finding objects. Other important services include authorization control (such as determining if one object has permission to invoke methods of another) and shielding applications from host heterogeneity (for instance, hosts may differ in the bit and byte ordering used to represent integers). Both authorization control and heterogeneity are particularly important when hosts are connected by large, open, wide area networks. Distributed object environments are not yet widely available but are the subject of much industrial and standards-related activity; see Nicol *et al.* (1993) for an overview. As a simple example of how such environments could be used for multimedia programming, consider the expression yourCdPlayer.PlayTrack(4). Using a distributed object environment, yourCdPlayer could be located on any of the connected hosts. When the PlayTrack method for yourCdPlayer is invoked, a message is sent across the network and directed to the remote object. The transfer of the message and the reply are transparent to the application, which can be constructed as if yourCdPlayer were a local object.

Class frameworks □ Class frameworks are groups of classes that work together in a variety of situations. A more precise and widely used definition is:

a framework is a set of classes that embodies an abstract design for so-
lutions to a family of related problems (Johnson and Foote, 1988).

Typically frameworks consist of abstract classes, serving to specify interfaces,
and suggested procedures (often informal) for using the classes. A standard example is the MVC framework found in Smalltalk-80. Here three abstract classes,
Model, View, and Controller help construct interactive applications: Model objects
represent application state, View objects produce visualizations of Model objects,
and Controller objects determine how Model and View objects respond to user input
events. A particular application is constructed largely by implementing Model,
View, and Controller subclasses. For example, a text editor could be based on Text-
DocumentModel, TextDocumentView, and TextDocumentController classes; these
would implement the methods of the abstract MVC classes in the context of modelling, viewing, and editing text documents. Further examples of frameworks are
presented by Deutsch (1989) and Johnson and Wirfs-Brock (1991).

4.3 MULTIMEDIA FRAMEWORKS

A compelling way of applying the ideas of object orientation to multimedia programming is to construct a framework encompassing the essential objects and operations that appear in multimedia applications. One can imagine the framework
as consisting of interrelated abstract classes which are tailored and specialized for
different multimedia platforms. Applications using the abstract classes adapt to
variations in platform performance and functionality, and so are highly portable.
Helping applications adapt to new platforms is an important goal since platforms
continually evolve as hardware improves and new standards are proposed.

A highly schematic and idealized view of the process of framework specialization is shown in Figure 4.1. Here the abstract classes of the framework present
an application programming interface, or API, that is available on multiple platforms. Each platform, a combination of hardware and operating system software,
offers a variety of low-level services through a platform-dependent systems programming interface. Examples of these services include scheduling and synchronization mechanisms for real-time processes, storage formats and storage access
operations, and network protocols for transferring audio and video data. When the
framework is specialized, concrete classes are introduced to implement the API
for the platform in question.

The API, the classes, both concrete and abstract, and the platform together
form a specific multimedia programming environment. Applications using the
API can be ported from one environment to another (see Figure 4.2) and so are
independent of the underlying platform.

The scenario just described is extremely simplified and in practice, unless
platform choices are constrained, application portability is likely to be limited.
Factors hindering portability include the following. First, platforms need not offer
the same capabilities and so certain parts of the API may be supported on some
platforms but not others. Second, the performance of platforms differs so certain

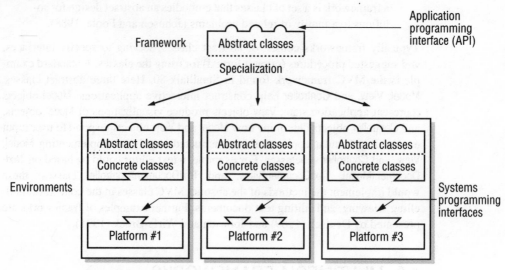

Figure 4.1   Specializing a framework.

operations may be feasible on some platforms but not on others. Third, it may be possible for applications to bypass the API and access platform-dependent interfaces. Finally, there is no consensus on system-level support for multimedia programming; instead the design of network and operating system services is currently an active research area. Since there can be great variation in the lower-level services, it may turn out that the objects and operations of the framework are inappropriate or inefficient for some platforms. So in summary, perhaps the most that can be said is that multimedia frameworks encourage, but do not guarantee, portability.

A framework, like any good programming library, should be robust, well-documented, and complete. Other requirements, more related to multimedia programming, include:

> *Economy of concepts:* A multimedia framework should be based on a small number of concepts, otherwise there is the danger of it becoming a maze of media-specific details. It is particularly important to identify any general concepts that apply across media types.

> *Open:* It should be possible to extend a multimedia framework to incorporate new media types, new data representations, and new hardware capabilities as they become available.

> *Queryable:* A multimedia framework should specify interfaces for querying environments concerning their capabilities. Applications can then recognize missing functionality and adapt their behavior.

> *Distribution:* A multimedia framework should help partition applications in a way that facilitates distribution. In particular, the objects within the framework should correspond to easy-to-distribute units or subsystems. Many

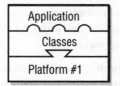
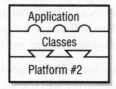
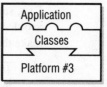

Figure 4.2   Platform independence.

future multimedia applications are likely to be distributed, so the utility of a framework is greatly diminished if it conflicts with distribution.

Scalable: A multimedia framework should support scalable media representations. Once media are in digital form, improvements in quality and capability are tied to advances in hardware. To take one example, an early version of a processor might handle digital video at quarter-screen resolution and a few frames per second, while the next version is capable of full-screen resolution and 30 frames per second. If media representations are scalable, applications can increase quality as platform performance increases.

High-level interfaces: A multimedia framework should provide high-level interfaces for media synchronization, media composition, device control, database integration, and concurrent media processing activities. These operations are central to multimedia programming, so development is simplified if easy to use high-level interfaces are available.

These requirements are very general, but they refer to multimedia frameworks rather than environments. When a framework is extended and specialized for a particular application platform, further, more specific, requirements emerge. For instance, there may be the need to support certain data formats or certain pieces of hardware. In satisfying such 'second generation' requirements, it is particularly important that the framework be designed to be open and extensible in the first place.

4.4 A NOTE ON C++

The following chapters describe the *design* of a set of classes in C++ (Ellis and Stroustrup, 1990; Stroustrup, 1991), a widely used object-oriented programming language. It may appear surprising that a programming language is used for design when a variety of high-level modelling techniques are available. There are two reasons for the choice of C++. First, C++ is probably more well known than any of the notations for object-oriented design. Second, this is a book on multimedia programming, and although classes and methods are not fully specified, we still want to give examples in code showing how the proposed classes could be used.

C++ can be difficult to read for those unfamiliar with its syntax and features. Furthermore, the static type-checking of C++ is constraining when the language is used for design. To reduce these problems, many of the advanced features of C++, such as user-defined operators, multiple inheritance, and templates will be avoided and we will take a few minor liberties with C++ syntax. In particular, we make the following changes and simplifications:

Terminology: The terminology of C++ differs from other object-oriented languages. We will use the more traditional and intuitive terminology derived from Smalltalk. There is a simple mapping from one to the other as shown below:

C++	Used here
Class	Class
Object	Object, instance
Data member	Instance variable
Static data member	Class variable
Member function	Method
Static member function	Class method
Virtual function	Virtual method
Base class	Superclass
Derived class	Subclass

Dynamic binding: In C++ dynamically bound methods are called 'virtual functions'; they allow a subclass to override a superclass method (and can be identifed by use of the virtual keyword in a class declaration). However, the signature of a virtual function as it appears in the subclass must match that in the superclass. We will weaken this requirement and allow subclasses to specialize the arguments (and return value) of virtual functions.

Abstract classes: In C++ abstract classes are identified by the presence of a 'pure virtual function' in their class declaration. Here we indicate an abstract class simply by placing the keyword abstract at the beginning of the declaration.

Type-checking: C++ distinguishes between method arguments and identifiers that are either objects, references to objects, or pointers to objects. Also arguments and identifiers may be declared as constant or volatile. These nuances are important for the performance of C++ programs and for getting the most out of the type-checker, but lead to unnecessary detail at the design phase and so are ignored here.

Virtual class methods: C++ does not have virtual class methods. Here virtual class methods are used and indicate that subclasses must provide a class method with the same name.

Sets: C++ does not have a built-in set constructor. Here the keyword setOf indicates set-valued arguments or identifiers.

4.5 AN EXAMPLE CLASS HIERARCHY

We conclude by giving an example of class definitions in the form used in the remaining chapters. The lines have been numbered for convenience.

```
1.        abstract class AudioPlayer { };
2.        abstract class CdPlayer : public AudioPlayer {
3.        public:
4.        static      int                        maxTrack;
5.                    int                        currentTrack;
6.                    virtual void               PlayTrack(int trackNumber);
7.                    // other methods ...
8.        };
```

The first line defines an abstract class called AudioPlayer, which has no methods or instance variables. Line 2 indicates that a second abstract class is being defined; the name of the class is CdPlayer and it is a subclass of AudioPlayer. Line 3 indicates that the following methods and instance variables belong to the 'public' interface to CdPlayer (and so are available for use outside the implementation of the class). Line 4 then declares a class variable (indicated by the static keyword) and line 5 an instance variable; both are integers. Line 6 declares a virtual method, which has no return value (indicated by void) and an integer-valued method argument. Line 7 is a comment and line 8 ends the definition of CdPlayer.

This section of code only defines interfaces, it does not provide an implementation. Both CdPlayer and AudioPlayer are abstract and implementation (of the PlayTrack method, for example) is deferred to subclasses.

5

A MULTIMEDIA FRAMEWORK

5.1 Framework overview

5.2 Media classes

5.3 Transform classes

5.4 Format classes

5.5 Component classes

5.6 An application – 'Hello World: The Video'

5.7 Framework summary

Class frameworks specify interfaces, leaving open their implementation. By adding new classes through specialization the interfaces can be extended; this ability makes frameworks well suited to constructing open-ended software environments. For example, a multimedia framework might contain two abstract classes, *Video* and *VideoProcessingComponent*, intended for representing video values and the software or hardware components that process video values. The interfaces to these classes can then be specified without concern for the details of particular video representations or processing components. Support for specific representations and components is achieved by implementing concrete subclasses of *Video* and *VideoProcessingComponent*.

This chapter explores one possible framework for multimedia programming. Other examples are found in *NeXTStep*, the *Andrew Toolkit*, recent industrial proposals for multimedia system services (Interactive Multimedia Assoc., 1994), and as parts of large new application frameworks (Udell, 1994). While not as fully specified as the others, the framework described here is relatively compact and intended to be easy to extend. This chapter focuses on the structure and organization of the framework, including questions of what classes are needed and how the inheritance hierarchy is arranged. The presentation is somewhat informal, since classes and methods are not completely specified. However, in several places code fragments will be used to illustrate various features. In essence this chapter follows a top-down approach where media are considered *collectively*. This differs from the more usual bottom-up approach that treats media in isolation, resulting in media-specific environments.

The framework has been heavily influenced by existing environments and research in multimedia programming. In particular, the central notion of components and component connection (discussed in Section 5.5) appears in AVK's 'digital production studio' model, QuickTime's component model, and numerous research efforts – for instance, Angebranndt *et al.* (1991), Gibbs (1991), Northcutt and Kuerner (1991), and Blair *et al.* (1992). This widespread use of 'components' suggests their role as a fundamental abstraction for multimedia programming.

5.1   FRAMEWORK OVERVIEW

The multimedia framework comprises what may first appear to be a large number of unrelated classes and methods. There is, however, an overall structure and the classes fall into four distinct groups – *media classes*, *transform classes*, *format classes* and *component classes*. Each of the four groups will be covered in a separate section. In essence, media classes correspond to audio, video, and the other media types; transform classes represent media operations in a flexible and extensible manner; format classes deal with external representations of media data; and components represent the devices and processes that modify media data. As the classes are introduced and the class machinery is built up, the design of the framework will be motivated by a series of examples that become progressively more elaborate.

5.2 MEDIA CLASSES

Following the classification of Chapter 2, media are divided into types; each type
is represented by a class. These are called *media classes* and form the hierarchy
shown in Figure 5.1.

Note to the Reader

In diagrams of class hierarchies used in this chapter, nodes depict classes
and edges depict superclass/subclass relationships. An edge points from
the superclass to the subclass. Shading is used to differentiate between
abstract classes (no shading) and concrete classes (shaded). Generally,
abstract classes are defined by the framework while concrete classes are
extensions of the framework for particular environments and platforms.

Instances of media classes are called *media objects*. A media object consists of a
descriptor and a *media value*. Descriptors bundle together attributes of media objects such as their size and date of creation, while media values correspond to the
actual data used to represent artifacts (recall the discussion of media data and media artifacts in Chapter 1). The relationship between media objects, descriptors,
media values, and artifacts is illustrated over for an image object:

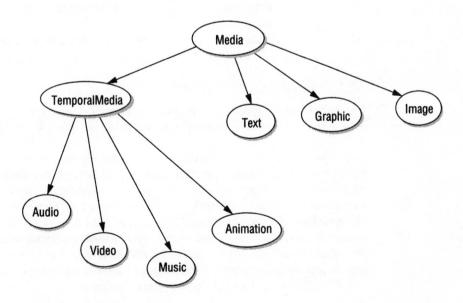

Figure 5.1   Media classes.

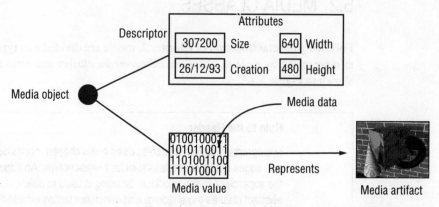

The most general media class is simply called Media. It is an abstract class that specifies methods which must be implemented by concrete media classes. A declaration for this class is:

```
abstract class Media {
public:
                    // querying
static   virtual setOf Media      KnownMedia( );
static   virtual Media            FindMedia(string mediaClassName);
         virtual MediaInfo        Descriptor( );

                    // editing
         virtual void             Cut(MediaSelection);
         virtual Media            Copy(MediaSelection);
         virtual void             Paste(MediaSelection, MediaContext);
};
```

5.2.1   GENERIC OPERATIONS

The methods of the Media class are divided into two categories, querying and editing. Interfaces to other generic operations would also appear in this class.

Querying □ The query methods allow applications to determine the media types present in an environment. The class method Media::KnownMedia[1] returns a set containing one representative of each concrete media class; FindMedia returns a representative of a named class. The objects returned by KnownMedia and Find-Media are special objects called media prototypes that can in turn be queried; they have descriptors but no media value. Both KnownMedia and FindMedia are overridden by subclasses. For instance Audio::KnownMedia returns a set of prototype Audio objects and Image::FindMedia("TrueColorImage") returns a prototype for the class called TrueColorImage (if a class of this name is defined).

---

[1]   Method names will be prefixed by the name of the class in which they are declared, unless the class is clear from the context.

Media and its subclasses have a Descriptor method used to obtain attributes of media objects. The class MediaInfo groups together those attributes possessed by all media objects; these include their type, size, and possibly author, date of creation, copyright holder, and so on. Subclasses of MediaInfo collect attributes of specific media types. (In other words, the MediaInfo hierarchy parallels the Media hierarchy.) For example, the Image class is declared as:

```
abstract class Image : public Media {
public:
            // querying
    static  virtual setOf Image      KnownMedia( );
    static  virtual Image            FindMedia(string imageClassName);
            ImageInfo                Descriptor( );

            // editing
            void                     Cut(ImageSelection);
            Image                    Copy(ImageSelection);
            void                     Paste(ImageSelection, ImageContext);

            // image specific methods
            ...
};
```

An ImageInfo object contains, in addition to the generic attributes found in MediaInfo, image-specific attributes such as image height, width, depth, and color model. The Image::Descriptor method overrides Media::Descriptor. As an example, if myImage is an Image instance then myImage.Descriptor( ) returns an ImageInfo object rather than a MediaInfo object.

Methods of MediaInfo are used to inspect and modify attribute values. For programming convenience it is useful if frequently accessed attributes of media objects are obtained directly rather than via invoking the Descriptor method and manipulating a MediaInfo object. This can be accomplished by adding methods such as Media::Size or Image::Width.

Editing □ The Media class declares three general editing methods: Cut, Copy, and Paste. As with the Descriptor method, the editing methods are implemented by subclasses. The arguments to Cut, Copy, and Paste include a MediaSelection – a 'subpart' of a media value, and a MediaContext – a 'location' within a media value. The form of MediaSelection and MediaContext depend on the media type. For example, Image::Cut takes an ImageSelection object while Text::Cut takes a TextSelection object. Both TextSelection and ImageSelection are subclasses of MediaSelection. Similarly, TextContext and ImageContext are subclasses of MediaContext (so here again are parallel class hierarchies).

Media subclasses □ The immediate subclasses of Media are the Image, Graphic, and Text classes and the TemporalMedia class. The purpose of a Media subclass is to group together media-specific operations. So the Image class specifies methods for images while the Text class specifies methods for text. These classes are abstract and have further subclasses. For example, some image operations may apply only to grayscale images (such as thresholding) while others apply only to color images (such as color separation). Thus subclasses of Image should include GrayScaleImage and ColorImage. Going further, ColorImage could have IndexedColorImage and TrueColorImage as its subclasses. In general, each Media subclass will have in turn a number of subclasses; this allows multiple representations for media types and enriches the variety of media-specific operations.

When the subclasses of Image and the other media types are taken into account, the Media hierarchy becomes considerably deeper than the hierarchy of Figure 5.1. It seems overly complicated to extend the parallel MediaInfo, MediaContext, and MediaSelection hierarchies to the same degree, and preferable if they 'bottom out' near the level of the main media types. These classes must then be designed with a high degree of generality so that, for example, ImageInfo can describe instances of GrayScaleImage, ColorImage, and any other Image subclass.

In some sense the Media hierarchy is unbalanced and it is tempting to group Image, Graphic, and Text as subclasses of a 'spatial media' class. However, it is not clear what methods would be provided by this class that are not also provided by the Media class. For example, a generic layout operation could be declared as SpatialMedia::PresentAt(Point p); the Image, Graphic, and Text classes would then provide media-specific implementations. But a layout operation also makes sense for video and animation objects (as when playback layout is specified) and these are instances of temporal media; hence a generic layout operation could be declared as Media::PresentAt(Point p). Unless operations can be identified that only apply to image, graphics, and text objects, a 'spatial media' class seems unnecessary.

5.2.2   TEMPORAL MEDIA SUBCLASSES

We now describe temporal media values, the TemporalMedia class, and its subclasses. In general, each temporal media value is a *temporal sequence* of *media elements*. A temporal sequence is one containing timing information for its elements. We first give examples of the underlying media elements and then look at their organization as temporal sequences.

Media elements ☐ Audio, video, and other temporal media values are built from sequences of simpler media elements. Each temporal media type has an associated element type (Table 5.1).

Table 5.1   Temporal media and underlying media elements.

Temporal media type	Media element type
Audio	AudioElement
Video	VideoElement
Animation	AnimationElement
Music	MusicElement

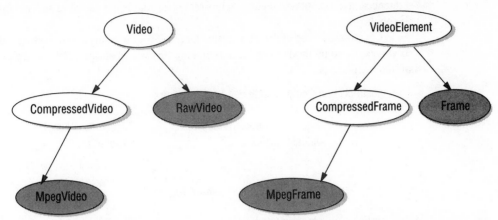

Figure 5.2   Examples of video classes and their sequence elements. Instances of the classes on the left are sequences whose members belong to the corresponding classes on the right.

Audio and video elements □ Conceptually, the elements of video values are frames, which are essentially images, and the elements of audio values are individual samples. In practice, frame and sample sequences are implemented in several ways, the primary difference being how elements are encoded. A class with multiple implementations can be modelled by an abstract class whose subclasses provide the alternate implementations. In this case, Audio and Video are the abstract classes, and their subclasses correspond to different forms of encoding. Figure 5.2 shows the relationship between Video subclasses and VideoElement subclasses. A similar organization would be used for Audio (Figure 5.3). Video has two immediate subclasses, RawVideo, a concrete class used for uncompressed or 'raw'

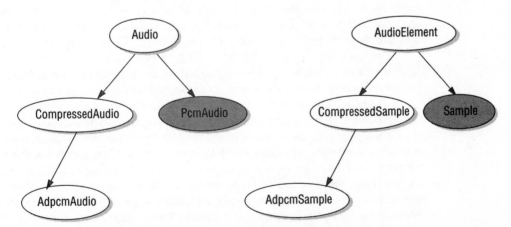

Figure 5.3   Examples of audio classes and their sequence elements. Instances of the classes on the left are sequences whose members belong to the corresponding classes on the right. (AdpcmAudio and AdpcmSample are abstract classes since there are many ADPCM representations for audio.)

sequences, and CompressedVideo, an abstract class that is the parent of further video subclasses.

CompressedVideo introduces virtual methods for encoding and decoding video values; these methods must be implemented by its subclasses. For example, a simple interface is:

```
abstract class CompressedVideo : public Video {
public:
static      virtual CompressedVideo          Encode(RawVideo);
            virtual RawVideo                 Decode( );
            // ...
};
class MpegVideo : public CompressedVideo {
public:
static      MpegVideo                        Encode(RawVideo);
            RawVideo                         Decode( );
            // ...
};
```

A RawVideo instance, rv, is then MPEG encoded by invoking MpegVideo::Encode(rv), which returns an instance of MpegVideo. Further methods would be defined for encoding and decoding particular frames and for specifying compression parameters.

One could argue that RawVideo, MpegVideo, and the other CompressedVideo subclasses break data encapsulation since aspects of the internal representation are now visible. But differences between the CompressedVideo subclasses are not just internal. There are external differences related to video quality, performance, and resource utilization that applications should be allowed to exploit.

Animation and music elements □ While the form of media elements for audio and video seems fairly apparent, identifying media elements for music and animation is more problematic. Again subclasses are used for different representations.

For animation, sequences of 2D or 3D geometric scenes and sequences of 'animation events' are two simple representations. In the first case, animation elements correspond directly to scenes, in the second they are changes to scenes. These forms of animation can be modelled by subclasses of Animation called SceneBasedAnimation and EventBasedAnimation (see Figure 5.4). Other representations would appear as additional subclasses to Animation or perhaps as refinements to existing subclasses. As an example of the latter, consider a representation using temporal functions. Here there is no explicit sequence of animation elements but, by 'sampling' the temporal function, scenes at different points in time are obtained. This suggests a specialization of SceneBasedAnimation where elements are not stored in some data structure but derived by functional evaluation.

The AnimationElement class hierarchy of Figure 5.4 parallels the Animation hierarchy. A similar approach is needed for music where a variety of representations is also possible. Families of representations, such as EventBasedMusic (based on sequences of musical events, for instance notes, tempo changes, and instrument changes) and ScoreBasedMusic (based on high-level structuring of musical

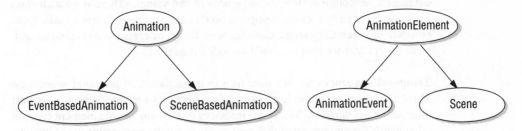

Figure 5.4   Examples of animation classes and their sequence elements. Instances of the classes on the left are sequences whose members belong to the corresponding classes on the right.

activities) form abstract subclasses of Music. Particular representations, such as MidiMusic, then appear as concrete subclasses (see Figure 5.5).

Media element descriptors ☐ Media elements have a descriptor identifying their size, type, and various pieces of media-specific information. For instance, a Sample descriptor would indicate the sample size and a Frame descriptor would indicate frame width and height. Given a sequence of media elements, their descriptors need not be identical. Compression and encoding parameters can vary between elements, as can element size.

Before discussing temporal sequences there is one further observation to make concerning media elements. Some media elements are media values themselves; they can be extracted from the sequence in which they are contained and treated autonomously. Other media elements require the context of a temporal sequence for interpretation. For example, a single frame can be extracted from a video sequence and displayed as an image, but it is not very meaningful to output a single audio sample. While not all media elements are media values, all nontemporal media values can be used as media elements. In particular, Graphic and Image values can be used as elements within Animation and Video sequences. One can also

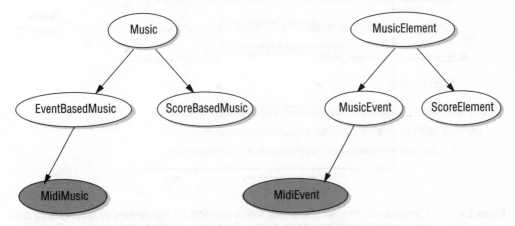

Figure 5.5   Examples of music classes and their sequence elements. Instances of the classes on the left are sequences whose members belong to the corresponding classes on the right.

envisage a TemporalText class for sequences of Text values. (There is no such class in Figure 5.1 simply because 'temporal text' is not a commonly used media type; however, it is certainly appropriate for such things as captions and subtitles and, since the framework is open, could be added if needed.)

Temporal sequences □ We now turn to a discussion of temporal sequences. These are sequences of the form $<e_i, s_i, d_i>$ where e_i is a media element, s_i its start time, and d_i its duration. The e_i are instances of the same media element type, in other words the combining of different media is not the responsibility of temporal sequences. Associated with each temporal sequence is a quantity called a *time-base*, which is a number indicating the units of measurement for the s_i and d_i. For example, if the timebase is 30, then start times and durations are measured in units of 1/30 sec.

Temporal sequences fall into several broad categories exhibiting various regularities in form and timing (see Figure 5.6). Four sets of quantities are used to define these categories: element sizes, element descriptors, element start times, and element durations.

- *Homogeneous* sequences: element descriptors are identical
  An example is CD audio, where all elements have the same form (16-bit PCM samples).

- *Heterogeneous* sequences: element descriptors vary
  Examples include compressed audio formats (such as ADPCM) where encoding parameters vary over the course of a recording.

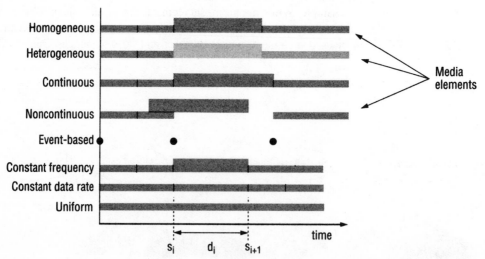

Figure 5.6   Categories of temporal sequences. Media elements are represented by rectangles (or dots in the case of event-based sequences). Four pieces of information are shown for each element: its start time (s_i) and duration (d_i), size (area of rectangle), and descriptor (shading of rectangle).

- *Continuous* sequences: $s_{i+1} = s_i + d_i$, for $i = 1, ..., n–1$
  In this case there is a unique element for every time value within the span of the sequence. Digital audio and digital video sequences are good examples.

- *Noncontinuous* sequences: $s_{i+1} \neq s_i + d_i$, for some i
  In this case there are 'gaps' and/or 'overlaps' among elements. Music and animation provide examples of this sort. For instance, if music is represented by sequences of notes and durations then a chord will require overlapping elements.

- *Event-based* sequences: $d_i = 0$, for $i = 1, ..., n$
  A special case of noncontinuous media occurs when media elements are duration-less events. An example is MIDI since elements are not notes with durations but events of the form 'Start Note' and 'Stop Note'.

- *Constant frequency sequences*: continuous and the d_i are constant
  In this common case the durations of media elements are constant; examples include fixed-frame rate digital video and many digital audio representations.

- *Constant data rate* sequences: continuous and $sizeof(e_i)/d_i$ is constant
  Some media sequences have a constant data rate (the data rate is the ratio of size in bytes, here indicated by *sizeof*, to duration of media elements).

- *uniform sequences*: continuous and both $sizeof(e_i)$ and the d_i are constant
  This is a common sub-case of constant data rate media. Examples include uncompressed digital audio and uncompressed digital video sequences.

Temporal media ☐ The framework represents temporal sequences by instances of the TemporalMedia class. This is an abstract class that declares methods supported by all temporal media types. These methods are divided into three categories – those dealing with time coordinates, access to media elements, and temporal transformations:

```
abstract class TemporalMedia : public Media {
public:
            // querying and editing methods ...


            // time coordinates
            int                          TimeBase( );
            void                         SetTimeBase(int timeBase);


            // element access
            int                          NumElements( );
            virtual MediaElement         Element(Time t);
            virtual MediaElement         Element(int index);
            virtual MediaElementInfo     Descriptor(int index);
            Time                         Start(int index);
            Time                         Duration(int index);
```

```
                    // temporal transformations
        void                        Translate(Time displacement);
        virtual void                Scale(float scaleFactor);
        void                        Invert(Time invertPoint);
};
```

Time coordinates and element access □ The TimeBase and SetTimeBase methods determine the current timebase and specify a new timebase (the timebase of a temporal sequence is initially set when the sequence is created). Media elements are accessed via the Element(Time) and Element(int) methods. If a temporal sequence contains overlapping elements, then Element(Time) is not well defined and individual elements must be accessed by their index number in the sequence.

   In practice, methods for element access are more elaborate than those found in TemporalMedia. Access to spans of consecutive elements is likely to improve performance. In addition, TemporalMedia subclasses can define alternative methods for element access. A Music subclass could allow elements to be accessed via tempo 'clicks', while an Animation subclass could use a notion of simulation time.

Temporal transformations □ The three methods, Translate, Scale, and Invert, are known as temporal transformations and are used to alter the timing of media elements. Translate shifts a sequence in time, but leaves the duration unchanged, Scale alters the overall duration of a sequence by a specified scale factor, and Invert 'flips' a sequence about a particular time point.

   The effect of the temporal transformations can be visualized by plotting media elements against time. Figure 5.7 shows what happens to a temporal sequence when it is translated by the amount displacement, scaled by a factor of 2, and inverted about its midpoint. The implementation of Translate and Invert is generic; both involve changing the start times of media elements. Scale is a virtual method and has media-specific implementations. In particular, it is possible to implement

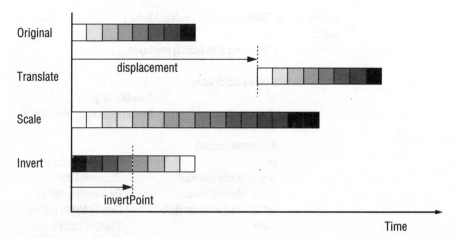

Figure 5.7   Temporal transformations.

Scale by simply changing the durations (and start times) of elements or by inserting new interpolated elements.

5.2.3   STRUCTURED MEDIA AND CONVERSIONS

Structured media □ Music, animation, and graphics are structured media. In the context of the framework this means that Graphic instances, and elements of Music and Animation instances, are composite objects that contain references to other objects. For each of the structured media, a number of associated *supporting classes* are needed (Table 5.2). Some of the supporting classes are in turn media classes. This allows, for example, a text string to be part of a graphics object. The rules for constructing a structured media object, and the form of the supporting classes, will depend on the class of the media object. For instance, the Graphic class could have subclasses for 2D and 3D graphics and then further subclasses such as PhigsGraphic and OglGraphic (referring to PHIGS and OpenGL). Each subclass would have its own set of supporting classes. So, to build a PhigsGraphic object one would use the methods and supporting classes related to PhigsGraphic, while to build an OglGraphic object different supporting classes and methods would be used. For a complete example of a graphics class hierarchy, and a discussion of issues in object-oriented graphics, the reader is referred to Wisskirchen (1990).

Table 5.2   Supporting classes for structured media.

Graphic	Primitive, Light, ViewPoint, Texture, Text, Font ...
Animation	Graphic, Trajectory, KeyFrame, ...
Music	Note, Instrument, ...

Conversions □ The media-specific methods belonging to a class generally produce objects of the same class. For example, many image-specific methods, such as Image::Rotate, produce images rather than instances of some other media type. However, there are also methods that involve several media classes. An important group are *conversion methods*, which convert from one media type to another. Some examples are:

Video	Animation::Render(...);
Image	Graphic::Render(...);
Audio	Text::Synthesize(...);
Audio	Music::Synthesize(...);
Text	Audio::Recognize(...);

These methods are declared as virtual and left to subclasses (of Animation, Graphic, Text, Music and Audio respectively) to implement.

5.2.4   MEDIA CLASS SUMMARY

This section has described a large number of classes, yet this set forms only the upper levels of the Media hierarchy and, with the inclusion of classes implementing particular representations of particular media types, the number of classes becomes many times larger. Figure 5.8 shows the organization of an expanded Media hierarchy and the places where new media classes are added. What is important is that as media-specific classes are designed and implemented, they be incorporated in the media hierarchy rather than left 'dangling'. In this way different media share a common organization and the foundations are laid for media composition.

5.3 TRANSFORM CLASSES

Adding new media classes is one way of extending the framework. A second possibility is through adding new *transform classes*. A transform class implements what are known as *function objects* – objects that encapsulate both a function and its parameters (function arguments will be called parameters to avoid confusion with method arguments). Typically the instance variables of a transform class are used to store parameters, and there is an 'apply' method which invokes the function and returns the result. A somewhat contrived example is:

```
class RaiseToPower {
public:
                      RaiseToPower(int); // constructs new RaiseToPower objects
         float        Apply(float);
};
```

```
cuber = new RaiseToPower(3);        // instantiate a RaiseToPower object

xcubed = cuber.Apply(x);            // apply it to some value
```

All media operations, including generic operations such as cut/copy/paste, the temporal transformations, conversions between media, and media-specific operations, can be represented by function objects. However, when it comes to implementation, function objects reveal several drawbacks, so the technique should be used with some caution. Implementation problems include performance penalties because of indirection and possible loss of static type-checking. In particular, it is difficult to specify a wide variety of function objects (in C++) and retain static type-checking of their invocation. The MediaInfo and MediaElementInfo objects found with media values contain type information and so can be used for run-time checks; however, operations where static type-checking or efficient invocation are considered essential should be 'promoted' to media class methods.

This being said, the reasons for introducing function objects include:

(1) Not all operations are known when media classes are defined. With function objects, new operations can be added without the need to modify existing classes (and existing applications).

(2) Image filters, audio filters, video effects, and video transitions are large in number. Rather than clutter media class declarations with additional methods, they can be represented by function objects.

```
Media
    Text
        AsciiText
        <other Text subclasses>
    Image
        BinaryImage
        GrayScaleImage
        ColorImage
            IndexedColorImage
            TrueColorImage
        <other Image subclasses>
    Graphic
        2dGraphic
            <2dGraphic subclasses>
        3dGraphic
            PhigsGraphic
            OglGraphic
            <other 3dGraphic subclasses>
    TemporalMedia
        Audio
            RawAudio
            CompressedAudio
                AdpcmAudio
                <other CompressedAudio subclasses>
        Video
            RawVideo
            CompressedVideo
                MpegVideo
                <other CompressedVideo subclasses>
        Animation
            EventBasedAnimation
                <EventBasedAnimation subclasses>
            SceneBasedAnimation
                <SceneBasedAnimation subclasses>
            <other Animation subclasses>
        Music
            EventBasedMusic
                MidiMusic
                <other EventBasedMusic subclasses>
            ScoreBasedMusic
                <ScoreBasedMusic subclasses>
            <other Music subclasses>
        <other TemporalMedia subclasses>
    <other Media subclasses>
```

MediaInfo ..., MediaSelection ..., MediaContext ...
MediaElement ..., MediaElementInfo ...
Supporting classes for Graphic, Animation and Music (see Table 5.2).

Figure 5.8   An expanded Media hierarchy and associated classes.

(3)   Function objects allow the efficient storage and processing of *derived media values*. (A derived media value is one that is calculated from existing values.) For instance, color separation produces one image from another. It is much more efficient to store the function object specifying the color separation than the separated image itself.

The interface to function objects is specified by an abstract class called Transform:

```
abstract class Transform {
public:
        // querying
static   virtual setOf Transform    KnownTransforms( );
static   virtual Transform          FindTransform(string transformClassName);
         TransInfo                  Descriptor( );

        // applying
        void                        SetParam(string paramName, void* paramValue);
        virtual bool                CanApply(...);
        virtual Media               Apply(...);
        virtual void                ApplyInPlace(...);
};
```

Transform has several abstract subclasses whose purpose is to group families of similar transformations such as image filters and video effects. These classes have, in turn, concrete subclasses representing specific transformations. The class method Transform::KnownTransforms returns a set containing one transform object from each concrete subclass. These objects can then be queried, using Transform::Descriptor, to obtain information concerning the name, number, and types of their parameters. The second query method, Transform::FindTransform, simply returns an instance of the concrete subclass with the specified name (if it exists).

After an instance of a concrete Transform subclass has been obtained, whether by querying or explicit construction, the Transform::SetParam method is used to assign values to its parameters. The remaining methods of Transform deal with applying the encapsulated function. Their arguments vary from subclass to subclass, but, in general, CanApply does a run-time type check, Apply produces a new media value, and ApplyInPlace 'overwrites' an existing value.

As an example, suppose a Transform subclass is declared as:

```
abstract class ImageTransform : public Transform {
public:
        // querying
static   setOf ImageTransform        KnownTransforms( );
static   ImageTransform              FindTransform(string name);

        // applying
        virtual bool                 CanApply(Image);
        virtual Image                Apply(Image);
        virtual void                 ApplyInPlace(Image);
};
```

Here ImageTransform::KnownTransforms and ImageTransform::FindTransform override the Transform methods; their purpose is to restrict queries to ImageTransform subclasses. ImageTransform also specifies the arguments needed for the CanApply, Apply, and ApplyInPlace methods. A specific image transformation, such as a filter used for embossing, can then be declared as:

```
class Emboss : public ImageTransform {
public:
            // applying
            bool                        CanApply(Image);
            Image                       Apply(Image);
            void                        ApplyInPlace(Image);
};
```

It is in the Apply methods of Emboss and other concrete classes that the real work gets done. Before invoking these methods, any needed parameters must be set. Suppose Emboss uses an imaginary light source whose direction can be adjusted. The following code shows how to apply this filter, and also shows how FindTransform is used:

```
emboss = ImageTransform::FindTransform("Emboss");
emboss.SetParam("Direction", 45);          // set the direction of the 'light source'
image2 = emboss.Apply(image1);             // apply the filter to image1 and
                                           //produce image2
```

Other Transform subclasses follow the same pattern as ImageTransform. For example, VideoTransition is a family of transformations used to produce transitions from one video value to another:

```
abstract class VideoTransition : public Transform {
public:
            // querying
static      setOf VideoTransition       KnownTransforms( );
static      VideoTransition             FindTransform(string name);

            // applying
            virtual bool                CanApply(Video, Video);
            virtual Video               Apply(Video, Video);
};
```

VideoTransition, like ImageTransform, overrides the Transform query methods and specifies the form of the Apply and CanApply methods. (There is no VideoTransition::ApplyInPlace since it is not clear which of the two video values should be modified; Video::Paste could be used for attaching the transition to the original values if need be.) A concrete subclass of VideoTransition is:

```
class Dissolve : public VideoTransition {
public:
        // applying
        bool                            CanApply(Video, Video);
        Video                           Apply(Video, Video);
};
```

Dissolve parameters should include the duration of the dissolve and the points (that is, the times) where the dissolve is to be applied. Code for applying a Dissolve instance to two video values will then resemble:

```
Dissolve                    dissolve;         // instantiate a Dissolve object
dissolve.SetParam("TimeBase", 30);           // measure time in 1/30 seconds
dissolve.SetParam("Duration", 60);           // set the duration to 2 seconds
dissolve.SetParam("In1",
        video1.Start(video1.NumElements( )) – 60);    // set where to begin the
                                                      // dissolve in video1
dissolve.SetParam("In2", video2.Start(1));   // similarly for video2
video3 = dissolve.Apply(video1, video2);     // apply the transition to video1 and
                                             // video2
```

5.4 FORMAT CLASSES

Media values are accessed and manipulated through methods found in the Media hierarchy. A well-designed class conceals the internal representation of media values from users, leaving the choice of data structures to class implementors. Not to be confused with the somewhat arbitrary internal representations, media values also have external representations allowing values to be saved in files or exchanged between applications. External representations are not at all arbitrary; instead they are determined by numerous standards and conventions.

External representations of media values are called *media formats*. There are two basic categories: *file formats*, used to store media values, and *stream formats*, used to send media values over communications links. File and stream formats are very similar, even identical in some cases, so rather than discuss both, this section focuses on the former.

What is required are methods for importing and exporting media values in different file formats (provided, of course, the media value is compatible with the format – it makes no sense to try to store images using an audio format). The obvious approach is to add import and export methods to media classes. For example, two common image formats are TIFF and GIF. The Image class could be declared as:

```
abstract class Image : public Media {
public:
        // import and export methods
static   Image        ImportTiff(string fileName);
```

```
static       Image              ImportGif(string fileName);
             void               ExportTiff(string fileName);
             void               ExportGif(string fileName);

             // other image methods
             ...
};
```

The following code then imports a TIFF image from one file and exports it in GIF format to a second file:

```
image = Image::ImportTiff("myImageFile.tiff");
image.ExportGif("myImageFile.gif");
```

Instead of having import and export methods for each image format, an alternate is to define general methods taking a 'format type' argument:

```
abstract class Image : public Media {
public:
             // general import and export methods
static       Image              Import(string fileName, formatType t);
             void               Export(string fileName, formatType t);
             // ...
};
```

There are problems with both approaches. First, not all formats are known when media classes are defined, and additional formats are likely to be needed by future applications. But supporting a new format requires either adding methods or modifying existing methods, which means classes are changed and software integration and portability are more difficult. Second, media formats evolve, but adding a new format version suffers the same problems as adding a new format – existing classes must be modified. Finally, media formats themselves contain useful information: they have names and possibly versions, and there are options which can be selected, or restrictions on the media types supported. For example, some image formats handle indexed color, others do not, some use compression, others do not. This information should be available for inspection by applications.

Media format classes address the above problems. Each format of interest is represented by a class that implements import and export methods. *Format objects*, that is, instances of format classes, are used to obtain information about formats and to exercise fine-grain control over importing and exporting.

Format classes are organized in a hierarchy with a structure similar to the hierarchy of media classes. The root of the hierarchy is an abstract class called MediaFormat; it has subclasses (also abstract) for each of the main media types. Actual formats are represented by concrete subclasses appearing as the leaves of the hierarchy. Some examples of format classes are shown in Figure 5.9. The names of the concrete (shaded) classes in this figure are not important; they refer to existing file formats, to existing formats for analog and digital streams, and to possible formats based on standard coding schemes.

The MediaFormat class is declared as:

```
        abstract class MediaFormat {
        public:
                    // querying
        static      virtual setOf MediaFormat      KnownFormats( );
        static      virtual MediaFormat            GuessFormat(string fileName);
        static      virtual bool                   IsFormatOf(string fileName);
                    virtual MediaFormatInfo        Descriptor( );
                    virtual MediaFormatInfo        Descriptor(Media val);
                    virtual bool                   SetDescriptor(MediaFormatInfo info);


                    // import, export
                    virtual bool                   CanImport(string fileName);
                    virtual MediaInfo              ImportInfo(string fileName);
                    virtual Media                  Import(string fileName);
                    virtual void                   CanExport(Media val);
                    virtual void                   Export(string fileName, Media val);
        };
```

Querying □ The class method MediaFormat::KnownFormats returns a set containing a format object for each defined format. This method is overridden by subclasses, for instance ImageFormat::KnownFormats will only return instances of subclasses of ImageFormat. The GuessFormat method attempts to identify the format of a specified file (perhaps by looking within the file or checking for a filename extension or suffix). Similarly, IsFormatOf attempts to determine whether an existing file uses the format represented by a particular format class. As an example, if TIFF is a subclass of ImageFormat then

TIFF::IsFormatOf("someFile.data");

would return true if someFile.data contains a TIFF image. (Although IsFormat has been declared as returning a Boolean value, allowing for 'unknown' replies is also needed.)

Once a format object has been obtained, whether by KnownFormats, GuessFormat, or by explicit instantiation, the Descriptor methods can be used. These return a MediaFormatInfo object, an auxiliary object containing attributes that describe formats.

MediaFormatInfo is the root of a class hierarchy. Like MediaInfo, MediaFormatInfo collects generic attributes (of media formats rather than media objects), while its subclasses collect attributes of specific formats.

The two descriptor methods, MediaFormat::Descriptor( ) and MediaFormat::Descriptor(Media), differ in that when no media value is supplied as an argument, format attributes refer to possible values, or default values, rather than actual values. For example:

```
tiff = new TIFF;                  // a format object
finfo = tiff.Descriptor( );       // possible and default values of format attributes
finfo = tiff.Descriptor(myImage); // values of format attributes appropriate for
                                  // myImage
```

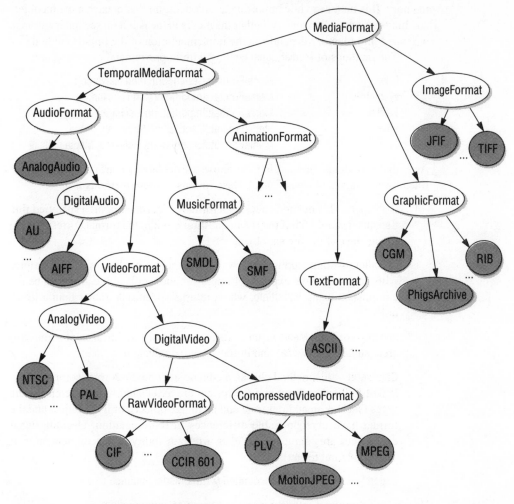

Figure 5.9   Some media format classes.

The final querying method, SetDescriptor, allows applications to override default settings of format attributes. For example, given a 24-bit image and a format supporting both 24- and 8-bit depths, the default behavior of the export method would be to use 24-bit depth. However, if the application sets the format attribute for image depth to indicate 8 bits, then the image would be exported with 8-bit depth (resulting in a loss of information).

In addition to the general-purpose SetDescriptor method, format classes can have methods allowing more convenient modification of commonly used attributes. For instance, a variable sample rate digital audio format could provide a SetSampleRate method.

Import and export □ The main purpose of format classes is importing and exporting media values. Note that importing does not imply loading data into memory. It is better to view importing as an operation that creates a media object and binds it to a media value. Whether the media value is left on secondary storage or loaded into memory depends on the implementation of the import method.

The methods of MediaFormat dealing with importing and exporting are:

```
bool                    MediaFormat::CanImport(string fileName);
MediaInfo               MediaFormat::ImportInfo(string fileName);
Media                   MediaFormat::Import(string fileName);
void                    MediaFormat::CanExport(Media val);
void                    MediaFormat::Export(string fileName, Media val);
```

As with the methods for querying, the above are declared as virtual and further refined by subclasses of MediaFormat. Descriptions of these methods follow:

CanImport – this method checks if a format object can import a specified file. CanImport should fail if the file in question is not in the format corresponding to the class of the format object.

ImportInfo – some applications want to inspect a media object's descriptor without going to the expense of importing the media value. This can be accomplished using ImportInfo, which returns a MediaInfo rather than a Media object.

Import – creates a Media instance (or, more exactly, an instance of some concrete subclass of Media) and initializes it using data in a file.

CanExport – this method checks media object / media format compatibility. It will fail if the object and the format are associated with different media types (such as an audio format and an image object), or if the object and the format have unreconcilable differences in representation. Deciding what differences are 'unreconcilable' is a responsibility of the implementor of CanExport (and Export).

Export – writes the data associated with a Media instance to a file.

Here is an example of importing and exporting an image value:

```
myCoder = ImageFormat::GuessFormat("someImage.data");
myImage = myCoder.Import("someImage.data");
// process myImage
myCoder.Export("someImage.data", myImage);
```

In this example we know that the file someImage.data contains an image but the format is unknown, so the class method ImageFormat::GuessFormat is used to find a format object. The Import method is then invoked and, depending on the contents of the file, will create an instance of one of the Image subclasses such as TrueColorImage or BinaryImage. The image is then processed and exported in the same format.

NPCMFF – a format class example □ As a more detailed example, suppose we invent an audio file format called 'NPCMFF' (New PCM File Format). It stores audio values as PCM samples; the sample rate, sample size, and number of channels are allowed to vary (from one audio value to another). The new format is represented by the class NPCMFF, a subclass of AudioFormat. Declarations for these classes are:

```
abstract class AudioFormat : public TemporalMediaFormat {
public:
                // querying
    static      setOf AudioFormat      KnownFormats( );
    static      AudioFormat            GuessFormat(string fileName);
    static      virtual bool           IsFormatOf(string fileName);
                virtual AudioFormatInfo  Descriptor( );
                virtual AudioFormatInfo  Descriptor(Audio val);
                virtual bool           SetDescriptor(AudioFormatInfo info);


                // import, export
                virtual bool           CanImport(string fileName);
                virtual AudioInfo      ImportDescriptor(string fileName);
                virtual Audio          Import(string fileName);
                virtual void           CanExport(Audio val);
                virtual void           Export(string fileName, Audio val);
};


class NPCMFF : public AudioFormat {
public:
                // querying
    static      bool                   IsFormatOf(string fileName);
                AudioFormatInfo        Descriptor( );
                AudioFormatInfo        Descriptor(PcmAudio val);
                bool                   SetDescriptor(AudioFormatInfo info);


                // import, export
                bool                   CanImport(string fileName);
                AudioInfo              ImportDescriptor(string fileName);
                PcmAudio               Import(string fileName);
                void                   CanExport(Audio val);
                virtual void           Export(string fileName, PcmAudio val);
};
```

Note how the argument and return values of various methods have been specialized (for instance, compare the Descriptor methods as found in the NPCMFF and MediaFormat classes). Also the two class methods, KnownFormats and GuessFormat, need only be declared in the AudioFormat class (since it does not seem to make sense to direct these queries to a specific format).

The class NPCMFF is concrete and can be instantiated to produce format objects. Suppose npcm is an instance of NPCMFF, the information provided by npcm.Descriptor( ) would resemble:

Attribute	Value
MediaFormatInfo attributes	
Name	"New PCM File Format"
Version	"1.0"
...	
TemporalMediaFormatInfo attributes	
NumberOfElements	> 0
ExplicitTiming[a]	false
...	
AudioFormatInfo attributes	
SampleRate	8000–48 000
SampleSize	8 or 16
NoOfChannels	1 or 2
...	

a.   If true elements have timestamps, otherwise element times are implicit from their position in the sequence.

Note that NPCMFF::Descriptor( ) provides information about MediaFormatInfo, TemporalMediaFormatInfo, and AudioFormatInfo attributes. Furthermore, some attributes, such as SampleRate, do not have a simple value but rather indicate the range of values supported by the format.

Now suppose we have a five-second audio object, myAudioClip, obtained from a CD recording. Using this object, we can invoke the second descriptor method, as in: npcm.Descriptor(myAudioClip). The information now provided shows what values would be bound to format attributes if myAudioClip were exported in NPCMFF format. Since myAudioClip is from a CD recording, this information would resemble:

Attribute	Value
MediaFormatInfo attributes	
Name	"New PCM File Format"
Version	"1.0"
...	
TemporalMediaFormatInfo attributes	
NumberOfElements	220,500
ExplicitTiming	false
...	
AudioFormatInfo attributes	
SampleRate	44,100
SampleSize	16
NoOfChannels	2
...	

Analog formats □ Stream format classes, in addition to describing digital streams, can describe analog signal formats. The AnalogVideo and AnalogAudio subclasses are examples. The purpose of analog formats is to aid in representing devices and analog media that might be under application control. For instance, consider using objects as handles to analog video clips. Here is a class for representing clips on a videodisc:

```
class VideoDiscClip {
public:
        string              DiscTitle( );
        string              Name( );
        int                 StartFrame( );
        int                 EndFrame( );
        AnalogVideo         Format( );
};
```

The VideoDiscClip::Format allows an application to determine whether a particular clip is in NTSC, PAL, or some other analog video format. A similar class could be defined for clips on video tape.

Analog formats play an important role in acquiring and presenting media values (their input and output). Analog formats do not have methods that import and export media values; instead analog formats are associated with components that convert between the digital and analog realms. This will be described in Section 5.5.

Media object / format compatibility □ What happens when a media format is not compatible with a media object? Looking at the NPCMFF example, suppose myAudioClip has a sample rate or sample size out of the ranges of possible values supported by NPCMFF. Or suppose we have a 24-bit image and an image format only supporting 8 bits, or a video value relying on one form of compression but a format using another. Handling these situations is the responsibility of the implementors of format classes. One possibility is simply to return an error when Descriptor(Media) is invoked. A second possibility is to convert the media value to something which can be exported. Conversion introduces the possibility of information loss (as when a 24-bit image is reduced to 8 bits); but the application can be forewarned if a 'WillBeLossy' format attribute is set when Descriptor(Media) is invoked.

Format conversion □ The process of importing a media value in one format and exporting it in another is called format conversion. It offers a means for compressing (or recompressing) a media value since many file formats, in particular those for images, audio, and video, are based on specific compression algorithms. The steps needed to achieve format conversion are related to the implementation of media classes. There are two basic alternatives:

(1)   Media values use a single 'canonical' internal representation, all import methods return the same type.

(2) Media values differ in their internal representation, import methods return different types.

When a media sub-hierarchy is implemented using the first alternative, format conversion reduces to importing and then exporting. For example, suppose Image and its subclasses are based on a 'canonical' representation. The following then converts from some arbitrary image format to a format based on JPEG compression:

```
JPEG                  jpegFormat;                    // a format object
ImageFormat           otherFormat ;                  // a format object
Image                 myImage;                       // a media object

otherFormat = ImageFormat::GuessFormat("someImage.data");
if(/* GuessFormat succeeded */) {
      myImage = otherFormat.Import("someImage.data");
      jpegFormat.SetQuality(80);                      // sets a format attribute
      jpegFormat.Export("someImage.jpeg", myImage);
}
```

Video, in comparison, has subclasses based on different internal representations. Format conversion now takes place in four steps: importing, decoding, encoding, and then exporting. This is shown in the next example where video format objects are used in tandem with the CompressedVideo::Decode and CompressedVideo::Encode methods to convert a video value in 'MPEG format' to one in 'PLV format':

```
MPEG                  mpegFormat;                    // a format object
PLV                   plvFormat ;                    // a format object
MpegVideo             mv;                            // a media object
PlvVideo              pv;                            // a media object
RawVideo              rv;                            // a media object

mv = mpegFormat.Import("someVideo.mpeg");
rv = mv.Decode( );
pv = PlvVideo::Encode(rv);
plvFormat.Export("someVideo.plv", pv);
```

It is worth noting that the functionality provided by the CompressedVideo::Decode and CompressedVideo::Encode methods can be made available via Transform classes:

```
abstract class VideoDecode : public Transform {
public:
           // ...
           // applying
           virtual bool              CanApply(Video);
           virtual RawVideo          Apply(CompressedVideo);
};
```

A concrete subclass of VideoDecode is:

```
class MpegDecode : public VideoDecode {
public:
        // applying
        bool                            CanApply(Video);
        RawVideo                        Apply(MpegVideo);
};
```

VideoEncode transform classes would have a similar form. The video format conversion example now becomes:

```
MPEG                    mpegFormat;         // a format object
PLV                     plvFormat ;         // a format object
MpegVideo               mv;                 // a media object
PlvVideo                pv;                 // a media object
RawVideo                rv;                 // a media object
MpegDecode              decode;             // a transform object
PlvEncode               encode;             // a transform object

mv = mpegFormat.Import("someVideo.mpeg");
rv = decode.Apply(mv);
pv = encode.Apply(rv);
plvFormat.Export("someVideo.plv", pv);
```

Note that in both examples, the entire MpegVideo value is decoded and the result then encoded. No timing behavior is implied by this sequence of operations, so the PlvVideo value is not produced in real time. Furthermore, the RawVideo value is temporary and probably very large so is basically an expensive waste of memory. It would be preferable if decoding and encoding were interleaved. This can be done by iterating over video elements (decoding and encoding frame-by-frame), but this is inelegant and likely to be inefficient. A more general approach is described in the next section where the concurrent processing of media values is addressed.

5.5 COMPONENT CLASSES

Temporal data, including audio, video, and other temporal media values, have a dual nature – they can be thought of as active 'streams' or passive 'pools'. The difference lies in whether operations are time-critical or not. When temporal data is operated on without regard to timing it plays a passive role – to a large extent it is the operation, rather than the data, that determines the amount of time needed to complete the operation. Consider copying a file containing a video value. As the file is copied there is no need to observe any of the timing information implicit within the video value (and in fact one of the advantages of digital, as opposed to analog, video is that copying a 30-minute clip need not take a full 30 minutes). In other words, copying a temporal media value is not a time-critical operation.

There are, of course, many operations on temporal media values that are time-critical. Real-time playback and recording are obvious examples. In these cases the media value resembles a *stream*: a rate can be associated with the value (such as a frame rate or sample rate), and the operation must process the data at, or at least near, this rate. Now the data has an active role – it, rather than the operation, determines the amount of time allowed to perform the operation.

The methods introduced in the previous sections do not perform time-critical operations. In particular, the methods of the TemporalMedia class and its subclasses deal only with passive media values. Additional objects, called *components*, are responsible for applying time-critical operations to media streams. A component is a special form of object that encapsulates a time-critical operation. For instance, consider playback of an audio value. Here samples are retrieved (perhaps from a file) and passed to a digital-to-analog converter. Since samples must arrive at the converter at a specific rate, the audio playback operation is clearly time-critical. A component capable of performing this operation, an 'audio player' component, would encapsulate both control of the digital-to-analog converter and the transfer of samples to the converter. Clients of the component could then control audio playback through high-level methods such as StartPlayback and StopPlayback and any other methods provided by the component interface.

As just mentioned, components are objects of a special form. They are examples of *active objects* (see page 155). Recall that active objects, like ordinary or passive objects, have state and behavior. In addition, active objects spontaneously perform actions, even if no messages have been sent to the object. Active objects introduce concurrency. This is clearly seen with the audio player component. Once an audio player is started it should continue to operate until either the audio value it is playing comes to an end or it is directed to stop. During playback both the component and the client of the component proceed in parallel. Schematically, the code for starting and stopping an audio player component could resemble:

```
// obtain an audio player object, ap
ap.StartPlayback( );          // the player is started and playback
// do other things            // proceeds in parallel with the client
ap.StopPlayback( );           // until the player is stopped
```

Components are instances of component classes, but components come in many shapes and sizes. Players, recorders, encoders, decoders, synthesizers, renderers, and special effects processors are all components. In addition, some components correspond to pieces of hardware (for instance, a video digitizer), others to pieces of software (for instance, a software-based JPEG decoder), and others to combinations of the two (for instance, an animation renderer that uses graphics hardware). This is clearly a situation where subclassing can be exploited to organize the large variety of components.

There are several ways to construct a component taxonomy through subclassing and inheritance. Components can be classified by the types of media they operate on and/or by the types of operations they provide. Many components have different implementations (such as similar hardware devices produced by different manufacturers), which adds a further dimension to a component taxonomy.

The framework uses a simple component hierarchy consisting of four levels (see Figure 5.10). The abstract class Component is the root of the hierarchy; it declares methods supported by components in general. Below Component are three abstract classes, Producer, Consumer, and Transformer, that divide components into families that produce streams, consume streams, and transform streams (in which case streams are both consumed and produced). The three families are also called *sources*, *sinks*, and *filters*. Concerning streams, generally these are flows of information. More precisely, a stream is either a timed data sequence, in the sense of temporal media values, *or* an analog signal. The inclusion of analog streams is important since many components are bridges between the analog and digital realms and their descriptions are incomplete if the analog half is excluded.

Returning to Figure 5.10, the level below Producer, Consumer, and Transformer contains *abstract component types*. These classes represent particular time-critical operations but do not provide implementations. For example, AudioPlayer is an abstract component type (the operation it represents is audio playback); furthermore, since it produces an (analog) audio stream it is a Producer subclass. Finally, the leaves of the hierarchy, the *concrete component types*, provide particular implementations of abstract component types. Continuing with the AudioPlayer example, suppose a hardware platform includes an 'XY Sound Board' for audio output. The interface to the board would be provided by a subclass of AudioPlayer named XYAudioPlayer (or something similar). The XYAudioPlayer class would appear on the fourth level of Figure 5.10; it would implement the methods of audio players in general plus any XY-specific methods.

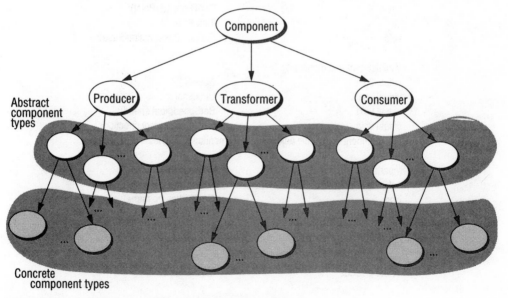

Figure 5.10   Component classes – a component taxonomy.

5.5.1   GENERIC OPERATIONS

The Component class is shown in Figure 5.11. Its methods have been divided into several categories and deal with: querying, power control and initialization, transport control, timing, adjustment and monitoring, ports, and events.

```
abstract class Component {
public:
                    // querying
static              virtual setOf Component          KnownComponents( );
static              virtual Component               FindComponent(string componentClassName);
                    virtual CompInfo                Descriptor( );

                    // power control and initialization
static              virtual Component               Open(string componentLocator);
                    virtual errCode                 PowerOn( );
                    virtual errCode                 PowerOff( );

                    // transport control
                    componentState                  State( );
                    virtual errCode                 Start( );
                    virtual errCode                 Stop( );
                    virtual errCode                 Pause( );
                    virtual errCode                 Resume( );

                    // timing
                    virtual Time                    CurrentTime( );
                    virtual                         Cue(Time cuePoint);
                    int                             TimeBase( );
                    void                            SetTimeBase(int timeBase);

                    // adjustment and monitoring
                    virtual float                   Speed( );
                    virtual bool                    Direction( );
                    virtual void                    SetSpeed(float speed);
                    virtual void                    SetDirection(bool direction);
                    // ... (component-specific adjustment and monitoring methods)

                    // ports
                    setOf Port                      KnownPorts( );
                    Port                            FindPort(string name);

                    // events
                    setOf Event                     KnownEvents( );
                    virtual errCode                 UnMask(Event ev);
                    virtual errCode                 Mask(Event ev);
};
```

Figure 5.11   The Component class

Querying □ The class methods Component::KnownComponents and Component::FindComponent allow applications to determine what components are available on the platform where they are running. The first returns a set containing representatives of each concrete component type that is supported by the current platform, the second returns a representative of the named concrete component type. As with other query methods, both KnownComponents and FindComponent are overridden by subclasses. So Consumer::KnownComponents returns a set of consumers, and AudioPlayer::FindComponent("XYAudioPlayer") returns an XYAudioPlayer instance (if this class has been defined and the current platform contains an 'XY Audio Sound Board').

Once a component has been obtained, whether by querying or through explicit instantiation, the Component::Descriptor method can be used to obtain a CompInfo object. CompInfo identifies such things as the component's name and type, the manufacturer and model number if the component is hardware-based, the name and number of the component's 'ports' (see below), and a description of the component's capabilities. The capability description is particularly important. There is great variation among even closely related components. For instance, all subclasses of AudioPlayer support audio playback, but they are likely to use different sample rates and samples sizes. Perhaps the XYAudioPlayer works with 8-bit samples at 8000 Hz, while other, more powerful, components support a range of sample rates and both 8-bit and 16-bit samples. The capability description should identify these variations.

Power control and initialization □ Components are created and initialized by calling the class method Component::Open and passing a *component locator*. The meaning and syntax of locator strings varies among component classes. For some components the locator might be a local device name, for others a format name, or the name of a network service. In addition, component locators may contain embedded host names. Possible examples are:

```
XYAudioPlayer::Open("/dev/xyaudio0");      // locator contains a device name
VideoPlayer::Open("MPEG");                 // locator contains a format name
VideoPlayer::Open("MPEG@someHost");        // locator contains a format name
                                           // and a host name
```

The above examples create sources of different kinds. The first produces an analog audio signal, while the second and third produce MPEG video streams.

Before a component can be used it is 'turned on' by invoking the PowerOn method. PowerOn allocates any resources needed by the component, and these are held until PowerOff is issued. PowerOn fails if insufficient computing resources (such as memory, bus bandwidth, processor cycles) are available or if any required hardware is already in use. As specified in Figure 5.11, the PowerOn method has no arguments. This is simplistic and does not account for components capable of operating with reduced 'power'. A more sophisticated PowerOn method might take a *Quality-of-Service* parameter, and depending upon the value of this parameter the component would allocate more or less power (that is, resources). The effect of reducing power varies from component to component. For example, an AudioPlayer operating at reduced power might drop every second sample, while

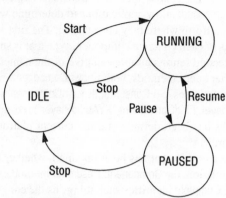

Figure 5.12   Component state diagram.

a renderer component might switch to a simpler shading method. In general, reducing power reduces quality, but a component needs fewer resources to operate.

Transport control □ Powering on a component allocates resources but does not make the component active; it is in an IDLE state. Two other states are possible, RUNNING and PAUSED. The transport control methods, Start, Stop, Pause, and Resume, alter a component's state as shown in Figure 5.12. When in the RUNNING state, components (that are sinks or filters) consume incoming streams and produce outgoing streams (components that are sources and filters). In the IDLE state no streams are either produced or consumed. In the PAUSED state streams are produced but 'held' at the same value (that is, media elements within the stream are repeated). For example, pausing a digital video player could cause the same frame to be repeated. For some components (such as an audio source) the PAUSED state is not very useful, in which case Pause and Resume may be replaced by Stop and Start.

Timing □ A component is like a clock: once turned on it measures what is called *component time*. When a component is running smoothly, component time changes in a regular fashion at a near constant rate. If the component is overloaded or resource-starved, component time is likely to stutter and jump about. The rate at which component time changes, and whether it increases or decreases, depends on the 'speed' and 'direction' of the component (which can be adjusted, see below). This current value of component time is returned by the Component::CurrentTime method. The timebase used to measure component time is obtained with Component::TimeBase and set using Component::SetTimeBase. Finally, the Component::Cue method positions a component at a particular point in time. The only circumstances when component time changes are when the component is in the RUNNING state or when a Cue is issued. The following example illustrates the use of the timing methods:

```
// ap is an AudioPlayer component
ap.PowerOn( );
ap.SetTimeBase(1000);          // set the timebase to 1000 units per second
ap.Cue(100);                   // position component time at 0.1 sec
ap.Start( );                   // start playback
// do other things
// ...
now = ap.CurrentTime( );       // ask the player where it is
```

Adjustment and monitoring ☐ This category of Component methods deals with the numerous parameters and settings that influence component operation. Most of the methods falling into this category are type-specific. For example, AudioPlayer might have methods for adjusting volume and balance, while a VideoPlayer component could have methods for adjusting brightness and window size. The methods found in the Component class under this category apply to a wide variety of components; they deal with the speed and direction of component operation. Speed is the rate at which component time changes, while direction indicates whether component time increases or decreases with respect to real time. These values are adjusted by Component::SetSpeed and Component::SetDirection, and a matching pair of methods returns the current settings. It is important to note that not all components support these methods (for instance, the speed of a 'live' source can never be changed), and furthermore, there are per-component constraints on possible speed values. In other words, the fact that a component can change speed does not guarantee that all speeds are attainable. A description of a component's possible speeds, and whether it can change direction and/or speed, should be included in the CompInfo object returned by Component::Descriptor. Another source of variation is whether speed, direction, and other operational parameters can be adjusted while the component is running or only when it is paused or idle. This again should be provided by CompInfo.

5.5.2   PORTS AND CONNECTORS

The notion of *ports* perhaps distinguishes media components most clearly from software components in general. Attached to each component are one or more ports. These can be thought of as places where streams enter or leave the component. (It is possible for a component to have no ports, but this is a less interesting situation and will not be considered here.) Ports are typed and have a name and direction. The direction is either 'input' for streams entering the component, or 'output' for streams leaving. The type of a port is a format class, in particular a stream format.

It will be convenient to use a graphical notation where components are represented by circles. Boxes attached to the circles indicate ports – extruding for output ports and intruding for input ports. Using this notation it is easy to identify producers (output ports only), consumers (input ports only), and transformers (both output and input ports), as seen in Figure 5.13.

Of course, the reason for introducing ports is that they are used to *connect* components. In general, two ports can be connected provided:

Producer/source   Transformer/filter   Consumer/sink

Figure 5.13   Graphical representation of components.

(1)   One is an output port and the other an input port.
Usually the two ports will reside on different components, but this is not necessary and feedback loops can be established – perhaps for testing or special effects (such as reverberation).

(2)   The two ports are *plug compatible*.
This means either their types are identical *or* the type of the output port is a subtype of the type of the input port. This latter case can be imagined using an analogy of a speaker and a listener where, provided the speaker uses a smaller vocabulary than known by the listener, what is said will be understood.

(3)   Adding the connection does not exceed the *fan-limit* on either port.
The fan-limit is a number indicating how many connections can be attached to the port. The simplest case is when ports allow only one connection at a time. But this is overly restrictive, and it is possible that some ports accept multiple connections.

There may be a question as to why directional ports are used, as opposed to ports allowing two-way communication. First, streams have a sense of direction so it is natural to speak of directional ports. This can be seen, for example, by looking at audio/video equipment where there are 'ports' for input and output connections. Second, directional ports increase component autonomy. A component should be unaffected by the presence or absence of connections to its output ports. It should also be possible to change these connections while the component is running. In other words, a component depends on other components upstream (which supply data to its input ports) but not on those downstream.

Both ports and the connections between ports are represented by objects. The Port class is declared as:

```
class Port {
public:
        // querying
        PortInfo                              Descriptor( );
        errCode                               SetDescriptor(PortInfo info);
        TemporalMediaFormat                   CurrentType( );
        setOf TemporalMediaFormat             PossibleTypes( );
        Component                             LocatedOn( );
        Port                                  ConnectedTo( );
        setOf Port                            ConnectedToSet( );
```

```
        errCode                         CanConnectTo(Port otherPort);

    // data transfer
    int                     Get(void* data, int nbytes);// used by Component
    int                     Put(void* data, int nbytes);// used by Component
};
```

PortInfo indicates a port's name, fan-limit, and whether it is an input or output port.
Some input ports are optional (in which case no connection is needed for the component to run), and some ports carry 'live' streams (streams that issue from a microphone, camera, or other real-time acquisition device). Port query methods also
return the current type of the port and the set of possible types. (If many types are
possible then one is selected when the port is matched with another port prior to
connection.) The remaining query methods return the component on which the
port is located, and the port, or set of ports, to which it is connected (if it is connected). It is also possible to test whether one port can be connected to another.
The two data transfer methods, Port::Get and Port::Put, are used to read and write
data through the port (provided the port is digital rather than analog). Get and Put
are for use by component implementors and would not normally be seen by applications.

Connections are represented by instances of a Connector class declared as
follows:

```
    abstract class Connector {
    public:
        // querying
        bool                    IsConnected( );
        Port                    From( );
        Port                    To( );


        // connection control
static  Connector               Match(Port from, Port to);
        virtual errCode         Connect( );
        virtual errCode         Disconnect( );

        // data transfer
        virtual int             Get(void* data, int nbytes);    // used by Port
        virtual int             Put(void* data, int nbytes);    // used by Port
};
```

A connector attaches two ports – called the 'from' port and 'to' port. The Connector query methods return the state of the connector (whether it is connected or not)
and the ports to which it is connected. Connections are established and removed
by invoking the Connector::Connect and Connector::Disconnect methods. Finally, the
data transfer methods are used to pass data over a connection; these would be invoked by the corresponding Port methods.

The class method Connector::Match is used to create a connector that is compatible with two ports; it does not, however, establish a connection. The reason

Match is needed is that Connector is an abstract class and has different subclasses corresponding to different communication mechanisms. For example, some components communicate by shared memory, others via network connection, and others via low-level device interfaces and operating system calls. In addition, components with analog ports are connected by physical cables. Match examines its two Port arguments, and the components to which they are attached, and creates a suitable connector object.

Some possible Connector subclasses are shown in Figure 5.14. These classes provide alternate implementations for the connection control and data transfer methods:

NetworkConnector: NetworkConnector::Get and NetworkConnector::Put perform reads and writes over a digital network. A NetworkConnector would be used to connect components running on different machines.

MemoryConnector: Components joined by a MemoryConnector bypass the Get and Put methods (of both Port and Connector) and access directly a region of shared memory. A MemoryConnector could be used by tightly coupled components running on the same machine.

DelegateConnector: The Put and Get methods of DelegateConnector relay the request to the port at the 'opposite' end of the connector. For example, DelegateConnector::Put is invoked by the port at the 'from' end, and the connector then simply invokes the Put method of the 'to' port. DelegateConnector allows software-based components (generally those implemented using a process) to be connected to hardware-based components (implemented using a device driver).

BufferConnector: BufferConnector::Put and BufferConnector::Get add and remove data from a shared buffer. A BufferConnector could be used by loosely coupled components running on the same machine.

CableConnector: A CableConnector object represents a physical cable connection. Implementing the Connect method requires a computer-controllable switch, if a switch is not available the appropriate cable must be plugged in

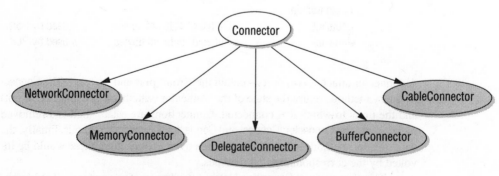

Figure 5.14   Possible Connector subclasses.

manually. CableConnector::Get and CableConnector::Put are null operations (or raise an error).

As an example of using ports and connectors, consider two components, vsource and vsink, with compatible ports. Suppose the ports are named 'Video Out' and 'Video In'. Possible code for connecting these components is listed below. The graphic representation of the situation is shown in Figure 5.15.

```
Connector        mycon;
Port             vout;
Port             vin;

vsource.PowerOn( );
vsink.PowerOn( );
vout = vsource.FindPort("Video Out");
vin = vsink.FindPort("Video In");
mycon = Connector::Match(vout, vin);
mycon.Connect( );
vsink.Start( );
vsource.Start( );
```

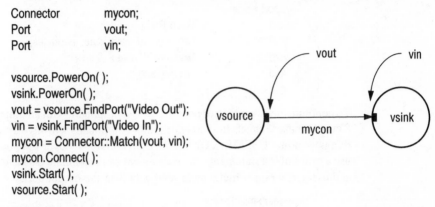

Figure 5.15   Connected components.

The above example shows how applications only need know the names of components in order to establish a connection (assuming port compatibility, which can be tested by the application). Details of how the components communicate, and the passing of data from one component to another, are completely hidden from application.

Port wrappers □ Users of components basically instantiate component classes and make connections; they control components from the outside and can ignore what happens internally. Implementing a component, on the other hand, is more difficult and requires knowledge of available communication mechanisms. One way to simplify inter-component communication, from the implementor's perspective, is by using *port wrappers*. A port wrapper is a format object of the same type as a component's output port. Furthermore, the format class declares methods which transfer data over a port. This is best illustrated by an example. Consider a 2D animation format where animation values are sequences of the following elements:

```
CREATE <int id> <2D geometric data>
MOVE <int id> <float x> <float y>
DELETE <int id>
```

Here a CREATE element specifies the geometric structure of a 2D object and assigns it an integer identifier. The object can then be moved and deleted. The following class represents this format:

```
class SimpleAnimationFormat : public AnimationFormat {
    // querying
    // ...

    // import, export
    // ...

    // port wrappers
    void                Wrap(Port p);
    void                Create(int id, void* data, int nbytes);
    void                Move(int id, float x, float y);
    void                Delete(int id);
}
```

To continue the example, suppose there is a component with an output port of type SimpleAnimationFormat. Implementing this component will involve (among other things) sending CREATE, MOVE and DELETE elements over the port. Rather than use a series of Put statements, the component can instantiate SimpleAnimationFormat and use port wrapper methods to send data over the output port:

```
// component initialization
//
SimpleAnimationFormat        saf;
Port                         outPort;
saf.Wrap(outPort);           // associates the format object with the Port object

// component execution
// ...
saf.Create(id, data, n);     // sends a CREATE element over outPort
// ...
saf.Move(id, x, y);          // sends a MOVE element over outPort
// ...
```

5.5.3   COMPONENT EVENTS

The final group of Component methods allows applications to respond to asynchronous events generated by components. Component events are bundles of information that reflect the conditions of component operation. Different components generate different types of events, and the different event types carry different attributes. Events in general are easily modelled by a class hierarchy. The root of the hierarchy, the class Event, provides generic methods, in particular a method for registering *event handlers*, while its subclasses add instance variables and access methods for type-specific attributes.

The Component class includes methods allowing an application to determine the types of events generated by a component and to mask or unmask the generation of specific event types. The following illustrates these methods. Consider an event class named FrameEvent. Suppose video sources generate events of this type each time a frame is sent over the output port. The code fragment:

```
FrameEvent                    ev;

ev.SetFrameNumber(1200);
ev.Register(handlerFunction);
vsource.UnMask(ev);
```

creates a FrameEvent object and sets an event attribute (the frame number) to a specific value. An event handler or 'callback function' is registered and the event is unmasked in the vsource component. The effect is that when vsource reaches frame number 1200 the event handler is called.

5.5.4   COMPONENT SUBCLASSES

The immediate subclasses of Component (the classes Producer, Consumer, and Transformer, see Figure 5.10) divide components into three large families, where the taxonomy is based on port topology – in particular whether a component has input ports, output ports, or both. There are also basic behavioral differences between the three families: producers create streams, transformers operate on streams, and consumers absorb streams. These differences in behavior are captured by methods found in the respective classes. First consider the Producer class:

```
abstract class Producer : public Component {
public:
            // loading, single-port source
            virtual errCode              Load(TemporalMedia val);
            virtual errCode              UnLoad( );


            // loading, multi-port source
            virtual errCode              Load(TemporalMedia val, Port p);
            virtual errCode              UnLoad(Port p);
};
```

The Producer::Load methods are used to specify temporal media values to be sent over a source's output port(s). The loaded value must be compatible with the port (specifically, it must be possible to export the value in a format used by the port). Additionally, ports that are the sources of 'live' data return an error if the application attempts a load. In such cases the value leaving the port comes from acquisition hardware rather than from an existing media value. Whether a port is live or not can be determined from its descriptor.

The Consumer class is declared as:

```
abstract class Consumer : public Component {
public:
            // shadowing, single-port sink
            virtual TemporalMedia        Shadow( );


            // shadowing, multi-port sink
            virtual TemporalMedia        Shadow(Port p);
}
```

The Consumer::Shadow methods allow applications to inspect the media value(s) entering a sink. The performance of the component can then be monitored by looking at intermediate results. The value returned by Shadow (and hence the method name) is read-only – allowing applications to modify the value would interfere with component operation. This method is only supported by sinks which record the data entering their ports. If the data is transient, as when used for presentation, there is no value to be returned by Shadow.

Perhaps the most interesting components are the transformers. The Transform class is declared as:

```
abstract class Transformer : public Component {
public:
                // loading, single output filter
                virtual errCode          Load(Transform tform);
                virtual errCode          UnLoad( );

                // loading, multiple output filter
                virtual errCode          Component::Load(Transform tform, Port p);
                virtual errCode          Component::UnLoad(Port p);
};
```

Here the Transformer::Load method associates one or more transform objects with a transformer component. This may sound redundant, but can be motivated as follows. A transform object represents an operation – its instance variables specify various pieces of information needed by the operation, and its Apply method performs the operation. However, Apply makes no guarantees regarding timing. In comparison a transformer component represents a time-critical operation. It does this by encapsulating both an operation *and* the computing resources needed to perform the operation (subject to the timing constraints in effect).

In many cases a transformer component is designed to perform a specific operation, and for such 'hardwired' components the Load method is not needed. But some transformers are capable of a variety of operations, and applications then select a member of the component's repertoire by invoking the Load method. Consider the following transformer:

```
abstract class VideoMixer : public Transformer {
public:
                // loading
                virtual errCode          Load(VideoTransition vtran);
                virtual errCode          UnLoad( );
};
```

A VideoMixer component performs the video transition specified by the Load method. The argument to Load will be an instance of a VideoTransition subclass (since VideoTransition is an abstract class). These subclasses represent specific transitions such as dissolves, wipes, and so on.

The VideoMixer example also illustrates what can be called transformer/transform compatibility. Transformers only perform certain operations and it is not possible to invoke Load with an arbitrary transform object. A necessary (but

not sufficient) condition is that there be a match between the ports of the transformer and the arguments of the Apply method for the transform object. Consider
a transform object with an Apply method of the form:

Audio   Apply(Audio, Audio);

This object could not be loaded on a transformer with video ports, or, for that matter, a transformer with only one audio input port. The general rule is that the media
types of the arguments to Apply must be compatible with the transformer's input
ports, and the media type of the value returned by Apply must be compatible with
the transformer's output port.

The three component categories, producers, consumers, and transformers,
accommodate many of the devices and processes needed for multimedia programming. There are situations, however, where the use of components appears problematic, for instance:

Components falling into none of the three categories: Strictly speaking
these are not components, in the sense of the framework, since the absence
of ports implies there is no encapsulated time-critical operation. However
there are many devices, such as scanners and printers, which process nontemporal data. For the sake of completeness it is worth extending the notion
of component to incorporate 'portless' devices and processes. For example,
image scanners could be represented by the class of the form:

```
abstract class Scanner : public PortlessComponent {
    // ...
    Image                    Grab( );
    // ...
};
```

The Scanner class would include methods for adjusting settings (such as
brightness and resolution). The Grab method performs a scan and acquires
an image. Note that Scanner::Grab, unlike video acquisition, is not a time-
critical operation.

Components that fall into multiple categories: Some components have multiple modes of operation where different modes place the component in different categories. For example, player/recorder components act as both
sources and sinks. Rather than add a new component category, these situations suggest what could be called 'composite components', that is, aggregates built from simpler components.

5.6 AN APPLICATION – 'HELLO WORLD: THE VIDEO'

The Media, Format, Transform, and Component classes play different roles in modelling a multimedia environment. Media classes are the most basic, as they represent

the available media, and instances of Media classes represent media values; Format classes are used to import and export media values, and represent external data formats; Transform classes provide a flexible way of adding new functionality, as they represent operations on media values; and finally Component classes encapsulate hardware devices and software services, and represent resources that perform time-critical operations.

Although the framework classes have different roles, they are meant to support each other and work together. To illustrate some aspects of this cooperation, and to give an idea of the style of programming fostered by the framework, we will look at a longer example. It is called 'Hello World' since, like the C program that prints out this greeting, it is a simple but complete application.

The application reads a compressed video value on one machine, and decodes and displays the value on another machine. Three components are used, instances of classes called VideoPlayer, VideoDecoder, and VideoWindow. Their ports are described below:

Component class	Input port (name/type)		Output port (name/type)	
VideoPlayer		(none)	Video Out	CompressedVideoFormat
VideoDecoder	Video In	CompressedVideoFormat	Video Out	RawVideoFormat
VideoWindow	Video In	RawVideoFormat		(none)

VideoPlayer, VideoDecoder and VideoWindow are abstract component types; this can be inferred by looking at the port types – CompressedVideoFormat and RawVideoFormat – both of which are abstract classes. The components used for 'Hello World' are connected to form a three-component chain: the player is connected to the decoder, and the decoder connected to the window. Possible code for the application is shown in Figure 5.16 (error-checking code has been excluded). The point to note here is the degree of abstraction and generality provided by the framework classes. For instance, although the stored video value could be in one of several formats, and although different communication mechanisms could be used between components, few indications of these possibilities percolate up to the level of the application programming interface. Variations in video format are concealed by using the abstract classes Video, VideoPlayer, VideoDecoder and VideoFormat. The appropriate concrete subclasses are determined when the application is running and the file containing the video data has been examined.

5.7 FRAMEWORK SUMMARY

After reading through all the preceding class descriptions and looking at the examples, the overall organization of the framework may no longer be clear. It is perhaps useful to give a summary of the framework by seeing how it fares in light of the requirements mentioned in Section 4.3.

Economy of concepts: The framework is based on two primary concepts: media values, the digital representations of artifacts; and components,

```
//              HelloWorld.cc                        play a video value in a window across the network
//
#include <Multimedia.h>                             // definitions for the framework classes

#define VIDEO_FILE          "HelloWorld.video"      // name of file with video data
#define HOST_NAME           "someHost"              // name of host machine to display on
#define FIRST_FRAME         1                       // index of first video frame
#define FRAME_RATE          15                      // want 15 frames per second

void            LastFrameHandler( );                // forward declaration of event handler

main( )
{
        VideoPlayer             player;             // a Producer component
        VideoDecoder            decoder;            // a Transformer component
        VideoWindow             viewer;             // a Consumer component
        Video                   movie;              // a Video object
        VideoDecode             decodeFunction;     // a Transform object
        VideoFormat             format;             // a Format object
        Connector               playerToDecoder;
        Connector               decoderToViewer;
        Port                    playerOut
        Port                    decoderIn;
        Port                    decoderOut;
        Port                    viewerIn;
        string                  formatName;
        string                  transformName;
        FrameEvent              lastFrameEvent;

        // import the video
        format = VideoFormat::GuessFormat(VIDEO_FILE);
        formatName = format.Descriptor( ).Name( );
        movie = format.Import(VIDEO_FILE);

        // instantiate the player, decoder, and viewer
        player = VideoPlayer::Open(formatName);
        decoder = VideoDecoder::Open(HOST_NAME);    // i.e., we want the viewer and decoder
        viewer = VideoWindow::Open(HOST_NAME);      // components to be located on the remote host

        // set decoding parameters and
        // load transform object on decoder component
        transformName = Concat(formatName, "Decode");
        decodeFunction = VideoDecode::FindTransform(transformName);
        decodeFunction.SetParam("Decoded Frame Rate", FRAME_RATE);
        decoder.Load(decodeFunction);
```

Figure 5.16   The 'Hello World' application

```
                    // allocate resources for components
                    player.PowerOn( );
                    decoder.PowerOn( );
                    viewer.PowerOn( );

                    // connect player to decoder
                    playerOut = player.FindPort("Video Out");
                    decoderIn = decoder.FindPort("Video In");
                    playerToDecoder = Connector::Match(playerOut, decoderIn);
                    playerToDecoder.Connect( );

                    // connect decoder to viewer
                    decoderOut = decoder.FindPort("Video Out");
                    viewerIn = viewer.FindPort("Video In");
                    decoderToViewer = Connector::Match(decoderOut, viewerIn);
                    decoderToViewer.Connect( );

                    // set a common timebase for movie and player
                    movie.SetTimeBase(30);
                    player.SetTimeBase(30);

                    // register event handler
                    lastFrameEvent.SetFrameNumber(movie.NumElements( ));
                    lastFrameEvent.Register(LastFrameHandler);
                    player.UnMask(lastFrameEvent);

                    // load movie, cue and play
                    player.Load(movie);
                    player.Cue(movie.Start(FIRST_FRAME));
                    viewer.Start( );
                    decoder.Start( );
                    player.Start( );

                    // wait for playback to finish
            }

            void LastFrameHandler(Event ev)
            {
                    player.Stop( );
                    decoder.Stop( );
                    viewer.Stop( );
            }
```

Figure 5.16   (continued) The 'Hello World' application.

active entities that produce, consume, and transform media values. There is a Media class hierarchy that encapsulates media values and a Component class hierarchy for components. Additional hierarchies for transforms and formats play supporting roles. Descriptors of several varieties are available. Many of the class hierarchies have a similar overall structure patterned on the breakdown of media into media types. Finally the classes fit together fairly naturally. This is seen in the dependencies between transformer components and transform objects, or between ports and format objects. Identifying and isolating such dependencies reduces the complexity of the framework.

Open: The framework is extended by adding classes. Typically these would be concrete classes that implement the methods specified in the more general abstract classes. The primary locations for new classes are the Media, Component, Format, and Transform hierarchies. By adding classes to these hierarchies a variety of extensions are accommodated, including: new media types or new representations of existing types, new devices, and new file and stream formats.

Queryable: Media and Component hierarchies, and those for transforms, formats, and descriptors, have methods that query classes and instances. Query methods allow applications to inspect media values, to determine what formats and transforms are available, and to inquire about components and their capabilities. If combined with a dynamic loading facility, queries allow existing applications to instantiate new classes without the need for recompilation. Applications can then adapt as the underlying platform changes.

Distribution: Components are natural units for building distributed applications. Components encapsulate autonomous activities that can be connected into cooperative assemblies. In addition, connectors and ports encapsulate low-level communication protocols and application protocols respectively.

Scalable: Scalability requires both scalable data representations and components that take advantage of this ability. Concrete component classes and concrete media classes supporting scalability can be added, but the abstract classes at the higher levels of the Component and Media hierarchies do not provide any generic methods for scalability. The notions of component power and media quality are both related to scalability and perhaps could form a conceptual basis for more general support.

High-level interfaces: A multimedia framework should provide high-level interfaces in five areas: media synchronization, media composition, device control, database integration, and concurrent media processing. Three of these (synchronization, composition, and database integration) are research topics and will be discussed in Chapter 6. Device control and concurrent processing are addressed by the methods found in component classes. There are two parts to a component interface – general methods provided by all components and component-specific methods. The former are designed to be high level and easy to use, the latter depend on the design of the particular component. While it is certainly possible to design low-level, implementation-dependent interfaces, the object-oriented approach promotes clean interfaces. Furthermore, an important property of components is that they encapsulate both devices and processes. As a result, device control and process control reduce (from the application's perspective) to the same thing – component control.

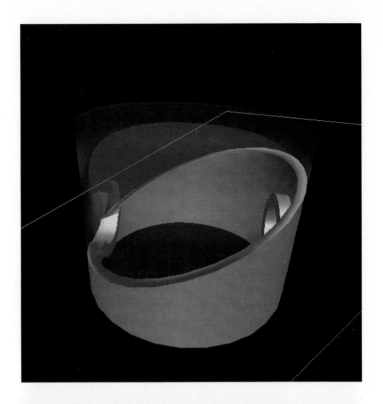

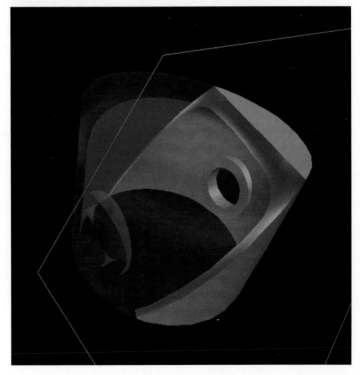

VII VOLUME IMAGES. Two views of a piston are shown, from slightly different perspectives and with different orientations of a cut plane.

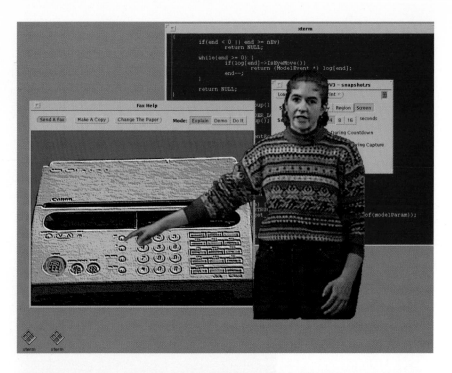

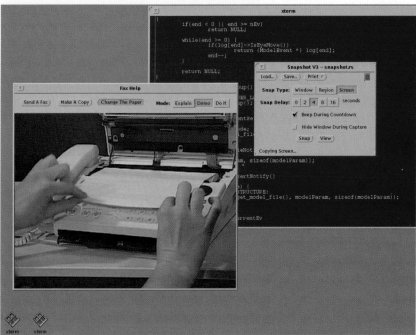

VIII THE FAX ASSISTANT. A prototype of a tool intended to help people learn how to use a computer-controlled fax machine. It has three modes: Explain, Demo and Do It. In Explain mode a video assistant (see Chapter 6) appears and explains various operations (top). In Demo mode, the picture of the fax machine is replaced by a video clip showing it in operation (bottom). Finally, in Do It mode the fax machine actually performs operations.

6

USING THE FRAMEWORK: TWO APPLICATIONS

6.1 Media processing platforms and component kits
6.2 A virtual museum
6.3 Video widgets and video actors
6.4 Summary

The multimedia framework described in the previous chapter is heavily influenced by the metaphor of plugging components together to build applications. The idea of implementation by connection, also called dataflow programming, has been used in many areas, notably scientific visualization systems (Upson *et al.*, 1989; Dyer, 1990) and environments for simulation and visual programming (Shu, 1988). Constructing applications from components that produce, consume, and transform streams of data is not appropriate for all application areas. However, this approach does appear to fit multimedia programming where, because of stream-like temporal media, components and connections are very natural.

6.1 MEDIA PROCESSING PLATFORMS AND COMPONENT KITS

Before building applications by connecting and configuring components, a set of components is first designed and implemented. Once available, components can be *reused* in different applications. Designing and implementing reusable software is a difficult task in general, but for the multimedia framework it is somewhat simplified since the design of new components is guided by the existing abstract classes. In particular, a new component class, and the same holds for media and format classes, must implement the virtual methods declared by its abstract superclasses. Concrete classes also introduce many new methods of their own, as these operations reflect the capabilities of particular platforms. For example, a component that encapsulates a hardware device may introduce methods specific to the device. Similarly, concrete media classes may introduce media-specific methods. The role of concrete classes and their relationship to the framework can be made more clear with the help of two definitions – media processing platforms and component kits.

Media processing platforms □ A media processing platform is a set of hardware and/or software resources that perform operations on media values. ('Multimedia platform' is an equivalent and more commonly used term; however, we want to emphasize that platforms have a computational dimension.) Depending on the range of operations supported, media processing platforms range from simple playback-only devices to more versatile and programmable platforms for media acquisition, manipulation, and interactive presentation. Specific examples are CD players, video editing suites, sets of MIDI devices, and workstations with audio and video processing hardware.

Component kits □ A component kit is the extension of the multimedia framework to encompass the functionality of a media processing platform. This means that concrete classes, in particular media types, transforms, formats, and components, are defined and implemented for the platform. For instance, a component kit for a MIDI platform would include a temporal media class for MIDI sequences, a MIDI file format class, a stream format class for exchanging MIDI values, a connector class for MIDI connections, and various components corresponding to such things as MIDI samplers, sequencers, and synthesizers.

We now look at two examples of constructing applications by connecting components. The two examples, a 'virtual museum' and 'video widgets', both derive from existing prototypes (de Mey and Gibbs, 1993; Gibbs *et al.*, 1993). The first demonstrates a virtual environment for exploring a multimedia information space. The second demonstrates a technique for integrating digital video with user interfaces. The examples are assembled from a component kit containing over forty components. This component kit, and the underlying media processing platform, are described in the appendices. We have chosen an elaborate platform that furnishes a rich set of components. While such platforms require many pieces of

equipment and are not widely available, they point to how more compact platforms may develop. Furthermore, a complex media processing platform allows us
to exercise the framework more fully by seeing whether it can be modelled by
framework classes.

Note to the Reader

This chapter refers to many classes for media types, formats, and
components. In addition, some sections contain diagrams where
components are identified by short three- or four-letter names. A
description of all classes appearing in this chapter and a list of component
names is found in Appendix B. An experimental hardware platform for
these components is described in Appendix A.

6.2 A VIRTUAL MUSEUM

The traditional museum is a setting allowing people to visit exhibits, often shown
in pleasant surroundings and often presented with information concerning their
history, origin, and so on. Like the traditional museum, a virtual museum contains
exhibits, but now these, and their surroundings, are digital constructs rather than
real objects and places. The concept of a virtual museum is very broad and has
been proposed as a model for 'large-scale information resources' (Hoptman,
1992). Virtual museums also provide an ideal opportunity for evaluating a multimedia programming environment – they are media-rich spaces where many forms
of digital media are called into play.

The virtual museum presented in this section has only a small number of exhibits and there are no facilities for linking exhibits with related information.
Rather than focus on issues of information structuring or information retrieval, the
aim is to combine real-time 3D animation with other forms of media. Another virtual museum, relying more on digital video, is described by Hoffert *et al.* (1992).

6.2.1   A TOUR OF THE VIRTUAL MUSEUM

The virtual museum is an example of a non-immersive virtual world. It is a virtual
world since it presents users with a view of a 3D world through which they navi-
gate interactively. It is non-immersive since the 3D world is viewed on a conventional, rather than a head-mounted, display. At the moment only one user at a time
can enter the virtual museum. However, as we will see, this is largely a consequence of lacking components and multi-user functionality can be added quite
easily.

The virtual museum itself is a 3D model of an existing building[1] with a few
pieces of furniture. Several 2D and 3D exhibits have been placed within this rather

---

[1] The Barcelona Pavilion, designed by Ludwig Mies van der Rohe for the 1929 World
Exhibition in Barcelona.

spartan model and considerably enrich its visual appearance (see Figure 6.1). Features of this virtual museum include:

Different views: The museum can be simultaneously viewed in 3D and 2D. As a museum visitor moves through the 3D model, a marker tracks their position on a 2D floor plan.

Different forms of interaction: As the visitors move around the museum, they enter and exit 'sensitive' regions which trigger the presentation of exhibits. The position of the sensitive regions is indicated on the 2D floor plan and through 3D visual cues. Navigation in the museum is principally done in 3D via an input device that allows six degrees of freedom in movement (although the interface can be constrained so that only motion in a horizontal plane is possible); it is also possible to 'teleport' by pointing within the 2D floor plan. The museum floor plan and the location of sensitive regions are shown in Figure 6.2.

Different media: Museum exhibits incorporate various media including still and moving video, digital images, surface images, and simple geometric objects. Some exhibits are animated, for example they may move or change their size. Images and video can be mapped onto 3D surfaces within the model or simply 'overlaid' on top of rendered views of the model.

Different levels of detail: Several exhibits, including digital images, video stills, and surface images, can be viewed in low resolution or high resolution. Low-resolution exhibits, called 'stand-ins', are rendered more quickly and so give the application an opportunity to improve performance by sacrificing quality.

Recorded tours: It is possible to record a path through the museum, edit the recording, and then play back in normal or reverse direction at various speeds. The path itself can be visualized by adding it to the 3D or 2D view of the museum.

Guides: Video-based museum 'guides' can be overlaid on the museum and then played back. Guides are examples of video actors and are discussed more fully in Section 6.3.

6.2.2   MEDIA CLASSES FOR THE VIRTUAL MUSEUM

The virtual museum is based on two media classes, PolyGraphic and PolyAnimation. The first is a simple 3D graphics class for hierarchical structures of polygons. The second supports temporal sequences of events; the events refer primarily to PolyGraphic objects but may also reference image and video objects. The geometry of the museum, its walls and floors, is modelled by a PolyGraphic object; PolyAnimation objects dynamically alter the rendering of this model. Additional media classes are used for exhibits, but these are less important to the overall design of the virtual museum and their description is left to the appendices (see Appendix B).

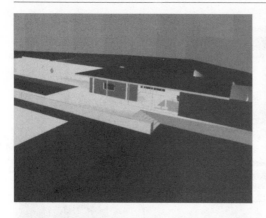

Figure 6.1   Four views of the virtual museum. Clockwise from top left are the museum viewed from above, an exhibit area showing a digital image, a vase represented by a surface image, and an example of a video frame mapped onto a cylinder.

Figure 6.2   The floor plan of the virtual museum. The rectangular areas are 'sensitive regions' where exhibits are displayed on entry. Within each sensitive region is a graphic symbol indicating the type of exhibit. For example the bottommost exhibit is a moving video clip. Other exhibits include digital images, surface images, geometric models, and video frames mapped onto simple geometrical solids.

```
typedef      float       GeoMatrix[4][4];        // coordinate transformation matrix
typedef      float       PosVec[3];              // position vector
typedef      short       TrueColor[3];           // RGB value

typedef struct {                                 // a set of polygons with vertex color
             int         npoly;                   // number of polys in the set
             ColorPoly*  polys;                   // vertex and color info for each poly
} ColorPolySet;

typedef struct {                                 // a single colored polygon
             int         nvertex;                 // number of vertices
             PosVec*     p;                        // position data
             TrueColor*  c;                        // color data
} ColorPoly;

class PolyGraphic : public 3DGraphic {
public:
             // querying
             GraphicInfo                Descriptor( );

             // editing
             void                       Cut(PolyGraphicSelection);
             PolyGraphic                Copy(PolyGraphicSelection);
             void                       Paste(PolyGraphicSelection, PolyGraphicContext);

             // Graphic methods
             TrueColorImage             Render(/* viewing and other parameters */);
             // ...

             // 3DGraphic methods
             GeoMatrix                  CoordTransform( );
             void                       SetCoordTransform(GeoMatrix xform);
             // ...

             // PolyGraphic-specific methods
             ColorPolySet               Polys( );
             PolyGraphic                Parent( );
             setOf PolyGraphic          Children( );
             // plus methods for modifying the polygon data, adding children and so on
             // ...
};
```

Figure 6.3   The PolyGraphic class – partial definition.

PolyGraphic

A skeleton declaration for PolyGraphic is shown in Figure 6.3. Instances of this class are groups of polygons with colored vertices; the data structure used to specify geometry and coloring is called ColorPolySet. It is possible to assemble hierarchies of PolyGraphic instances; for example, a cup and saucer might be grouped together in a hierarchy as is shown in Figure 6.4. Generally only leaf nodes refer to geometry data, while non-leaf nodes act as containers for structuring more complex objects. Geometry data can be shared among PolyGraphic objects. For example, to create a car with four identical wheels it is not necessary to duplicate four sets of polygons. Rather one set can be shared by the four wheels (however, subsequently modifying the geometry data will influence the appearance of each wheel). Using geometry sharing it is also possible for PolyGraphic objects to act as templates when creating new objects; this is done by passing the new object a reference to the template object's geometry data.

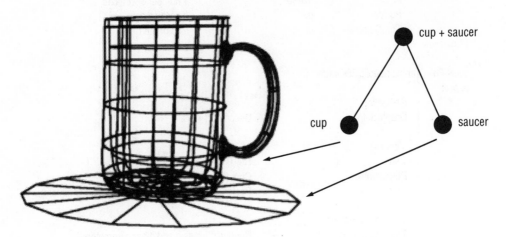

Figure 6.4   A PolyGraphic hierarchy. (The heavy circles represent PolyGraphic objects, the arrows indicate references to geometry data.)

Within a PolyGraphic hierarchy, the position and orientation of each object is specified relative to its parent. Per-object coordinate transformation matrices are used for this purpose. A special predefined PolyGraphic object, called the 'world' object, is the root of all visible PolyGraphic hierarchies. Its coordinate system is known as world coordinates.

PolyAnimation

The PolyAnimation class is the key to building the virtual museum. This is a subclass of EventBasedAnimation and is used for temporal sequences of PolyAnimation-Event (in turn a subclass of AnimationEvent). A partial declaration for PolyAnimation is shown in Figure 6.5. Notice how the declaration overrides virtual methods inherited from the four superclasses: Media, TemporalMedia, Animation, and EventBasedAnimation. There are also two PolyAnimation-specific methods. The first, PolyAnimation::MakePath, returns a PolyGraphic object representing the trajectory of a selected animated object within the sequence. The second, PolyAnimation::Normalize, removes relative motion from the sequence and replaces this with absolute motion. This simplifies editing operations (for instance, cutting a sub-sequence) and also simplifies cueing and reverse playback.

```
class PolyAnimation : public EventBasedAnimation {
public:
                // querying
                AnimationInfo                   Descriptor( );

                // editing
                void                            Cut(PolyAnimationSelection);
                PolyAnimation                   Copy(PolyAnimationSelection);
                void                            Paste(PolyAnimationSelection, PolyAnimationContext);

                // time coordinates
                int                             TimeBase( );
                void                            SetTimeBase(int timeBase);

                // element access
                int                             NumElements( );
                PolyAnimationEvent              Element(Time t);
                PolyAnimationEvent              Element(int index);
                AnimationEventInfo              Descriptor(int index);
                Time                            Start(int index);
                Time                            Duration(int index);

                // temporal transformations
                void                            Translate(Time displacement);
                void                            Scale(float scaleFactor);
                void                            Invert(Time invertPoint);

                // Animation methods
                RawVideo                        Render( );
                PolyGraphic                     SceneAt(Time samplePoint);
                PolyGraphic                     SceneAt(int index);

                // EventBasedAnimation methods
                void                            InsertEvent(PolyAnimationEvent ev, Time insertPoint);
                void                            InsertEvent(PolyAnimationEvent ev, int index);
                void                            DeleteEvent(Time deletePoint);
                void                            DeleteEvent(int index);

                // PolyAnimation-specific methods
                PolyGraphic                     MakePath(PolyAnimationSelection);
                void                            Normalize( );
};
```

Figure 6.5   The PolyAnimation class – partial definition.

Generally the events appearing within a PolyAnimation instance refer to changes in PolyGraphic objects and their hierarchies; however, events can also refer to other media objects such as images and videos. References from events to media objects are called *structure identifiers* and *structure type identifiers*. These are integer values that must be mapped to media objects by components that process PolyAnimation values. The difference between the two identifiers is that the first refers to actual visual elements appearing within the animation, while the second refers to templates used to create other objects.

There are a number of subclasses of PolyAnimationEvent; these are listed in Table 6.1 along with a brief description of what different events signify. The descriptions should be interpreted in the context of *rendering* a PolyAnimation stream (as we will see, there are components which do exactly this). Other actions may be taken in other contexts.

Table 6.1   PolyAnimationEvent subclasses.

Class name (event type)	Description
DefineStructureTypeEvent	event contains geometry data, assign it a structure type id
LoadStructureTypeEvent	load geometry data from a file, assign it a structure type id
CreateEvent	create a PolyGraphic object, assign it a structure id
DeleteEvent	delete a PolyGraphic object
InstallEvent	install a PolyGraphic object in a hierarchy
UnInstallEvent	remove a PolyGraphic object from a hierarchy
MoveAbsoluteEvent	move a PolyGraphic object in world coordinates
MoveInLocalSpaceEvent	move a PolyGraphic object in local coordinates
MoveInParentSpaceEvent	move a PolyGraphic object relative to its parent
LoadGridEvent	load grid data from a file, create a PolyGraphic object, assign it a structure id
LoadImageEvent	load an image from a file, assign it a structure id
LoadSurfaceImageEvent	load a surface image from a file, assign a structure id for the image data, create a PolyGraphic grid object for the surface data, assign it a structure id
GrabImageEvent[a]	grab a video frame as an image, assign it a structure id
MapVideoOnGridEvent[a]	color a grid with video
MapImageOnGridEvent	color a grid with an image
OverlayVideoEvent[a]	overlay video with the graphics as a background
SelectViewPointEvent	select a PolyGraphic object to serve as the viewpoint
FlashEvent	flash the display

a. Events of type GrabImageEvent, MapVideoOnGridEvent and OverlayVideoEvent are ignored if no video value is available; see the discussion of the R3 component.

Once the PolyAnimation and PolyAnimationEvent classes are available it is possible to create PolyAnimation values. One such value is shown in Table 6.2; it is a sequence of six events that produce a graphics object and move it about.

Table 6.2   A PolyAnimation value (time values are h:mm:ss:ff, fps = 30).

Time	Event Type	Attributes
0:00:00:00	LoadStructureTypeEvent	fileName = /vm/PolyGraphic/cup.pg StructureTypeId = 12
0:00:00:01	CreateEvent	StructureTypeId = 12 StructureId = 44
0:00:00:02	InstallEvent	parent StructureId = WORLD_SID child StructureId = 44
0:00:00:03	MoveInParentSpaceEvent	StructureId = 44 coordinate transformation matrix = [...]
0:00:00:06	MoveInParentSpaceEvent	StructureId = 44 coordinate transformation matrix = [...]
0:00:01:00	MoveInParentSpaceEvent	StructureId = 44 coordinate transformation matrix = [...]

This value can be created by the following code:

```
PolyAnimation        anim;              // a PolyAnimation value
StructureTypeId      cupDef = 12;       // a structure type identifier
StructureId          myCup = 44;        // a structure identifier

anim.SetTimeBase(30);                              // measure time in 1/30 sec units
anim.InsertEvent(new LoadStructureTypeEvent("/vm/PolyGraphic/cup.pg",
                    cupDef), 0);
anim.InsertEvent(new CreateEvent(cupDef, myCup), 1);
anim.InsertEvent(new InstallEvent(WORLD_SID, myCup), 2);
anim.InsertEvent(new MoveInParentSpaceEvent(myCup, someGeoMatrix), 3);
anim.InsertEvent(new MoveInParentSpaceEvent(myCup, someGeoMatrix), 6);
anim.InsertEvent(new MoveInParentSpaceEvent(myCup, someGeoMatrix), 30);
```

6.2.3   TRANSFORM CLASSES FOR THE VIRTUAL MUSEUM

Several Transformer components will be used to construct the virtual museum but these components (such as a renderer used to convert PolyAnimation values to digital video) have 'hardwired' rather than loadable transforms. Thus no transform classes are needed.

6.2.4   FORMAT CLASSES FOR THE VIRTUAL MUSEUM

The virtual museum is built by importing PolyGraphic objects and then positioning the objects in world coordinates. The import operation is provided by a format class called, as one might expect, PolyGraphicFileFormat. The exhibits found in the museum are also imported from files and make use of the following formats:

RGBImageFileFormat: A file format for importing and exporting color images.

GridFileFormat: A file format for importing and exporting PolyGraphic values that are rectangular grids. GridFileFormat is more compact for large grids than PolyGraphicFileFormat.

DepthImageFileFormat: A file format for importing and exporting color images with a depth channel. Data stored in this format resembles an image stored in RGBImageFileFormat followed by a grid stored in GridFileFormat.

The above handle graphics and image data and are all file formats. The PolyAnimation media class has a stream format and, since some components of the virtual museum import and export PolyAnimation values (as when loading and saving recorded walk-throughs), a file format is also needed. The two formats are called PolyAnimationFileFormat and PolyAnimationStream; their declarations are shown in Figure 6.6. Since this is the first example of a stream format we will look at these two classes in more detail.

PolyAnimationFileFormat

The file format is the simpler of the two PolyAnimation formats. Like other file format classes it has methods for querying and import/export. The query methods use AnimationFormatInfo objects which include the following attributes:

Attribute	Value
MediaFormatInfo attributes	
Name	"Poly Animation File Format"
Version	"1.0"
TemporalMediaFormatInfo attributes	
NumberOfElements	> 0
ExplicitTiming	true
AnimationFormatInfo attributes	
FormatSpecific	undefined

Subclasses of AnimationFormat are free to use the FormatSpecific attribute as they see fit. PolyAnimationFileFormat uses this attribute to flag whether a PolyAnimation value is normalized or not. The ExplicitTiming attribute is true, which indicates that elements are stored with timestamps.

PolyAnimationStream

In general, stream formats are intended for component implementors. The main service they provide is 'port wrapper' methods, used to send data over output ports. The port wrappers found in PolyAnimationStream include one method for each PolyAnimationEvent subclass; arguments to these methods match the arguments needed to create such events. In addition the SendEvent method accepts previously constructed PolyAnimationEvent instances.

The following example uses both PolyAnimationFileFormat and PolyAnimationStream. It is meant to be part of a component that 'replays' PolyAnimation values. It does so by importing a value and then sending the constituent events, at the proper time, over an output port (which is assumed to be connected to a component responsible for their rendering):

```
class PolyAnimationFileFormat : public AnimationFormat {
public:
        // querying
        AnimationFormatInfo             Descriptor( );
        AnimationFormatInfo             Descriptor(PolyAnimation val);
        bool                            SetDescriptor(AnimationFormatInfo info);

        // import, export
        bool                            CanImport(string fileName);
        AnimationInfo                   ImportInfo(string fileName);
        PolyAnimation                   Import(string fileName);
        void                            CanExport(Media val);
        void                            Export(string fileName, PolyAnimation val);
};


typedef         int             StructureTypeId;                // structure type identifier
typedef         int             StructureId;                    // structure identifier
class PolyAnimationStream : public AnimationFormat {
public:
        // querying
        AnimationFormatInfo             Descriptor( );
        AnimationFormatInfo             Descriptor(PolyAnimation val);
        bool                            SetDescriptor(AnimationFormatInfo info);

        // port wrapper methods
        //      send any event
        void                    SendEvent(PolyAnimationEvent ev);
        //      send graphics related events
        void                    DefineStructureType(StructureTypeId stype, ColorPolySet polys);
        void                    LoadStructureType(string fileName, StructureTypeId stype);
        void                    Create(StructureTypeId stype, StructureId sval);
        void                    Delete(StructureId sval);
        void                    Install(StructureId parent, StructureId child);
        void                    UnInstall(StructureId sval);
        void                    MoveAbsolute(StructureId sval, GeoMatrix xform);
        void                    MoveInLocalSpace(StructureId sval, GeoMatrix xform);
        void                    MoveInParentSpace(StructureId sval, GeoMatrix xform);
        //      send image and video related events
        void                    LoadGrid(string fileName, StructureId grid);
        void                    LoadImage(string fileName, StructureId image);
        void                    LoadSurfaceImage(string fileName, StructureId grid, StructureId image);
        void                    GrabImage(StructureId image);
        void                    MapVideoOnGrid(StructureId grid);
        void                    MapImageOnGrid(StructureId grid, StructureId image);
        void                    OverlayVideo( );
        //      send events for 3DRenderer methods accessed via a port interface
        void                    SelectViewPoint(StructureId sval);
        void                    Flash( );
};
```

Figure 6.6   File and stream format classes for PolyAnimation.

```
PolyAnimation            animRec;        // a media object
PolyAnimationFileFormat   file;          // a file format object
PolyAnimationStream       rdr;           // a stream format object
Port                      outPort;       // an output port

// import the recording
animRec = file.Import("recording.pa");

// create an output port and associate the stream object with the port
outPort = ...
rdr.Wrap(outPort);

// send animation events over the port
for(/* i = each element in animRec */) {
        // wait until animRec.Time(i)
        rdr.SendEvent(animRec.Element(i));
}
```

6.2.5   COMPONENTS FOR THE VIRTUAL MUSEUM

The virtual museum application relies on a large number of interconnected components driven by PolyAnimation values. Different extensions, involving the rearranging and rerouting of components, are possible. Common among the various configurations are three components critical to the operation of the museum: R3, a renderer of PolyAnimation values, NAV, used for interactive navigation through the museum, and MOD, the modeller of the museum itself.

R3 – a 3D renderer component

R3 is a transformer with two input ports and one output port. The first input is a PolyAnimation stream (that is, the port type is PolyAnimationStream). The second input port takes an NTSC video signal. (Although R3 uses analog video, a similar component could be implemented with digital video.) The video port, which need not be connected for the component to operate, provides a series of video frames used to color parts of a PolyGraphic hierarchy. The hierarchy is built up as events arrive in the PolyAnimation stream. The output of R3 is a sequence of images depicting the PolyGraphic hierarchy rendered at successive times. In other words, R3 produces video – a temporal sequence of images; the specific format used is called RGBVideoStream. Typically the resulting images are deposited in a framebuffer and then displayed; however, they can also be saved in files.

Figure 6.7 visualizes the operation of R3. Here we see PolyAnimationEvent instances and video frames entering, and rendered images emerging. This figure conceals some of the difficulties in realizing such a component. For example, rendering times depend on the complexity of the PolyGraphic hierarchy and the performance of the underlying platform. Furthermore, it is likely that the events are not arriving at a fixed rate. Since the input rate varies, in general there is not a one-to-one correspondence between rendered images and incoming events or video

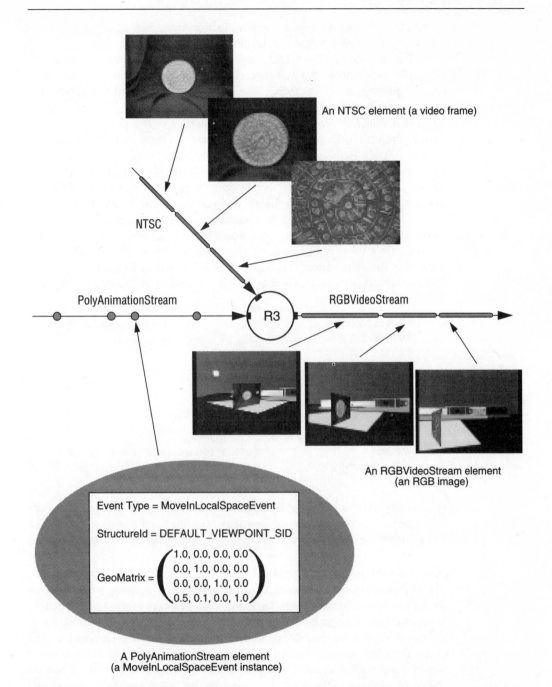

An NTSC element (a video frame)

NTSC

PolyAnimationStream

R3

RGBVideoStream

An RGBVideoStream element
(an RGB image)

Event Type = MoveInLocalSpaceEvent

StructureId = DEFAULT_VIEWPOINT_SID

$$\text{GeoMatrix} = \begin{pmatrix} 1.0, 0.0, 0.0, 0.0 \\ 0.0, 1.0, 0.0, 0.0 \\ 0.0, 0.0, 1.0, 0.0 \\ 0.5, 0.1, 0.0, 1.0 \end{pmatrix}$$

A PolyAnimationStream element
(a MoveInLocalSpaceEvent instance)

Figure 6.7   The R3 (3D renderer) component – a transformer of PolyAnimationStream and (optionally) NTSC to RGBVideoStream.

frames. Instead the component may have to drop video frames, merge events, or take some other action that avoids lagging behind the incoming data.

The class declaration for R3 is shown in Figure 6.8. Using the terminology of the previous chapter, this is a concrete component type. It inherits from three classes: 3DRenderer, its immediate superclass, Transformer, and Component. The methods of interest are those coming from 3DRenderer and the R3-specific methods. The first includes setting the viewing transformation (for instance, the type of viewing projection, the size of the viewport) and other parameters of 3D renderers in general. There is also a method that returns the current frame rate – the time taken in rendering the last completed image. The R3-specific StereoOn and StereoOff methods toggle between a stereo mode (when the mode is selected the PolyGraphic hierarchy is rendered from two slightly different viewpoints as determined by Focus). VideoOn and VideoOff direct the component to accept or ignore incoming video frames. SelectViewPoint identifies a PolyGraphic object whose local coordinate system defines the current viewpoint; Flash causes a few blank red images to be inserted in the output stream (giving the illusion of red flashes). Both Flash and SelectViewPoint can be invoked explicitly or by PolyAnimationStream port wrappers:

```
R3                       r3;          // a component
PolyAnimationStream      rdr;         // a stream format object
FlashEvent               flash;       // an event

// explicit invocation
r3.Flash( );

// invoke by sending an event, assumes that rdr
// wraps a port connected to r3
rdr.Flash( );             // use the port wrapper that sends a Flash event
rdr.SendEvent(flash);     // or use the port wrapper that sends any
                          // PolyAnimationEvent
```

In summary, R3 is a real-time 3D renderer accessed via ports and methods. The port interface carries streams of geometry, shading[1] and viewpoint data. The method interface allows overall control and monitoring of the renderer.

NAV – a navigator component

The NAV, or navigator, component is responsible for transforming a *tracker event stream* to a PolyAnimation stream (see Figure 6.9). Tracker events indicate changes in position and/or orientation. Tracker events are easily obtained from mouse or joystick input; it is also possible to implement components which generate tracker events from keyboard input or by playing back a 'dribble file' (a file containing timestamped tracker events). The platform of Appendix A contains a natural source of tracker events, a ball-like input device which can be displaced and

---

[1] R3 uses a very simple lighting model (constant ambient light). For this reason no lighting-related methods appear in the port or method interface.

```
class R3 : public 3DRenderer {
public:
                    // Component methods
                    CompInfo              Descriptor( );
                    errCode               PowerOn( );
                    errCode               PowerOff( );
                    componentState        State( );
                    errCode               Start( );
                    errCode               Stop( );
                    errCode               Pause( );
                    errCode               Resume( );
                    Time                  CurrentTime( );
                    virtual               Cue(Time cuePoint);
                    int                   TimeBase( );
                    void                  SetTimeBase(int timeBase);
                    float                 Speed( );
                    bool                  Direction( );
                    void                  SetSpeed(float speed);
                    void                  SetDirection(bool direction);
                    setOf Port            KnownPorts( );
                    Port                  FindPort(string name);
                    setOf Event           KnownEvents( );
                    errCode               UnMask(Event ev);
                    errCode               Mask(Event ev);

                    // Transformer methods
                    // not present since the transform is 'hardwired' and not loadable

                    // Renderer methods
                    void                  SetView(/* viewing parameters */);
                    int                   CurrentFrameRate( );
                    // ...

                    // R3-specific methods (adjustment and monitoring category)
                    void                  StereoOn( );
                    void                  StereoOff( );
                    void                  Focus(/* viewing parameters */);
                    void                  VideoOn( );
                    void                  VideoOff( );
                    void                  SelectViewPoint(StructureId sval);
                    void                  Flash( );
};
```

Figure 6.8   The R3 component class.

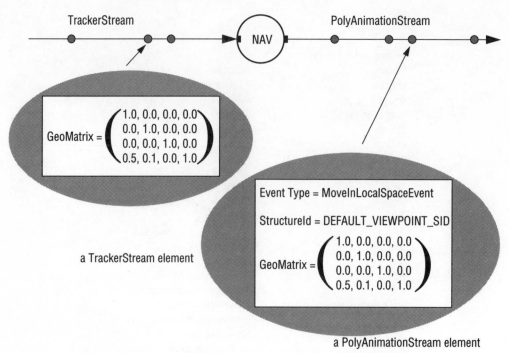

Figure 6.9   The NAV (navigator) component – a transformer of TrackerStream to PolyAnimationStream.

twisted along three axes. (This device is encapsulated by a component called 6DOF, referring to its six degrees of freedom.)

As Figure 6.9 indicates, tracker events are simply coordinate transformation matrices. In order to have a renderer component interpret this data as a change in viewpoint, NAV inserts the matrix in an instance of MoveInLocalSpaceEvent. The structure id appearing in the event is set to DEFAULT_VIEWPOINT_SID; this value identifies the PolyGraphic object currently selected as the viewpoint.

MOD – a modeller component

Neither NAV nor R3 contain code specific to the virtual museum, consequently both can be used in other applications. All museum-specific code is isolated within a third component. This component, called MOD or the modeller, intercepts one PolyAnimation stream and produces two slightly altered PolyAnimation streams (see Figure 6.10). The output ports are named 3Dout and 2Dout. The first is intended for connection to a component which renders perspective views of the museum, while the second is intended for connection to a component which renders the museum floor plan. Typically 3Dout is connected to the R3 component, and 2Dout is connected to a similar component called R2. (R2, despite its name, is a 3D renderer, but its rendering performance is limited and so it is used for simple 2D-like models such as the museum floor plan.)

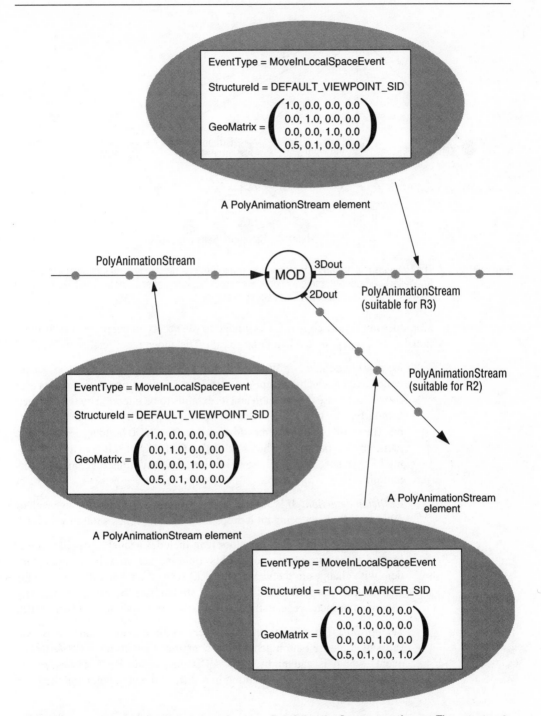

Figure 6.10   The MOD (modeller) component – a PolyAnimationStream transformer. The output ports are called 3Dout and 2Dout.

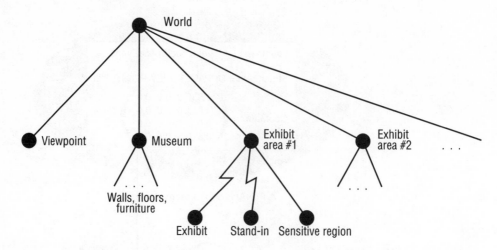

Figure 6.11 The PolyGraphic hierarchy for the virtual museum. The hierarchy is maintained by the MOD (modeller) component, the only component with museum-specific data. The links between an exhibit area and its exhibit and stand-in are dynamic.

MOD does not simply copy from its input port over to its output ports. It adds functionality by processing the incoming stream. The added functionality includes:

Museum initialization: When a MOD component is first 'powered on' it generates events which are sent out over its two output ports. The events sent over 3Dout cause the museum and its exhibits to be imported by the receiver. Similarly, events sent over 2Dout cause the museum floor plan to be imported. The result is that renderers downstream from MOD build up a PolyGraphic hierarchy similar to that shown in Figure 6.11. MOD itself constructs a parallel PolyGraphic hierarchy; however, it needs only limited geometry information.

Collision detection: If MOD detects an incoming event resulting in a wall or other 'solid' object being hit it drops the event and sends a flash over 3Dout.

Floor marker movement: The floor plan includes a small cross-like object located at the current viewpoint. This 'floor marker' must be moved in tandem with changes to the viewpoint. MOD scans the input stream for events altering the viewpoint and, in the 2Dout stream, sets the structure identifier contained in such events to that of the marker (this is shown in Figure 6.10).

Teleporting: The component that renders the floor plan is mouse-sensitive. Pressing a mouse button generates a component event (not a PolyAnimation event) which is caught by MOD. MOD then sends PolyAnimation events through 3Dout and 2Dout, resulting in a shift of the viewpoint and the floor marker.

Sensitive regions: MOD detects entry to and exit from the sensitive regions surrounding exhibits. When a sensitive region is entered its exhibit is 'activated'. Depending on the nature of the exhibit this may involve triggering other components (such as a video source or a component responsible for animating an exhibit) or replacing the exhibit with its 'stand-in'. A stand-in is a simple PolyGraphic object installed within the PolyGraphic world hierarchy in place of the exhibit; using stand-ins reduces the load on renderers.

6.2.6   COMPONENT NETWORKS FOR THE VIRTUAL MUSEUM

We now look at a series of progressively more complex configurations, or 'component networks', made from NAV, R3, MOD, and other components. Component networks are groups of connected components; they correspond to entire applications or large subsystems used by applications. Component networks can be reconfigured as applications proceed; this is demonstrated by a component network for noninteractive rendering discussed below.

Noninteractive rendering

As a starting point we take the component network shown in Figure 6.12. Here an R3 renderer is connected to a framebuffer component (FB) which is in turn connected to a workstation monitor (WM). The result is the display of the image sequence being produced by R3.

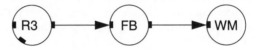

Figure 6.12   A component network for noninteractive rendering.

As this network stands, the display would be uninteresting because R3 has no input and so nothing to render. The following code sequence implements an R3 'client' which simply makes a connection to the PolyAnimation input port of an R3 component and then sends some data:

```
R3                    r3;         // a component
PolyAnimationStream   rdr;        // a stream format object
Connector             toR3;       // a connector object
Port                  myOut;      // the local port
Port                  r3In;       // the remote port


r3 = R3::Open(HOST_NAME);         // get a handle to an R3 renderer located on
                                  //   HOST_NAME, assume it is running
r3In = r3.FindPort("PolyAnimation In");  // want its PolyAnimation port
myOut.SetDescriptor(...);         // setup local port
                                  // (set type to PolyAnimationStream)
rdr.Wrap(myOut);                  // wrap it
toR3 = Connector::Match(myOut, r3In);  // create an appropriate connector
toR3.Connect();                   // and connect

rdr.LoadStructureType(...);       // start sending
```

```
rdr.Create(...);              // PolyAnimation data to
rdr.Install(...);             // r3 using its port
rdr.MovelnLocalSpace(...);    // interface
```

Interactive rendering

Interactivity can be added to the previous component network by connecting an interactive source to the renderer. One way to do this is shown in Figure 6.13, where a NAV component and a 6DOF component (a source of tracker events) are added to the network.

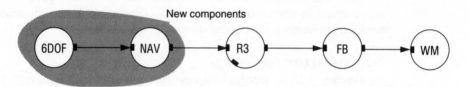

Figure 6.13   A component network for interactive rendering.

The effect of the new components is to couple an input device to the viewpoint used when rendering. It is still necessary for R3 to be supplied with geometric data. This can be done by other clients; since the PolyAnimation port of R3 has *multiple fan-in* it is possible for several clients to simultaneously connect to R3.

Basic virtual museum

Rather than relying on transient clients to provide geometry data to R3, we can add a MOD component as shown in Figure 6.14. Here a source has also been added for R3's video port. This is the minimum set of components needed to run the virtual museum; such a configuration supports interactive navigation and display of the museum and its exhibits.

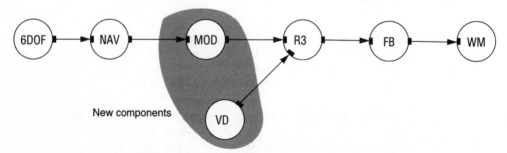

Figure 6.14   A component network for the virtual museum.

Extended virtual museum

An extension to the basic configuration is shown in Figure 6.15. Here an 'animator' (ANI) adds dynamism by transforming or displacing parts of the museum (for instance, it could rotate an exhibit), and a model recorder (MOR) logs museum walk-throughs (by exporting the PolyAnimation value arriving at its input port).

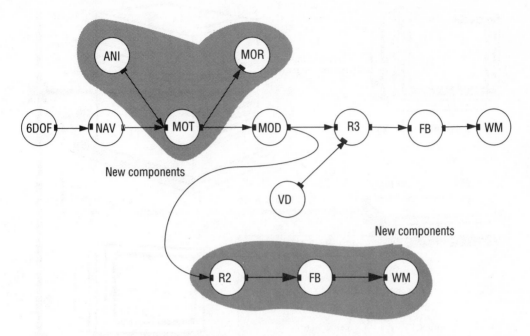

Figure 6.15   An extended component network for the virtual museum. The additional components add dynamics, recording ability, and the display of the floor plan.

Since the streams from NAV and ANI are fed to two components (MOD and MOR), an intermediate 'tee' is needed. This component, the model tee (MOT), simply duplicates its input on two output ports. The MOT input port, like that of MOD and R3, allows multiple connections. The remaining new components display the museum floor plan. This involves the R2 renderer, a second framebuffer and a second monitor.

When looking at component networks keep in mind that components are abstractions of services provided by a media processing platform. To emphasize this point, Figure 6.16 shows a *mapping* of the network of Figure 6.15 to the particular platform described in Appendix A.

Further extensions for the virtual museum

The final member of this series of virtual museum networks is shown in Figure 6.17. Again functionality is added by 'patching in' components. In this case the extensions are the ability to play back previously recorded walk-throughs (MOP), a video overlay window on the display being used for the floor plan (VOV), and a video-based museum guide (VDRW, SCON, CKEY).

The first extension is straightforward. MOP simply imports a PolyAnimation value and sends it though its output port. To the rest of the network this data is indistinguishable from actual input by a user. Control of the model recorder and model player can be combined in a single tool. For instance, Figure 6.18 shows a prototype that allows recording, editing and playback of PolyAnimation values.

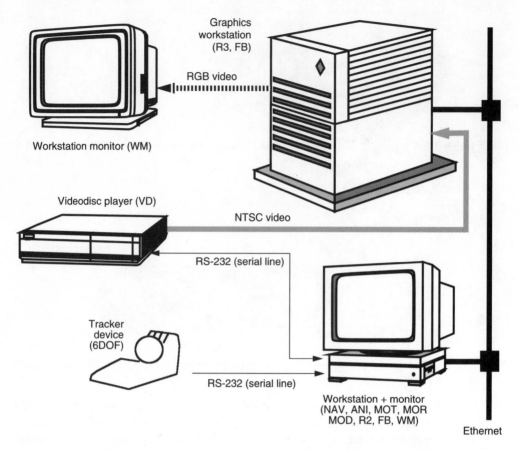

Figure 6.16   A component-to-platform mapping. The platform of Appendix A is capable of running the component network of Figure 6.15. Shown are the actual locations of components on the platform and the physical paths underlying component connections.

The second extension involves VOV, a component used to overlay analog video signals. The component is inserted between a framebuffer and monitor; it also receives the video signal sent to R3 (no video tee is needed since the video source has multiple fan-out[1]). The result is that the video signal overlays the images in the framebuffer. By drawing an empty window in the framebuffer and suitably positioning and clipping the overlaid video (both functions are part of the VOV's method interface) the illusion of the video appearing in the window is achieved.

---

[1]   The video routing switch used in the platform described in Appendix A allows a single video source to be connected to multiple sinks. This is reflected by video ports with multiple fan-out at the component level.

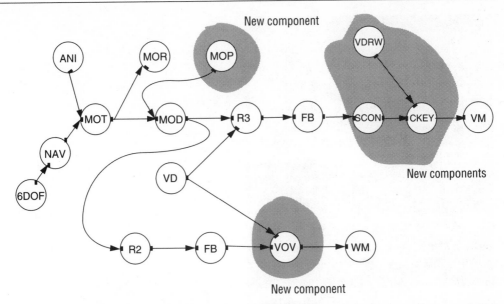

Figure 6.17   Further extensions for the virtual museum component network. The additional components play back recorded tours, overlay a video-based museum guide on the 3D view of the museum, and add a video overlay window to the 2D view of the museum.

The third extension, the addition of the VDRW, SCON and CKEY components, gives the ability to display 'guides' for the museum. This is one particular use of the 'video actors' described in the following section.

If, as this series of component networks suggest, certain kinds of multimedia applications can be constructed by connecting and configuring components then it seems a component network 'editor' would be a useful prototyping tool. Figure 6.19 shows how such a tool may appear (de Mey and Gibbs, 1993). This editor represents components by icons. Icons can be connected to form a graph and opened to adjust internal parameters. As the graph is constructed, actual components are instantiated and connected. Thus the editor does not simply manipulate icons, but dynamically configures and controls running component networks.

6.3 VIDEO WIDGETS AND VIDEO ACTORS

We now look at a second and very different example of multimedia programming. Rather than building a complete application, such as the virtual museum, we shall see how to construct *video widgets* – user-interface components rendered using video information. Like graphics-based widgets, video widgets come in a variety of forms. For example, a video button widget might use a video sequence, instead of an icon or character string, for the face of the button (imagine a button that is a burning flame or fountain of water). Instead of discussing video widgets in general, we will concentrate on a family of video widgets called *video actors*.

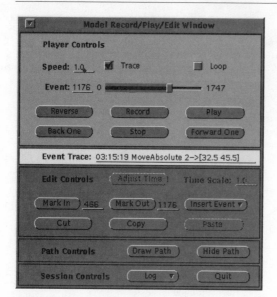

Figure 6.18 The model record/play/edit tool.

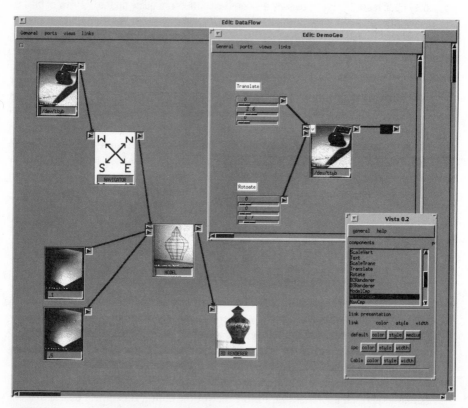

Figure 6.19 A component network editor.

These widgets are characterized by human-like behavior and can be used to provide assistance or help information – an example is the fax assistant shown in Plate VIII.

6.3.1   VIDEO ACTORS – CONCEPTS

A video actor consists of layered video material that appears on top of application windows. Applications create and manipulate video actors by instantiating a VideoActor class. Before describing the interface provided by this class we first introduce some of the terms and concepts relevant to video actors:

> *Multiple video sources:* A video actor is composed from one or more video layers. Layers are separate video values and are accessed by separate players, that is, there is one player for each video layer and each player can be controlled independently of the others.

> *Layer mixing:* A video actor's layers are *mixed* (composited), using techniques such as chroma-keying and luminance keying, into a single video stream. Application graphics and the single video stream are then mixed so that the graphics appears *behind* the video. Thus windows, icons, menus, and other graphics are in the background and the video actor is in the foreground.

> *Non-linear/random-access video:* Within a layer, individual video frames can be randomly accessed and displayed; in other words, playback is nonlinear. Low frame access times are crucial for nonlinear playback and will depend on the format and size of the video and the performance of the player.

> *Actions, postures and events:* Each video actor has a repertoire of actions and postures. An action is a path through the frames contained within a video layer. Actions need not be sequential (see Figure 6.20) and may have accompanying audio. A posture is a particular frame (or set of frames – in order to reduce access times, postures can be replicated and scattered through a video layer). It is possible for a video actor to perform several actions simultaneously, provided each is on a different layer. As video actors perform actions they generate PostureHit and EndOfAction events. Applications can request notification of these events, allowing synchronization of application activities with the actor.

The basic functionality of video actors is provided by a VideoActor class. An outline of this class follows; here, in addition to the public interface, we also show the 'private' interface (visible only from methods of VideoActor) and the 'protected' interface (visible from methods of VideoActor and its subclasses):

```
class VideoActor {
private:
        int        nlayers;            // how many layers for this actor
        VideoPlayer       player[ ];   // player components for each layer
        LayerInfo         layer[ ];    // state information for each layer protected:
```

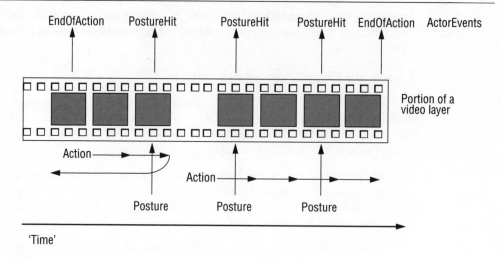

Figure 6.20   A video layer showing ActorEvents, Actions and Postures.

```
// protected instance variables include chroma-key information
// plus tables defining actions and postures for this actor
//
VideoPlayerPlayer(LayerId lay);
        public:
                VideoActor(int n);              // create an actor with n layers
                ~VideoActor( );                 // destroy it

        int     LoadLayer(LayerId lay, string fileName);
        void    Map(LayerId lay);               // make a layer visible
        void    UnMap(LayerId lay);             // make it invisible
        void    Mute(LayerId lay);              // make a layer inaudible
        void    UnMute(LayerId lay);            // make it audible

        videoKeyBackgroundKey(Layer Id lay);// identifies background in layer
        int     RepertoireSize( );              // how many things can it do?
        void    Repertoire(ActorRepertoire ar);     // what are they?

        int     Perform(LayerId lay, ActionId a, float speed, bool block);
        int     Pose(LayerId lay, PostureId p);

        void    Register(ActorEvent e, ActorEventHandler h);
        void    UnRegister(ActorEvent e);
};
```

Here layers, actions and postures have unique identifiers. When using the VideoActor class directly, applications must be aware of these identifiers. It is also possible, as we will see, to create subclasses of VideoActor which encapsulate this information.

After creating an actor, the first step is to bind video values to its layers. This is done by the LoadLayer method which indicates the name of a file containing a video value. The player for the specified layer then imports the value. LoadLayer invokes the Producer::Load method (see page 201) so has no effect on players not supporting selective loading (such as a videodisc player – unless part of a juke-box).

The BackgroundKey method returns a value, the videoKey, that separates background from foreground in a video layer. The content of videoKey will depend upon how mixing is performed. For instance, using luminance keying only a single value, a threshold luminance level, is needed, while chroma-keying requires specification of a key color or color range (for instance, maximum and minimum values for red, green, and blue).

The RepertoireSize and Repertoire methods are used to query an actor and determine the actions and postures of which it is capable. In addition to returning valid action and posture identifiers, Repertoire indicates the layers used, and, for actions, whether there is speech, and if so, the language spoken.

Perform is the crucial method. It directs an actor to start an action on the specified layer (and at the specified speed). Perform takes a Boolean parameter indicating whether the method should block. By using non-blocking invocations, it is possible for an application to direct an actor to perform more than one action at a time (provided the actions are on different layers). Alternately, blocking invocations allow applications to synchronize with the end of actions. The Pose method simply requests that the actor assume a specific posture.

Finally, the Register and UnRegister methods are used to set and remove event handlers. An ActorEvent includes an event type (for example, EndOfAction, PostureHit), a layer identifier, an action or posture identifier, and data to be passed to the application. (To catch all events of a particular type, the application uses wildcards for action or posture identifiers.)

As an example, consider an actor with two layers: one showing the torso of a person and the other the head (see Figure 6.21). The head layer has an accompanying audio track containing a number of utterances. Actions are defined for particular utterances. The body layer has a number of body positions, such as pointing in a particular direction, which correspond to postures. The following gives an idea of how an application could invoke this actor:

```
vact = new VideoActor(2);                    // create a two-layer actor
vact->LoadLayer(TORSO_LAYER, "Torso Track");
vact->LoadLayer(HEAD_LAYER, "Talking Head Track");
vact->Pose(TORSO_LAYER, GESTURE_POINT_LEFT);
vact->Perform(HEAD_LAYER, ACTION_SAY_HELLO, someSpeed, FALSE);
```

Here the Perform does not block, so the application can continue responding to user input events. These could result in changes of posture, allowing, for example, the actor to follow the movement of a window or cursor.

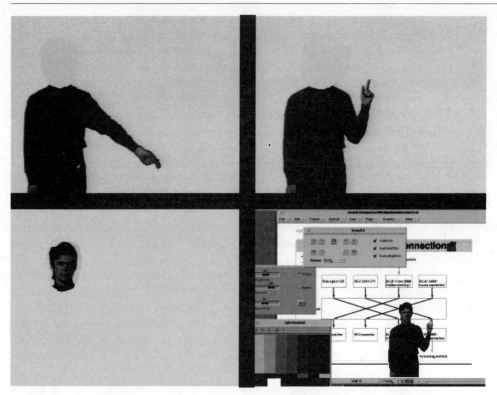

Figure 6.21   A multi-layer video actor. Clockwise from top-left are two frames from the torso layer, the actor after composition with an application, and a frame from the head layer.

6.3.2 IMPLEMENTATION OF VIDEO ACTORS

We now present component networks for video actors and describe how they can be realized on different media processing platforms. First we discuss the application programmer's view of video actors.

Application level

Rather than appearing in a 'playback window', video actors are overlaid on top of the windows, icons, menus, and other graphics drawn by applications. This allows video and graphics information to be more tightly coupled than when each appears in separate windows. Assume that graphics rendering is done by a window server and that the server is encapsulated by a transformer component. This component consumes a stream of requests specifying operations on windows and produces a video stream depicting the rendered windows. A second video stream, containing the composed layers of the video actor, is produced by a group of video player components. The players are managed by the VideoActor class and not visible outside the class, so to the application programmer a video actor resembles a single producer component. A third component, a source of window server requests, is the application itself (Figure 6.22). During initialization the application connects to the window server and registers for both window server events and events generated by the actor. It controls the window server by sending requests over its output port and controls the actor by invoking methods of VideoActor. The streams produced by the window server and the actor are mixed before display; however, the components used for mixing are not visible to the application.

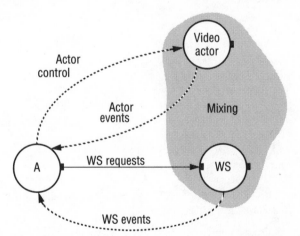

Figure 6.22   Multi-layer video actor: application level. (A is the application component, WS the window server component.)

Component level

Several strategies for implementing video actors can be identified (Gibbs, 1994); they differ primarily in where mixing of the video actor stream and window server graphics takes place. Other factors include whether video streams are analog or digital, whether mixing is performed by hardware or software, the number of actor layers supported, and how easily layers can be added. We will look at examples of component networks for two implementation strategies: *server-resident mixing* and *post-server mixing*.

Server-resident mixing □ This approach relies on extending the window server with video mixing capabilities. The extensions are: (1) the server must have at least one video input port, and (2) server requests are needed for controlling mixing of the graphics background with the incoming video stream (for example, the additional requests could be StartMixing, StopMixing and SetChromaKey). Suppose the extended window server is encapsulated by a component called WS*. A component network for a multi-layer video actor based on WS* is shown in Figure 6.23. Here a Player is a digital video source (such as a process which reads compressed video frames from a file and produces decompressed frames) and DVMIX is a digital video mixer (such as a process which receives frames from several sources and produces a single composite frame). The other components make explicit the connections between the extended window server, the framebuffer, and the display. A word of explanation concerning framebuffers: these are modelled by transformer components that convert incoming digital video frames to an analog RGB signal suitable for display on a workstation monitor. The connection between the framebuffer component and the window server component is an abstraction. In reality, complete frames are not exchanged; instead the window server issues low-level raster operations that modify the contents of a hardware framebuffer.

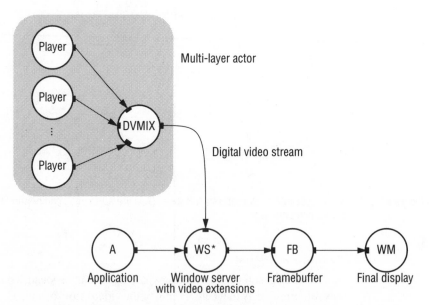

Figure 6.23   Multi-layer digital video actor: component level, server-resident mixing.

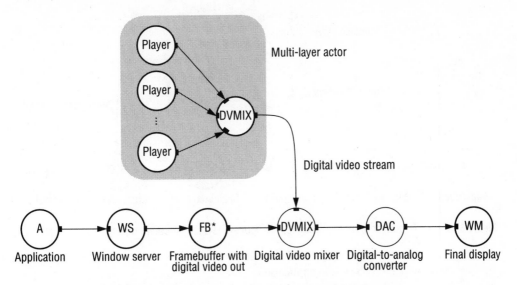

Multi-layer digital video actor: component level, post-server mixing.

Post-server mixing ☐ While the component network of Figure 6.23 can be implemented without special hardware it does require fairly significant modifications to the window server. An alternative is to leave the window server unchanged and perform the final mix 'downstream' from the window server. This is the basis of the component network shown in Figure 6.24. The critical component for this network is FB*, a framebuffer with a digital output port. In normal operation (no video actor) FB* would be connected to a digital-to-analog converter that produces the display signal. A video actor is introduced by splicing in a mixer component between the framebuffer and the digital-to-analog converter.

If we restrict ourselves to the components provided by the experimental platform of Appendix A, it is not possible to build either of the two preceding networks. The component kit for this platform lacks both WS* and FB*. However, the component kit does contain two NTSC video mixers and a scan converter that transforms RGB video to NTSC. This allows a two-layer video actor to be built as shown in Figure 6.25. Here two video sources, such as a videodisc player and a QuickTime player, produce analog video signals for two actor layers. These signals pass through AVMIX, an analog video mixer, whose output is in turn mixed with an analog signal coming from the scan converter. The result is then displayed on an NTSC monitor. Although this hybrid implementation relies on analog video and suffers from the problems of RGB to NTSC conversion, such as loss of resolution and color bleeding, applications see the same VideoActor interface as with the preceding component networks.

Platform level

There are several ways of mapping each of the above component networks to actual hardware and software. For instance, the network for server-resident mixing (Figure 6.23) can be mapped to a simple platform consisting of a workstation,

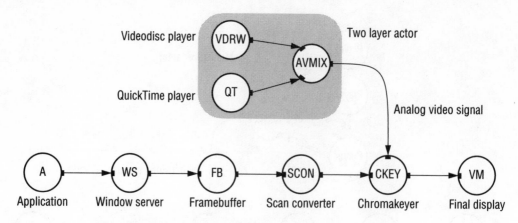

Figure 6.25   Two-layer analog video actor: component level, post-server mixing.

framebuffer, display, and a group of processes for the players, mixer, extended window server, and application.

A more interesting platform is shown in Figure 6.26. Here a 'video studio' subsystem, motivated by the Audio/Video Kernel architecture of DVI, routes uncompressed video streams between video producers, consumers, and transformers. The component network of Figure 6.24 can be mapped to this platform. Player processes would extract compressed video frames from storage (magnetic disk or CD) and pass these across the system bus to the decompressor. The uncompressed video would be routed to the mixer and composited with the background stream (containing application graphics) produced by the framebuffer. The output of the mixer would then be routed to the digital-to-analog converter for display.

Finally, Figure 6.27 shows the communication and signal paths when the component network of Figure 6.25 is mapped to the experimental platform of Appendix A. Here three NTSC video sources, called F (front), M (middle) and B (back) are synchronized and mixed. The B signal is produced by scan-converting the RGB video output of a workstation framebuffer; M is produced by a read/write videodisc player; and F is produced by a video board on a Macintosh. The signals contain, respectively, application graphics rendered by a window server running on the workstation (B), material from the videodisc (M), and material rendered by a QuickTime server running on the Macintosh (F). The central part of the configuration is a video routing switch allowing video sources and sinks to be connected under computer control. The TBCs (timebase correctors) synchronize video signals against some reference signal (coming here from a sync generator) and are needed when video signals are mixed. The two mixers overlay the F, M, and B signals using chromakeying and luminance keying.

Although the platforms of Figure 6.26 and Figure 6.27 are strikingly different, they allow similar components to be realized. The point to note is that since applications deal with components rather than platforms directly, porting an application from one platform to another is possible provided the components needed by the application are available on the new platform.

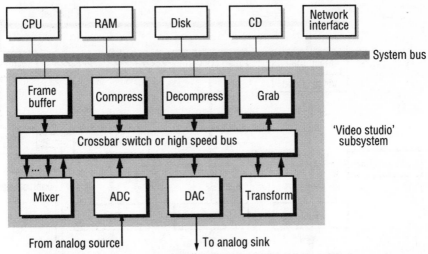

Figure 6.26   Multi-layer digital video actor: platform level, post-server mixing. Heavy lines indicate high data rate streams. The analog-to-digital converter (ADC) and digital-to-analog converter (DAC) connect the video processing hardware to external analog sources (such as video cameras) and sinks (such as monitors).

6.3.3   EXAMPLES OF VIDEO ACTORS

The VideoActor class provides the general methods needed to control actors, but Perform and Pose are somewhat low-level since they refer to layer, posture, and action identifiers. One way to avoid the identifiers is by specializing the VideoActor class and then introducing more meaningful methods. This approach is the basis of the following examples.

The fax assistant, videodisc assistant, and museum guide

These three video actors are very similar. The first (shown in Plate VIII) provides information about using a fax machine. A user selects an operation, such as 'send fax', causing the fax assistant to appear over an image of the fax machine and explain the function of various buttons. It is also possible to replace the image of the fax with a video sequence demonstrating a fax operation. The class for this actor is declared as:

```
class FaxAssistant : public VideoActor {
public:
        void        SendFax( );      // have actor explain how to send a fax
        void        ChangePaper( );  // have actor explain how to change paper
        // ... other explanations
};
```

When an explanation is requested by the user, the application activates the fax assistant by invoking one of the FaxAssistant methods rather than a lower-level VideoActor method.

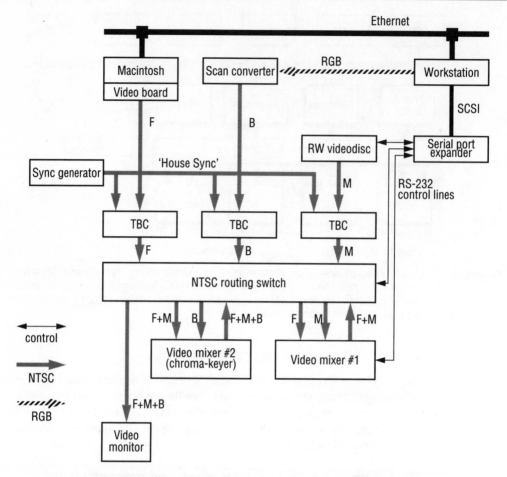

Figure 6.27   Two-layer analog video actor: platform level, post-server mixing. The three video signals F (front), M (middle), B (back) come from the two actor layers and the application respectively.

The videodisc assistant is shown in Figure 6.28. The tool in the background controls a videodisc player (output from the player is visible in the small window in the figure). If the user does not understand a control button then he or she presses the '?' followed by the button in question. The videodisc assistant then appears. The assistant first gives a verbal explanation of the button and then *demonstrates* the button by pressing it himself. Implementing this interaction requires both the application to control the actor (causing the actor to appear when needed) and the actor to control the application. The first is done by invoking Perform methods, the second requires an event handler. The handler is triggered when the videodisc assistant reaches a posture with the hand over the button; on receiving control the handler simulates a button press and executes the associated videodisc command for a short time period.

The VideoDiscAssistant class implements the behavior of this actor. The declaration for this class is:

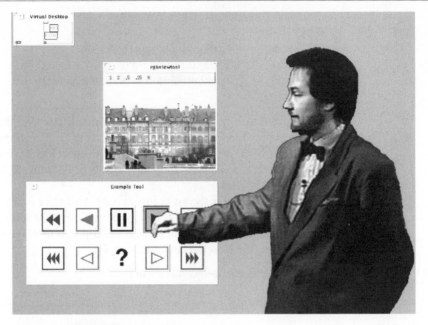

Figure 6.28   The video disc assistant.

Figure 6.29   The museum guide.

```
class VideoDiscAssistant : public VideoActor {
public:
        bool            CanExplainButton(int buttonId);
        void            ExplainButton(int buttonId);
        void            RegisterHitButtons(ActorEventHandler h);
};
```

The CanExplainButton tests if the video actor has an explanation for the chosen button in its repertoire. The ExplainButton method starts the explanation of some button. The RegisterHitButtons is used for registering an event handler for the buttons. These methods are implemented using the Repertoire, Perform and Register methods of the VideoActor class.

The museum guide is shown in Figure 6.29. This actor is activated when a user enters sensitive regions in the virtual museum. One of the features of this actor is that it is multilingual and can provide descriptions of museum exhibits in several languages. The class declaration is simply:

```
class MuseumGuide : public VideoActor {
public:
        void   Explain(Exhibit, Language);        // have a guide explain a museum
                                                  // exhibit
};
```

The hand tracker

The actions performed by the fax assistant, videodisc assistant, and museum guide are sequences of frames where the order is the same as recorded. Random-access is needed for cueing the actor (moving quickly to a start frame), but during playback access is linear. Our next video actor, the hand tracker, requires nonlinear playback. This actor has a repertoire of arm postures. It can be programmed to point to a place on the screen, or to follow the mouse as it moves across the screen (see Figure 6.30). The class declaration is again very simple:

```
class HandTracker : public VideoActor {
public:
        void            PointTo(int x, int y);        // point the arm at a screen location
};
```

The PointTo method finds the posture where the hand is closest to the indicated position, and then invokes the VideoActor::Pose method to move the arm to the desired position.

The basic gesture actor

The above actors are formed from a single video layer; we now look at a multi-layer example. We will use two video layers, one for the head of the actor and the other for the torso. This means that the head and torso can be moved independently. This actor is called a basic gesture actor since it has a small repertoire of common gestures; its class declaration is:

Figure 6.30   The hand tracker.

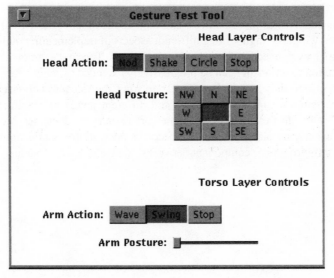

Figure 6.31   A tool for testing the methods of BasicGesturerActor.

```
class BasicGestureActor : public VideoActor {
public:
        void    HeadNod( );             // perform an action on the head layer
        void    HeadShake( );           // perform an action on the head layer
        void    HeadCircle( );          // perform an action on the head layer
        void    LookAt(int x, int y);   // assume a posture on the head layer
        void    ArmWave( );             // perform an action on the torso layer
        void    ArmSwing( );            // perform an action on the torso layer
        void    PointTo(int x, int y);  // assume a posture on the torso layer
};
```

The PointTo method is the same as that of HandTracker. There is a similar method, LookAt, for the head layer, and a number of actions that are 'synthesized' by playing through postures in particular orders. Because there are two layers the actor can perform two actions simultaneously. For example, using the tool in Figure 6.31 to test gestures, if both the 'Nod' and 'Swing' buttons are pressed then the actor will nod its head and swing an arm. In general, composing multiple layers gives a combinatorial increase in the number of playback possibilities over single-layer video.

6.4 SUMMARY

This chapter has presented two example applications – the virtual museum and video widgets – highlighting different aspects of implementing multimedia applications by connecting framework components. The first example shows how application functionality can be progressively extended by adding new components. The second shows how a high-level construct, the VideoActor class, can be mapped to different component networks and different media processing platforms. In both cases the flexibility of the framework reduces the dependency of applications on underlying platforms since it becomes possible for applications to adapt, by reconfiguring their component networks, to available components.

PART III

7

SOME RESEARCH PROBLEMS IN MULTIMEDIA PROGRAMMING

7.1 Composition
7.2 Synchronization
7.3 Interaction
7.4 Database integration

Developers of multimedia applications are faced with several challenges. First, the requirements of future applications are not clear – some features, such as digital video and high-quality audio, are expected to be needed but the extent and nature of their use is uncertain; second, platform architectures and supporting software are changing and not likely to be stable, at least in the near future; and third, design choices are highly interrelated, so choices made in one area influence many others. Thus developers must seek a balance between the evolving demands of multimedia applications on the one hand and the evolving capabilities of multimedia platforms on the other.

Despite the volatility of multimedia programming, it is possible to identify some general problems confronting environment developers. These include: *composition* – how to structure and aggregate digital media; *synchronization* – how to specify timing constraints and ensure their satisfaction during presentation; *interaction* – how to add interactivity to digital media; and *database integration* – how to access large shared collections of digital media. This chapter explores these areas using the framework notions of media objects and components to guide the discussion.

7.1 COMPOSITION

Combining and composing diverse media lies at the heart of multimedia. Some combinations are common – we are accustomed to documents containing text and graphics and to audio accompanying video. Traditionally special equipment, such as printing presses and video editing decks, is used, in effect, to physically couple media. With digital media, on the other hand, composition reduces to a computational process rather than a physical process. This opens up experimentation with many new forms of composition: once in digital form, video and animation can be embedded in documents, music and audio can have textual annotations (or vice versa), text and image elements can appear in animated sequences, video and images can be used to texture graphics models, and so on.

Since composition is such a basic aspect of multimedia, one would expect a multimedia programming environment to support composition in a general and open way. The problem is to identify just what 'support' is needed and just what should be left to the application programmer. Before discussing this further we need to introduce a few terms. Suppose we call the result of composition a *composite*, and a composite's primitive building blocks *elements*. The problem of composition is how, and to what extent, to support such activities as the creation, editing, presentation, and capture of composites, and also to identify appropriate elements and mechanisms for grouping elements.

7.1.1 MECHANISMS

Different application areas have different approaches to multimedia composition and it is possible to identify several commonly used composition mechanisms. Examples include spatial, temporal, semantic, procedural, and component-based composition.

Spatial composition ☐ Media objects presented on display screens or on the printed page are composed by assigning spatial locations and regions. An example is document layout where text, graphics, and images are positioned on pages. Another example is assembling complex graphics composites by grouping and positioning graphics elements. In general, spatial composition produces a hierarchical structure. For instance, a 'glyph' (a small image) representing a special character may be grouped with text as part of a figure caption; the caption is then grouped with an image to form the figure, which is finally grouped with other text and image elements on a page. The relative positioning of composites and elements can be constrained. This occurs when a figure is 'anchored' to a piece of text. Constraints on relative positioning are also common in graphics and animation modelling. For instance, a door might be attached to a wall and only allowed to rotate about its hinges.

Temporal composition ☐ Analogous to spatial composition is the layout of elements along a timeline. In this case elements include audio, video, and animation sequences and nontemporal media which have been 'extended' in time. An example of the latter is taking an image and specifying a time interval for its presentation. The positioning of elements may be absolute, in which case explicit 'start times' are given, or relative, such as when one element starts after another finishes.

Semantic composition □ Spatial and temporal composition produce structures that govern the presentation of information; they are more concerned with form than content. Semantic composition, in comparison, explicitly links related material. For example, a picture might be linked to a description of its author, an historical novel to examples of music and art from the relevant period, or a documentary video to information about the people and places shown. The end points of links may be simply media objects or composites of some sort. Semantic composition is the mechanism used to build *hypermedia webs*; it is also used, on a smaller or more localized scale, when cross-references are embedded within a document.

Procedural composition □ With procedural composition, high-level commands act as the glue between media objects. Commands include simple control structures and primitives for manipulating media objects, handling user interaction, and controlling presentation. For instance, parts of an image may be made sensitive to user input so that when selected (such as by a mouse click) a sound plays and an animation sequence begins.

Component-based composition □ A final form of composition is associated with situations when multiple sources are activated and coordinated. An orchestra is an example: here each instrument contributes during a performance and is coordinated with respect to other elements of the orchestra. We call this 'component-based' composition since framework components produce (and consume or transform) media values. Component-based composition is closely related to temporal composition. One can view composite components (that is, assemblies of components such as component networks) as generalized players of temporal composites. For instance, in analogy to how an orchestra *plays* a symphony, a group of MIDI synthesizers and sequencers (a composite component) *plays* a multi-track MIDI sequence (another temporal composite). In other situations, much like a group of improvising musicians, a composite component may be less 'score-driven' and more open to user interaction. The various component networks underlying the virtual museum in the previous chapter are of this nature, as are component networks where some sources are 'live' rather than players of recorded material.

7.1.2 METAPHORS

Composition mechanisms are further categorized by several metaphors reflecting the user's view, or model, of composition (see Table 7.1).

Document metaphor □ Spatial composition is often realized as 'multimedia documents' – tree-like structures of embedded media objects. Examples include the document formats used by desktop publishing systems (for instance, Frame-

Table 7.1   Composition mechanisms and metaphors.

Mechanism/metaphor	Representation	Composite	Elements
Spatial/document	Tree	Multimedia document	Document elements (text, image, graphic objects)
Temporal/movie	Linear	Multi-track aggregate	Tracks (audio, video, music, animation objects)
Semantic/web	Graph	Hypermedia web	Nodes (media objects in general)
Procedural/script	Various (linear, graph)	Multimedia script	'Cast members' (media objects in general)
Component-based/ circuit	Graph	Component network	Producers, consumers, transformers

Maker, PageMaker, Interleaf) capable of combining text, images, and graphics; and proposed standards for electronic documents such as ODA and HyTime.

Movie metaphor □ Temporal composition lends itself to a movie metaphor; examples include QuickTime and authoring systems such as Director. The movie metaphor is based on the notion of tracks, which are sequential in nature and organized along a timeline.

Web metaphor □ Hypertext and hypermedia have given us the vivid metaphor of a 'web' of interconnected information. Here the underlying representation is essentially a graph where nodes are media objects, and edges indicate semantic links. Probably the most extensive example is the *World-Wide Web* (Berners-Lee *et al.*, 1992), a collection of 'pages' spanning the Internet. World-Wide Web pages consist of marked-up text containing links to audio, image, or video files and to other pages.

Script metaphor □ In multimedia authoring systems one finds the scripting metaphor of procedural composition. Scripts are procedural specifications involving operations on media elements. Scripting languages have both linear textual representation (in which case scripts are sequences of commands) and graph-like representations (as when scripts are 'attached' to images, graphics objects, sounds, and so on). Popular multimedia scripting languages include HyperTalk and Lingo.

Circuit metaphor □ Finally, component-based composition leads to the 'circuit metaphor' where, much like the flow of current in an electrical circuit, streams of data flow through components. An example are LOUDs, or 'logical audio devices' (Angebrannt *et al.*, 1991), which process audio streams and may be connected to form more complex devices. The example is given of constructing a telephone answering machine from LOUDs representing audio players, recorders, and a telephone.

Research related to multimedia composition looks at ways of extending and generalizing the above mechanisms. The goal is to define composition techniques that apply across application domains and across media types. One approach is to combine different mechanisms, which could be called the 'mixed-metaphor' model. Examples include embedding temporal composites in spatial composites (such as a movie in a document) and adding spatial structure to a temporal composite (such as a movie with several video tracks, each having different spatial locations). Procedural composition can also be combined with the other mechanisms. For instance, Director supports temporal, spatial, and procedural composition through its score window, stage window, and scripting language. As another example, with 'active multimedia documents' (Zellweger, 1992), in addition to spatial and temporal composition one finds scripts used to specify paths through related documents. So in this case scripts provide a form of semantic composition.

A second approach to extending and generalizing composition is to look for new forms of composition. For instance, the Muse authoring system introduces a flexible mechanism based on 'dimensions' (Hodges *et al.*, 1989). Composition takes place in a multidimensional space, each dimension representing a spatial, temporal, or a more abstract degree of freedom. For example, two spatial dimensions might be used to link a map with images of sites on the map. If desired, a 'seasons' dimension could be added to allow viewing of the sites at different times of the year.

7.2 SYNCHRONIZATION

Temporal composition establishes timing constraints between elements which need to be respected by producers, consumers, and other components. This is often called *inter-stream synchronization* – a familiar example is the simultaneous playback of audio and video material where what is heard coincides with what is seen. Timing constraints can also apply to media objects in isolation; the frame rate of a video sequence is such a constraint. Ensuring that single streams meet their timing goals is called *intra-stream synchronization*. Overviews of multimedia synchronization are provided by Steinmetz (1990) and Little *et al.* (1991).

When streams are composed for further processing, timing constraints may be very tight. For example, digital audio mixers require samples to arrive in lockstep. During presentation, constraints are less tight since limits to the accuracy of human perceptual resolution allow a degree of imprecision in timing. While nearly everyone notices lags when they are tenths of a second or longer, audio slipping a few milliseconds behind a video track is not likely to be caught even by the most sensitive ear. The amount of leeway afforded components as they produce, consume, or transform a stream is called the stream's *synchronization tolerance*. Tolerances during presentation are clearly subjective; interestingly, tolerances are also media type and content dependent. For example, slight timing errors are more noticeable in a music stream than a video stream, and tolerances are tighter when sound sources are visible, or are correlated with visual content (such as lip sync with a voice track).

Stream synchronization is continuous in the sense that there is a need to continually monitor and adjust stream flow. Other forms of media synchronization are discrete; these are sometimes called *event synchronization*. This is the case when activities must be started and stopped at specific times. For instance, consider an interactive application where a button push or menu selection triggers the display of an image and the playback of an audio sequence. Here we want the image to appear and the sound to start at the same time (or, more accurately, within some tolerance interval).

7.2.1   ASPECTS OF SYNCHRONIZATION

Media timing constraints are either inherent (for instance, the sample rate governs the timing of an audio stream) or appear as the result of composition (as when temporal composition correlates the timing of several streams). The problem of media synchronization deals with how to satisfy media timing constraints.

To be more specific, suppose we frame the synchronization problem in terms of components – the producers, consumers, and transformers of media values. A multimedia system is then an assembly of connected components, a component network, where connections carry media values from one component to another. Using this view of multimedia systems, called the 'circuit metaphor' above, we can relate synchronization to timing measurements made on component networks. A measurement occurs when a single media element (a frame, sample, image) enters or leaves a port. Each measurement produces two values: the *timestamp* for the element at the port in question and a *reference value*. The first derives from the stream, the second from a *reference signal* associated with the port. In practice, timestamps can be obtained either from metering, whether by byte counting or element counting, or from time code embedded in streams; reference values are often obtained from an external source such as a clock.

Timing constraints on a multimedia system can be expressed as constraints on element timestamps and reference values. The timing of an element (at a particular port) is 'within specs' if its timestamp differs from the reference signal by no more than the synchronization tolerance. More specifically, if TS and RV are timing measurements at some port, and T the tolerance for this port, we must have:

$$| TS - RV | < T$$

Note that both the reference signal and synchronization tolerance are specific to the port where the timestamp is measured (see Figure 7.1). Furthermore, depending upon circumstances, the reference signal may be either a clock signal *or* timestamps from some other port. Inter-stream timing constraints can be expressed by taking timestamps from one stream as the reference for the other; intra-stream synchronization uses a clock reference; and event synchronization uses either a clock or stream reference (for instance, 'do event *e* at time *t*' and 'do event *e* when stream *s* completes').

The informal model of multimedia systems just described serves as a context for introducing some of the factors that complicate synchronization. These include:

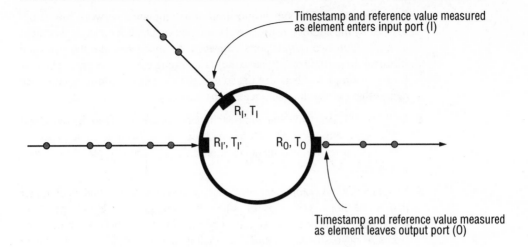

Timestamp and reference value measured
as element enters input port (I)

R_I, T_I

$R_{I'}, T_{I'}$ R_O, T_O

Timestamp and reference value measured
as element leaves output port (O)

Figure 7.1   Timing measurements. Synchronization timing constraints refer to element timestamps,
and to port reference signals (R) and tolerances (T).

- Clock errors: Components may not have a common clock (because of distribution or because of the hardware architecture); consequently there can be errors between reference signals.

- Communication and processing delays: Component connections and components themselves introduce delays; the timestamp of an element entering a connection or component may not be the same as when it leaves.

- Response delays: Components may delay in responding to requests (such as to start and stop) and require some form of cueing or pre-loading.

- Tolerance ranges: Synchronization tolerances vary from component to component. Furthermore, it may be useful to allow change in tolerances (while a component network is active) as a way of adjusting presentation quality.

- Changes in playback speed and direction: Some applications allow users to control playback speed (normal, slow-motion) and playback direction (forward, reverse). Synchronization technniques must cope with such changes.

- Changes in component load: Certain components have variable load and consequently varying resource requirements. An example is a renderer component where, as model complexity increases, more memory and processing time is needed.

- Graceful degradation: As the resources available to a component network decrease, or its load increases, some form of graceful degradation in presentation quality is needed. Furthermore, maintaining the quality of some streams can have higher priority than others. For example, some digital audio/video playback systems reduce video quality (by dropping frames) while striving to maintain audio quality.

- Reconfiguration: The synchronization of a component network can be destroyed by the addition (or removal) of components. For example, consider a source with two output ports connected to sinks. Assume the sinks are identical; in particular they have the same timing reference signal. Then inserting a component between the source and one of the sinks may introduce delays that exceed the tolerances of the network.

- Stability: It is desirable that component networks are stable in the sense that if they start 'out-of-sync', or lose synchronization owing to some perturbation, then correction and feedback mechanisms come into play and restore synchronization.

- Virtual clocks: A component network can be synced to a virtual clock rather than a real clock. This is useful when some components do not operate in real time. For instance, consider a component network that compresses and stores a video stream: suppose an analog (and frame addressable) video source is connected to a video digitizer, the digitizer is connected to an MPEG compressor, and the compressor is connected to a component that writes compressed frames to disk. If the compressor cannot operate in real time then one possibility is to make it 'master' of the component network and 'slave' the other components to the progress of the compressor.

7.2.2   TECHNIQUES

Clock errors, communication and processing delays, and the other factors just listed make media synchronization a difficult problem in general. Design and evaluation of techniques for media stream synchronization is an area of intense research. Some existing and proposed techniques include:

Interleaving □ One way to simplify inter-stream synchronization is by interleaving the storage of elements from several streams. In this way media elements are retrieved together and so at least start out in sync. This technique is the basis of CD-i layout and the 'audio/video interleave' (AVI) file format; another example is the optimization of QuickTime movies by interleaving tracks at the level of the media to storage mapping. As a side-effect of exploiting physical storage layout, interleaving 'hardwires' the timing relationships between streams. This is appropriate when presentation timing is known and unlikely to change, but ineffective if inter-stream timing can be modified or is not known prior to presentation.

Time code □ Streams with embedded time code can act as references for other streams. Inter-stream synchronization is then achieved by having components continually adjust their production and/or consumption relative to the time code, an ability known as 'time code chase'. For example, professional video tape drives can chase SMPTE time code; when two such drives are connected and one is made the 'master', video frames emerge from the drives in step. Time code synchronization also appears in software. An example is QuickTime where time code chase is realized by extending and dropping the display of video frames.

Synchronization components □ Consider a transformer component that encapsulates a 'timed' queue – elements arrive at the input port, are added to the queue, remain in the queue a certain time interval, and then are sent through the output port. This component is the digital version of a *delay line*, a device that shifts an analog signal backwards in time (see Figure 7.2). Delay lines are used in audio and

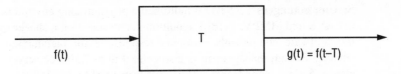

f(t)   T   g(t) = f(t–T)

Figure 7.2   A delay line. The output signal (g) is the input signal (f) delayed by the amount T.

video studios to make fine adjustments in signal timing – by adding delays it is possible to ensure that comparable times are taken by signals arriving at the same point over alternate paths. In a similar fashion, a digital delay line, or 'delay component', delays one stream so it remains in sync with another stream suffering a comparable delay (see Figure 7.3). Other forms of specialized 'synchronization components' have been proposed. For example, the 'software phase-locked loop' (Northcutt and Kuerner, 1991) uses a reference clock and a regulation process to adjust the rate at which elements are emitted from an output port. An average output rate is fed back to the regulation process to help ensure stability. It is also possible to create components that remove delay. An example is given by Friedmann *et al.* (1992) where a 'Kalman filter' compensates for delay caused by an input device with a slow response time. The filter predicts future elements by extrapolating from current elements. (The predicted values are optimal, but their calculation requires a 'state evolution function'. Obtaining a plausible function is the key to this technique.)

Load scaling □ In situations where delays within components lead to timing errors, it may be possible to recover synchronization by reducing component load.

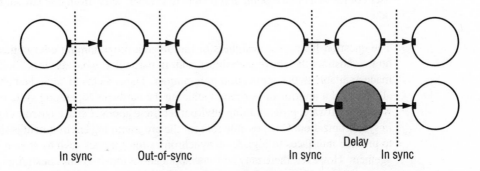

In sync   Out-of-sync   In sync   In sync

Figure 7.3   A delay component. Streams in the component network at left are out of sync when they arrive at the consumer components. Adding a delay restores synchronization.

Consider a transformer which receives elements from an input port, performs some processing, and then outputs modified elements. If the component cannot satisfy the timing constraints on its output port it may ignore occasional input elements or simplify its processing task (and so perhaps reduce the quality of its output stream). In either case the effect is to scale down component load.

Stream managers ☐ Several multimedia programming environments, noticeably AVK and MMPM/2 (IBM's multimedia presentation manager for OS/2) contain software components explicitly responsible for maintaining the flow of streams. Stream management is also central to audio/video servers (see, for instance, Anderson and Homsy (1991) and Rowe and Smith (1992)); and to file systems supporting time-based media (see, for instance, Vengat Rangan *et al.* (1991)). Stream managers offer applications high-level interfaces to stream services, including, for instance, the ability to start, stop, pause, fast-forward, and cue streams. Internally a stream manager may rely on interleaving, time code, some other synchronization technique, or some combination of techniques. This is a choice made by the designers of the stream manager and is largely hidden from applications.

Intelligent scheduling ☐ If delays can be anticipated then one can ensure that streams arrive in sync by careful scheduling of source start-up times. For example, using the left-hand side of Figure 7.3, suppose the start of the lower source is deliberately delayed. If this delay is chosen to balance the delay caused by the transformer component then the streams will arrive in sync (assuming negligible connection delays). A more sophisticated use of scheduling is described by Little and Ghafoor (1991) who obtain an optimal start-up schedule for media sources taking into account network delays and limits on bandwidth. Another example of 'intelligent scheduling' is the Tactus time server (Dannenberg *et al.*, 1993). Tactus synchronizes the presentation of streams received from applications. Streams are buffered on the server prior to presentation – the latency caused by buffering, and network transfer, is overcome by setting application clocks to run slightly ahead of real time. The drawback is a lag in responding to user input; however, applications can start several alternate streams, which reduces response time when the user comes to a choice point and results in cleaner 'cuts' from one stream to another.

The question facing the designers of multimedia programming environments is how to abstract the above techniques and, in particular, what services should be made available to the application programmer. There seems to be agreement that all layers of a multimedia system, including the hardware, operating system, networking software, programming environment, and applications, have roles to play in synchronization. One possible role for the programming environment is simply to provide interfaces to high-level synchronization services such as stream management. However, there may be some applications that find this constraining and require direct interfaces to operating system and network services.

7.3 INTERACTION

During the 1980s there was a move from character-based command-language interfaces to a visual style of interaction distinguished by windows, icons, and direct manipulation. A second shift may now take place as audio, video, and animation become more prominent in the user interface.

This section discusses abstractions needed at the level of the programming environment to simplify adding multimedia to user interfaces. Topics such as the 'look and feel' of multimedia user interfaces and appropriate uses of various media are more related to user-interface design than programming environment design. Instead, the problem we look at is identifying abstractions and generic mechanisms that enable many styles of interaction and give free rein to interface designers. For instance, graphics environments have a general-purpose 'pick' operation for interactively selecting graphics objects, and other environments provide generic mechanisms for cut/copy/paste and for event notification. Although multimedia interfaces are at an early stage, some areas where software abstractions appear needed can be identified. Several are listed below:

Multimodal interaction ☐ The media types now appearing on computing platforms (including desktops and palmtops) are likely to change the form of human–computer communication. Audio opens up the possibility of voice recognition and speech synthesis – interactive animation can be driven by pen-based and gesture-based input. Furthermore, new input devices such as 3D mice, eye trackers, and datagloves are expanding the range of channels available for human–computer communication. Harnessing these channels, exploiting their simultaneous and complementary use, is called multimodal interaction. An early example is 'Put-That-There' (Bolt, 1980), a landmark system combining voice commands and hand gestures to query a visual database. A number of more recent examples are described by Blattner and Dannenberg (1992). Software support for multimodal interaction seems a key provision of multimedia programming environments; it involves such problems as characterizing input devices – see, for instance, Card *et al.* (1990) – and providing uniform interfaces to devices (as provided by MCI, see page 135).

Input streams versus input events ☐ The current user-interface paradigm of windows, icons, menus, the mouse, and pointing is largely event-driven. Input devices generate events, such as keystrokes and mouse clicks, and applications respond to input events via 'event-handlers'. Events tend to be processed in isolation and *ad hoc* techniques are used for timing and synchronization. This rather static and discrete view of interaction is somewhat at odds with the continuous flows common to multimedia applications. It may be that many new input devices, including pressure-sensitive pens and position trackers, are more naturally handled in a context of input streams and processes than in a context of input events and event handlers. An early example of process abstractions as an aid in implementing user interfaces is found in the *squeak* language (Cardelli and Pike, 1985). This language is based on communicating concurrent processes that encapsulate devices and exchange timed events. More recently, toolkits for dynamic virtual reality applications, such as described by Shaw *et al.* (1993), have illustrated the use of multiple processes for device handling. The notion of components introduced in the previous chapters can also be used to model stream-like input devices.

Dialogue independence ☐ One of the traditional problems in user-interface development is ensuring changes in the user interface have minimum impact on application structure; this is known as dialogue independence (Hartson and Hix, 1989). Multimedia applications, because of the range of input devices and styles, stand to benefit from a high degree of dialogue independence. It would be nice, for instance, if a document editor allowed the same operation to be selected by mouse click, voice command, or pen gesture. Programming environments can help promote dialogue independence by providing abstractions that help isolate input operations and interaction tasks. Examples include 'virtual events', where device-specific input events are mapped to device-independent abstractions, and Smalltalk's MVC framework (see page 156) which aids in decomposing applications and their user interfaces. It remains to be seen whether these and other existing techniques, perhaps with minor extension, are sufficient for multimedia interfaces or whether totally new approaches are needed.

Interaction embedding ☐ With interactive multimedia one sees a shift in the roles of applications and their data. Usually we think of interactivity as originating in the application, since it is during application design that interaction style and dialogue structure are specified. However, the view of interaction being 'embedded' in applications does not always hold for interactive multimedia. The various multimedia authoring and scripting languages, and hypermedia formats such as MHEG, illustrate ways of embedding interaction directly in the data. Several examples are given by Bier (1992). In this view applications reduce to generic players, and the real task facing developers becomes designing the titles (that is, the data) to be played. Representing interaction by scripts or data structures has many implications for the programming environments used to implement authoring tools, players, and other generic applications. It should be possible to import and export user interface components, to specify new components, to test their behavior and presentation, and to inspect and modify their attributes. Here the object-oriented approach, since it naturally couples state and behavior, appears well suited for representing user-interface components containing embedded interaction.

7.4 DATABASE INTEGRATION

A fourth research area concerns database integration, or the nature of the interface between multimedia programming environments and multimedia databases. The problem of database integration should be considered early on in environment design as it is particularly crucial for multimedia applications. There are several reasons why this is so. First, and most obviously, the size of audio, video, and image data makes local storage difficult. While it is a simple matter to store a few text documents on a local disk, doing so with a few video documents is likely to be impractical. Second, the authors of multimedia material want their titles made available to as wide an audience as possible. Large shared multimedia databases, accessed over network connection, are one means by which titles can be widely distributed. Also, by offering query facilities, multimedia databases help both title designers and end users in locating material. Finally, multimedia databases can control access to their contents and so help safeguard copyrights and data integrity.

Currently, two approaches to database integration are predominant: database interface languages and database programming languages. The first, common to relational database systems and other traditional database systems, more clearly separates applications from the database. In this case the database usually consists of a collection of simple and regular structures such as tables. Applications use the interface language to send queries and data manipulation requests to the database system; the database responds by executing the query or request and passing data back to the application. SQL (Date and Darwen, 1993), a standard interface language for relational database systems, typifies this approach.

One drawback of database interface languages is the fragmentation of application logic. This results when code written in the programming language is interleaved with database requests and queries. Furthermore, since the two languages have different structuring mechanisms and data types, the application must specify conversions when exchanging data. Code fragmentation and conversion are particularly severe when the database contains complex nested or hierarchial structures rather than flat tables.

The incompatibilities between programming languages and database interface languages are collectively referred to as the 'impedance-mismatch' problem. Much work in the database community has been directed towards smoothing out the differences and providing 'seamless' interfaces. Database programming languages, which extend existing programming languages with database operations, offer a higher degree of integration. Of particular note are object-oriented database systems (Cattell, 1991) where often a single object-oriented programming language underlies both the programming environment and the database system. In this case application objects have the same form as objects residing in the database, and communication between applications and the database is via method invocation.

A highly figurative illustration of the two approaches to database integration is shown in Figure 7.4. The left-hand side depicts queries and other requests passing across a fairly rigid and well-defined database interface; there is a clear notion of where the database ends and where the application begins. The right-hand side shows a set of objects, separated by a 'seamless' interface, and communicating by method invocation and reply. Here the separation between application and database is more blurred.

A basic question for multimedia programming environments is whether either of the above approaches is appropriate or whether multimedia database extensions, like earlier database extensions for objects and complex structures, require our concept of the database interface to change. The latter seems the case since the existing approaches tend to deal in terms of discrete units of data rather

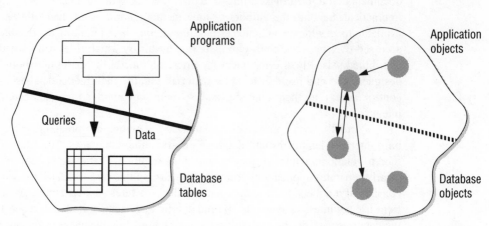

Figure 7.4   The application/database interface: traditional database systems (left), and object-oriented database systems (right).

than the continuous flows common to multimedia. It is certainly easier to discuss issues of multimedia database integration in the context of a natural model for multimedia applications and databases than to try to coerce the existing approaches to this end.

One possible model, based on the notion of media components, is shown in Figure 7.5. As with object-oriented databases, objects here are distributed among applications and the database. The essential difference is that the objects are divided into two groups – media objects and components. Instead of exchanging media objects directly with the database, the application loads media objects onto components that perform the transfer over connections to other components. For instance, to play back a video object from the database the application first locates the object, perhaps by issuing a query or perhaps by following a link from another object. The video object is then loaded onto a producer component within the database and this component is connected to a consumer within the application (this two-node network is the simplest playback configuration; in general, several components, both in the database and in the application, may be needed). When the components are started, transfer and playback of the video object begins.

The use of components to mediate data transfers between applications and databases has many implications for database integration. In particular, a range of new issues must be addressed by the database interface. These include:

Data quality □ A central tenet of database systems is *physical independence*, the idea that applications should be protected from changes in the physical storage structures and formats used within the database. This conflicts with the notion of data quality: multimedia applications need the ability to specify audio fidelity, image resolution, frame rates, and other aspects of the 'quality' of data presented to the user. As a result, applications may wish to negotiate with the database over the quality of data to be stored and retrieved. Data quality can be specified in terms of compression formats, timing delays, sample sizes, pixel depths, and so on, but doing so reduces physical independence – applications become directly involved

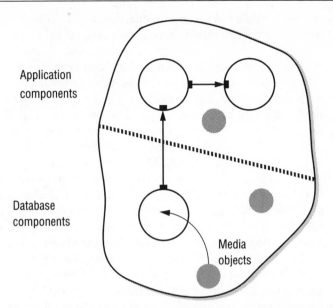

Application
components

Database
components

Media
objects

Figure 7.5   The application/database interface: multimedia database systems with components.

with storage choices. Thus mechanisms are needed allowing applications to specify data quality in high-level descriptive terms (for instance, 'HiFi quality audio',
'broadcast quality video') which can then be translated by the interface software
to storage and network requirements.

Asynchrony, concurrency and notification □ With conventional database
interfaces, data transfers are synchronous and discrete. The application issues a request and then receives a reply. With media data this form of interaction is not
very suitable. For example, consider an application that requests an audio value.
The programmer is not interested in handling the reply stream sample-by-sample,
but rather simply wants to direct it to a suitable component such as a digital-to-
analog converter. (Of course, at some level, there would be software on the application side that transfers samples to the converter; the point is that inner details of
this activity need not be visible at the level of the database interface.)

    As another example, consider timing. Here again the issue-request/receive-
reply mode of interaction seems unsuitable. Some media values require significant
lengths of time for their transfer. Now it is possible, by rapidly exchanging highly
compressed data, to obtain transfer durations similar to those experienced with
traditional database systems. For instance, given an extremely high-speed network, a 90-minute video clip, compressed to a few hundred Mbytes, can be transferred in a few seconds. However, this requires very considerable capacity (in the
database system, the network, and application platform) and is not possible if the
value is being produced by a 'live' source. When long transfer times occur, then,
it is important that the application does not simply block during the transfer. Rather it needs to initiate the transfer and then proceed to other tasks, perhaps being
informed when the transfer is complete. Thus the database interface should

support multiple tasks, stream redirection, and asynchronous notification rather than a simple issue-request/receive-reply protocol.

Request scheduling □ Traditional databases perform various scheduling activities. For instance, read and write requests are scheduled by the concurrency control subsystem and disk accesses are scheduled by the storage subsystem. With multimedia databases, scheduling of database operations is particularly important owing to timing constraints (Little and Ghafoor, 1991; Little, 1993). Some forms of scheduling should be visible at the database interface and under application control. For instance, it should be possible to request 'play video X now' or 'play video X at 8 pm.' There are several reasons why playback scheduling, and other examples of request scheduling, are needed. First, media values often have long durations (of the order of minutes or hours). Second, shared use of special-purpose hardware needed by database-resident components may not be possible. Third, system resources (buffers, processor cycles, bus bandwidth, network bandwidth) are limited. The result is that application requests can tie up resources, and the database itself, for significant periods of time. Consequently, concurrent access to media data may involve explicit scheduling (in particular, resource pre-allocation) by applications. The database interface should thus allow applications to express resource requirements and negotiate terms for their usage.

Configuration □ A further ability needed in the database interface is flexible configuration and connection of components. As an example, consider the virtual museum from the previous chapter, where video imagery is displayed within a 3D virtual world. For instance, one of the exhibits might involve mapping video onto the walls of the museum. Suppose, rather than using local video sources, the video material is obtained from a remote database. Figure 7.6 shows some of the components that could be used and their connections; the components include a 3D renderer (R3), a navigator (NAV), a video source, and display components. The important point is that, depending upon the capabilities of the database system and the application platform, rendering (that is, mapping the video onto geometry in the virtual world) is done either at the database site or by the application. When the application platform is equipped with 3D graphics hardware, it requests a video stream from the database and renders it locally; this is shown at the top of Figure 7.6. If 3D hardware is not available, the application requests that rendering occur at the database site (bottom of Figure 7.6). This example also illustrates the need for multimedia databases to play an active role in data handling. Instead of being static repositories, multimedia databases must actively engage in production (playback), consumption (recording) and *processing*. The last point is perhaps the most surprising – multimedia databases do not simply store and retrieve media values, but should also be capable of processing media values. The types of processing could include: compression and decompression; conversion from one format to another; mixing (for instance, if an application requires simultaneous playback of two audio streams then network load is reduced if they are mixed down to a single stream prior to transfer); and, as the virtual museum example shows, rendering. As a result, the database interface should allow applications to connect and create components, both locally and at the database site.

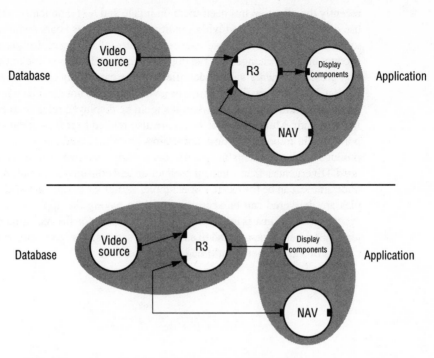

Figure 7.6   Alternative component networks for a virtual world application.

Query streams ☐ Consider the lower component network of Figure 7.6 where the navigator component (NAV) sends information about the user's current position to the database. The connection between NAV and the database can be considered a *query stream* – a continuous sequence of requests sent to the database. In this case the requests essentially say 'send me a view of the museum from my current position.' Query streams have many properties similar to those of data streams. For instance, the *query rate* is the number of requests issued per unit time, and a *query quality* specification might be used to guide the database system in processing the stream. Suppose queries are issued at a rate of 10 per second but the database system is only prepared to evaluate five per second. Depending upon the quality specification of the query stream, the database system might consider simply ignoring queries (this could be called 'query dropping'), or increasing the rate at which they are evaluated. The latter case could involve obtaining more processing resources or reducing the per-query processing duration (such as by only performing partial evaluations or by producing the resulting media value at a lower quality). These examples suggest that query rates and other properties of query streams should be part of the database interface.

Database systems that provide applications with the above capabilities are only in the early stages of design and so are not commercially available. Although the database community has been interested in multimedia for some time, until recently the attention has been more on image and text than temporal media. The use of timing information within multimedia databases bears some resemblance to work in temporal databases where attributes of an object, for instance a bank account balance, change over the object's life span. However, the timing information present in media values identifies what is essentially synchronization information. For instance, the start time of a video frame is not the time when the frame was captured or created, but when it should be displayed relative to other frames in the stream. Multimedia databases are also related to real-time databases. Temporal media impose real-time constraints since the database must consume and produce media elements at specific rates. Note, however, the deadlines are not *hard*. Divergences from element production and consumption deadlines, although undesirable, can be tolerated. For example, variations in rates at which audio samples are delivered can be accommodated by having the application re-establish synchronization just prior to presentation. Support for the real-time playback of temporal media is now found in audio/video servers. These systems are likely precursors of more general multimedia databases.

8

INTEGRATED MULTIMEDIA SYSTEMS

8.1 Polikom overview
8.2 The Communication Wall
8.3 Summary

For many people multimedia immediately brings to mind notions of entertainment, or at least a combination of entertainment and learning ('edutainment'). In this chapter we will try to point out that multimedia has many other, perhaps more mundane and more traditional, applications. Multimedia technology can be applied to diagnosis in medicine, to visualization of complex molecules in chemistry and biology, to long-distance learning, to cooperative design and prototyping, and to many other areas. We will pick as an example 'tele-administration', that is, the ability to provide virtual offices for a geographically divided public administration and its employees.

8.1 POLIKOM OVERVIEW

Large and complex organizations, whether in business, industry, or public administration, are increasingly dependent on the use of the latest telecommunications technology, owing to their distribution, frequently worldwide, and the need to save resources and to perform tasks more quickly and more efficiently.

A major challenge to computing and telecommunications can be found in Germany where, in the coming years, a large number of government functions and the parliament itself will move to Berlin while other ministries and departments are to stay in Bonn. When announcing the decision to move, the parliament stated that 'use of the most modern information and communications technology is of particular importance for the functioning and cooperation of the constitutional bodies.' The goal is 'transmission, further processing and representation of information between all concerned at the separate sites as far as possible without technical restrictions,' in other words, to create an innovative information link between Bonn and Berlin. This requirement was the impetus for starting the **Polikom** research and development program. (The name derives from *polis*, the Greek word for city, and the German word *Kommunikation*. Thus, communication uniting cities.) The German National Research Center for Information Technology, GMD, has been commissioned by the government to develop the concepts of the **Polikom** program and to create a context for its implementation. The planned budget for the program amounts to several tens of millions of dollars per year over a period of several years.

The governmental directive to create the Bonn–Berlin information link creates a unique challenge for the application of telecommunications and computing technology in Germany and Europe. Innovative techniques and new organizational procedures will be needed to support government units working at different places at different times. It is an opportunity for research institutes, industry, and users in government organizations to build up the technological and organizational infrastructure for public administration services and activities.

In terms of technology, developments in **Polikom** are based on innovations currently under way and those that can be anticipated. In networks, transmission bandwidths of several megabits per second or even gigabits per second are expected through the development of broadband ISDN and ATM. In computers, in the near future multimedia workstations will be available with processing speeds of GIPS (giga instructions per second), high-resolution screens, stereo sound, handwritten input (pen-based computing), and a memory capacity of many gigabytes. These systems will also be suitable for use as high-quality audio-visual input and output devices for purposes such as television, videophone, and other forms of personal and group communication.

Polikom concentrates on several research and development areas to form *integrated multimedia systems*. Possible functions to be developed include:

Telepresence functions: To provide communication channels that increase the sense of presence and allow flexible participation. Examples are a group tele-workroom and a personal tele-workstation.

Telecooperation functions: To aid in coordinating the activity of distributed groups. Examples in this category include cooperative document processing tools, office procedure processing, and group coordination and meeting preparation tools.

Personal assistance functions: To develop an integrated suite of desktop tools including a task organizer, an appointment manager, and fax and electronic mail tools.

Information systems functions: To develop the overall information infrastructure. Components include an organizational filing system and multimedia archive, an organizational knowledge base, and a distributed information management system.

Security and reliability functions: To address privacy issues. Functions include electronic signature creation and verification, access control and authorization, and encrypting and decrypting services.

One challenge is to integrate these functions in an open system on heterogeneous hardware platforms with gateways to local and wide area networks. A second challenge is to ensure acceptance of the new technology among its users. To help achieve this goal, general system requirements, including a common user interface for all functions and an ergonomic design, are being evaluated by consulting user groups during all stages of research and development.

8.1.1   STRUCTURE AND STATUS OF THE POLIKOM PROGRAM

The **Polikom** program spans the entire development process from research and development of components, through system and product development, to pilot and field tests. The strategy of concurrent engineering (interlinking activities in research and industry) is expected to help reduce the time until the new technologies are introduced. **Polikom** therefore has several parallel undertakings:

- Demonstration of new technologies to help educate and increase the awareness of potential users.

- Prototyping and product development of promising technologies.

- Pilot and field tests to gain user acceptance and feedback for further development.

- Medium- and long-term research on **Polikom** goals, in close cooperation with development projects and oriented to user requirements.

The first pilot applications and field tests were started at GMD a few years ago. The GMD sites at Bonn, Berlin and Darmstadt are linked via a national switched broadband network called VBN (Figure 8.1). Each VBN connection provides a bandwidth of 140Mbits/s, sufficient for very high-quality audio/video links. To date, over fifty **Polikom** stations have been installed at GMD sites. A **Polikom** station consists of a workstation with audio and video hardware, desktop conferencing software, and assorted multi-user applications (see Figure 8.2 and Plate III).

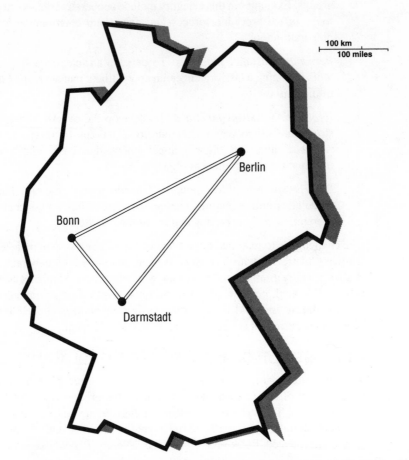

Figure 8.1   VBN links used by Polikom field tests. VBN is a regular service provided by the German telecom. It supports 140 Mbit/s connections between approximately 800 sites in Germany.

VBN functionality is not limited to high-quality audio and video links. The possibility of conferences with several participants is offered, as well as joint editing functions allowing different conference participants to edit the same document simultaneously. VBN offers a data channel with a bandwidth of 2 Mbits/s in parallel to the video channel; the data channel is used for this function. Additionally, **Polikom** workstations are connected via WAN (wide area network) and LAN (local area network). In the pilot application, one of the greatest technical problems was integrating these heterogeneous systems in a consistent environment with different local and regional networks, protocols, and platforms.

Several GMD prototype applications have already been used on **Polikom** workstations; these include a desktop video conferencing tool, a multimedia mail service, a hypermedia system for cooperative work, an organizational knowledge base, an activity assistant, and an 'intelligent card' security system for electronic signatures. The **Polikom** workstations are installed at the desks of different GMD

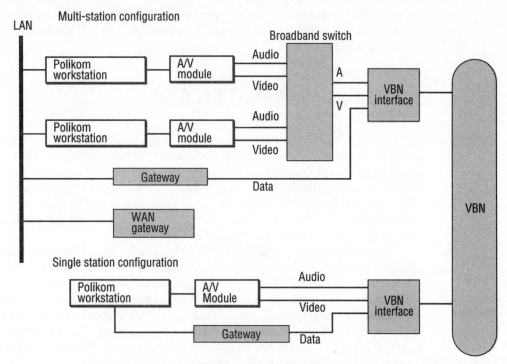

Figure 8.2 Polikom workstations and network connections. The A/V modules allow attachment of cameras, microphones, and speakers.

employees and are used for day-to-day work. For example, they help structural engineers at Bonn and Berlin sites draw up and revise blueprints using joint editing techniques. By means of the prototype systems, valuable experience is gathered in working with telepresence. However, **Polikom** is still far away from a polished technology that would gain user acceptance. Areas requiring further research and development include integration, security, availability, user convenience, and the design of distributed applications for specific governmental tasks and services.

8.1.2 ATM OUTLOOK

As the world's first switched broadband network offered on a commercial basis, VBN has provided a valuable testbed for future broadband applications. However, VBN is not an international standard and is now being superseded by ATM. The first wide area ATM pilot in Germany, parallel to a European pilot, will start in late 1994; three cities – Berlin, Hamburg and Cologne/Bonn – are to be included in the initial phase. But, despite the efforts of the national telecom providers, ATM is not expected to be available throughout Europe for several years and, if current cost estimates are accurate, is likely to be extremely expensive. So for the next few years, **Polikom** will use alternative communications facilities between geographically distant locations. Where ATM can play an immediate and important role in **Polikom** is in the backbone LAN infrastructure for departments and other organizational units. When an organization is geographically dispersed, a wide area broadband network, suitable for such multimedia applications as video conferencing and video-on-demand, can be formed by using leased lines or satellite to interlink the ATM backbones.

8.2 THE COMMUNICATION WALL

We now consider how the multimedia framework might aid in constructing large integrated multimedia systems such as envisaged in the **Polikom** project. The experimental nature of **Polikom** and the need to carry out field tests at an early stage place emphasis on the ability to rapidly construct and reconfigure system prototypes. The multimedia framework lends itself to extensible architectures, and so encourages experimentation and enhancement. To illustrate this point, we look at one specific aspect of **Polikom** – video conferencing.

Video conferencing is planned as one of the main facilities of **Polikom**. Several configurations are likely to be available for different tasks. Generally each **Polikom** workstation will run *desktop conferencing* software supporting two-way video (and audio) connections between small groups of co-workers and also broadcasts to arbitrarily sized groups. Traditional video conferencing, involving high-cost and specialized facilities, has not been particularly successful; Egido (1988) discusses its failures. Desktop conferencing, however, offers many advantages over traditional forms of video conferencing, as it is:

Self-contained: A single piece of equipment, the workstation, both displays video of remote participants and captures video of the local participant (using an attached camera).

Integrated: Conferences are set up using tools on the workstation; other tools, such as multi-user editors, can be shared by participants.

On demand: The service is continuously available to users; it is not necessary to reserve special rooms or special equipment.

High-quality: Networks like ATM allow transmission of high-quality full-motion video rather than low frame rate and low-resolution video as often found in traditional video conferencing systems.

Non-intrusive: Users can engage in video conferences from their offices; there is no need to disrupt their work by moving to a special room.

Flexible: Each participant can position and control his or her local camera, attach other video sources (such as a VCR) for transmission, and select the size and position of display windows.

Despite the many advantages of desktop video conferencing, for some situations it is not appropriate. First, when more than two people are involved, what can be called 'coherency of observation' breaks down. For example, when A looks at B, one would like B, and other participants, to see that A is looking at B. But if each remote participant appears in a window on the local workstation, who is paying attention to whom is not immediately apparent. Another drawback is that the small size of the video window by itself breaks down the sense of a shared physical space. If participants are displayed as life-sized, or near life-sized, there is only enough space for the head and perhaps shoulders, so information about body position and gestures is lost, while if the entire body appears in the window then participants are reduced to miniature doll-like figures. In either case the sense of speaking to another person as if in the same room is minimal. Finally, for some users the workstation is superfluous. For example, executives and government ministers may not feel comfortable using workstations and may prefer a technology that blends in with their accustomed working environment.

One of the alternate forms of video conferencing that may be explored in **Polikom** is the *Communication Wall*. The central idea is that wall-sized displays rather than workstation windows are used for conferencing (Figure 8.3).The goals are: (1) to increase the degree of realism and sense of presence and (2) to provide better observational coherency for multi-participant meetings.

Figure 8.3   A Communication Wall.

The notion of a Communication Wall derives from proposals for high-resolution display walls (Woodward, 1993) and from previous work on video collaboration and 'shared video spaces'. Experiments at Xerox PARC (Bly *et al.*, 1993), Bellcore (Fish *et al.*, 1990) and in Japan (Ishii and Miyake, 1991) have investigated several forms of video linkages between single users and between small groups. Of particular note is Bellcore's 'VideoWindow' where pairs of very large displays (8ft × 3ft) support the illusion of windows placed between adjacent rooms. Taking such systems as a starting point, we now speculate on a series of scenarios exhibiting a progressively increasing sense of presence.

8.2.1 COMPONENTS FOR THE COMMUNICATION WALL

In a fashion similar to the series of virtual museum configurations presented in Chapter 6, the Communication Wall scenarios are based on a component network which is successively extended by adding components. For sake of completeness, the 'component kit' used is listed in Table 8.1. Some of these components have appeared in previous examples; for example, the kit includes a 3D renderer (R3) and a video mixer (VMIX). Others are self-explanatory (for instance, MIC, a microphone). Components that are unique to the Communication Wall will be explained as they are encountered in the various scenarios.

Table 8.1 Communication Wall components and their port types.

Component description	Name	Input port(s)	Output port(s)	Base
Microphone	MIC		AnalogAudio	HW
Amplifier & speakers	SPK	AnalogAudio		HW
Audio digital-to-analog converter	DAC	PCM	AnalogAudio	HW
Audio analog-to-digital converter	ADC	AnalogAudio	PCM	HW
Audio net reader	ANR	PCM	PCM	SW
Audio net writer	ANW	PCM	PCM	SW
Video camera	VCAM		NTSC	HW
Display surface	WALL	NTSC		HW
Video digital-to-analog converter	VDAC	RGBVideoStream	NTSC	HW
Video analog-to-digital converter	VADC	NTSC	RGBVideoStream	HW
Video net reader	VNR	RGBVideoStream	RGBVideoStream	SW
Video net writer	VNW	RGBVideoStream	RGBVideoStream	SW
Videodisc player	VD		NTSC	HW
Multi-layer video mixer	VMIX	3 × NTSC	NTSC	HW
Video framebuffer	VFB	RGBVideoStream	NTSC	HW
2D video transform	V2	NTSC	NSTC	HW
3D renderer	R3	PolyAnimationStream	RGBVideoStream	SW+HW
Navigator	NAV	TrackerStream	PolyAnimationStream	SW
Position tracker	POS		TrackerStream	HW

8.2.2 BASIC COMMUNICATION WALL

The first scenario consists of two connected Communication Walls located at two sites – room #1 and room #2. The sites communicate over a broadband network such as ATM; each room contains a wall-sized display, and camera, microphone, and speaker assemblies.

Basic component networks for connected Communication Walls are shown in Figure 8.4 where symmetric pairs of audio and video streams join the two rooms. For instance, the top stream links the camera (VCAM) in room #1 to an analog-to-digital to converter (VADC) which is in turn linked to a component that sends a digital video stream over the network (VNW). These components could be implemented using an off-the-shelf video camera, a video board on a **Polikom** workstation (for digitizing the analog signal coming from the camera), and a process on the workstation that writes digital frames to the network. At room #2, the incoming video stream is read from the network (VNR), passed through a digital-to-analog converter (VDAC), and then sent to the wall-sized display (WALL). Identical components are used for the video stream from room #2 to room #1. In a similar fashion, two symmetric audio streams link the rooms.

In terms of component networks, what sets the Communication Wall apart from desktop conferencing systems is simply the choice of the display surface. If the WALL component is replaced by a component encapsulating a window on a workstation, then the component networks of Figure 8.4 become those needed for desktop conferencing. Thus the WALL component is central to this (and the remaining) scenarios. Alternatives for WALL components include rear-projected video displays and 'video walls' constructed from arrays of modular video screens. The latter are more expensive but are brighter and have better resolution.

This brief description has overlooked many of the design problems associated with the Communication Wall. Camera placement and optics need to be

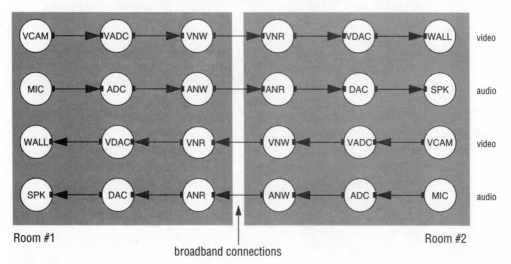

Room #1   Room #2

broadband connections

Figure 8.4   Component networks for two connected Communication Walls.

considered, as do lighting and furniture placement. Several important issues arise in the design of the audio components. One wants to allow two-way simultaneous conversation but avoid echoes and feedback. Also the spatial localization of sound sources adds realism, but requires multiple microphones and speakers in each room and multiple audio streams between the rooms. However, the component networks of Figure 8.4 provide the basic functionality of Communication Walls and offer the basis for further expansion.

8.2.3   COMMUNICATION WALL WITH STATIC VIDEO BACKGROUND

There are many directions that can be explored for improving and refining the preceding component networks. One avenue is to focus on increasing the sensation, among users of connected Communication Walls, of being in the same place. This

Background video frame

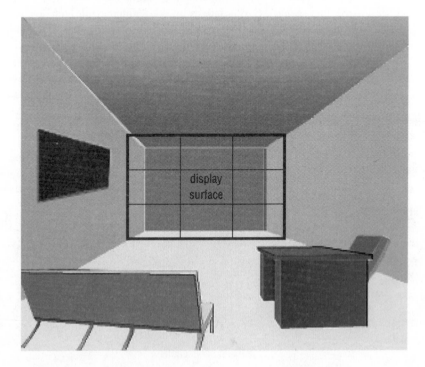

Figure 8.5   A Communication Wall displaying a matching background video frame.

sensation is easily lost in the previous scenario: if the two rooms are not identical and the video signal from one room is simply projected on a wall of the other there will be visual discontinuity at the edges of the display – where one room ends and the other begins becomes very noticeable.

Suppose users of Communication Walls are not particularly interested in the contents of opposing rooms, but would like to carry on conversation as if face-to-face in the same room. Furthermore, assume that it is possible to process the video signal coming from each room and separate the foreground (the person or people in the room) from the background (primarily the wall opposite the Communication Wall). One can then replace the background portion of the signal with some other video signal that more closely matches the room where the altered signal is displayed. For instance, the new background could continue the real walls back into the display surface (Figure 8.5).

An extended component network for replacing the background is shown in Figure 8.6. (Here just changes along the video path from room #1 to room #2 are shown; similar changes would be needed for the video path in the opposite direction.) The new background is produced by a single frame video source such as a paused videodisc player (VD). This source and the signal from the remote room are passed through a video mixer (VMIX) and the output is then displayed.

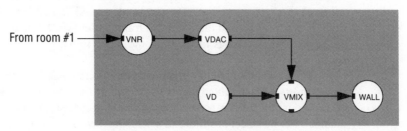

Room #2

Figure 8.6   Component network for Communication Wall with static video background.

The key challenge with this scenario is separating foreground and background video signals. A simple solution is to use chroma-keying; however, this requires that the rooms be specially designed (for example, blue screens might be placed in the background) and the quality of the foreground/background separation would be sensitive to lighting conditions. A more promising alternative is some form of 'intelligent keying' based on image processing techniques. In this case the design of the rooms may again be constrained (perhaps only certain colors allowed for walls and furniture) but the appearance of the rooms should be more natural than when using chroma-keying.

8.2.4   COMMUNICATION WALL WITH DYNAMIC COMPUTER-GENERATED BACKGROUND

A problem with the preceding scenario is that the replacement background is static and so only appears correctly aligned when viewed from within a small region of the room. The component network of Figure 8.7 incorporates perspective tracking

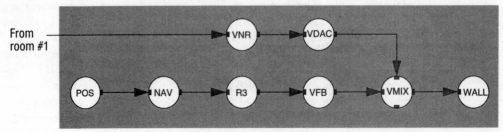

Figure 8.7   Component network for Communication Wall with dynamic computer-generated backgrou

and motion cues to increase depth perception. First, rather than a static background, the background is continually generated by a 3D renderer using a model of room geometry. Second, the location of the viewpoint used when rendering the background is determined from a position tracking device attached to a (single) observer. This device, encapsulated by the POS component, produces a data stream indicating the observer's current location in the room. The stream is transformed by a navigator component (NAV, see page 224) to animation events specifying changes of viewpoint. The 3D renderer (R3) consumes this stream and renders new background images into a framebuffer (VFB). Finally, the video output of the framebuffer is mixed with the video signal coming from the remote room.

The result of adding the position tracking and rendering components is that as the observer moves about the room the background image is continually adjusted to account for the new perspective. A similar technique is used to create 'virtual studios'. For instance, position and orientation sensors can be attached to a video camera and a 3D model then rendered in sync with camera movement. The signal coming from the camera, typically of actors and other objects in front of a blue screen or curtain, is chroma-keyed with the rendered frames. The composited video then has the actors in the foreground and the rendered frames in the background (Shimoda *et al.*, 1989; Shibata, 1992).

8.2.5   MULTI-PARTICIPANT COMMUNICATION WALL

Without very high-resolution video, some form of stereo display giving depth perception, and photorealistic rendering, the computer-generated background in the previous scenario is not likely to be very convincing. However, what is gained by the last scenario is that we come to a point where it is fairly simple to add additional participants, that is, to connect several Communication Walls.

A modified component network for three connected Communication Walls is shown in Figure 8.8. A new component, V2, applies 2D transformations to video signals. It translates, and perhaps scales, the signals coming from the remote rooms. For example, the room #1 signal could be translated to the left and the room #3 signal to the right. Both signals are then mixed with the background and the result appears on the wall display.

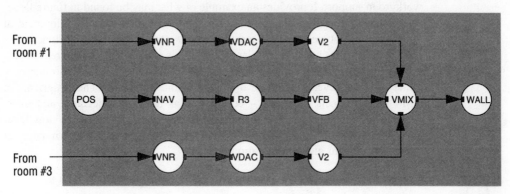

From
room #1

From
room #3

Room #2

Figure 8.8   Component network for multi-participant Communication Wall with dynamic computer-
generated background.

   If each room shifts incoming signals in a consistent manner it is possible to
approximate a triangular arrangement of the three participants. For example, room
#2 sees room #1 to the left and room #3 to the right, so room #1 should see room
#3 to the left and #2 to the right:

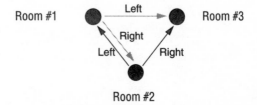

   Looking back over the four Communication Wall scenarios, there has been
a steady progression towards the original design goals: to increase the degree of
realism and sense of presence, and to provide better observational coherency for
multi-participant meetings. It may be that none of the configurations would be
successful in practice, and perhaps further steps in the direction of virtual reality
need to be explored. However, the point of the exercise was not to produce a final
design but to demonstrate how functionality is added by introducing new components. The multimedia framework and component networks promote an experimental approach to application development where design choices are guided by
the form and availability of components.

8.3 SUMMARY

The **Polikom** project is a research and development effort in combining several
technologies, in particular broadband networking and software for distributed

workgroup support. It provides an example of what may be found in future large-scale integrated multimedia systems. The project requires rapid development of application prototypes for field tests, so new strategies for implementing multimedia applications are of particular interest. This chapter has considered one aspect of **Polikom**, video conferencing, and has applied the multimedia framework to the design of several variations of a 'Communication Wall'. The designs are in terms of component networks – configurations of interconnectable and interchangeable components. Well-constructed components encapsulate low-level tasks of multimedia programming and leave the developer free to experiment with alternative designs and configurations.

APPENDIX A
A MEDIA PROCESSING
PLATFORM

At the University of Geneva we have assembled a media processing platform for the purpose of experimenting with application development based on connecting and composing what the framework calls components. The equipment was gathered several years ago at a cost of a few hundred thousand dollars; however, a similar platform could now be realized for a fraction of this amount. The platform is not intended solely for authoring or playback; rather it is a set of media processing elements and user-interface devices that can be configured in a variety of ways. At the moment such platforms are not the type of thing one finds on the desktop. But there is a trend where more and more media processing tasks are transferred from external devices to PCs and workstations. Following this trend we expect that desktop-based systems will gradually approach and exceed the functionality of this experimental platform.

In setting up the platform, the desire to exercise the framework dictated the selection of equipment. Among the requirements were:

Heterogeneous: Component classes are meant to encapsulate hardware dependencies. In order to test encapsulation realistically, the platform contains equipment from several manufacturers. For instance, the workstations and PCs include those from Sun, Silicon Graphics, Digital, NeXT, Apple, and Commodore.

Highly connectable: An early goal and motivation in designing the framework was to explore a new type of application, the essential characteristic being the presence of many simultaneous media streams. Thus equipment was sought that had flexibility in terms of inter-component connection.

Analog and digital media: Analog media and analog devices should not be overlooked. First, analog is unavoidable. At some point, whether just prior to presentation or at an earlier stage, digital values are converted to analog signals (for instance, audio coming from a digital source must be in analog form by the time it reaches the speakers). Additionally a large number of audio and video processing devices have only analog inputs and outputs. For these reasons a mix of analog and digital equipment was selected, with the view of moving towards a greater dependence on digital audio and video as the technology matured.

Time-based media: Another factor in gathering the equipment was the ability to support a variety of media types. Particular attention was paid to time-based media and selecting equipment for working with audio, video, music, and animation.

The configuration of the platform is shown in Figure A.1 through Figure A.5. These diagrams reflect very closely the existing configuration at the University of Geneva. Manufacturer and model names have been largely excluded (except when used to emphasize diversity).

Digital connections □ Figure A.1 is a computer-oriented view of the platform, showing various workstations and PCs, peripheral devices, and their digital connections. Some of the processors are reserved for special purposes; for instance, the Silicon Graphics workstation is used for real-time animation, the video mixer is a dedicated Amiga with a video processing board, and the Alpha is reserved primarily for computationally intensive components.

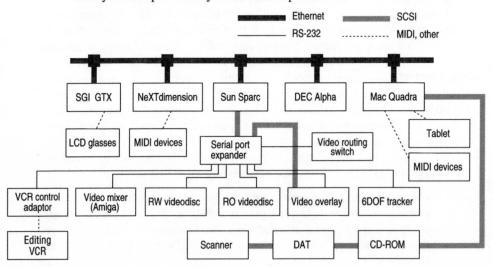

Figure A.1   Digital connections.

Video connections □ Many of the devices shown in Figure A.1 are sources or sinks of analog video signals. Analog video is easy to exchange between equipment, and it is possible to prototype applications without waiting for multimedia networking to mature. However, the platform's video network is essentially a number of dedicated lines, and when assembling the platform it soon became apparent that there was a cabling problem – different applications required different connections and it was awkward to reconnect equipment manually. This prompted the installation of a computer-controllable 16×16 NTSC video routing switch (see Figure A.2[1]) and also a patch panel for reconfiguring RGB video connections (see Figure A.3).

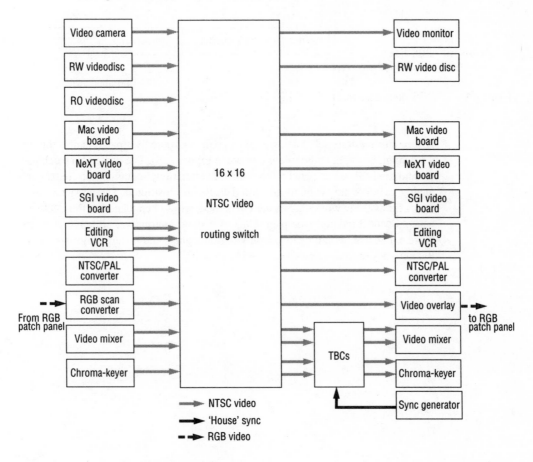

Figure A.2   NTSC video connections.

[1] In Figure A.2, video sources appear to the left of the switch and sinks to the right. Some components act as both sink and source and so appear twice. The situation is similar in the other figures.

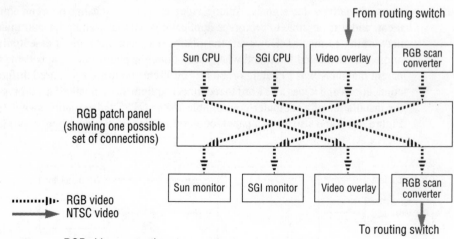

Figure A.3   RGB video connections.

Audio connections □ Analog audio signals are routed via patch panels through a 12-input, 8-output audio mixer (shown in Figure A.4). The two audio patch panels and the RGB patch panel require manual operation, but computer-controllable analog switches are available and could easily be substituted. The impact of doing so, as far as framework classes are concerned, would be isolated in the CableConnector::Connect method (see page 198). A second alternative, although currently more expensive, would be to use only digital signals and install a high-speed digital network (perhaps based on an ATM switch).

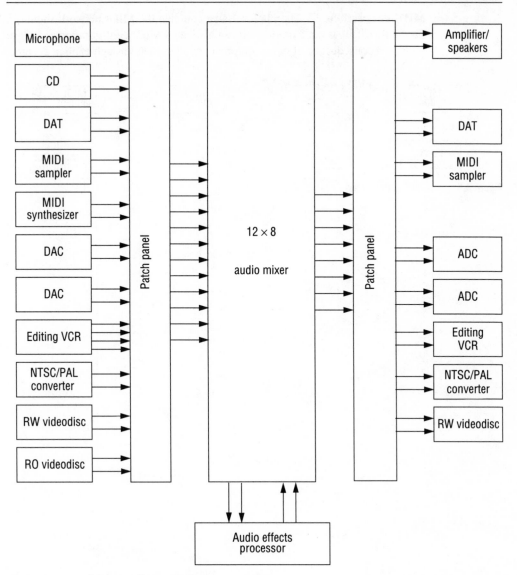

Figure A.4   Analog audio connections.

MIDI connections ☐ The platform also contains the MIDI network shown in Figure A.5. This is not a particularly sophisticated MIDI configuration and arose more as a consequence of other equipment choices than through explicit design.

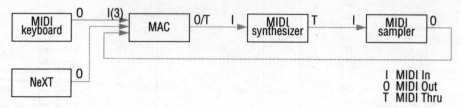

Figure A.5   MIDI connections.

APPENDIX B
A MEDIA COMPONENT KIT

In order to develop applications using the framework, the functionality of a media processing platform must be represented by a set of media types, media formats, components, and possibly transforms. Clearly certain classes will not be available on all platforms, but application portability can be improved by using query methods and programming in terms of abstract rather than concrete classes.

This appendix describes how the framework would be specialized by introducing concrete classes appropriate for the platform described in Appendix A. Also included are several software-based, or platform-independent classes. The resulting set of classes is called a media *component* kit since, although media types, media formats and transforms are included, components are often the starting point of application development. Many of the classes listed here have been partially implemented and used to construct prototypes of the virtual museum and the VideoActor class described in Chapter 6.

B.1 CONCRETE MEDIA CLASSES

The concrete media subclasses are shown in Figure B.1 (recall that concrete classes are shaded). These classes are:

RawAudio: Temporal sequences of audio samples. Sample rate, sample size and number of channels vary from sequence to sequence. This is one of the basic framework classes.

RawVideo: Temporal sequences of images (frames). Pixel depth, image width and height, and color model vary from sequence to sequence.

PolyAnimation: Temporal sequences of polygon animation events. This class is described in detail in Chapter 6.

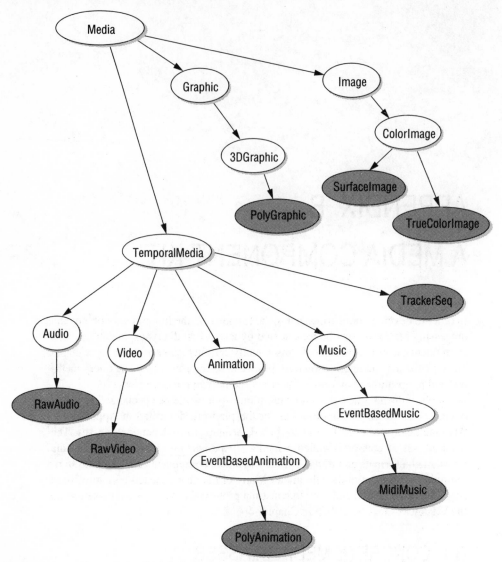

Figure B.1   Concrete media subclasses.

MidiMusic: Temporal sequences of MIDI events.

TrackerSeq: Temporal sequences of data elements generated by position and orientation tracking devices. Elements are 3D geometrical transformations such as scaling, rotation, and translation (or their combination).

PolyGraphic – 3D polygons with vertex color information.

TrueColorImage: Color images. Pixel depth, image width and height, and color model vary from image to image.

SurfaceImage: Color images with an additional channel giving surface depth (see section 2.3.1 on page 72). Depth values refer to cylindrical or Cartesian coordinates.

Subclassing is not restricted to the media sub-hierarchies (Image, Audio, Video, and so on), but can also take place at the level of the Media and TemporalMedia classes. An example is TrackerSeq, a direct subclass of TemporalMedia for encapsulating temporal sequences of sensor data.

B.2 CONCRETE TRANSFORM CLASSES

Two families of transform classes are used to capture the functionality of the platform's video mixer and audio effects processor. The video mixer provides hardware support for real-time video transitions, and the audio effects processor performs a variety of audio effects in realtime. Specific transitions and effects are represented by concrete subclasses of VideoTransition and AudioEffect (see Figure B.2). The immediate subclasses of VideoTransition and AudioEffect, for instance Wipe and Delay, have software-based implementations. These classes are platform-independent but cannot be loaded on a transformer component and so cannot be used for real-time effects or transitions. Instead the subclasses of Wipe and Delay override the Apply method and provide hardware-based, but platform-dependent, implementations. For example, suppose the platform uses manufacturer M's 'Model x' video mixer and manufacturer N's 'Model y' audio effects processor. This is represented by the hardware-based classes, such as MxWipe and NyExcite, also shown in Figure B.2. MxWipe implements a wipe using the 'Model x' video mixer (and so could be loaded onto a component representing the mixer).

B.3 CONCRETE MEDIA FORMAT CLASSES

The concrete stream and file format classes shown in Figure B.3 support the import, export, and exchange of values from the concrete media classes of Figure B.1. The media processing platform uses analog signals so the stream format classes include several classes for analog formats. The following lists the concrete format classes and gives a brief description of each format.

AnalogAudio: An analog signal format used as a port type.

PCMF: A file format for importing and exporting sequences of PCM-encoded audio samples. PCMF files have a header indicating the sample size, sample rate and number of channels.

PCM: A stream format for exchanging sequences of PCM-encoded audio samples. Format attributes include the sample size, sample rate, and number of channels.

NTSC: An analog signal format used as a port type.

PAL: An analog signal format used as a port type.

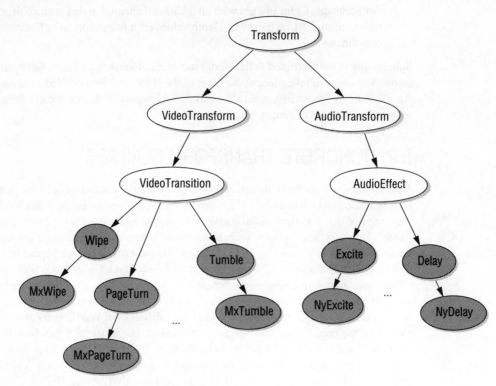

Figure B.2   Concrete transform classes.

AnalogRGB: An analog signal format used as a port type.

RGBVideoStream: A stream format for exchanging sequences of 24-bit RGB images. Format attributes include image width and height.

PolyAnimationFileFormat: A file format for importing and exporting polygon animation values. These values are temporal sequences of polygon animation events (see Chapter 6). A file header indicates the number of events and whether the sequence is 'normalized'. (Recall the PolygonAnimation class has a Normalize method for converting all relative movements to absolute movements.) The header is followed by a timestamp and data for each event.

PolyAnimationStream: A stream format for exchanging polygon animation values. This format resembles PolyAnimationFileFormat minus the header and timestamps.

MIDI: A stream format corresponding to the standard for MIDI messages.

SMF: A file format corresponding to the 'standard MIDI file' format.

TrackerStream: A stream format for exchanging tracker sequences. This format is a stream of 4×4 matrices. Matrix elements are floating point values.

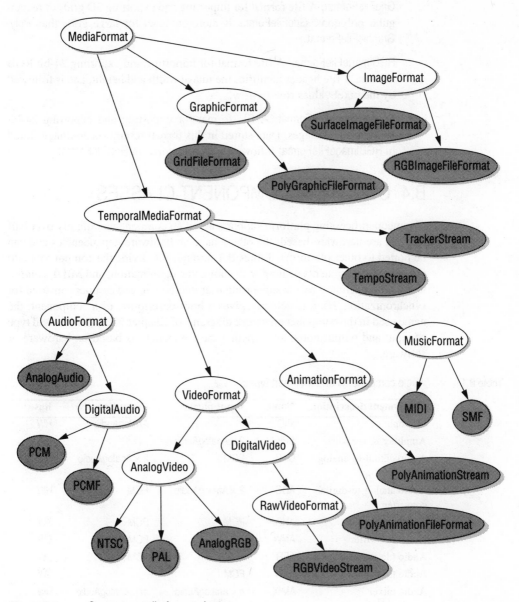

Figure B.3   Concrete media format classes.

PolyGraphicFileFormat: A file format for importing and exporting 3D polygons with vertex color information. A file in this format consists of a list of
vertex definitions followed by a list of polygon definitions. A vertex definition is three floating point numbers and an integer, which represent the vertex position and color respectively. A polygon definition is a list of
references to vertex definitions.

GridFileFormat: A file format for importing and exporting 3D grids of rectangular polygons. GridFileFormat is more compact for large grids than PolyGraphicFileFormat.

RGBImageFileFormat: A file format for importing and exporting 24-bit RGB images. A file header identifies the image width and height, and is followed by the pixel values row-by-row.

SurfaceImageFileFormat: A file format for importing and exporting 24-bit RGB surface images. Data stored in this format resembles an image stored in RGBImageFileFormat followed by a grid stored in GridFileFormat.

B.4 CONCRETE COMPONENT CLASSES

The media processing platform supports about 40 components. Slightly over half of these are hardware-based; the others have no hardware dependencies and can be ported to other platforms. Tables B.1 through B.6 divide the components into six groups: components dealing with audio, video, animation, and MIDI, components whose primary role is supporting user interaction, and components used for synchronization. Each table entry gives a brief description of a component, the name used in the component network diagrams of Chapter 6, the number and type of input and output ports, and whether the component is based on hardware or software.

Table B.1   Audio components and their port types.

Component description	Name	Input port(s)	Output port(s)	Base
Microphone	MIC		AnalogAudio	HW
Amplifier & speakers	SPK	2 × AnalogAudio		HW
Audio digital-to-analog converter	DAC	PCM	2 × AnalogAudio	HW
Audio analog-to-digital converter	ADC	2 × AnalogAudio	PCM	HW
Audio net reader	ANR	PCM	PCM	SW
Audio net writer	ANW	PCM	PCM	SW
Audio file reader	AFR		PCM	SW
Audio file writer	AFW	PCM		SW
Audio mixer	AMIX	n × AnalogAudio	m × AnalogAudio	HW
Audio effects processor	AEF	2 × AnalogAudio	2 × AnalogAudio	HW
Sound player	SND		PCM	SW
CD player	CD		2 × AnalogAudio PCM	HW
DAT player/recorder	DAT	2 × AnalogAudio PCM	2 × AnalogAudio PCM	HW

The audio components (see Table B.1) include microphone, speakers, stereo analog-to-digital and digital-to-analog converters, and processes that read and write digital audio. There is a hardware-based mixer and a hardware-based effects processor, but similar components could be implemented in software. The sound player is a source of short PCM sequences, and the CD (with analog and digital output ports) and DAT player/recorder are sources of longer PCM sequences.

Table B.2   Video components and their port types.

Component description	Name	Input port(s)	Output port(s)	Base
Video camera	VCAM		NTSC	HW
Workstation monitor	WM	AnalogRGB		HW
Video monitor	VM	NTSC		HW
Read-only videodisc player	VD		NTSC 2 × AnalogAudio	HW
Read-write videodisc player	VDRW	NTSC 2 × AnalogAudio	NTSC 2 × AnalogAudio	HW
Video editor	VED	NTSC 2 × AnalogAudio	2 × NTSC 4 × AnalogAudio	HW
Analog video mixer	AVMIX	2 × NTSC	2 × NTSC	HW
Chroma-keyer	CKEY	2 × NTSC	NTSC	HW
QuickTime player	QTP		NTSC	SW+HW
QuickTime recorder	QTR	NTSC		SW+HW
Video overlay	VOV	AnalogRGB NTSC	AnalogRGB	HW
Framebuffer	FB	RGBVideoStream	AnalogRGB	HW
NTSC/PAL video converter	VCON	NTSC I PAL 2 × AnalogAudio	NTSC I PAL 2 × AnalogAudio	HW
Scan converter	SCON	AnalogRGB	NTSC	HW

The video components (see Table B.2) include camera, monitors, and tape and videodisc equipment. There is a general-purpose video mixer used primarily for video transitions and a component whose only function is chroma-keying. The QuickTime player encapsulates a server running on a Macintosh. The server plays QuickTime movies on the Mac's display. The display signal is converted to NTSC, so although QuickTime is a digital video environment, this component has an analog video output port. Finally there is a set of components for converting between video formats. The framebuffer component is somewhat artificial; its purpose is to represent the conversion from digital to analog RGB video.

The animation components (see Table B.3) deal with the generation and rendering of PolyAnimation values. Examples of their use are the various virtual museum configurations discussed in Chapter 6.

Table B.3   Animation components and their port types.

Component description	Name	Input port(s)	Output port(s)	Base
Animator	ANI		PolyAnimationStream	SW
Modeller	MOD	PolyAnimationStream	PolyAnimationStream	SW
Model tee	MOT	PolyAnimationStream	PolyAnimationStream PolyAnimationStream	SW
Model recorder	MOR	PolyAnimationStream		SW
Model player	MOP		PolyAnimationStream	SW
2D renderer	R2	PolyAnimationStream	RGBVideoStream	SW
3D renderer	R3	PolyAnimationStream NTSC	RGBVideoStream	SW+HW

Table B.4   MIDI components and their port types.

Component description	Name	Input port(s)	Output port(s)	Base
MIDI synthesizer	MSY	MIDI	AnalogAudio	HW
MIDI keyboard	MKB		MIDI	HW
MIDI sampler	MSAM	MIDI AnalogAudio	MIDI AnalogAudio	HW
MIDI sequencer	MSQ	MIDI	MIDI	SW

The platform includes a fairly standard set of MIDI devices (see Table B.4); these are represented by keyboard, synthesizer and sampler components. The final MIDI component is a software-based sequencer – it is also possible to find hardware-based sequencers.

Table B.5   Interaction components and their port types.

Component description	Name	Input port(s)	Output port(s)	Base
6DOF tracker	6DOF		TrackerStream	HW
Navigator	NAV	TrackerStream	PolyAnimationStream	SW

The first of the interaction components (see Table B.5) encapsulates a six degrees-of-freedom tracking device. The navigator is a software-based component that transforms tracker data to a form used by the animation components.

Table B.6   Synchronization components and their port types.

Component description	Name	Input port(s)	Output port(s)	Base
Video time-base corrector	TBC	2 x NTSC	NTSC	HW
Video sync generator	VSY		NTSC	HW

Finally there are two components that correspond to devices used for video synchronization (see Table B.6).

APPENDIX C

ONLINE MULTIMEDIA

INFORMATION SOURCES

A large number of information sources related to multimedia are found on the Internet. An index of pointers to many of these sources is located at:

http://cui_www.unige.ch/OSG/MultimediaInfo/index.html

To access the index, a World-Wide Web browser and an Internet connection are needed. Browsers have been developed for several platforms. One popular browser, called *Mosaic*, runs on PCs, the Mac, and UNIX systems. Mosaic is available via anonymous ftp from ftp.ncsa.uiuc.edu.

The index is divided into several sections:

- Ratings and Guides

- FAQs (frequently asked questions)

- Software

- Media Delivery Services

- Companies

- Media Archives

- Research

- Conference Announcements

- Bibliographies

- Newsgroup Archives

- Standards
- The CD Family
- Digital Galleries and Museums
- Educational
- Magazines, Books and Journals
- Publishers
- Hypertext and Hypermedia
- Virtual Reality
- Miscellaneous Information

Suggestions for new entries can be sent to SimonGibbs@gmd.de.

GLOSSARY

ADC	analog-to-digital converter.
ADPCM	(adaptive delta pulse code modulation) a form of audio compression.
ANSI	American National Standards Institute.
API	application programming interface.
ASCII	(American Standard Code for Information Interchange) a standard character encoding scheme.
ATM	(asynchronous transfer mode) a form of fast packet switching used in B-ISDN.
AVI	(Audio/Video Interleaved) a file format supported by Video for Windows.
AVK	(Audio/Video Kernel) the second generation of DVI software.
AVSS	(Audio/Video Support System) the first generation of DVI software.
B-ISDN	broadband ISDN.
BLOB	binary large object.
BPM	beats per minute.
CAV	constant angular velocity.
CCIR	(*Comité Consultatif International des Radio Communications*) a broadcasting standards organization.
CCIR 601	a standard for uncompressed digital component video.
CCITT	(*Comité Consultatif International Télégraphique et Téléphonique*) a telecommunications standards organization.
CD	compact disc.
CD+G	compact disc plus graphics.
CD+MIDI	compact disc plus MIDI.
CD-DA	compact disc, digital audio.
CD-i	compact disc interactive (formerly CD-I).
CD-R	compact disc, recordable.

CD-ROM	compact disc, read-only-memory.
CD-ROM XA	CD-ROM, extended architecture.
CD-RTOS	(compact disc, real-time operating system)　the operating system used by CD-i players.
CD-V	compact disc, video.
CD-WO	compact disc, write-once.
CGM	(computer graphics metafile)　a file format for 3D graphics information.
CIE	(*Commission Internationale de l'Éclairage*)　an international organization and standards body for matters related to light.
CIF	(Common Intermediate Format)　a digital video format.
CLUT	(color lookup table)　a table of color values; the color of a pixel of an 'indexed image' is determined by using the pixel value as an index to the table.
CLV	constant linear velocity.
CMYK	(cyan, magenta, yellow, black)　a color model used for color printing.
CRT	cathode ray tube.
CSG	(constructive solid geometry)　a method for modelling 3D solids by combining union, intersection and difference operations.
D1, D2, D3, D5	digital video tape formats.
DAC	digital-to-analog converter.
DAT	digital audio tape.
DCT	(digital component technology)　a digital video tape format.
DCT	(discrete cosine transform)　a mathematical transform used for image compression.
DIB	(Device Independent Bitmap)　an image format supported by MME.
DVE	(digital video effect)　video effects produced by digital processing.
DVI	(Digital Video Interactive)　a pioneering system for compressed digital video.
DVTR	digital video tape recorder.
DYUV	(differential YUV)　an image format supported by CD-i.
EBU	European Broadcasting Union.
EDL	(edit decision list)　a list of audio or video editing operations.
EPS	(encapsulated PostScript)　a standard format for PostScript files.
FMV	(full-motion video)　video at rates of about 25 or more frames per second.
FTP	(file transfer protocol)　a network protocol and software utility for transferring files over the Internet.

G.721	a CCITT recommendation for audio encoding at 32 Kbits per second using adaptive pulse code moduation.
GIF	(Graphics Interchange Format) a compressed image file fomat.
GKS	(Graphic Kernel System) an early standard for 3D graphics programming.
GM	(General MIDI) an extension to MIDI including a program number assignment.
H.261	a CCITT recommendation for a very low data rate digital video format used for conferencing over ISDN lines.
HD-MAC	European analog HDTV.
HDTV	high-definition television.
Hi-Vision	Japanese analog HDTV.
HSB	(hue, saturation, brightness) a color model.
HyTime	an ISO standard for structuring time-based media.
IEC	(International Electrotechnical Commission) a standards body for the electrical and electronics industries.
IMA	(Interactive Multimedia Association) a trade association that promotes multimedia technology.
ISDN	integrated services digital network.
ISO	International Organization for Standardization.
JPEG	(Joint Photographic Experts Group) an ISO standard for image compression.
LAN	local area network.
LCD	liquid crystal display.
LD	(Laser Disc) 8-inch and 12-inch Laser Vision videodiscs with digital audio.
LPC	(linear predictive coding) a compression technique.
LPC-10	a standard for encoding speech at a very low data rate.
LTC	(longitudinal time code) time code placed in a track running along the length of video (or audio) tape.
LV	(Laser Vision) an analog videodisc format.
LZW	(Lempel-Ziv and Welsh) refers to a widely used compression algorithm.
MCI	(Media Control Interface) a high-level interface for controlling media devices under MME.
MD	(Mini Disc) a recordable magneto-optical disc half the diameter of the CD but with similar audio capacity.
MHEG	(Multimedia and Hypermedia Information Coding Experts Group) an ISO standard for encoding hypermedia documents.
MIDI	(Musical Instrument Digital Interface) an industry defined standard for communicating with musical equipment and other devices.

MME	(Microsoft Multimedia Extensions) a set of software components and services found in Windows 3.1.
MMPM	(Multimedia Presentation Manager) multimedia extensions for IBM's OS/2.
MPC	(Multimedia PC) an industry standard identifying the hardware and software for a multimedia platform based on the PC.
MPEG	(Motion Pictures Expert Group) a group of standards for compressing digital video (and accompanying audio).
MTC	MIDI time code.
MVC	(model/view/controller) a class framework in Smalltalk.
NTSC	(National Television Systems Committee) a video standard developed in the U.S.
ODA	(Office Document Architecture) an ISO standard for electronic documents.
OMF	(Open Media Framework) a group of animation software companies and broadcast equipment manufacturers concerned with interoperation of their products.
OpenGL	an industry standard for 3D graphics programming.
PAL	(phase alternation line) a European video standard.
PAL	(Palette File Format) an image format supported by MME.
PCM	(pulse code modulation) a technique for digitally encoding analog signals.
PHIGS	(Programmer's Hierarchical Interactive Graphic System) an ISO standard for 3D graphics programming.
PHIGS+	extension to PHIGS allowing more complex geometry and lighting.
PICT	a Macintosh file format for images and graphics.
PLV	(production-level video) the higher quality format of DVI's two video formats.
PPQ	(parts per quarter note) a measure of timing granularity, used by MIDI devices.
px64	a very low data rate digital video format used for conferencing over ISDN lines, also known as H.261.
QCIF	(quarter-CIF) a digital video format with quarter the resolution of CIF.
QuickTime	the software subsystem supporting time-based media on the Macintosh.
RAM	random access memory.
RGB	(red, green, blue) a color model.
RGB 5:5:5	an image format supported by CD-i.
RIB	(RenderMan Interface Binary) a format for specifying 3D rendering operations.
RIFF	(Resource Interchange File Format) a structured file format supported by MME.

RL-3, RL-7	CD-i image formats using run-length coding.
ROM	read-only memory.
RTF	(Rich Text Format) a file format for formatted text and graphics.
RTV	(real-time video) the lower quality format of DVI's two video formats.
RTX	(real-time executive) a component of AVSS responsible for scheduling and synchronization.
S-VHS	(separated VHS) a consumer video tape format.
SECAM	(*séquentiel couleur avec mémoire*) a video standard developed in France.
SGML	(Standard Generalized Markup Language) an ISO standard for document markup and structuring.
SMDL	(Standard Music Description Language) an application of SGML for musical scores.
SMF	Standard MIDI File.
SMPTE	Society of Motion Picture and Television Engineers.
SQL	(Structured Query Language) a standard query language for relational database systems.
TBC	(timebase corrector) a device used to remove timing errors from video signals.
TIFF	Tagged Image File Format.
UNIX	an operating system used primarily on workstations and in client/server environments.
UV	'chroma' (color difference) signals or values.
VBI	(vertical blanking interval) portion of a video signal that separates fields.
VCR	video cassette recorder.
VGA	(video graphics array) a video display adapter used by PCs; provides resolutions of 640×480 4-bit pixels or 320×240 8-bit pixels.
VHS	(video home system) a consumer video tape format.
VITC	(vertical interval time code) a method for inserting time code data in the vertical blanking interval of video signals.
VRAM	video RAM.
VTR	video tape recorder.
WAN	wide area network.
WAVE	(Waveform Audio File Format) an audio file format supported by MEE.
WORM	(write once, read many) recordable optical disc technology.
X11	a widely used window server primarily found on UNIX systems.
YUV	refers to both a color model and a video signal format containing luminance (Y) and chroma (UV) components.

BIBLIOGRAPHY

Abelson H. and diSessa A. (1981). *Turtle Geometry: The Computer as a Medium for Exploring Mathematics*. Cambridge, MA: MIT Press

Adie C., ed. (1993). *A Survey of Distributed Multimedia Research, Standards and Products* RARE Project OBR(92)046v2. Amsterdam: Réseaux Associés pour la Recherche Européenne (Available on the Internet by anonymous ftp from ftp.edinburgh.ac.uk:pub/mmsurvey.)

Adobe Systems Incorporated (1990). *PostScript Language Reference Manual* 2nd edn. Reading, MA: Addison-Wesley

Adobe Systems Incorporated (1991). *Adobe Photoshop User's Guide* Version 2

Aho A. and Ullman J. (1972). *The Theory of Parsing, Translation and Compiling, Vol. I: Parsing*. Englewood Cliffs, NJ: Prentice Hall

Ambron S. and Hooper K., eds. (1988). *Interactive Multimedia*. Redmond, Washington: Microsoft Press

American National Standards Institute (1988a). *Standard Music Description Language, Part One: Objectives and Methodology (X3V1.8M/SD-6 Journal of Development)*

American National Standards Institute (1988b). *Standard Music Description Language, Part Two: Technical Description and Formal Definition (X3V1.8M/SD-7 Journal of Development)*

Anderson D.P. and Homsy G. (1991). A continuous media I/O server and its synchronization mechanism. *IEEE Computer*, **24**(10), 51–7

Angebranndt S., Hyde R.L., Luong D.H., Siravara N. and Schmandt C. (1991). Integrating audio and telephony in a distributed workstation environment. In *Proc. Summer 1991 USENIX Conference*, Nashville, Tennessee, 10–14 June 1991, 419–35

Apple Computer Inc. (1989). *The Visual Alamanac Companion*

Apple Computer Inc. (1992). *QuickTime 1.5 Developer's Kit*

Arnold D.B. and Bono P.R. (1988). *CGM and CGI: Metafile and Interface Standards for Computer Graphics*. Berlin: Springer-Verlag

Association of Computing Machinery (1985). Special Issue on Computer Music. *Computing Surveys*, **17**(2)

Association of Computing Machinery (1989). Interactive technologies. *Comm. ACM*, **32**(7)

Association of Computing Machinery (1990a). Alphabets and languages. *Comm. ACM*, **33**(5)

Association of Computing Machinery (1990b). HDTV. *ACM SIGGRAPH Video Review*, Special Issue 60

Association of Computing Machinery (1991). Digital multimedia systems. *Comm. ACM*, **34**(4)

Association of Computing Machinery (1992). Hypermedia. *Comm. ACM*, **35**(1)

Association of Computing Machinery (1993a). Multimedia in the workplace. *Comm. ACM*, **36**(1)

Association of Computing Machinery (1993b). Debating digital telephony legislation. *Comm. ACM*, **36**(3)

Barrett E., ed. (1992). *Sociomedia*. Cambridge, MA: MIT Press

Becker J. (1987). Arabic word processing. *Comm. ACM*, **30**(7), 600–10

Bell T., Witten I. and Cleary J. (1989). Modeling of text compression. *Computing Surveys*, **21**(4), 557–91

Berners-Lee T. and Connolly D. (1993). Hypertext Markup Language. Internet Draft. Internet Engineering Task Force (IETF)

Berners-Lee T., Cailliau R. and Groff J. (1992). The World-Wide Web. *Computer Networks and ISDN Systems*, 454–9

Bier E.A. (1992). EmbeddedButtons: Supporting buttons in documents. *ACM Trans. Information Systems*, **10**(4), 381–407

Blair Benson K. and Whitaker J. (1990). *Television and Audio Handbook for Technicians and Engineers*. New York, NY: McGraw-Hill

Blair G., Coulson G., Auzimour P., Hazard L., Horn F. and Stefani J.B. (1992). An integrated platform and computational model for open distributed multimedia applications. In *Proc. Third Intl. Workshop on Network and Operating System Support for Digital Audio and Video* (Venkat Rangan P., ed.), Lecture Notes in Computer Science, No. 712. Berlin: Springer-Verlag

Blattner M.M. and Dannenberg R.B., eds. (1992). *Multimedia Interface Design*. Reading, MA: ACM Press

Bly S.A., Harrison S.R. and Irwin S. (1993). Media spaces: Bringing people together in a video, audio, and computing environment. *Comm. ACM*, **36**(1), 28–47

Bolt R.A. (1980). Put-That-There: Voice and gesture at the graphics interface. *Computer Graphics (Proc. SIGGRAPH'80)*, **14**(3), 262–70

Borenstein N.S. (1990). *Multimedia Applications Development with the Andrew Toolkit*. Englewood Cliffs, NJ: Prentice Hall

Bove T. and Rhodes C. (1990). *Que's Macintosh Multimedia Handbook*. Carmel, IN: Que Corp.

Boyer R. and Moore J. (1977). A fast string searching algorithm. *Comm. ACM*, **20**(10), 762–72

Brand S. (1987). *The Media Lab*. New York, NY: Viking

The British Computer Society (1993). Special Issue on Multimedia. *The Computer Journal*, **36**(1)

Brown M. (1991). *Desktop Video Production*. Blue Ridge Summit, PA: Windcrest

Bruckman A. (1991). The electronic scrapbook: Towards an intelligent home-video editing system. *Master's thesis*, The Media Laboratory, MIT

Bryan M. (1988). *SGML: An Author's Guide to the Standard Generalized Markup Language*. Reading, MA: Addison-Wesley

Burger J. (1993). *The Desktop Multimedia Bible*. Reading, MA: Addison-Wesley

Card S.K., Mackinlay J.D. and Robertson G.G. (1990). The design space of input devices. In *Proc. CHI'90*, 117–24, New York: ACM Press

Cardelli L. and Pike R. (1985). Squeak: a language for communicating with mice. *Computer Graphics (Proc. SIGGRAPH'85)*, **19**(3), 199–204

Cattell R.G.G. (1991). *Object Data Management*. Reading, MA: Addison-Wesley

Clifford W.H., McConnell J.I. and Saltz J.S. (1988). The development of PEX, a 3D graphics extension to X. In *Proc. Eurographics'88*, 21–30. Berlin: Springer-Verlag

Conklin J. (1987). Hypertext: An introduction and survey. *IEEE Computer*, **20**(9), 17–41

Dannenberg R.B., Neuendorffer T., Newcomer J.M. and Rubine D. (1993). Tactus: Toolkit-level support for synchronized interactive multimedia. *Multimedia Systems*, **1**(2), 77–86

Date C.J. and Darwen H. (1993). *A Guide to the SQL Standard*. Reading, MA: Addison-Wesley

de Mey V. and Gibbs S. (1993). A multimedia component kit. In *Proc. ACM Multimedia'93*, 291–300. New York: ACM Press

De Poli G., Piccialli A. and Roads C., eds. (1991). *Representations of Musical Signals*. Cambridge, MA: MIT Press

de Prycker M. (1991). *Asynchronous Transfer Mode: Solution for Broadband ISDN*. Chichester, England: Ellis Horwood

Deutsch L.P. (1989). Design reuse and frameworks in the Smalltalk-80 programming system. In *Software Reusability* Vol. II. (Biggerstaff T.J. and Perlis A.J., eds.), pp. 57–71. Reading, MA: Addison-Wesley

Digital Equipment Corporation (1991). *XMedia Technical Summary*

Dyer D.S. (1990). A dataflow toolkit for visualization. *IEEE Computer Graphics & Applications*, **10**(4), 60–9

Egido C. (1988). Videoconferencing as a technology to support group work: A review of its failures. In *Proc. of the Conf. on Computer-Supported Cooperative Work*, 13–24. New York: ACM Press

Ellis M.A. and Stroustrup B. (1990). *The Annotated C++ Reference Manual.* Reading, MA: Addison-Wesley

Faloutsos C. (1985). Access methods for text. *Computing Surveys*, **17**(1), 49–74

Ferrari D., Banerjea A. and Zhang H. (1992). Network Support for Multimedia: A Discussion of the Tenet Approach. *Technical Report TR-92-072*, International Computer Science Institute, University of California at Berkeley

Fish R.S., Kraut R.E. and Chalfonte B.L. (1990). The VideoWindow System in informal communications. In *Proc. of the Conf. on Computer-Supported Cooperative Work*, 1–11. New York: ACM Press

Foley J., van Dam A., Feiner S. and Hughes J. (1990). *Computer Graphics Principles and Practice* 2nd edn. Reading, MA: Addison-Wesley

Fournier A., Fussel D. and Carpenter L. (1982). Computer rendering of stochastic models. *Comm. ACM*, **25**(6), 371–84

Fox E.A. (1991). Advances in interactive digital multimedia systems. *IEEE Computer*, **24**(10), 9–21

Frenkel K.A. (1989). HDTV and the computer industry. *Comm. ACM*, **32**(11), 1301–12

Friedmann M., Starner T. and Pentland A. (1992). Device synchronization using an optimal linear filter. *Computer Graphics*, 57–62 (Special Issue: Proc. 1992 Symposium on Interactive 3D Graphics.)

Fuhrt B. (1994). Multimedia systems: An overview. *IEEE Multimedia*, **1**(1), 47–59

Furuta R., Scofield J. and Shaw A. (1982). Document formatting systems: Survey, concepts, and issues. *Computing Surveys*, **14**(3), 417–72

Gemmell J. and Christodoulakis S. (1992). Principles of delay-sensitive multimedia storage and retrieval. *ACM Trans. Information Systems*, **10**(1), 51–90

Gibbs S. (1991). Composite multimedia and active objects. In *Object-Oriented Programming: Systems, Languages and Applications* (OOPSLA'91), pp. 97–112. New York: ACM Press

Gibbs S. (1994). Video widgets: Implementation strategies. In *Proc. IS&T/SPIE Conf. on High-Speed Networking and Multimedia Computing*. Springfield, VA: IS&T

Gibbs S., Breiteneder C., de Mey V. and Papathomas M. (1993). Video widgets and video actors. In *Symp. User Interface Software and Technology* (UIST'93), 179–85. New York: ACM Press

Goldberg A. and Robson D. (1983). *Smalltalk-80: The Language and Implementation.* Reading, MA: Addison-Wesley

Goldfarb C.F. (1990). *The SGML Handbook.* Oxford: Clarendon Press

Green J. (1992). The evolution of DVI system software. *Comm. ACM*, **35**(1), 53–67

Grimes J. and Potel M. (1991). What is multimedia? *IEEE Computer Graphics & Applications*, **11**(1), 49–52

Grosvenor J., Morrision K. and Pim A., eds. (1992). *The PostScript Font Handbook*. Reading, MA: Addison-Wesley

Harney K., Keith M., Lavelle G., Ryan L.D. and Stark D.J. (1991). The i750 video processor: A total multimedia solution. *Comm. ACM*, **34**(4), 64–78

Harrington S. (1987). *Computer Graphics – A Programming Approach* 2nd edn. New York, NY: McGraw-Hill

Hartson H.R. and Hix D. (1989). Human–computer interface development: Concepts and systems. *Computing Surveys*, **21**(1), 5–92

Herrtwich R.G., ed. (1991). *Proc. Second Intl. Workshop on Network and Operating System Support for Digital Audio and Video*, Lecture Notes in Computer Science, No. 614. Berlin: Springer-Verlag

Hodges M.E. and Sasnett R.M., eds. (1992). *Multimedia Computing: Case Studies from MIT Project Athena*. Reading, MA: Addison-Wesley

Hodges M.E., Sasnett R.M. and Ackerman M.S. (1989). A construction set for multimedia applications. *IEEE Software*, **6**(1), 37–43

Hoffert E., Miller G., Chen S.E., Patterson E., Blackketter D., Rubin S., Applin S.A., Yim D. and Hanan J. (1992). *The Virtual Museum: Interactive 3D Navigation of a Multimedia Database*. Apple Computer Inc.

Höhne K.H., Bomans M., Riemer M., Schubert R., Tiede U. and Lierse W. (1992). A volume-based anatomical atlas. *IEEE Computer Graphics & Applications*, **12**(4), 72–8

Holzmann G. (1988). *Beyond Photography – The Digital Darkroom*. Englewood Cliffs, NJ: Prentice Hall

Hoptman G. (1992). The virtual museum and related epistemological concerns. In *Sociomedia* (Barrett E., ed.), pp. 141–59. Cambridge, MA: MIT Press

Horak W. (1985). Office Document Architecture and Office Document Interchange formats: Current status of international standardization. *IEEE Computer*, **18**(10), 50–60

Howard T., Hewitt W., Hubbold R. and Wyrwas K. (1991). *A Practical Introduction to PHIGS and PHIGS PLUS*. Reading, MA: Addison-Wesley

Howell P., West R. and Cross I., eds. (1991). *Representing Musical Structure*. London: Academic Press

IEEE Computer Society (1985a). Chinese/Kanji text and data processing. *IEEE Computer*, **18**(1)

IEEE Computer Society (1985b). Multimedia communications. *IEEE Computer*, **18**(10)

IEEE Computer Society (1991). Multimedia information systems. *IEEE Computer*, **24**(10)

Interactive Multimedia Association (1991). IMA Compatibility Project Proceedings. *Tech. J. of the IMA Compatibility Project*, **1**(1)

Interactive Multimedia Association (1994). Middleware system services architecture. In *Multimedia Systems* (Koegel Buford J.F., ed.), pp. 221–44. Reading, MA: Addison-Wesley

International Organization for Standardization (1985). *Information Processing Systems: Computer Graphics – Graphical Kernel System (GKS), Functional Description (ISO 7942)*.

International Organization for Standardization (1986). *Information Processing – Text and Office Systems – Standard Generalized Markup Language (ISO 8879)*.

International Organization for Standardization (1987a). *Metafile for the Storage and Transfer of Picture Information (ISO 8632)*.

International Organization for Standardization (1987b). *Information Processing – 8-bit single-byte coded graphic character sets – Part 6: Latin/Arabic alphabet (ISO TC/97 8859-6 0)*.

International Organization for Standardization (1988). *Volume and File Structure of CD-ROM for Information Exchange (ISO/DIS 9660)*.

International Organization for Standardization (1989a). *Programmer's Hierarchical Interactive Graphic System (PHIGS) (ISO/IEC 9592)*.

International Organization for Standardization (1989b). *Office Document Architecture (ODA) and Interchange Format (ISO 8613)*.

International Organization for Standardization (1992a). *Hypermedia/Time-based Structuring Language (HyTime) (ISO/IEC IS 10744)*.

International Organization for Standardization (1992b). *Coded Representation of Multimedia and Hypermedia Information Objects (MHEG) (ISO/IEC JTC1/SC29/WG12 Working Document S.7)*.

International Organization for Standardization (1993). *Office Document Architecture (ODA) and Interchange Format – Temporal Relationships and Nonlinear Structures (ISO/IEC DIS 8613-14)*.

Ishii H. and Miyake N. (1991). Toward an open shared workspace: Computer and video fusion approach of TeamWorkStation. *Comm. ACM*, **34**(12), 36–50

Johnson R. and Foote B. (1988). Designing reusable classes. *J. Object-Oriented Programming*, **1**(2), 22–35

Johnson R. and Wirfs-Brock R. (1991). Object-oriented frameworks. In *Object-Oriented Programming: Systems, Languages and Applications (OOPSLA'91) (Tutorial Notes)*. New York: ACM Press

Kay D.C. and Levine J.R. (1992). *Graphics File Formats*. New York, NY: Mc-Graw-Hill

Kjelldahl L., ed. (1992). *Multimedia Systems, Interaction and Applications*. Eurographic Seminar Series. Berlin: Springer-Verlag

Knuth D. (1973). *The Art of Computer Programming, Vol. 3: Sorting and Searching*. Reading, MA: Addison-Wesley

Knuth D. (1984). *The TEXbook*. Reading, MA: Addison-Wesley

Knuth D. (1986). *The METAFONTbook*. Reading, MA: Addison-Wesley

Koegel J.F., Rutledge L.W., Rutledge J.L. and Keskin C. (1993). HyOctane: A HyTime engine for an MMIS. In *Proc. ACM Multimedia'93*, 129–36. New York: ACM Press

Koegel Buford J.F., ed. (1994). *Multimedia Systems*. Reading, MA: Addison-Wesley

Krupnick M. (1990). *The Electric Image*. White Plains, NY: Knowledge Industry

Lambert S. and Ropiequet S., eds. (1986). *CD ROM: The New Papyrus*. Redmond, WA: Microsoft Press

Lamport L. (1986). *LATEX User's Guide and Reference Manual*. Reading, MA: Addison-Wesley

Le Gall D. (1991). MPEG: A video compression standard for multimedia applications. *Comm. ACM*, **34**(4), 46–58

Liou M. (1991). Overview of the px64 kbit/s video coding standard. *Comm. ACM*, **34**(4), 59–63

Lippman A. (1991). Feature sets for interactive images. *Comm. ACM*, **34**(4), 92–102

Little T.D.C. (1993). A framework for synchronous delivery of time-dependent multimedia data. *Multimedia Systems*, **1**(2), 87–94

Little T.D.C. and Ghafoor A. (1991). Scheduling of bandwidth-constrained multimedia traffic. In *Proc. Second Intl. Workshop on Network and Operating System Support for Digital Audio and Video* (Herrtwich R.G., ed.), pp. 120–31. Lecture Notes in Computer Science, No. 614.Berlin: Springer-Verlag

Little T.D.C., Ghafoor A., Chen C.Y.R., Chang C.S. and Berra P.B. (1991). Multimedia synchronization. *IEEE Data Eng. Bulletin*, **14**(3), 26–35

Luther A. (1991). *Digital Video in the PC Environment*. New York, NY: McGraw-Hill

MacroMind Inc. (1991). *Director Studio Manual* Version 3.0.

Magnenat-Thalmann N. and Thalmann D., eds. (1989). *State-of-the-art in Computer Animation*. Tokyo: Springer-Verlag

Magnenat-Thalmann N. and Thalmann D. (1990). *Computer Animation: Theory and Practice* 2nd edn. New York, NY: Springer-Verlag

Markey B.D. (1991). Emerging hypermedia standards: Hypermedia marketplace prepares for HyTime and MHEG. In *Proc. Summer 1991 USENIX Conference*, Nashville, Tennessee, 10–14 June 1991, 59–74

McLuhan M. (1964). *Understanding Media*. New York, NY: McGraw-Hill

Meyer B. (1988). *Object-oriented Software Construction*. Englewood Cliffs, NJ: Prentice Hall

Meyrowitz N. and van Dam A. (1982). Interactive editing systems: Part I and Part II. *Computing Surveys*, **14**(3), 321–415

Microsoft Corporation (1987). *Rich Text Format Specification*.

Microsoft Corporation (1991a). *Microsoft Windows Multimedia Programmer's Reference*. Microsoft Press

Microsoft Corporation (1991b). *Microsoft Windows Multimedia Programmer's Workbook*. Microsoft Press

Microsoft Corporation (1991c). *Microsoft Windows Multimedia Authoring and Tools Guide*. Microsoft Press

Moline J., Benigini D. and Baronas J., eds. (1990). *Proceedings of the Hypertext Standardization Workshop*. National Institute of Standards and Technology (NIST Special Publication 500-178)

National Bureau of Standards (1977). *Data Encryption Standard (Federal Information Processing Standard (FIPS) Publication 46)*. US Department of Commerce

Nelson M. (1991). *The Data Compression Book*. Redwood City, CA: M&T Books

Netravali A. and Limb J. (1980). Picture coding: A review. *Proceedings of the IEEE*, **68**(3), 366–406

Newcomb S.R., Kipp N.A. and Newcomb V.T. (1991). The 'HyTime' hypermedia/time-based document structuring language. *Comm. ACM*, **34**(11), 67–83

Newmann W.M. and Sproull R.F. (1979). *Principles of Interactive Computer Graphics* 2nd edn. New York, NY: McGraw-Hill

NeXT Inc. (1992). *NeXTstep General Reference*. Reading, MA: Addison-Wesley

Nicol J.R., Wilkes C.T. and Manola F.A. (1993). Object orientation in heterogeneous distributed computing systems. *IEEE Computer*, **26**(6), 57–67

Northcutt J.D. and Kuerner E.M. (1991). System support for time-critical applications. In *Proc. Second Intl. Workshop on Network and Operating System Support for Digital Audio and Video* (Herrtwich R.G., ed.), pp. 242–54. Lecture Notes in Computer Science, No. 614. Berlin: Springer-Verlag

OpenGL Architecture Review Board (1993). *The OpenGL Reference Manual*. Reading, MA: Addison-Wesley

Ossana J. (1976). NROFF/TROFF User's Manual. *Technical Report 54*, Bell Laboratories

Pennycock B.W. (1985). Computer–music interfaces: A survey. *Computing Surveys*, **17**(2), 267–89

Philips (1982). Special Issue on the Compact Disc. *Philips Technical Review*, **40**(6)

Phillips R. (1991). MediaView: A general multimedia digital publication system. *Comm. ACM*, **34**(7), 74–83

Pohlmann K. (1989). *Principles of Digital Audio* 2nd edn. Carmel, IN: H.W. Sams and Co.

Pohlmann K. (1992). *The Compact Disc Handbook* 2nd edn. Madison, WI: A-R Editions

Porter T. and Duff T. (1984). Compositing digital images. *Computer Graphics (Proc. SIGGRAPH'84)*, **18**(3), 253–9

Poynton C.A. (1994). High definition television and desktop computing. In *Multimedia Systems* (Koegel Buford J.F., ed.), pp. 383–402. Reading, MA: Addison-Wesley

Preston J.M., ed. (1987). *Compact-Disc Interactive: A Designer's Overview*. Deventer NL: Kluwer

Price R. (1993). MHEG: An introduction to the future international standard for hypermedia object interchange. In *Proc. ACM Multimedia'93*, 121–8. New York: ACM Press

Reeves W.T. (1983). Particle systems – a technique for modelling a class of fuzzy objects. *Computer Graphics (Proc. SIGGRAPH'83)*, **17**(3), 359–76

Reynolds C. (1982). Computer animation using scripts and actors. In *Computer Graphics (Proc. SIGGRAPH'82)* (3), July 1982, 289–96

Ripley G.D. (1989). DVI – A digital multimedia technology. *Comm. ACM*, **32**(7), 811–22

Rivest R., Shamir A. and Adelman L. (1978). A method for obtaining digital signatures and public-key cryptosystems. *Comm. ACM*, **21**(2), 120–6

Roads C. and Strawn J., eds. (1987). *Foundations of Computer Music* 3rd edn. Cambridge, MA: MIT Press

Rona J. (1987). *MIDI: The Ins, Outs & Thrus*. Milwaukee, WI: Hal Leonard

Rona J. (1990). *Synchronization From Reel to Reel*. Milwaukee, WI: Hal Leonard

Rothstein J. (1992). *MIDI: A Comprehensive Introduction*. Madison, WI: A-R Editions

Rowe L.A. and Smith B.C. (1992). A continuous media player. In *Proc. Third Intl. Workshop on Network and Operating System Support for Digital Audio and Video* (Venkat Rangan P., ed.), pp. 376–86. Lecture Notes in Computer Science, No. 712. Berlin: Springer-Verlag

Rowe R. (1993). *Interactive Music Systems: Machine Listening and Composing*. Cambridge, MA: MIT Press

Schnorf P. (1993). Video as a high-level data type. *Multimedia Systems*, **1**(3), 132–40

Shaw C., Green M., Liang J. and Sun Y. (1993). Decoupled simulation in virtual reality with the MR Toolkit. *ACM Trans. on Information Systems*, **11**(3), 287–317

Shepherd D. and Salmony M. (1990). Extending OSI to support synchronization required by multimedia applications. *Computer Communications*, **13**(7), 399–406

Shibata M. (1992). Proposal for desktop program production. In *134th SMPTE Technical Conf.*, Toronto, Nov. 1992

Shimoda S., Hayashi M. and Kanatsugu Y. (1989). New chroma-key imaging technique with Hi-Vision background. *IEEE Trans. on Broadcasting*, **35**(4), 357–61

Shu N. (1988). *Visual Programming*. New York, NY: Van Nostrand Reinhold

Smith A.R. (1984). Plants, fractals and formal languages. *Computer Graphics (Proc. SIGGRAPH'84)*, **18**(3), 1–10

Smith P.D. (1990). *An Introduction to Text Processing*. Cambridge, MA: MIT Press

Stallings W. (1992). *ISDN and Broadband ISDN*. New York, NY: Macmillan

Steinmetz R. (1990). Synchronization properties in multimedia systems. *IEEE Journal on Selected Areas in Comm.*, **8**(3), 401–12

Steinmetz R. (1994). Data compression in multimedia computing – Standards and systems. *Multimedia Systems*, **1**(5), 187–204

Stenzel H., Kansy K., Herman I. and Carson S. (1994). Premo – An architecture for presentation of multimedia objects in an open environment. In *Proc. 1st Eurographics Symp. on Multimedia*, Graz, Austria

Stroustrup B. (1991). *The C++ Programming Language* 2nd edn. Reading, MA: Addison-Wesley

Terry D.B. and Swinehart D.C. (1988). Managing stored voice in the Etherphone system. *ACM Trans. on Computer Systems*, **6**(1), 3–27

Thanos C., ed. (1990). *Multimedia Office Filing*. Amsterdam: North-Holland

Thorell L.G. and Smith W.J. (1990). *Using Computer Color Effectively: An Illustrated Reference*. Englewood Cliffs, NJ: Prentice Hall

Tinker M. (1989). DVI parallel image compression. *Comm. ACM*, **32**(7), 844–51

Tokuda H. (1994). Operating system support for continuous media applications. In *Multimedia Systems* (Koegel Buford J.F., ed.), pp. 201–20. Reading, MA: Addison-Wesley

Udell J., (1994). A Taligent update. *Byte*, July, 183–4

Upson C., Faulhaber T., Kamins D., Laidlaw D., Schlegel D., Vroom J., Gurwitz R. and van Dam A. (1989). The Application Visualization System: A computational environment for scientific visualization. *IEEE Computer Graphics & Applications*, **9**(4), 30–42

Upstill S. (1990). *The RenderMan Companion*. Reading, MA: Addison-Wesley

USENIX Association (1991). *Proc. Summer 1991 USENIX Conference*. Berkeley, CA: USENIX Association

van de Meer J. (1992). The Full Motion System for CD-I. Philips Corp.

Venkat Rangan P., ed. (1992). *Proc. Third Intl. Workshop on Network and Operating System Support for Digital Audio and Video*, Lecture Notes in Computer Science, No. 712. Berlin: Springer-Verlag

Venkat Rangan P., Burkhard W.A. and Bowdidge R.W. (1991). A testbed for managing digital video and audio storage. In *Proc. Summer 1991 USENIX Conference*, Nashville, Tennessee, June 1991, 199–208

Vince J. (1992). *3D Computer Animation*. Reading, MA: Addison-Wesley

Von Ehr J. (1988). Kerning, tracking, and letterspacing. In *Real World PostScript* (Roth S., ed.), pp. 75–86. Reading, MA: Addison-Wesley

Wallace G. (1991). The JPEG Still Picture Compression Standard. *Comm. ACM*, **34**(4), 30–44

Waterworth J. (1991). *Multimedia Technology and Applications*. Chichester, England: Ellis Horwood

Watkinson J. (1990). *The Art of Digital Video*. Stoneham, MA: Focal Press

Wayner P. (1991). Inside QuickTime. *Byte*, Dec., 189–96

Wegner P. (1990). Concepts and paradigms of object-oriented programming. *OOPS Messenger*, **1**(1), 7–87

Weinstock N. (1986). *Computer Animation*. Reading, MA: Addison-Wesley

Wirfs-Brock R., Wilkerson B. and Wiener L. (1990). *Designing Object-Oriented Software*. Englewood Cliffs, NJ: Prentice Hall

Wisskirchen P. (1990). *Object-Oriented Graphics*. Berlin: Springer-Verlag

Witten I. (1982). *Principles of Computer Speech*. New York, NY: Academic Press

Wolberg G. (1990). *Digital Image Warping*. Washington, DC: IEEE Computer Society Press

Woodward P.R. (1993). Interactive scientific visualization of fluid flow. *IEEE Computer*, **26**(10), 13–25

Yavelow C. (1992). *Macworld Music & Sound Bible*. San Mateo, CA: IDG Books

Yawitz M., O'Sullivan D. and Mills M. (1992). Navigable movies: An overview. *The QuickTime Forum*, **3**(1)

Zeleznik R.C., Brookshire Conner D., Wloka M.M., Aliaga D.G., Huang N.T., Hubbard P.M., Knep B., Kaufman H., Huges J.F. and van Dam A. (1991). An object-oriented framework for the integration of interactive animation techniques. *Computer Graphics (Proc. SIGGRAPH'91)*, **25**(4), 105–11

Zellweger P.T. (1992). Toward a model for active multimedia documents. In *Multimedia Interface Design* (Blattner M.M. and Dannenberg R.B., eds.), pp. 39–52. Reading, MA: ACM Press

Zettl H. (1984). *Television Production Handbook*. Belmont, CA: Wadsworth Publishing Company

INDEX

Numerics

1125/60   36–37
1250/50   36–37
6DOF component   226, 232, 284, 296
82750DA/DB   105
82750PA/PB   105

A

A-B roll editing   43
abstract classes   *see* classes, abstract
abstract component types   191
abstract keyword   160
ActionMedia   103, 105–108
active objects   *see* objects, active
adaptive delta pulse code modulation (ADPCM)
   57
   CD-ROM XA   85
   use in DVI   104
ADPCM   *see* adaptive delta pulse code modulation
A-law   58
alpha channels   24
analog formats   187
analog video
   conversion   45
   editing   43
   mixing   43
   retrieval   41
   storage   39
   synchronization   42
   tape formats   39
analog video tape   39–40
AnalogAudio class   291
AnalogRGB class   292
Andrew   14, 80, 163
animation
   non-temporal   74
   playback   72
   rendering   71
animation models
   cels   69
   empirical   71
   event-based   70
   hierarchical   70
   key frames   70
   physically based   71
   procedural   71
   scene-based   70
articulated objects   70
artifacts   *see* media artifact
ASCII 17
asynchronous transfer mode (ATM)   8, 270, 286
ATM   *see* asynchronous transfer mode
audio cross-fade   60
audio segments   59
audio/video interleaved (AVI)   133
audio/video kernel (AVK)   111–113, 242, 260
audio/video servers   260, 268
audio/video support system (AVSS)   108–111
AudioFormat class   185
AVI   *see* audio/video interleaved
AVK   *see* audio/video kernel
AVSS   *see* audio/video support system
AVSS file format   105

B

BasicGestureActor class   248
B-ISDN (broadband ISDN)   8, 270
blobs   13
BufferConnector class   198
bump mapping   31

C

C++   159–160
CableConnector class   198
CAV   *see* constant angular velocity
CCIR 601   47
CD
   capabilities   88
   frame format   82
   multisession discs   86
   multi-speed drives   84
   physical characteristics   82
   storage capacity   82